SEVENTH EDITION

Improving Reading Skills

CONTEMPORARY READINGS FOR COLLEGE STUDENTS

Deanne Spears

City College of San Francisco

The McGraw-Hill Companies

Connect
Learn
Succeed™

For David

IMPROVING READING SKILLS, SEVENTH EDITION

Published by McGraw-Hill, a business unit of McGraw-Hill Companies, Inc., 1221 Avenue of the Americas, New York, NY, 10020. Copyright © 2013 by The McGraw-Hill Companies, Inc. All rights reserved. Printed in the United States of America. Previous editions © 2010, 2004, and 2000. No part of this publication may be reproduced or distributed in any form or by any means, or stored in a database or retrieval system, without the prior written consent of the McGraw-Hill Companies, Inc., including, but not limited to, in any network or other electronic storage or transmission, or broadcast for distance learning.

Some ancillaries, including electronic and print components, may not be available to customers outside the United States.

This book is printed on acid-free paper.

1 2 3 4 5 6 7 8 9 0 DOC/DOC 1 0 9 8 7 6 5 4 3 2

ISBN: 978-0-07-340731-9
MHID: 0-07-340731-3

Senior Vice President, Products & Markets: *Kurt L. Strand*
Vice President, General Manager, Products & Markets: *Michael Ryan*
Vice President, Content Production & Technology Services: *Kimberly Meriwether David*
Director of Developmental Services: *Lisa Pinto*
Managing Director: *David Patterson*
Brand Manager: *Kelly Villella*
Development Editor: *Penina Braffman*
Director, Content Production: *Terri Schiesl*
Senior Project Manager: *Joyce Watters*
Buyer: *Sandy Ludovissy*
Media Project Manager: *Sridevi Palani*
Cover Designer: *Studio Montage, St. Louis, MO*
Cover Image: *Yellowdog Productions/Lifesize/Getty Images*
Typeface: *10/12 Palatino*
Compositor: *Lachina Publishing Services*
Printer: *R.R. Donnelley*

All credits appearing on page or at the end of book are considered to be an extension of the copyright page

Library of Congress Cataloging-in-Publication Data

Milan Spears, Deanne.
   Improving reading skills : contemporary readings for college students / Deanne Spears. — 7th ed.
      p. cm.
   ISBN 978-0-07-340731-9 (acid-free paper)
   1. Reading (Higher education) 2. College readers. 3. Vocabulary. I. Title.
   LB2395.3.M56 2012
   428.4071'1—dc23
                                                                                          2012030245

www.mhhe.com

About the Author

Deanne Spears is originally from Portland, Oregon, but she now considers herself a native Californian, having moved to Los Angeles when there were still orange groves in the area and only a couple of freeways. After receiving a B.A. and an M.A. in comparative literature from the University of Southern California, she began teaching composition and reading at City College of San Francisco. She continues to tutor students in reading and composition and to conduct teacher-preparation workshops for the college. She is married to fellow English teacher and jazz musician, David Spears. In addition to her primary interests—reading and studying Italian—she and David enjoy cooking, watching movies (they have over 100 titles in their Netflix queue), kayaking and camping (especially in the Gold Lakes Basin area of Northern California), walking their Queensland heeler, Katie, on the bluffs around Half Moon Bay, and discovering new and inexpensive ethnic restaurants. Deanne is the author of *Developing Critical Reading Skills*, (9th edition, 2013) and, with David, *In Tandem* (1st edition, 2008).

Contents

DAVE BARRY

**PRACTICE
SELECTION**

Tips for Women: How to Have a Relationship with a Guy 21

We're not talking about different wavelengths here. We're talking about different planets, in completely different solar systems. Elaine cannot communicate meaningfully with Roger about their relationship any more than she can meaningfully play chess with a duck. Because the sum total of Roger's thinking on this particular topic is as follows: Huh?

PART ONE

Getting Started: Practicing the Basics 31

1

DAVID SEDARIS

Hejira 43

It wasn't anything I had planned on, but at the age of twenty-two, after dropping out of my second college and traveling across the country a few times, I found myself back in Raleigh,

7

CAROLINE HWANG

The Good Daughter 101

My parents didn't want their daughter to be Korean, but they don't want her fully American, either. Children of immigrants are living paradoxes.

8

STUDS TERKEL

Somebody Built the Pyramids 109

Mike Fitzgerald . . . is a laborer in a steel mil!. "I feel like the guys who built the pyramids. Somebody built 'em. Somebody built the Empire State Building, too. There's hard work behind it. I would like to see a building, say The Empire State, with a foot-wide strip from top to bottom and the name of every bricklayer on it, the name of every electrician. So when a guy walked by, he could take his son and say, 'See, that's me over there on the 45th floor. I put that steel beam in.'"

9

SHERRY TURKLE

The Nostalgia of the Young 118

One high school senior recalls a time when his father used to sit next to him on the couch, reading. "He read for pleasure and didn't mind being interrupted." But when his father, a doctor, switched from books to his BlackBerry, things became less clear. "He could be playing a game or looking at a patient record, and you would never know . . . . He is in that same BlackBerry zone."

10

ELIZABETH BERNSTEIN

How Facebook Ruins Friendships 129

Notice to my friends. I love you all dearly.

But I don't give a hoot that you are "having a busy Monday," your child "took 30 minutes to brush his teeth," your dog "just ate an ant trap" or you want to "save the piglets." And I really, really don't care which Addams Family member you most resemble.

11

CHRIS ROSE

Hell and Back 136

For all of my adult life, I regarded depression and anxiety as pretty much a load of hooey. I never accorded any credibility to the idea that they are medical conditions. Nothing scientific about it. You get sick, get fired, fall in love, get laid, buy a new pair of shoes, join a gym, get religion, seasons change, whatever; you go with the flow, dust yourself off, get back in the game. I thought antidepressants were for desperate housewives and fragile poets.

The work is backbreaking, but it takes less physical dexterity than many other jobs on the line. At the same time, the job is multifaceted and cannot be quickly learned. The harinero *adjusts the breader and rebreader, monitors the marinade, turns the power on and off, and replaces old flour with fresh flour. All this would be relatively manageable if the lines ran well. They never do.*

a creature of temperature, and upon man's frailty in general, able only to live within certain narrow limits of heat and cold; and from there on it did not lead him to the conjectural field of immortality and man's place in the universe.

Alternate Contents
Arranged by Theme

TRENDS IN CONTEMPORARY AMERICAN LIFE

Preface

Past users of *Improving Reading Skills* will find many changes in the seventh edition, which I elaborate on a bit later. The book's rationale, however, remains the same: Students improve their reading by reading, rather than by reading about techniques and strategies, just as one becomes a better driver by driving a lot or learns to make a good omelet by making dozens of omelets. Like the preceding six editions, the seventh edition tries to give students insightful, engaging, contemporary selections that challenge them and make them want to turn the page. The book's subtitle, *Contemporary Readings for College Students*, reflects this emphasis. In addition to acquiring skills, students will learn something about the world as they read.

In response to several reviewers' suggestions, in this edition I have incorporated more readings that students will find relevant to their lives, including the following: A blog posting by an Iraq War veteran who describes what it's like to return to the college classroom (Colby Buzzell); the psychological effects of the excessive use of cell phones, Facebook, and World of Warcraft (Sherry Turkle, Elizabeth Bernstein, and Tamara Lush); a unique way of finding marriage partners in China (Olivia Wu); an examination of whether online education is appropriate for K–12 students (Stephanie Banchero and Stephanie Simon); and finally, various commentaries on materialism and consumerism (John Bussey, Martin Lindstrom, Laurence Shames, and Guy de Maupassant).

More traditional analytical readings are here, as well, to get students' reading skills up to college level, some reprinted from earlier editions, many new. Among them are two pieces about learning to read: Sherman Alexie, "Superman and Me," and Carla Rivera, "From Illiterate to Role Model." Three selections are about the world of work: Studs Terkel, "Somebody Built the Pyramids"; an excerpt from a blog written by "The Waiter," pseudonym of Steve Dublanica, "Why Be a Waiter?"; and Steve Striffler, "Undercover in a Chicken Factory."

Other topics include psychological and social behavior: Chris Rose's battle with depression after Hurricane Katrina; Americans' preoccupation with hygiene (Martin Lindstrom); an experiment with college students about the problem of procrastination (Dan Ariely); and finally, Marc Ian Barasch's examination of empathy concerning the homeless. Human interest and adventure selections are included as well, represented by Dave Barry, David Sedaris, Joe Abbott, Caroline Hwang, Val Plumwood, and Debra J. Dickerson.

The readings are accompanied by a variety of practice exercises to reinforce good reading skills and to help students develop a college-level vocabulary. This basic principle—high-interest contemporary readings and useful exercises—has accounted for the book's success in the past and remains the guiding principle for this edition. A brief discussion of the book's important components follow. Former users of the text will see that most of these components remain the same, while new ones have been incorporated, which I hope will make the book more enjoyable and helpful.

An Overview of the Text

The seventh edition contains 41 reading selections—book, magazine, and newspaper articles and essays, online and newspaper editorials, two short textbook excerpts, and new to this edition, short fiction and everyday reading material (explained in detail further on). For Parts One through Six, I chose the readings using several criteria: They must be well written and relatively easy to understand (especially in the beginning readings); they must be a reasonable length so that students can complete the reading and accompanying exercises in one sitting; and they must be of sufficient interest to appeal to the most reluctant of readers.

I want students to see that they are members of a larger community and that reading can be instrumental in helping them fill this role. Reading also provides students with a way for them to understand the world around them and to search for meaning in their own lives. The book seeks to help students improve their reading comprehension and to read with better concentration, enjoyment, and confidence.

VOCABULARY DEVELOPMENT

As in the preceding six editions, the seventh edition continues to stress vocabulary development in the context of each reading. In my experience both teaching and tutoring reading at City College of San Francisco, a weak vocabulary—perhaps even more than poor concentration or lack of interest—is a major stumbling block for our students. Because the interrelationship between comprehension and vocabulary is so strong, intensive emphasis on vocabulary was an immediate concern when I prepared the first edition. My current tutoring job on campus and the workshops I teach for prospective teachers have only strengthened this conviction. Thus, vocabulary remains an integral part of the text.

To this end, a section titled "Vocabulary Analysis" precedes each selection (Parts One through Five). Each preview introduces students to one or two words that they will encounter in the reading. Typically divided into Word Parts and Word Families, these introductory sections introduce the reader to prefixes, roots, and suffixes, and illustrate a systematic way to analyze and to acquire new words. This vocabulary is taught in the context of the reading and should be useful both for English speakers and for English-language learners alike.

Finally, Parts One through Five include two vocabulary exercises, the forms of which vary from selection to selection, as a glance through the text will show. My aim is to make the vocabulary exercises more challenging and engaging than merely multiple-choice questions. Many exercises ask students to locate a word in the paragraph that matches a given definition. Others ask them to show their mastery of the meanings of several words by inserting them into a paragraph correctly; still others ask students to provide variant forms of some of the selection's most important words.

READING SKILLS AND THE EXERCISE MATERIAL

Each section of the book begins with an overview and explanation of various skills necessary for good reading comprehension and analysis. These topics are arranged so that students encounter the most fundamental skills at the beginning of the course before progressing to the next level. The introductions contain short examples and excerpts to familiarize students with these skills. In response to reviewers' suggestions, I have expanded these introductory sections for the most part, giving students an opportunity to practice with short exercise material.

The exercises in the seventh edition are extensive and cover a wider range of skills than those in most other college reading texts. Step by step, each exercise provides students an opportunity to practice these skills at a level appropriate for each reading. Instructors should feel free to choose exercises from among those offered and not feel compelled to assign them all. By the end of the course, these exercises will have helped to improve students' comprehension and analytical skills. In addition to the aforementioned vocabulary exercises, after each selection students are given intensive practice in the following skills: comprehending main ideas, identifying the writer's purpose, annotating and paraphrasing, sequencing (rearranging scrambled sentences to form a logical passage), locating information, distinguishing between main ideas and supporting details, making inferences and drawing conclusions, and distinguishing between fact and opinion. Emphasis on summary writing, paraphrasing, and annotating occurs throughout the text as well.

WEBSITE MATERIAL—HELP FOR INSTRUCTORS

To help in course planning, instructors will find a great deal of help on the website accompanying the book. For each selection, they will find a brief summary, some suggestions for teaching the reading selection, information about word lengths, grade levels, readability scores, and where relevant, answers to exercises (Parts One through Five and Part Seven). The address is www.mhhe.com/spears. Click on the cover of the book to access the Instructor's Manual.

Changes in the Seventh Edition

The most significant change is the inclusion of Parts Six and Seven—Reading Short Fiction and Everyday Reading—which give students an opportunity to read short stories for pleasure and to develop techniques for reading material outside the usual classroom experience. This latter section includes suggestions for reading newspaper articles, blogs, credit card inserts, recipes, labels on processed food packages, graphic material, and a discussion of e-readers. Brief exercises are included for most of these.

I have incorporated almost without exception the many excellent suggestions made by the reviewers of the previous edition. Here are the most significant changes in the seventh edition:

- Expanded Part Introductions that now precede each of the book's first five parts, including more short exercises.
- More easy, short readings, especially in Parts One and Two, and a balance between multiple-choice and fill-in answers. Many selections are between 600 and 1,000 words long.
- Where appropriate, for several readings students will find a group activity to define slang and idiomatic expressions, particularly helpful for English-language learners.
- Increased emphasis on annotating, paraphrasing, and summarizing.
- In Part Five, Reading About Issues, I have included a section called What More Do I Need to Know? giving students a chance to ask questions about the reading that go beyond the reading. The point here is that being educated doesn't mean having knowledge about a subject; it also means knowing what questions to ask.
- Each selection ends with Explore the Web, giving students a task to perform or a topic to explore in more depth that relates to the reading.
- The inclusion of short fiction and practical reading material.

Acknowledgements

I wish to thank all of the reviewers of the sixth edition, who offered many fine suggestions about how to improve the book, and I am grateful for their help. If this edition is better than previous ones, it is because of them:

Karin Alderfer, Miami Dade College
Jehane Brown, Santa Barbara City College
Marie Eckstrom, Rio Hondo College
Mary Ann Weyandt, Alan Hancock College
Janice Wiggins-Clarke, Passaic County Community College

I must also thank Steven Penzinger, formerly of Random House, who believed in my original proposal enough to take a chance on publishing the first edition. Janice Wiggins-Clarke, my developmental editor, supervised the revision process and handled innumerable details efficiently and with good humor. Wes Hall cleared the permissions and solved a number of thorny issues surrounding their clearance. Thanks also to Joyce Watters, Project Manager, and Allison Morgan and Chris Black at Lachina Publishing Services, who efficiently handled the book's production. To all of them, I am most grateful.

Instructors should feel free to send suggestions, comments, or questions via e-mail to me at dkspears@gmail.com. I can also be reached through the McGraw-Hill Higher Education website at http://www.mhhe.com/spears. I will do my best to answer all correspondence within a day or two.

Deanne Spears
Half Moon Bay, California

To the Student

The Aims of the Text

This is the seventh edition of *Improving Reading Skills*. Because the book has evolved in many ways—both large and small—since the first edition, you will benefit from the many changes it has undergone. If you work through the readings diligently and attentively, with your instructor's help you will achieve several goals: better concentration, improved reading comprehension, an advanced level of vocabulary, a knowledge of major word elements, and most important, a way to tie the content of the readings to the outside world. Finally, you can pursue subjects that particularly interest you by accessing relevant websites.

Your instructor and I hope that you will derive the ultimate benefit from the instruction provided in the text: an enjoyment of reading that becomes a lifelong pursuit. Reading well allows you to travel from the comfort of your home, to dream, to escape, to learn, to understand the important issues of the day, to question, and—most crucially as a student and citizen—to think.

The selections in this edition are drawn from books, magazines, newspapers, online sources, blogs, and college textbooks. Parts One through Five and Part Seven represent nonfiction, the kind of reading required in your other college courses (in particular, English courses), and reading material you will encounter the rest of your life. I have tried to choose high-interest readings reflecting a variety of topics and writing styles. Some are entertaining, some are informative, some are provocative. Most will give you something to think about—and to write about. The selections are arranged in order of difficulty, which means that as you work through them, you will be able to refine your comprehension, vocabulary, and analytical skills with increasingly more challenging material.

New to the seventh edition is Reading Short Fiction (Part Six) and Everyday Reading (Part Seven); the latter shows you how to tackle such mundane reading tasks as contracts, graphic material, recipes, and blogs, along with some thoughts about e-readers.

The Structure of the Text

The book is divided into seven parts. Each part begins with instruction in a particular reading skill. Since the material moves from simple to moderate to more difficult, the introductions conform to that system so that the most important skills are taken up first; each provides you with an opportunity to practice the skills with short excerpts before going on to the longer readings. It is worth taking a few minutes to look over the table of contents to see the overall organization of the contents. And even if your instructor doesn't assign it, be sure to read and to work through the exercises accompanying the Practice Selection in Part One by Dave Barry, which will familiarize you with the exercise material throughout the text.

Post-Reading Exercises

The exercise material following each reading will help you to practice a variety of important reading skills. Taken together, they will show you how to read systematically and will provide a structure and direction for your reading. Some of the exercises are multiple-choice, while others require you to formulate answers in your own words. Although the types of exercises vary from selection to selection, each skill is reinforced throughout the text as the material becomes more difficult. Further, these exercises break the process of comprehension and analysis down into small, separate steps, so that little by little, you will understand better what to look for when you read, whether you are reading for an academic course or for pleasure. A side benefit is that you should find it easier to concentrate and to focus as you read.

The questions for writing or discussion ask you to respond to reading in a short essay or to consider an important question that the selection raises. You should look over these two sections even if your instructor does not assign them, since they might provide inspiration for essays that you have to write in other courses.

The Skills You Will Learn

The skills that, apart from vocabulary, you will work on during the term include understanding the main idea, identifying the writer's purpose, distinguishing between main ideas and supporting details, making accurate inferences and conclusions, learning to annotate, paraphrasing and summarizing, distinguishing between fact and opinion, analyzing structure, patterns of development and placement of transitions, and identifying the claim and the evidence in editorial (persuasive) writing.

Exploring on Your Own—Explore the Web

Opportunities to search the Web on topics relevant to the selections' themes are integrated throughout the text in the many sections called Explore the Web. In some instances, I provide websites for you to explore; in other instances, I suggest how to conduct a search of a particular topic, using Google or your favorite search engine. I point you in some direction so that if you are particularly intrigued by a selection and want to read more, you can find a starting place. Many of the recommended sites include links to related sites.

Vocabulary—The Crucial Element

Even if your instructor doesn't assign it, be sure to read the introductory material on improving your vocabulary. This section offers some techniques for acquiring new vocabulary words and introduces you to context clues and to efficient ways of using the dictionary. Good vocabulary is essential for good comprehension skills. Stated another way, if you don't know the meanings of many words a writer uses, it's very difficult to know exactly what he or she is saying. All that you can hope for is to come away with a hazy idea of the main point.

The best way to improve your vocabulary is to commit yourself during the term to looking up many unfamiliar words that you encounter in your reading. At first this task may seem overwhelming, but as you work through the material, you will see that the job is not as daunting as it might at first have appeared.

Each selection opens with a Vocabulary Analysis, which is explained in detail in Part One's Practice Selection. As you work through the vocabulary exercises, remember that it is not cheating to look up unfamiliar words in the dictionary.

As will be demonstrated throughout the text, good comprehension and good vocabulary skills are interdependent. As the weeks go by, you will be pleasantly surprised to find that words you have met in the earlier selections will turn up again in later ones and in your other reading, as well. For example, one student told me that every morning while riding on a San Francisco Muni bus, she had seen an advertisement over the window which used a word previously unfamiliar to her—*nostalgia*. One day she encountered the word in a Vocabulary Preview section, and suddenly the ad made sense to her!

CALCULATING YOUR COMPREHENSION SCORE

Some of the selections contain only comprehension questions, followed by the regular exercises. However, the majority of selections in Parts One through Four ask you to do Exercises A and B without looking back at the selection. Your instructor may ask you to disregard these instructions. Not looking back, however, will force you to read with greater attention and concentration than you would if you knew you could look back at the passage to refresh your memory. When you are finished with all the exercises, calculate your comprehension score by counting your correct answers for the first two exercises, according to the formula.

Since the two questions on determining the main idea and writer's purpose are most crucial, each is worth two points, while the main-idea questions in Exercise B are each worth one point. Your final score will be a percentage of 100, the total number of points. Study this example of a hypothetical student who got both questions in section A correct and four questions in section B correct:

A. No. right ___2___ × 2 = ___4___

B. No. right ___4___ × 1 = ___4___

Total points from A and B _____8_____ × 10 = _____80_____ percent

Since the selections become progressively more difficult, maintaining a score of 70 percent or higher indicates steady improvement. A chart on which you can keep track of your progress is included at the back of the text. Again, note that some selections are missing from this chart because the comprehension questions are open-ended, requiring you to fill in the answers.

Finally, to be sure that you get the most out of the text and the course, be sure to ask your instructor for help with anything you do not understand. If you have questions, comments, or suggestions, you can reach me via e-mail at dkspears@gmail.com and also through McGraw-Hill's homepage at http://www.mhhe.com/spears. I will do my best to reply within a day or two.

Deanne Spears
Half Moon Bay, California

Improving Your Vocabulary

When my students complain in the reading classes I teach that they often have difficulty concentrating and maintaining focus as they read, we discuss the problem at length. Although poor concentration may be the result of many factors—going to school and working at the same time, personal problems, lack of sleep, financial worries—the problem is more often caused by lack of vocabulary. Reading is tedious if there are many unfamiliar words on the page, and having to look up lots of words in the dictionary is time-consuming and discouraging. A weak vocabulary is indeed a significant obstacle to good reading comprehension. Therefore, acquiring new vocabulary words is crucial if you hope to become a better reader. After all, if you do not know what key words on the page mean, you may not understand what a writer is saying.

Acquiring a solid reading vocabulary is a lifelong proposition, and I hope that this text will be of great use as you expand this most necessary of skills. Your goal during the course should be to acquire as many college-level vocabulary words as you can while you read each selection. Your goal after the course ends should be to continue to acquire words as you read in your everyday life.

And acquiring new words will have more benefits besides making you a better reader. Fair or not, people do judge others by their level of vocabulary, and surely as you acquire new words, you can begin to use some of them when you speak. Educated speakers tend to have good vocabularies, and they usually command respect and admiration for this quality. Beware, though. You don't want to come off as pretentious or sound like a walking dictionary.

For these reasons, it is important that you embark on a systematic vocabulary-acquisition program. Several features in this text will help you accomplish this. As you work through the selections, you will learn to identify common prefixes and roots, to break words down into their meaningful parts, and to use context clues to determine the meaning of unfamiliar words. When context clues aren't helpful, you can turn to your dictionary, as even the best readers do from time to time. This introductory portion of the text explores some techniques to increase your *recognition vocabulary*—words you can readily define from both your college and your everyday reading. Everything will work together to give you measurable immediate and long-term results. This introduction discusses these topics:

- Five techniques for acquiring words
- Breaking words down into their component parts
- Using context clues
- Using the dictionary effectively
- Comparing print and online dictionaries

As I prepared the selections and the accompanying exercises, I quickly saw that many words from the early selections—actually a surprising number—turned up in subsequent ones. Of course, I did not plan it this way; it just happened. This is the reason I stress that you read the Vocabulary Preview sections preceding each selection, even if your instructor doesn't assign them, and that you work through the two vocabulary exercises after each selection. If you do this conscientiously, not only will your stock of vocabulary words grow, but your reading of the later pieces will be easier and more enjoyable. The thrill of recognition does wonders for one's reading morale.

The single best way to improve your vocabulary is to read a lot. There is no shortcut or substitute for this method. The idea is simple and obvious: The more you read, the more you will be exposed to important vocabulary words. Memorizing long lists of words in isolation or working through vocabulary self-improvement books may fool you into thinking you are learning new words, but their meanings won't stick, and such activities deprive you of encountering words in real writing. The following are a few suggestions for learning new words.

Five Techniques for Acquiring Words

This section introduces some techniques to help you learn new words and retain them better.

TECHNIQUES FOR ACQUIRING WORDS
• Use the Three-Dot Method • Use Vocabulary Note Cards • Break New Words Down into Their Component Parts • Develop an Interest in Etymology • Subscribe to a Word-of-the-Day Website

USE THE THREE-DOT METHOD

The three-dot method works like this: When you look up a word in the dictionary, make a small dot in pencil next to the entry word. The second time you look it up, make another dot. The third time you look it up, add a third dot, and this time, learn the word! Any word that crops up three times within a short amount of time is obviously an important word that belongs in your permanent and active reading vocabulary.

THE THREE-DOT METHOD
• • • **eu • tha • na • sia** (yo͞o-thə -nā′ zhə, zhē-ə) *n*. The act or practice of ending the life of an individual suffering from a terminal illness or an incurable condition. [Gk., a good death: *eu-*, +*thanatos*, death]

USE VOCABULARY NOTE CARDS (OR KEEP A VOCABULARY NOTEBOOK)

When I studied German in college, our instructor suggested that we use 3″ × 5″ index cards to help us learn important vocabulary words. I did this religiously and found the cards' compact size perfect. Index cards can be easily secured with a rubber band and carried in your backpack, pocket, or purse. I could quickly review vocabulary words that we were to be tested on, sorting through the stack, omitting those I already knew, and concentrating on those that I wasn't so sure of. When the stack of cards became too unwieldy, I organized them into parts of speech (nouns in one stack, verbs in another, and so on), and continued my study.

I can suggest the same method for improving your reading vocabulary. It takes just a minute to write each card, whether you use index cards or a notebook. First, write the word (underline it for emphasis), the context in which it occurred (meaning the original sentence), and if you wish, the part of speech and pronunciation. On the other side, write the definition and etymology. Study this example from Selection 3 by Joe Abbott, "To Kill a Hawk":

Front side of card—word in original context, part of speech, and pronunciation

> . . . the <u>epiphany</u> was in part a result of something that happened the day before
>
> noun
>
> ĭ - pĭf′ə - ne

Reverse side of card—major definitions and the etymology (language from which English word is derived, and its meaning)

> (1) a revelatory manifestation of a divine being
> (2) <u>perception of reality by means of a sudden intuitive realization</u>
>   from Greek— "to appear"

ESL students who are struggling to master the complexities of the English language might be interested in learning *variant word forms*. In fact, most of the reading selections throughout Parts One through Four include an exercise in which you have to determine which form of the root word to use. ESL students might profit from including these variant forms on their vocabulary card, as you see in the following example from this excerpt that appears in the introduction to Part One:

> One of the few hues that can be *perceived* as both light and dark, blue defines our many moods. (James Sullivan, *Jeans: A Critical History of an American Icon*)

Study the front and back sides of this sample index card:

Front side of card—word in original context, part of speech, and pronunciation

can be _perceived_ as both light and dark

verb

pər - sēv.

Reverse side of card—appropriate definition, etymology (the language the word comes from), and some variant forms

become aware of through the senses

etymology: Latin [per + capere ("to seize")

variant forms: perception (noun)

perceptive (adjective)

perceptively (adverb)

An alternate method is to write new words in a vocabulary notebook, for example in an inexpensive spiral notebook. Using the notebook means that you can record the words in the order in which they appear, along with the page number where the word appeared in the selection. When you reread the selection, you can easily locate the definitions to refresh your memory in case you can't remember a particular word.

Which words should you write down? You don't want to overwhelm yourself with hundreds of unfamiliar words, so I would suggest—at least at first—noting those words that you have seen before in your reading but that you can't readily define. (This is called your recognition vocabulary.) Because you have seen these words before, they are not completely unfamiliar, and they are probably common enough in adult prose to make them a worthwhile addition to your vocabulary. As your command of new words grows, you can then focus on learning more unusual words.

BREAK NEW WORDS DOWN INTO THEIR COMPONENT PARTS

In Dave Barry's humorous essay that follows this introduction, after a disastrous date with Roger, Elaine calls her closest friend, and as Barry writes, "In _painstaking_ detail, they will analyze everything she said and everything he said, going over it time and time again, exploring every word, every expression, and gesture. . . ." Even if you have never seen the word _painstaking_, you can perhaps determine the meaning by separating the two parts of the word and then reversing them: _pains taking_ becomes "taking pains" or "taking great care"—in other words, analyzing the conversation in great detail.

Here is a second example from Selection 3 by Joe Abbott, "To Kill a Hawk." In describing the sudden revelation, or epiphany, that he experienced, Abbot writes:

> . . . even though the thing forgotten was the kind of experience, an epiphany, really, that marks a person's life, a moment which designates an *irrevocable* turning point.

You are probably already familiar with the verb *revoke*, as when one's license is revoked or when some privilege is revoked; in other words, when something is cancelled or taken back. *Irrevocable* (the accent is on the second syllable) can be broken down like this:

ir- (prefix, meaning "not")   +voc- (root, meaning "to call")   +-able (suffix, "able to")

Put this all together, and you will get something like this:

a literal definition   not able to be called

a better definition   not able to be cancelled or withdrawn

It's not a perfect definition, since *irrevocable* describes something that can't be taken back, but it's good enough to give you the sense of what Abbott means.

DEVELOP AN INTEREST IN ETYMOLOGY

Etymology refers to the study of word origins, and paying attention to them is not only interesting for its own sake; in addition, word origins can be helpful for remembering the meanings of new words. Something like 60 percent of English words come from Latin via French, one of the several Romance languages derived from Latin; another 15 percent derive from Greek, often through Latin, as well. Many words have unusual origins.

Hejira or hegira "Hejira" is the title of Selection 1 by David Sedaris. This word is unusual because it derives from Arabic, meaning "flight." Specifically, it is used to describe the prophet Mohammed's flight from Mecca to Medina and is also used to signify the beginning of the Muslim era. When you read Sedaris's selection, you will understand the title's significance in context of his narrative.

narcissism The word *narcissism* has become quite current with the enormous popularity of Facebook and other social media. Elizabeth Bernstein addresses this phenomenon in Selection 10, "How Facebook Ruins Friendships," which you will read in Part 2. The etymology of *narcissism* is provided in the Vocabulary Preview section. Briefly, the word derives from Greek mythology. One version of the myth says that Nemesis, the goddess of revenge, decreed that Narcissus would fall in love with himself. When Narcissus, who was a handsome young man, leaned over a pool of water one day, he saw his own reflection and became completely infatuated with himself. There's more to the story, but you will read the rest of it later.

If 75 percent of the words in English are derived from Latin, French, and Greek, what of the remaining 25 percent? Many, of course, derive from the original English language, known as Anglo-Saxon. These tend to be the very basic building-block words of the language, words like *sun, moon, walk, boy, daughter, house,* and so on. But many words come from more exotic and unusual languages.

WORDS WITH UNUSUAL ETYMOLOGIES	
Arabic	algebra, tariff, alchemy, alkali, hejira
Native American languages	canoe, hammock, succotash, moccasin, skunk, chile
Malay	amok (an uncontrolled state)
Tamil	pariah (an outcast)
Alaskan Russian	parka
Hungarian	coach (a type of carriage)
Old Norse	sky, skirt

SUBSCRIBE TO A WORD-OF-THE-DAY WEBSITE

Word-of-the-day websites offer a painless, entertaining, and free way to learn new words. Most of them have the same features: An e-mail or text message is sent to your inbox (or to your Twitter or Facebook account, in some cases). Each day you receive a new word. Typically, the information includes pronunciation symbols, a definition, a sentence or two showing how the word is used, and the word's etymology. Some sites include pronunciation. By clicking on the megaphone, you will hear the word pronounced by a native speaker. Here are four current word-of-the-day websites to check out, with four sample words for each. All these sites were current in summer 2012. If you are unable to locate one of them, go to Google and in the search box type in "Word of the Day Websites."

WORD-OF-THE-DAY WEBSITES
Dictionary.com Word of the Day
www.dictionaryreference.com
Sample words: altruistic, churlish, glower, bonanza
Merriam-Webster Word of the Day
http://www.merriam-webster.com/word-of-the-day/
Sample words: diligent, genuflect, sustain, QWERTY
WordThink.com
www.wordthink.com
Sample words: incongruous, assiduous, anecdotal, pragmatic
Merriam-Webster's Learner's Dictionary (for ESL English-language learners)
www.learnersdictionary.com
Sample words: gamble, reserve, crucial, secure

Using Context Clues

We begin this section with an exercise called a *cloze test*. Here is a passage from a selection you will read in Part 1, Sherman Alexie, "Superman and Me." Approximately every sixth word has been left out. None of the omitted words is difficult, and some of them are structure words like "a" and "the." Your task is to fill in the words that make sense and complete the meaning of the sentence. Be sure to pay attention both to the meaning and to grammar and sentence structure. The passage describes how Alexie learned to read.

I learned to read with _____ Superman comic book. Simple enough, _____ suppose. I cannot recall which particular _____ comic book I read, nor _____ I remember which villain he _____ in that issue. I cannot _____ the plot, nor the means _____ which I obtained the comic _____. What I can remember is _____: I was 3 years old, _____ Spokane Indian boy living with _____ family on the Spokane Indian Reservation _____ eastern Washington state. We were poor _____ most standards, but one of my _____ usually managed to find some minimum-_____ job or another, which made us middle-_____ by reservation standards. I had a _____ and three sisters. We lived _____ a combination of irregular paychecks, hope, fear _____ government surplus food.

Here is the passage again, this time with the missing words restored and boldfaced.

I learned to read with **a** Superman comic book. Simple enough, **I** suppose. I cannot recall which particular **Superman** comic book I read, nor **can** I remember which villain he **fought** in that issue. I cannot **remember** the plot, nor the means **by** which I obtained the comic **book**. What I can remember is **this**: I was 3 years old, **a** Spokane Indian boy living with **his** family on the Spokane Indian Reservation **in** eastern Washington state. We were poor **by** most standards, but one of my **parents** usually managed to find some minimum-**wage** job or another, which made us middle-**class** by reservation standards. I had a **brother** and three sisters. We lived **on** a combination of irregular paychecks, hope, fear **and** government surplus food.

There are nineteen answers. Give yourself a point for each answer that matches the correct ones above. Do not subtract a point if you used *recall* instead of *remember* or *defeated* instead of *fought*. You should consider 14 out of 19 correct a very acceptable score.

It's *context* that accounts for your ability to identify these words. *Context* refers to the words and phrases that surround a particular word and that *may* help you to figure out its meaning. In the preceeding passage, you used grammatical and word context clues to help you choose the right word. For example, following the phrase "Spokane Indian Reservation," the only English preposition that will work is *in*. We don't say *on eastern Washington state*, or *near* eastern *Washington State*.

The author of a book I am currently reading explains and illustrates context very succinctly. Daniel L. Everett, a linguist and anthropologist, wrote *Don't Sleep, There Are Snakes*, a fascinating account of his experiences living with and studying the Pirahã Indians who inhabit a region in Brazil's Amazonian jungle. Everett struggled to learn their difficult language, unique in the world for various reasons that he explains in the book. Here is the relevant part about context. He begins by talking about *sense*, which is defined as "the relations between words and the way that they are used":

> Think of what *break* means in examples like *John broke his arm*, *John broke the ice in the frigid conversation*, *John broke the sentence down for me*, or *John broke into the house*, for example. The only way that we can know what *break* means is to know how it is used. And using a word means selecting a particular context, a set of background assumptions shared by the speaker and the hearer, including how particular words should be used, and the other words that the word in question is used with.

This is the magical part about reading, and of course, the challenge. Getting at the underlying meaning of a sentence isn't just a matter of decoding the words one at a time (i.e., pronouncing them); it's a matter of sorting out and understanding the words' meanings in relation to the other words around them. When everything clicks, when we understand clearly what a writer says, we make a great leap forward, and more important, reading becomes much more enjoyable.

While you were growing up, you learned words by absorption, from the way people used them around you. You certainly didn't learn them from a dictionary. No one leans over a baby's crib and says, "My, what a good vocabulary she has." You figured out their meanings because of the several contexts in which you encountered them.

But a lot of words that appear in higher-level reading material—the language used in college reading material and in adult reading—aren't commonly used in speech. You might encounter them only in your reading. People who read a lot usually have a good reading vocabulary because they have exposed themselves to new words for years. Absorbing new words by reading a lot (i.e., practice) has one major drawback: It takes years to accomplish. Since time is of the essence if your vocabulary isn't up to the task of college assignments, you need to adopt some shortcuts. Here are a couple of suggestions:

First, try to break down the word into its component parts, which is demonstrated throughout the book in the Vocabulary Analysis sections. For example, when Sherman Alexie describes how Indian children behaved with their teachers, he writes: "They were *monosyllabic* in front of their non-Indian teachers but could tell complicated stories and jokes at the dinner table."

If you've never encountered the word *monosyllabic* before, you can perhaps figure it out by considering this. You probably know *monarchy* (rule by one) and you know *syllable*. *Syllabic* is simply the adjective form. So putting these two parts together you get this:

mono- (prefix meaning "one" or "single") + *syllable* (a part of a word containing one vowel) = an adjective that describes words of only one syllable

So word analysis is one possibility for determining the meaning of unfamiliar words. Draw on your knowledge of related words to help you figure out new words. The second suggestion is to use context clues, discussed previously, which may also yield a sufficiently acceptable meaning. Context clues free you from having to look up every unfamiliar word in the dictionary. It's tedious to have to look up so many words, and it detracts from the pleasure of reading. (However, the more you read, the fewer new words you will meet. It won't be tedious forever!)

Let's see how context clues work with an example you will encounter in the introduction to Part 1. Study this excerpt by poet and essayist Leslie Marmon Silko, a Native American of the Laguna Pueblo:

> As a person of mixed ancestry growing up in the United States in the late 1950s, I knew all of the cruel *epithets* that might be hurled at others; the knowledge was a sort of *solace* that I was not alone in my feelings of unease, of not quite belonging to the group that clearly mattered most in the United States.

If the words *epithets* and *solace* are unfamiliar to you, see if you can determine their meaning from the context: What would people hurl at others that are cruel? You might think of rocks, but rocks aren't cruel in and of themselves. More likely, *epithets* refer to abusive terms, often used against people of another race or ethnicity. And *solace* is something that reduced her "feelings of unease," so that sounds as if she was comforted or consoled. Relying on context clues isn't foolproof, and even though using them requires some thought, they can help you expand your knowledge of higher-level vocabulary.

Let's look at some specific types of context clues so that you are familiar with how they work before you begin the book. Each example is taken from some of the readings in the text. I have identified the writer and selection number in each instance and, where appropriate, drawn arrows from the context clue to the unfamiliar word printed in italics.

Synonyms A *synonym* is a word that is close in meaning to the word in question. This is the easiest type of context clue to recognize. For example, consider again this excerpt from Selection 3 by Joe Abbott:

> . . . even though the thing forgotten was the kind of experience, an *epiphany*, really, that marks a person's life, a moment which designates an irrevocable turning point.

Abbott's definition is good enough to give you an understanding of the word.

Antonyms An *antonym* is a word that means the opposite of the one you are unsure of. The antonym isn't as common as the other types of context clues, however, because writers have a tendency to use synonyms as clues rather than antonyms. Here is one example from Selection 6 by John Bussey, "Old Hat for the New Normal," in which he describes the new "buzz-phrase"—the "new normal":

> It springs from the discovery that—big surprise!—we've been living beyond our means. Three years of economic crisis gave life to our new cliché, chastened as we are now to be more cost-conscious, more *prudent*.

The phrase "living beyond our means" refers to spending too much money. The opposite of that is being *prudent*—careful with our money, also suggested by the related phrase "cost-conscious."

Examples or Series of Details   An *example*—a particular instance of something more general—or a cluster of details in a sentence may reveal the meaning of an unfamiliar word. In "How Facebook Ruins Friendships" (Selection 10), Elizabeth Bernstein writes this:

> Typing still leaves something to be desired as a communication tool; it lacks the *nuances* that can be expressed by body language and voice inflection. "Online, people can't see the yawn," says Patricia Wallace, a psychologist at Johns Hopkins University. . .

Meaning "shades of meaning" or "subtle degrees of difference," the examples of body language and voice inflection suggest a sufficiently accurate definition.

Situation   The *situation* or circumstance in which the word is used may give you a hint as to its meaning. In Selection 25 Mark Ian Barasch describes his experience living on the streets of Denver for a week as a homeless person as an exercise in developing compassion. Consider this excerpt:

> It's a different map of the world. Which Starbucks has a security guard who'll let you use the bathroom? How long can you linger in this place or that before you're *rousted*?

Even if you have never seen the word *rousted* before, the situation Barasch describes indicates that it means to be forced out of a place, asked to leave.

Emotion   The emotional attitude evident in a passage—its mood or atmosphere— may provide a good enough clue to save you from turning to the dictionary. In Selection 29, "The Seat Not Taken," the African-American writer and professor John Edgar Wideman writes about the odd experience of other passengers never sitting next to him in the Amtrak train he rides between New York and Providence, Rhode Island, where he teaches:

> Of course, I'm not registering a complaint about the privilege, conferred upon me by color, to enjoy the luxury of an extra seat to myself. I *relish* the opportunity to spread out, *savor* the privacy and quiet and work or gaze at the scenic New England woods and coast.

Relish and *savor* mean nearly the same thing—a positive emotional enjoyment of something pleasurable. Both the emotion and the situation suggest the meaning of both words, and of course, if you know one, you can easily figure out the other.

EXERCISE 1—USING CONTEXT CLUES

Try your hand at these passages that contain some words that might be unfamiliar to you. Study the passage carefully, paying attention to the context surrounding the italicized word. Then write your best estimation of the word's meaning in the first space. Finally, look the word up in the dictionary and write the definition in the second space. See how close your definition is to the dictionary's.

1. Never let up, women. Pound away *relentlessly* at this concept, and eventu-ally it will start to penetrate the guy's brain. (Practice Selection—Dave Barry, "Tips for Women: How to Have a Relationship with a Guy")

    Your definition _____
    Dictionary definition _____

2. If any aspect of the economic squeeze is hitting American workers across the board—white collar and blue-collar, high-income and low-income, chief executives and janitors—it is the phenomenon of increased stress on the job, a combination of longer workweeks and having to *toil* harder and faster dur-ing one's hours at work. (Introduction to Part 1, Steven Greenhouse, *The Big Squeeze: Tough Times for the American Worker*)

    Your definition _____
    Dictionary definition _____

3. At home all I had was an ancient English/Spanish dictionary my father had used to teach himself English, but its tiny print and archaic language did more to *obscure* meaning than to shed light on it. (Selection 4, Rose Guilbault, "School Days")

    Your definition _____
    Dictionary definition _____

4. The writer is describing a fellow student, a Navy veteran, who had been stationed in the Middle East during the Iraq war: "He tells me that he was in the Middle East early on in the war around the same time I was. A job brought him up to the Bay Area and when he saw how much money he could receive by going back to school, he jumped on it. I asked him if he misses the military, and with a slight hint of regret he *reminisces*: 'Oh yea, I thought it was going to be a career but . . .'" (Selection 5, Colby Buzzell, "Johnny Get Your Textbook")

    Your definition _____
    Dictionary definition _____

5. Of the few *hues* that can be perceived as both light and dark, blue defines our many moods. (Improving Your Vocabulary, James Sullivan, *Jeans: A Cultural History of an American Icon*)

    Your definition _____
    Dictionary definition _____

6. I stopped talking to Kelly, my wife. She *loathed* me, my silences, my distance, my inertia. I stopped walking my dog, so she hated me, too. (Selection 11, Chris Rose, "Hell and Back")

    Your definition _____
    Dictionary definition _____

7. Yolanda Leif graphically describes the trials of a waitress in a quality restaurant. They are compounded by her refusal to be *demeaned*. Yet pride in her
skills helps her through the night. "When I put the plate down, you don't
hear a sound. When I pick up a glass, I want it to be just right. When someone says, 'How come you're just a waitress?' I say, 'Don't you think you
deserve being served by me?'" (Selection 8, Studs Terkel, "Somebody Built
the Pyramids")

Your definition _____

Dictionary definition _____

8. The speculators, next, would hire people to pass out handbills in the Eastern
and Midwestern cities, *tracts* limning the advantages of relocation to "the Athens of the South" or "the new plains Jerusalem." When persuasion failed, the
builders might resort to bribery, paying people's moving costs and giving them
houses, in exchange for nothing but a pledge to stay until a certain census was
taken or a certain inspection made . . . The speculators' idea, of course, was to
lure the railroad. (Selection 19, Laurence Shames, "The Hunger for More")

tracts   Your definition _____

Dictionary definition _____

lure   Your definition_____

Dictionary definition _____

EXERCISE 2—USING CONTEXT CLUES

Here is an excerpt from a newspaper article. Read the passage carefully, paying
attention to possible context clues for the italicized vocabulary words. Then complete the exercise that follows.

The average American consumes 50 gallons each year of sugar-
sweetened beverages.

A double cheeseburger from McDonald's is packed with 440 calories.
Yet staying away from fast food is not necessarily the answer. A spicy tuna
roll packs 461 calories.

We live in a culture *glutted* with fatty foods. Small wonder that the average American is 23 pounds overweight and consumes 250 more calories
than two to three decades ago.

Many scientists have characterized obesity as a problem with multiple
causes. They cite a *mosaic* of biological *vulnerabilities*, family upbringing,
psychology (e.g., using food for comfort), and the environment. Genetics
studies show that weights of adopted children more closely resemble those
of their biological rather than adoptive parents, raising the possibility that
genes *trump* the environment.

Genes help determine which individuals within a population might be
most vulnerable, but how many people become overweight is determined
by *external* factors. Stated another way, obesity is caused by *toxic* food and
activity conditions that lead to too many calories consumed and too few

expended. Beginning first in countries like the U.S., this toxic environment has spread around the world and is now like a script being acted out time and again with completely predictable consequences—*rampant* obesity and diabetes. Overnutrition and obesity are not bigger problems in countries like India and China than are hunger and *malnutrition*. . . .

—From Kelly D. Brownell, "Nature and Nachos: How Fat Happens," *The Wall Street Journal*, May 1, 2010. Reprinted by permission of *The Wall Street Journal*, Copyright © 2010 by Dow Jones & Company, Inc. All Rights Reserved Worldwide. License numbers 2923230610525 and 2923230717498.

Choose the best definitions for each of the italicized words according to the context.

_____ 1. *glutted*:   (a) flooded   (b) characterized by   (c) satisfied by

_____ 2. *mosaic*:   (a) artistic design   (b) complicated pattern
(c) research study

_____ 3. *vulnerabilities*:   (a) susceptibilities; weaknesses
(b) factors, reasons
(c) persuasions, temptations

_____ 4. *trump*:   (a) reveal   (b) are more important than   (c) illustrate

_____ 5. *external*:   (a) on the inside   (b) surrounding   (c) on the outside

_____ 6. *toxic*:   (a) highly processed   (b) unhealthy
(c) literally poisonous

_____ 7. *expended*:   (a) saved up   (b) used up through activity
(c) digested

_____ 8. *rampant*:   (a) occurring without restraint   (b) universal
(c) declining

_____ 9. *overnutrition*:   (a) eating expensive food beyond what one can afford
(b) eating food that is healthy and nutritious
(c) eating too much food, especially unhealthy food

_____ 10. *malnutrition*:   (a) average nutrition   (b) excessive nutrition
(c) poor nutrition

Using the Dictionary

Whether you use a print or an online dictionary, you will need to become familiar with their features. If you do not have a desk dictionary (print format), ask your instructor to recommend one, or choose one from this list:

The American Heritage College Dictionary
The Random House College Dictionary
Webster's New World Dictionary

THE FEATURES OF A DICTIONARY

No matter which dictionary you choose, all contain the same features. Here is a brief overview of the important ones.

Guide Words *Guide words* are printed in boldface in the top margin of each page; they indicate the first and last words and help you locate words quickly. For example, if you are looking up the word *emulate*, the guide words at the top of the page—which could be *empress* and *enantiomorph*—show you quickly that you're on the right page.

Entry The word *entry* is simply a fancy term for the word that you are looking up. It is printed in boldface type in the left margin; dots separate the syllables, for example:

o • blit • er • ate

Obliterate, therefore, has four syllables.

Pronunciation Symbols *Pronunciation symbols* are printed in parentheses and follow the entry. English has a complicated pronunciation system. Unlike Spanish, for example, in which every letter always has the same sound, English has approximately 75 different sounds but only 26 letters to represent them. A single vowel letter like *a*, for example, can be pronounced seven ways, as in these words: *cat* (ă); *lake* (ā); *bar* (är); *bare* (âr); *part* (är); *law* (ô); and *father* (ä). The pronunciation symbols follow a standardized system to show you how each letter or combination of letters should be pronounced in an unfamiliar word. Ask your instructor for help if you don't know how to pronounce these symbols. In the college edition of *American Heritage Dictionary*, these symbols are printed in the lower-right corner of each *right* page. Other dictionaries print them across the bottom of both pages.

Stress Marks *Stress*, or *accent*, marks are as important as pronunciation symbols for pronouncing words correctly. Referring to the relative degree of loudness of each syllable, stress marks are printed *after* the syllable to be stressed within the pronunciation symbols, as you can see in this word: *solid* (sŏl′id). In this case, the first syllable, *sol*, receives primary stress or emphasis.

English has three kinds of stress. Primary, or heavy stress, is shown by a heavy boldface mark, like this: ′. Secondary, or weak stress, is shown by the same mark printed in lighter type, like this: ′. Unstressed syllables are often those containing a neutral vowel sound—symbolized by a pronunciation symbol called a *schwa*—which is written like an upside down "e" (ə). For example, the word *magnification* contains all three types of stress:

măg′nə-fĭ-kā′shən.

The first syllable takes the secondary stress, the fourth syllable takes the primary stress, and the second and fifth syllables (each with a schwa) are unstressed.

Parts of Speech and Inflected Forms Following the dictionary pronunciation symbols is an abbreviation indicating what part of speech the entry word is. For example, *n.* = noun; *v.* = verb, *adj.* = adjective, *adv.* = adverb, and so forth. As you will see at the end of this section, many words cross over and represent several parts of speech. It's important to know what kind of word (noun, adjective, and so forth) is used in the passage.

Inflected forms—the forms of the word that take inflections or word endings—are also included. Thus, you can look up the proper way to spell the present participle and past tense of a word like *gratify*. In *gratified* (the past tense form), the *y* changes to *i*, and the ending signifying the past tense (*-ed*) is added. In *gratifying* (the present participle), the ending *–ing* is added. Finally, in *gratifies* (the present tense for the third-person form, that is, the form used with "he," "she," or "it") the *y* changes to *i*, and the ending *–es* is added. Similarly, if you want to find the plural of the word *ox*, the dictionary indicates it like this: *n. pl.* oxen. The plural forms of *deer* and *sheep*, however, remain *deer* and *sheep*. The dictionary tells you this, as well.

Order of Definitions The one significant difference in dictionaries is in the order of definitions if a word has more than one meaning. The *American Heritage* and the *Random House* college editions follow this system: If a word has multiple senses (two or more meanings, in other words), the central and often the most commonly sought meaning is listed first. Less common senses, older forms, and obsolete senses are listed next. *However*, this does not mean that you should read the first meaning listed and look no further. The context is crucial in determining which sense best fits a particular word's meaning. This concept will be illustrated in more detail later in this section.

In contrast, the *Merriam-Webster's Collegiate Dictionary* organizes its definitions historically, which means that the earliest sense or senses of a word come first, with more modern senses following. If you are unsure about which method your particular dictionary uses, ask your instructor for help or refer to the early pages of the dictionary, called the *front matter*, where there will be a description of the *Order of Senses* or something similar.

Variant Forms If the word has other grammatical forms, the dictionary will list those after the last definition. If you look up *incorrigible* (an adjective), for example, the dictionary lists as variants *incorrigibility* and *incorrigibleness* (nouns) and *incorrigibly* (adverb).

Etymology A word's *etymology* refers to its linguistic origin, that is, the language from which it came into English. Etymology also refers to the word's history. It is printed in brackets [ ], either before or after the definitions, depending on your dictionary. Some dictionaries abbreviate the language or languages of origin. For example, *OF* indicates Old French, *ME* indicates Middle English, *L* or *Lat* refers to Latin, and *Gk* means Greek. A complete list of those abbreviations can be found in the front matter of your dictionary.

Other Features Some dictionaries include useful drawings in the margins. The *American Heritage* dictionaries (both the college and unabridged editions) are particularly generous in this regard, allowing you to see, for example, the location of El Salvador on a small map of Central America, what a French chateau (castle) looks like, and what Princess Diana looked like, just to cite three random examples from my dictionary. Thus the dictionary goes far beyond being merely a resource for looking up words: It is also a mini-atlas, a biographical index, and a provider of all manner of useful information from the world around you.

Entries

Pronunciation symbols

Variant forms

Parts of speech

Usage note

Definitions

Guide words

Etymology

Pronunciation key

in charge of domestic arrangements and the administration of servants; a steward or major-domo. [Middle English < Old French, of Germanic origin.]

Sen·ghor (säN-gôr′), **Léopold Sédar** 1906–2001. Senegalese poet and politician who served (1960–1980) as the first president of Senegal following independence from France. The author of many volumes of poetry, he contributed to the development of the concept of negritude.

se·nile (sē′nīl′, sĕn′īl′) *adj.* **1a.** Relating to or having diminished cognitive function, as when memory is impaired, because of old age. **b.** Being a disease or condition whose cause is primarily advanced age: *senile cataracts.* **2.** *Geology* At the end of an erosion cycle: *senile soil.* [Latin *senilis,* proper to or characteristic of old people, aged < *senex, sen-,* old; see **sen-** in App. I.] —**se′nile′ly** *adv.* —**se·nil′i·ty** (sī-nĭl′ĭ-tē) *n.*

senile dementia *n.* A progressive, abnormally accelerated deterioration of mental faculties and emotional stability in old age, occurring especially in Alzheimer's disease.

sen·ior (sēn′yər) *adj.* **1.** *Abbr.* **Sr.** Of or being the older of two, especially the older of two persons having the same name, as father and son. **2.** Of or relating to senior citizens. **3a.** Being in a position, rank, or grade above others of the same set or class: *a senior officer; the senior ship in the battle group.* **b.** Having precedence in making certain decisions. **4.** Of or relating to the fourth and last year of high school or college: *our senior class.* **5.** Relating to or being a class of corporate debt that has priority with respect to interest and principal over other classes of debt and equity by the same issuer. ❧ *n.* **1a.** A person who is older than another: *She is eight years my senior.* **b.** A senior citizen. **2a.** One that is of a higher position, rank, or grade than another in the same set or class. **b.** A student in the fourth year of high school or college. [Middle English < Latin, comparative of *senex,* old; see **sen-** in App. I.]

◆ **USAGE NOTE** *The Oxford English Dictionary* traces the use of *senior* in the sense of "an older person" to the 15th century. In contemporary American English, however, this sense of *senior* is generally taken to be a shortening of the more recent *senior citizen,* and those who object to the compound may object to the shorter term as well. However, as the *OED* makes clear, *senior* has always evoked the positive qualities of aging, including wisdom, dignity, and superior position, and it is less likely to sound condescending than the obviously coined term *senior citizen.* In any case, there is often no clear alternative to *senior* other than constructions such as *older person* or *older adult.* See Usage Notes at **elderly, old.**

senior airman *n.* **1.** A noncommissioned rank in the US Air Force that is above airman first class and below staff sergeant. **2.** One who holds this rank.

senior chief petty officer *n.* **1.** A noncommissioned rank in the US Navy that is above chief petty officer and below master chief petty officer. **2.** One who holds this rank.

senior citizen *n.* A person of relatively advanced age, especially a person who has retired. —**sen′ior-cit′i·zen** *adj.* —**senior citizenry** *n.*

senior high school *n.* A high school usually including grades 9, 10, 11, and 12.

sen·ior·i·tis (sēn′yə-rī′tĭs) *n. Informal* A reduction of academic focus or worsening of academic performance characteristic of some high-school seniors, especially after acceptance into college.

sen·ior·i·ty (sēn-yôr′ĭ-tē, -yŏr′-) *n.* **1.** The state of being older than another or others or higher in rank than another or others. **2.** Precedence of position, especially precedence over others of the same rank by reason of a longer span of service.

senior master sergeant *n.* **1.** A noncommissioned rank in the US Air Force that is above master sergeant and below chief master sergeant. **2.** One who holds this rank.

senior moment *n. Informal* An instance in which one is unable to remember something or to focus adequately on the matter at hand, viewed as typical of aging.

sen·i·ti (sĕn′ĭ-tē) *n., pl.* **seniti** A Tongan unit of currency equal to 1/100 of the pa'anga. [Tongan < English CENT.]

Sen·lac (sĕn′lăk′) A hill in southern England near Hastings. The battle fought here in 1066, in which William the Conqueror defeated Harold II, is known as the Battle of Hastings.

sen·na (sĕn′ə) *n.* **1.** Any of various plants in the pea family, chiefly of the genera *Senna* and *Chamaecrista,* having pinnately compound leaves and showy, nearly regular, usually yellow flowers, used as ornamentals and for medicinal purposes. **2.** A preparation of the dried leaves of *Senna alexandrina,* used as a laxative. [New Latin < Arabic *sanā;* akin to Aramaic *sanyā,* a thorn-bush.]

Sen·nach·er·ib (sĭ-năk′ər-ĭb) Died 681 BC. King of Assyria (705–681) who invaded Judah, destroyed Babylon (689), and rebuilt Nineveh.

sen·na·chie (sĕn′ə-kē) *n. Chiefly Scots* Variant of **shanachie.**

sen·net¹ (sĕn′ĭt) *n.* A call on a trumpet or cornet signaling the ceremonial exits and entrances of actors in Elizabethan drama. [Perhaps variant of SIGNET.]

sen·net² (sĕn′ĭt) *n.* Either of two small barracudas (*Sphyraena borealis* or *S. picudilla*) of the western Atlantic. [Origin unknown.]

sen·night (sĕn′ĭt′) *n. Archaic* A week. [Middle English *senight,* contraction of *seveniht* < Old English *seofon nihta,* seven nights : *seofon,* seven; see SEVEN + *nihta,* pl. of *niht,* night; see NIGHT.]

sen·nit (sĕn′ĭt) *n.* **1.** Cordage formed by braiding several strands of rope fiber or similar material. **2.** Braided straw, grass, or palm leaves for making hats. [Origin unknown.]

se·no·pi·a (sĭ-nō′pē-ə) *n.* Improvement of near vision sometimes oc-

ă	pat	oi	boy
ā	pay	ou	out
âr	care	ŏŏ	took
ä	father	ŏŏr	lure
ĕ	pet	ōō	boot
ē	be	ŭ	cut
ĭ	pit	ûr	urge
ī	bite	th	thin
îr	pier	*th*	this
ŏ	pot	zh	vision
ō	toe	ə	about,
ó	paw		item
ôr	core		

Stress marks: **′** (primary);
′ (secondary), as in
dictionary (dĭk′shə-nĕr′ē)

SAMPLE DICTIONARY COLUMN

Now that you are familiar with some of the more important dictionary terminology, reprinted in Figure 1 is one column from the *American Heritage College Dictionary*. Study the arrows to identify the key features discussed previously.

CHOOSING THE RIGHT DEFINITION

The tricky part about using a dictionary is determining which definition to use when several meanings are listed. English is especially complicated because the same word can be a noun and a verb, or a noun and an adjective. To illustrate this problem, consider these two examples. The first is from Rose Guilbault's "School Days" (Selection 4); the second is from John Stossel's opinion piece, "The College Scam" (Selection 28).

> At home all I had was an ancient English/Spanish dictionary my father had used to teach himself English, but its tiny print and archaic language did more to *obscure* meaning than to shed light on it.

Here are some of the definitions for *obscure* from the *American Heritage Dictionary*:

> **ob · scure** (ob sky oor) *adj.* **1.** Deficient in light; dark. **2a.** so faintly perceptible as to lack clear distinction; indistinct. See synonyms at **dark. b.** Indistinctly heard, faint. **c.** *Linguistics* Having the reduced, neutral sound represented by schwa. **3a.** Far from centers of human population: *an obscure village.* **b.** out of sight; hidden: *an obscure retreat.* **4.** Not readily noticed or seen: *an obscure flaw.* **5.** Of undistinguished or humble station or reputation: *an obscure poet; an obscure family.* **6.** Not clearly understood or expressed; ambiguous or vague. *tr.v.* **1.** To make dim or indistinct: *Smog obscured our view.* See synonyms at **block. 2.** To conceal in obscurity; hide: "*Unlike the origins of most nations, America's origins are not obscured in the mists of time*" (National Review). . . .
>
> Copyright © 2011 by Houghton Mifflin Harcourt Publishing Company. Reproduced by permission from *The American Heritage Dictionary of the English Language, Fifth Edition.*

You might want to throw up your hands when faced with this many choices. But before you despair, first consider the part of speech *obscure* represents in Guilbault's sentence: The little word *to* preceding *obscure* is a verb or infinitive marker, and recognizing that fact will save you a lot of time and lead you to the correct definition. Next, you have to locate the verb definitions. If you scan through the definitions in the preceeding box, you will quickly see that the first six are the adjective definitions (indicated by *adj.*), followed by the verb definitions. It's easy to miss this, however, because you have to see the abbreviation *tr.v*, which stands for *transitive verb* (this means that the verb requires a direct object). Now you can zero in on the correct definition, in this case the second one. To *obscure* meaning means to hide it.

In the second instance, *obscure* is clearly an adjective, modifying the noun *journals*, so you should focus only on the adjective definitions. In this case, the best answer is the fourth one, as Stossel means that these journals are not widely known among the general public.

Now study this passage that also contains *obscure*.

> The origins of bread, like those of most important culinary customs, are *obscure*. The best guess at present is that flat breads were a common feature of late Stone Age life; surviving versions include the tortilla, Indian Johnny-cake, and Chinese pancake. (Harold McGee, *On Food and Cooking: The Science and Lore of the Kitchen*)

Obscure here is an adjective (a subject complement of the subject, *origins*). If you study the six adjective definitions in the preceeding box, you will see that none of them exactly fits the way the word is used here, but you can mix and match a couple of them to produce a good definition. Definitions 3b and 4 are probably the closest. *Obscure* in this context means "not immediately obvious," "vague," or "uncertain." These examples are meant to emphasize the importance of knowing a given word's part of speech, not only to save time but to locate the precise definition.

And what of "*culinary* customs" in the first sentence? If you aren't familiar with the word *culinary*, consider the title of the book from which the sentence comes as well as the subject—flat bread. Putting two and two together, then, gives you a good definition: the adjective *culinary* describes food and cooking.

Here's a final example: In Olivia Wu's article, "Alfresco Marriage Market" (Selection 13), she describes the outdoor marriage markets that have sprung up all across China, where parents congregate on pleasant days in a public park to find marriage partners for their unmarried adult children. She writes:

> Clipped to shopping bags, taped to purses, laid on a low bush, pinned to a tree trunk, or just sitting in a lap, the signs are the springboard for the sign carriers to screen and negotiate *potential* partners for their subjects.

Which part of speech is *potential* in this sentence? How do you know? Here are some of the dictionary definitions for *potential*.

---

po·ten·tial (pə-'ten(t)-shəl) *adj.* **1.** Capable of being but not yet in existence; latent: *a potential problem*. **2.** Having possibility, capability, or power. **3.** *Grammar* Of, relating to, or being a verbal construction with auxiliaries such as *may or* can; for example, *it may snow.* *n.* **1.** The inherent ability or capacity for growth, development, or coming into being. **2.** Something possessing the capacity for growth or development. **3.** *Grammar*. A potential verb form. . . .

In this context *potential* is an adjective, because it describes the noun that follows it, *partners*. This means that you can safely ignore the noun definitions and focus only on the adjective ones, which follow the abbreviation *adj.* Either the first or second adjective definition works in the context.

To sum up: There is no need to read through all the definitions when looking up a word. Try to determine the word's part of speech first, locate the appropriate little abbreviation, and then choose the definition that best fits the context. Here is a list of the common part-of-speech labels. You can find these in the front pages of your print dictionary:

adj.	adjective	*n.*	noun	*prep.*	preposition
adv.	adverb	*pron.*	pronoun	*tr.v*	transitive verb
conj.	conjunction	*v.*	verb	*intr.v.*	intransitive verb
interj.	interjection				

EXERCISE IN LOCATING THE CORRECT DEFINITION IN THE DICTIONARY

These two excerpts, again from readings in the book, contain words each of which has multiple meanings. First, determine the part of speech. Then write the most accurate definition. For the purposes of this exercise, use a print, not an online, dictionary.

1. [This buzz-phrase] springs from the discovery that—big surprise!—we've been living beyond our *means*. (Selection 6, John Bussey, "Old Hat for the New Normal")

   Part of speech _____
   Dictionary definition _____

2. It tore me up inside to suppress my dream, but I went to school for a Ph.D. in English literature, thinking I had found the perfect *compromise*. (Selection 7, Caroline Hwang, "The Good Daughter")

   Part of speech _____
   Dictionary definition _____

3. To encourage marriage, or to get better *prospects*, the family itself becomes the search engine. (Selection 13, Olivia Wu, "Alfresco Marriage Market")

   Part of speech _____
   Dictionary definition _____

4. This brings us to our first dilemma: Amidst all this heightened *chatter*, we're not saying much that's interesting, folks. Rather, we're breaking a cardinal rule of companionship: Thou Shalt Not Bore Thy Friends. (Selection 10, Elizabeth Bernstein, "How Facebook Ruins Friendships")

   Part of speech _____
   Dictionary definition _____

5. Phones, before they become an essential element in a child's own life, were the competition, one that children didn't necessarily feel they could *best*. (Selection 9, Sherry Turkle, "The Nostalgia of the Young")

   Part of speech _____
   Dictionary definition _____

Armed with this information and a new-found appreciation for the dictionary and the pleasures of learning new words, you're ready to begin the hard work of becoming a successful college reader.

Practice Selection

Part One begins with a practice selection in which all the features you will find throughout this book are explained. Before you begin the readings in Part One, work through this selection and complete the exercises following it. Answers are provided for all of the exercises except for topics for discussion and writing. Explanations for each element are highlighted in color. These will show you how to get the most that you can out of this book, will help you focus and concentrate, and will help you learn what to look for when you read. To start, each reading selection begins with a brief headnote, offering biographical information about each author as well as necessary background information, where helpful, to ensure good comprehension.

Dave Barry has written a column for *The Miami Herald* since 1983. In 1988 he received a Pulitzer Prize for commentary. Besides writing, Barry plays with a literary band called Rock Bottom Remainders, along with fellow writers Amy Tan and Stephen King. His latest book is *I'll Mature When I'm Dead: Dave Barry's Amazing Tales of Adulthood* (2010). In this excerpt reprinted from *Dave Barry's Complete Guide to Guys*, we are introduced to a fictitious couple named Roger and Elaine, who have been dating for a while.

Vocabulary Analysis

This section constitutes a preview of one or two words in the reading. These generally are divided into two sections—Word Parts, which discusses an important prefix, root, or suffix, and Word Families, which introduces you to a Latin or Greek root so that you can recognize other words in the same family.

WORD PARTS

Answers

spectrometer: a device that measures wavelengths

hydrometer: an instrument that uses fluid to measure gravity

-meter [paragraph 7] As they are driving home, instead of paying attention to what Elaine is saying, Roger checks the *odometer* (pronounced ō - dŏm' -ĭ - tər) and wonders if his car needs an oil change. People often confuse a car's odometer with its speedometer. An odometer measures the distance that a vehicle has traveled, while a speedometer measures the speed at which it is moving.

Odometer joins two Greek word parts: *hodos* ("journey") + *metron* ("measure"). Besides the word *meter* itself (as in a water or gas meter), this Greek word part is attached to other roots referring to instruments that measure all sorts of things, among them *thermometer* (heat), *chronometer* (time), and *barometer* (atmospheric pressure). What do these two words ending in *-meter* mean? Look them up if you are unsure and write their meanings in the space.

spectrometer _____

hydrometer _____

WORD FAMILIES

Transmission [paragraph 9] Roger also worries about his car's *transmission*. This word is formed by two Latin word parts: the prefix *trans* ("across") and the root *mittere* ("to send"). A car's transmission literally transmits or "sends across" power from the engine to the axle. In English, many other words derive from *mittere*, although the idea of "sending" is lost in some of them, for example, *admission*, *commission*, *permission*, and *submission* ("sending under").

Now the selection: Follow your instructor's suggestions or requirements for reading. Otherwise, use these directions: Read through the selection once; then answer the questions in Exercises A, B, and C. After finishing these, follow the instructions that appear later to complete the assignment.

DAVE BARRY

Tips for Women: How to Have a Relationship with a Guy

Before you read, ask yourself: Do you know anything about this subject or about the author? What does the title suggest to you? Who is his audience?

1   Contrary to what many women believe, it's fairly easy to develop a long-term, stable, intimate, and mutually fulfilling relationship with a guy. Of course this guy has to be a Labrador retriever. With human guys, it's extremely difficult. This is because guys don't really grasp what women mean by the term *relationship*.

2   Let's say a guy named Roger is attracted to a woman named Elaine. He asks her out to a movie; she accepts; they have a pretty good time. A few nights later he asks her out to dinner, and again they enjoy themselves. They continue to see each other regularly, and after a while neither one of them is seeing anybody else.

3   And then, one evening when they're driving home, a thought occurs to Elaine, and, without really thinking, she says it aloud: "Do you realize that, as of tonight, we've been seeing each other for exactly six months?"

4   And then there is silence in the car. To Elaine, it seems like a very loud silence. She thinks to herself: Geez, I wonder if it bothers him that I said that. Maybe he's been feeling confined by our relationship; maybe he thinks I'm trying to push him into some kind of obligation that he doesn't want, or isn't sure of.

5   And Roger is thinking: Gosh. *Six months.*

6   And Elaine is thinking: But, hey, *I'm* not sure I want this kind of relationship, either. Sometimes I wish *I* had a little more space, so I'd have time to think about whether I really want us to keep going the way we are, moving steadily toward . . . I mean, where *are* we going? Are we just going to keep seeing each other at this level of intimacy? Are we heading toward *marriage*? Toward *children*? Toward a *lifetime* together? Am I ready for that level of commitment? Do I really even *know* this person?

7   And Roger is thinking . . . so that means it was . . . let's see . . . *February* when we started going out, which was right after I had the car at the dealer's which

means . . . lemme check the odometer . . . *Whoa!* I am *way* overdue for an oil change here.

8   And Elaine is thinking: He's upset. I can see it on his face. Maybe I'm reading this completely wrong. Maybe he wants *more* from our relationship, *more* intimacy, *more* commitment; maybe he has sensed—even before *I* sensed it—that I was feeling some reservations. Yes, I bet that's it. That's why he's so reluctant to say anything about his own feelings: He's afraid of being rejected.

9   And Roger is thinking: And I'm gonna have them look at the transmission again. I don't care *what* those morons say, it's still not shifting right. And they better not try to blame it on the cold weather this time. *What* cold weather? It's eighty-seven degrees out, and this thing is shifting like a goddamn *garbage* truck, and I paid those incompetent thieving cretin bastards *six hundred dollars.*

10   And Elaine is thinking: He's angry. And I don't blame him. I'd be angry, too. God. I feel so *guilty*, putting him through this, but I can't help the way I feel. I'm just not *sure.*

11   And Roger is thinking: They'll probably say it's only a ninety-day warranty. That's exactly what they're gonna say, the scumballs.

12   And Elaine is thinking: Maybe I'm just too idealistic, waiting for a knight to come riding up on his white horse, when I'm sitting right next to a perfectly good person, a person I enjoy being with, a person I truly do care about, a person who seems to truly care about me. A person who is in pain because of my self-centered, schoolgirl romantic fantasy.

13   And Roger is thinking: Warranty? They want a warranty? *I'll* give them a goddamn warranty. I'll take their warranty and stick it right up their . . .

14   "Roger," Elaine says aloud.

15   "What?" says Roger, startled.

16   "Please don't torture yourself like this," she says, her eyes beginning to brim with tears. "Maybe I should never have . . . Oh *God*, I feel so . . ." (*She breaks down, sobbing.*)

17   "What?" says Roger.

18   "I'm such a fool." Elaine sobs. "I mean, I know there's no knight. I really know that. It's silly. There's no knight, and there's no horse."

19   "There's no horse?" says Roger.

20   "You think I'm a fool, don't you?" Elaine says.

21   "No!" says Roger, glad to finally know the correct answer.

22   "It's just that . . . It's that I . . . I need some time," Elaine says.

23   (*There is a fifteen-second pause while Roger, thinking as fast as he can, tries to come up with a safe response. Finally he comes up with one that he thinks might work.*)

24   "Yes," he says.

25   (*Elaine, deeply moved, touches his hand.*)

26   "Oh, Roger, do you really feel that way?" she says.

27   "What way?" says Roger.

28   "That way about time," says Elaine.

29   "Oh," says Roger. "Yes."

30   (*Elaine turns to face him and gazes deeply into his eyes, causing him to become very nervous about what she might say next, especially if it involves a horse. At last she speaks.*)

31   "Thank you, Roger," she says.

32   "Thank *you*," says Roger.

33   Then he takes her home, and she lies on her bed, a conflicted, tortured soul, and weeps until dawn, whereas when Roger gets back to his place, he opens a bag of Doritos, turns on the TV, and immediately becomes deeply involved in a rerun of a tennis match between two Czechoslovakians he has never heard of. A tiny voice in the far recesses of his mind tells him that something major was going on back there in the car, but he is pretty sure there is no way he would ever understand *what*, and so he figures it's better if he doesn't think about it. (This is also Roger's policy regarding world hunger.)

34   The next day Elaine will call her closest friend, or perhaps two of them, and they will talk about this situation for six straight hours. In painstaking detail, they will analyze everything she said and everything he said, going over it time and time again, exploring every word, expression, and gesture for nuances of meaning, considering every possible ramification. They will continue to discuss this subject, off and on, for weeks, maybe months, never reaching any definite conclusions, but never getting bored with it, either.

35   Meanwhile, Roger, while playing racquetball one day with a mutual friend of his and Elaine's, will pause just before serving, frown, and say: "Norm, did Elaine ever own a horse?"

36   We're not talking about different wavelengths here. We're talking about different *planets*, in completely different *solar systems*. Elaine cannot communicate meaningfully with Roger about their relationship any more than she can meaningfully play chess with a duck. Because the sum total of Roger's thinking on this particular topic is as follows:

37   Huh?

38   Women have a lot of trouble accepting this. Despite millions of years of overwhelming evidence to the contrary, women are convinced that guys must spend a certain amount of time thinking about the relationship. How could they not? How could a guy see another human being day after day, night after night, sharing countless hours with this person, becoming physically intimate—how can a guy be doing these things and *not* be thinking about their relationship? This is what women figure.

39   They are wrong. A guy in a relationship is like an ant standing on top of a truck tire. The ant is aware, on a very basic level, that something large is there, but he cannot even dimly comprehend what this thing is, or the nature of his involvement with it. And if the truck starts moving, and the tire starts to roll, the ant will sense that something important is happening, but right up until he rolls around to the bottom and is squashed into a small black blot, the only distinct thought that will form in his tiny brain will be, and I quote.

40   Huh?

41   Which is exactly what Roger will think when Elaine explodes with fury at him when he commits one of the endless series of petty offenses, such as asking her sister out, that guys are always committing in relationships because they have virtually no clue that they are in one.

42   "How *could* he?" Elaine will ask her best friends. "What was he thinking?"

43   The answer is, He *wasn't* thinking, in the sense that women mean the word. He can't: He doesn't have the appropriate type of brain. He has a guy brain, which is basically an analytical, problem-solving type of organ. It likes things to be definite and measurable and specific. It's not comfortable with nebulous and imprecise relationship-type concepts such as *love* and *need* and *trust*. If the guy brain has to form an opinion about another person, it prefers to form that opinion based on something concrete about the person, such as his or her earned-run average.

44   So the guy brain is not well-suited to grasping relationships. But it's good at analyzing and solving mechanical problems. For example, if a couple owns a house, and they want to repaint it so they can sell it, it will probably be the guy who will take charge of this project. He will methodically take the necessary measurements, calculate the total surface area, and determine the per-gallon coverage capacity of the paint; then, using his natural analytical and mathematical skills, he will apply himself to the problem of figuring out a good excuse not to paint the house.

45   "It's too humid," he'll say. Or: "I've read that prospective buyers are actually attracted more to a house with a lot of exterior dirt." Guys simply have a natural flair for this kind of problem-solving. That's why we always have guys in charge of handling the federal budget deficit.

46   But the point I'm trying to make is that, if you're a woman, and you want to have a successful relationship with a guy, the Number One Tip to remember is:

1. Never assume that the guy understands that you and he have a relationship.

47   The guy will not realize this on his own. You have to plant the idea in his brain by constantly making subtle references to it in your everyday conversation, such as:

- "Roger, would you mind passing me a Sweet 'n' Low, inasmuch as we have a relationship?"
- "Wake up, Roger! There's a prowler in the den and we have a relationship. You and I do, I mean."
- Good news, Roger! The gynecologist says we're going to have our fourth child, which will serve as yet another indication that we have a relationship!"
- "Roger, inasmuch as this plane is crashing and we probably have only about a minute to live, I want you to know that we've had a wonderful fifty-three years of marriage together, which clearly constitutes a relationship."

48   Never let up, women. Pound away relentlessly at this concept, and eventually it will start to penetrate the guy's brain. Some day he might even start thinking about it on his own. He'll be talking with some other guys about women, and, out of the blue, he'll say, "Elaine and I, we have, ummm . . . We have, ahhh . . . We . . . We have this *thing*."

49   And he will sincerely mean it.

Exercises

Do not refer to the selection for Exercises A, B, and C unless your instructor directs you to do so.

The first two exercises measure your overall comprehension.

A. DETERMINING THE MAIN IDEA AND PURPOSE

Choose the best answer.

_____ 1. The main idea of the selection is that men and women
   a. are interested in different activities.
   b. think and communicate on completely different wavelengths.
   c. should date for a long time before they begin to think about a long-term commitment.
   d. are not clear about what they want from relationships with the opposite sex.

Exercise A asks you to identify the writer's main idea and purpose. Part One will help you with this. For now, see how well you can do on your own.

_____ 2. With respect to the main idea, the writer's purpose is to
   a. explain why so many relationships fail.
   b. criticize men and women for not understanding the opposite sex.
   c. entertain the reader with an amusing story.
   d. poke fun at men and women's styles of communicating.

B. COMPREHENDING MAIN IDEAS

Choose the correct answer for the multiple-choice items. Write the fill-in answers in the space provided using your own words.

Exercise B measures how well you understand the main ideas in the supporting paragraphs. It is not meant to be tricky but meant to determine how well you understand the important ideas in the selection.

_____ 1. Roger and Elaine, the couple in this hypothetical story, have been seeing each other for exactly
   a. six days.
   b. six weeks.
   c. ninety days.
   d. six months.

_____ 2. Roger realizes that he and Elaine have been together for this length of time because he is overdue
   a. for a pay raise.
   b. for an oil change.
   c. for a transmission check.
   d. in his rent.

3. According to Barry, guys have trouble understanding what women mean by the term _____.

4. What is Roger's reaction after Elaine tells him that "there's no knight, and there's no horse"? _____

_____ 5. Barry describes men's brains as
   a. analytical and problem-solving.
   b. incapable of thinking about two thoughts at the same time.

Note: The answers appear only for the practice selection.

    c. well-equipped to understand relationship terms like *love* and *need*.

    d. poorly suited to solving mechanical problems, preferring to call in experts.

_____ **6.** Barry humorously advises a woman who wants to have a relationship with a guy to

    a. choose a guy who enjoys the same activities as she does.

    b. nag and criticize him until she finally wears him down.

    c. give up the idea as hopeless and accept his inability to understand.

    d. plant the idea in his brain by constantly making subtle references to it.

ANSWERS TO EXERCISES A AND B

A. Determining the Main Idea and Purpose

    1. b   **2.** d

B. Comprehending Main Ideas

    1. d   **2.** b   **3.** the term relationship

    4.   He has no idea what she's talking about   **5.** a   **6.** d

Now check your answers. If you disagree with an answer or are unsure about an error, ask your instructor for an explanation. Then fill in the Comprehension Scoring chart below.

COMPREHENSION SCORE

Next, you can figure out your comprehension score.

Score your answers in Exercises A and B as follows:

A. No. right _____ $\times$ 2 = _____

B. No. right _____ $\times$ 1 = _____

Total points from A and B _____ $\times$ 10 = _____ percent.

Try to maintain a score throughout the book of 70 percent or higher.

C. SEQUENCING

This sequencing exercise gives you practice in seeing how sentences in a paragraph must be arranged to produce a logical discussion.

The sentences from the selection's opening paragraph have been scrambled. Read the sentences and choose the sequence that puts them back into logical order. Do not refer to the original selection.

    1 With human guys, it's extremely difficult. **2** Contrary to what many women believe, it's fairly easy to develop a long-term, stable, intimate, and mutually fulfilling relationship with a guy. **3** This is because guys don't really grasp what women mean by the term *relationship*. **4** Of course this guy has to be a Labrador retriever.

Now read the
selection again and
circle words you
don't know and
can't figure out
from the context.
Then look up the
words you circled.
Now complete
the remaining
exercises.

_____ Which of the following represents the correct sequence for these
sentences?

a. 1, 3, 2, 4

b. 2, 4, 1, 3

c. 3, 4, 1, 2

d. Correct as written.

You may refer to the selection as you work through the remaining exercises.

D. INTERPRETING MEANING

Write your answers to these questions in your own words.

1. Barry's humor in this piece relies on *overstatement*, sometimes called *hyperbole*
   (hī-pûr bə -lē) or deliberate exaggeration for effect. Here is one example: Barry
   states in paragraph 36, "We're not talking about different wavelengths here.
   We're talking about different *planets*, in completely different *solar systems*."
   Look through the selection and find two other examples of overstatement.

   _____

   _____

Exercise D asks you
to go beyond the
surface ideas. Later
you will be asked to
study the structure
and organization
of particular
selections.

2. From Elaine's response in paragraph 18 about there being no knight and no
   horse, what has occurred in her thinking process?

   _____

   _____

3. Barry writes in paragraphs 36 and 37 that the sum total of Roger's thinking on the subject of his and Elaine's relationship is *"Huh?"* What does this
   response mean?

   _____

   _____

4. At the end of paragraph 48, what is Barry poking fun at when Roger says,
   "Elaine and I, we have, ummm . . . We have, ahhh . . . We . . . We have this
   thing."

   _____

   _____

E. UNDERSTANDING VOCABULARY

Choose the best definition according to an analysis of word parts or the context.

_____ **1.**   this level of *intimacy* [paragraphs 6 and 8]:
   a. privacy
   b. long-term commitment
   c. closeness, familiarity
   d. friendship

Exercise E tests
your understanding
of some of the most
important words in
the selection. Since
you have looked
up the words you
didn't know, you
should be able
to complete this
section quickly.

_____ **2.** in *painstaking* detail [34]:
    a. simple
    b. exaggerated
    c. sketchy
    d. extremely careful

_____ **3.** *nuances* of meaning [34]:
    a. slight variations
    b. intentions
    c. direct expressions
    d. examinations

_____ **4.** every possible *ramification* [34]:
    a. interpretation
    b. consequence
    c. use of the imagination
    d. cause or reason

_____ **5.** pound away *relentlessly* [48]:
    a. harshly
    b. angrily
    c. persistently
    d. politely

Exercise F varies
from selection to
selection. This
one asks you to
consider forms of
words that are in
the same family
but have endings
that change their
grammatical
function. (That is,
they are inflected
forms.) If you aren't
sure which form
to use, try reading
the sentence out
loud and inserting
each choice to see
which one "sounds
right," or consult
your dictionary for
further help.

F. USING VOCABULARY

In parentheses before each sentence are some inflected forms of words from the selection. Study the context and the sentence. Then write the correct form in the space provided.

1. (*commit, commitment*) Roger and Elaine's imaginary dialogue suggests that

neither of them is ready for a _____.

2. (*incompetence, incompetent, incompetently*) Roger is convinced that the

mechanic who worked on his car was guilty of dishonesty and _____.

3. (*pettiness, petty, pettily*) A guy like Roger can never understand why a woman would make a big deal out of something _____ like asking Elaine's sister out.

4. (*subtlety, subtle, subtly*) Barry suggests that a woman can instill the idea of having a relationship by _____ referring to the concept in her everyday conversation.

ANSWERS TO EXERCISES C–F

C. Sequencing b

D. Interpreting Meaning

1. Here are some possible answers: Roger watches a tennis match between two unknown Czech players, rather than contemplate what went on between him and Elaine in the car [paragraph 33]. Roger commits a "petty offense" by asking Elaine's sister out [paragraph 41]. A guy figures out calculations

Now check
answers. Any
wrong answers?
Ask your instructor
for an explanation.

for painting a house and then devises excuses for not doing the job [para-graphs 44–45].

2. Elaine's mistake is assuming that Roger, in his silence, is thinking about the same thing as she is.

3. "Huh?" means that Roger has no idea what Elaine is talking about.

4. Barry means that men have difficulty even saying the word *relationship* per-haps because it may imply a commitment they are not yet ready to make.

E. Understanding Vocabulary

   1. c   **2.** d   **3.** a   **4.** b   **5.** c

F. Using Vocabulary

   1. commitment   **2.** incompetence   **3.** petty   **4.** subtly

G. TOPICS FOR DISCUSSION

Whether or not your
instructor assigns
these questions,
you should look the
questions over in
Exercise G. They
ask you to respond
to what you read
and to extend your
thinking, perhaps to
similar situations in
your own life. One
of the topics might
be the perfect
choice for a paper
in your composition
class.

1. Aside from Barry's observation that guys' brains are different from wom-en's, what might be some other reasons that men have difficulty talking about relationships and abstract concepts like love and need and commit-ment?

2. Is Barry being fair to men? to women?

3. To what do you attribute the differences in communication styles between men and women?

H. TOPICS FOR WRITING

1. Write an imaginary dialogue between Roger and Elaine that represents your past experience in a relationship. The situation is this: Elaine wants to have a relationship with Roger, and she wants him to make a commitment, but Roger isn't so sure that he's ready to make this leap.

2. Barry's essay deals with two different communication styles between men and women. Choose another activity that men and women do differently, such as cooking, studying, shopping, or watching television, and write an essay describing these differences.

EXPLORE THE WEB

• A collection of Dave Barry's *Miami Herald* columns can be found at:
  www.davebarry.com

On the next page is a Comprehension Worksheet for those who wish to have an alternative to the text's multiple-choice questions. The page can easily be dupli-cated for use with any of the text selections.

Comprehension Worksheet

1. Author's name and title of the selection: _____

   _____

2. Topic of the selection (What or who is it about?): _____

3. Main idea (What is the main point of the selection?): _____

   _____

   _____

4. Purpose (Why did the writer write it?): _____

   _____

5. Supporting ideas (List two or three points that support the main point.):

   a. _____

   b. _____

   c. _____

6. Evaluation (What was your reaction to the selection? Why do you feel this way?):

   _____

   _____

7. Does your experience and/or observation correspond to the ideas expressed in the selection? Explain. _____

   _____

8. What other information would you like to have on this subject? _____

   _____

9. Where would you look for that information? _____

10. Would you recommend this selection to someone else? Why or why not? Try to go beyond saying that you liked it or that you didn't like it.

   _____

Getting Started: Practicing the Basics

Identifying the Main Idea and the Writer's Purpose

Before beginning this section, be sure to read "To the Student" at the beginning of the book. This material previews the book's organization and content and explains what you will, with hard work, accomplish during the term. In addition, each of the book's seven parts begins with an introduction that discusses a particular skill or set of skills that will make you a better reader; these skills are organized in order of importance. In Part One you will work on the following areas, the most important ones in the course:

• Identifying the varieties of reading you will do in this book
• Finding the main idea in paragraph, both stated and implied
• Locating thesis statements in articles and essays
• Identifying the writer's purpose

THE VARIETIES OF READING YOU WILL DO IN THIS BOOK

Writing comes in three types: prose, poetry, and drama. This book is concerned with prose—ordinary writing that consists of words grouped into sentences and sentences grouped into paragraphs—just like the print that you are reading on this page. Prose is further divided into two types: nonfiction and fiction.

Your college textbooks are nonfiction; the daily newspaper is nonfiction; magazine articles and essays are nonfiction. Nonfiction writing discusses real people with real problems and real events in their lives, real issues and ways to resolve them, real events in the world and their consequences. This chart lists some common types of nonfiction.

COMMON TYPES OF NONFICTION
• Books on history, politics, social problems, and so on
• Editorials or opinion pieces
• Material on websites (information sites, blogs, and the like)
• Essays
• Memoirs and journals
• Textbooks
• Practical reading material like credit card inserts, contracts, nutritional information on processed food items, and recipes

Part Seven, new to this edition, offers an example of each type of practical reading material, the last item listed in the preceeding chart.

Most of the readings in this book are nonfiction articles and essays. Do not worry too much about the difference between them. Briefly, you can think of an article as being more contemporary, dealing with current issues and problems, whereas an essay is generally more timeless and universal, offering the reader a writer's perceptions on an age-old concern that affects all culture, all humans. When you finish the course, you might want to go back through the readings assigned to you and see if you can decide which might be classified as articles and which might be classified as essays.

Fiction, on the other hand, is writing that is imaginative. Generally fiction is divided into two types according to length—short stories and novels. And of course, fiction can also be subdivided into genres, a word meaning literary types, for example, science fiction, mystery, "chick-lit," historical, coming-of-age novels, and so forth. Part Six gives you an opportunity to enjoy four examples of short fiction.

IDENTIFYING THE MAIN IDEA IN SHORT PASSAGES

With those important definitions out of the way, we now turn to the comprehension skill that is at the heart of your college reading—how to locate the main idea. Let's say you have just returned from a meeting with your academic counselor. Your girlfriend asks you what you discussed. Obviously, you're not going to bore her by reciting the complete twenty-minute conversation. Instead, you tell her two most significant points you came away with after the discussion—that you will need to complete both organic and inorganic chemistry before you transfer to Rockport State University next year and that you are only 10 credits away from completing your Associate of Arts degree in science. In other words, you tell her only the most essential information—the main points.

In reading, however, finding the main idea is a bit more difficult than simply reporting a conversation. All you have are print and paper, so it's up to you to work through the words and sentences and make sense of it all. Step-by-step, this book—its readings and exercises—will help you make sense of what you're reading and give you the practice to perfect your reading skills.

Consider this simple diagram of a typical paragraph:

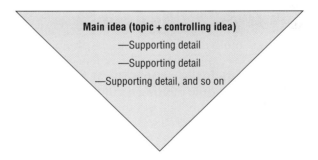

Main idea (topic + controlling idea)
—Supporting detail
—Supporting detail
—Supporting detail, and so on

This diagram suggests that the typical paragraph moves from a general statement (the main idea) to the supporting details or reinforcing points. This is why the triangle is printed with the larger side at the top.

As you will see in the reading selections in this text, paragraphs are the building blocks of an essay. As the writer moves through the discussion, each paragraph makes a point, though as you will see later, some paragraphs have *implied* (unstated) main ideas. Further, the point has to be supported, developed, and backed up. No idea is so good on its own that it can stand undefended.

Another way to visualize the main idea of a paragraph is to imagine an umbrella that covers everything beneath it, as you see in this diagram:

Main idea

Supporting details

Occasionally in the exercises following the selections in this text, you will be asked to choose a title for a paragraph. This kind of question is just another way of asking you to identify the topic and the controlling idea—what the writer wants us to understand about the topic. Here, for example, is a paragraph from an article that appears in Part Two. The title is "Minds of Their Own" by Virginia Morell, which appeared in *National Geographic*. Alex, mentioned in the last sentence, was an African gray parrot who learned to "speak" English. Study the annotations (notes) in the left margin as you read the paragraph. Then answer the questions that follow.

skills associated with intelligence

these skills don't exist only in humans

examples of intelligence in various species of animals

(1) Certain skills are considered key signs of higher mental abilities: good memory, a grasp of grammar and symbols, self-awareness, understanding others' motives, imitating others, and being creative. (2) Bit by bit, in ingenious experiments, researchers have documented these talents in other species, gradually chipping away at what we thought made human beings distinctive while offering a glimpse of where our own abilities came from. (3) Scrub jays know that other jays are thieves and that stashed food can spoil; sheep can recognize faces; chimpanzees use a variety of tools to probe termite mounds and even use weapons to hunt small mammals; dolphins can imitate human postures; the archerfish, which stuns insects with a sudden blast of water, can learn how to aim its squirt simply by watching an experienced fish perform the task. (4) And Alex the parrot turned out to be a surprisingly good talker.

Which of the following best represents the main idea of the passage?

1. Animals are smarter than humans in many respects.
2. Our intelligence derived from animal behavior.
3. Animal species display complex mental abilities similar to those in humans.

4. Self-awareness and creativity are two essential kinds of mental abilities present in both humans and animal species.

Which of the following would be the best title for this paragraph?

1. "Humanlike Mental Abilities in Animals"
2. "Animal Research"
3. "Who Is Smarter—Animals or Humans?"
4. "Ingenious Experiments with Animals"

The answers are 3 and 1, respectively.

    Notice that the main idea in this paragraph is followed by a series of logical statements—first, that scientific research allows us to recognize mental abilities in animals, and second, a list of representative animal species and various behaviors that indicate these mental abilities. The sentences work together to form a coherent and unified discussion that is relatively easy to follow. Let's look at the structure of this paragraph in another way. Study this diagram:

> Skills associated with mental abilities—good memory, grasp of grammar and symbols, and so on.
>   Researchers have devised experiments to show
>   how these abilities are present in animals.
>   Examples of various animal species' behaviors that reflect these
>   mental abilities (scrub jays, sheep, chimps, dolphins, archerfish, and
>   Alex the parrot).

This diagram shows that the paragraph moves from the very general to the more specific so that the specific supporting details both prove and reinforce the central point.

    It's relatively easy to locate the main idea in a paragraph structured like the preceding examples, where the main idea is stated prominently in the first sentence, followed by supporting details. But here are some words of caution: A writer is under no obligation to make your reading experience easy, and few professional writers structure their paragraphs according to a neat formula. Some do, but many don't. In longer essays, the main idea in supporting paragraphs can come anywhere—at the beginning, certainly, but also in the middle or even at the end. In the following exercise, locate the main idea in each passage and write the sentence or sentences that represent it in the space that follows.

Exercises

A. One of the few hues that can be perceived as both light and dark, blue defines our many moods. It is the eggshell shade of a baby's blanket and the stern authority of the uniforms of the police, umpires, and many military troops. The appeal of blue is near universal, spanning geography, culture, age, gender, and disposition. Though it is a comparative rarity in living nature—blueberries, the blue jay, forget-me-nots—blue is the color of both the sky and the sea. It covers the whole earth.

James Sullivan, *Jeans: A Cultural History of an American Icon*

B. I once read an article whose author stated that racism is the only form of mental illness that is communicable. Clever but not entirely true. Racism in the U.S. is learned by us beginning at birth.

As a person of mixed ancestry growing up in the United States in the late 1950s, I knew all of the cruel epithets that might be hurled at others; the knowledge was a sort of solace that I was not alone in my feelings of unease, of not quite belonging to the group that clearly mattered most in the United States.

Leslie Marmon Silko, "Fences Against Freedom,"
Yellow Woman and a Beauty of the Spirit

C. Boise City is in Oklahoma. The passage is set during the Great Depression.

Cash was scarce in Boise City. It was a hard-shelled, stiff little town that clung to a sense of destiny despite all evidence to the contrary. A visitor from Denver, getting off the train, said rusted cans scattered over the dusty plain would be an improvement. People swapped a hen—live and clucking—for a year's subscription to the *Boise City News*. They bartered a bushel of wheat for an oven stove wick. They brought in fifteen dozen eggs and got back a pair of overalls. They traded turnips for two cans of Franco-American spaghetti. Or they took the quarter they had been staring at for five days and went down to the little cafe run by Mrs. Skaggs, where two bits could buy a hamburger, a piece of pie, and a glass of milk. The Palace Theater closed, cutting off the one source of reliable fantasy, and then reopened after considerable pleadings, with ten-cent picture shows. The joy had gone out of living. Subsistence was a trial. But even though people were hurting, the town refused to slouch or cower. Boise City did not need help from anybody. The town was too proud to take anyone's charity. Pain was submerged until it screamed to the surface, as with one local businessman who had lost his life savings. He shot his wife first, then put the gun to his head and blew his own brains out.

Timothy Egan, *The Worst Hard Time: The Untold Story
of Those Who Survived the Great American Dust Bowl*

Here are two more passages for further practice in identifying the main idea. In these passages, however, you are given some choices for the main idea, but first you have to classify them before you choose the one that best states the main point.

The subject of the first passage is big-box stores like Wal-Mart and Costco. If there are any words that you don't know, look them up before doing the two exercises that follow. In particular, be sure that you know the meaning of *synonymous* in sentence 1, as the meaning of the entire passage centers on this word.

> "Think big-box stores and bargains are synonymous? Think again," declared a report on buying appliances in the September 2005 issue of *Consumer Reports.* "None of the major retailers outpriced the independents for ranges, refrigerators, and other large appliances, and only two were clear winners for small ones such as grills and vacuums. What's more, readers found Wal-Mart no cheaper than other stores overall, despite its low-price slogan." The report compared prices, service, selection, product quality, and checkout ease at independent appliance dealers, Best Buy, Costco, Home Depot, Lowe's, Sears, Target, and Wal-Mart. Overall, the local stores outscored their big competitors by a significant margin. Not only were they price-competitive—only Costco and Target beat them on price for small appliances and none of the chains did better on large appliances—but they offered a broader selection and better service. "Seventy-five percent of small-appliance buyers thought independent-store staffers were pleasant, informed, or helpful; five percent or fewer felt that way about Costco, Target, or Wal-Mart workers," noted *Consumer Reports.* Wal-Mart ranked the lowest in terms of quality and selection; 40 percent of those who bought appliances at the chain had to settle for a different brand than they had planned to buy.
>
> —Stacy Mitchell, *Big-Box Swindle*

Here are some sample main-idea statements. Before choosing which one most accurately restates the main idea, complete this exercise first by labeling the choices with a, b, c, or d according to these descriptions:

_____ **1.** Big-box stores and independent stores both offer competitive prices.

_____ **2.** Local independent stores are generally cheaper, and they offer a broader selection of appliances and better service than big-box stores.

_____ **3.** Big-box stores like Wal-Mart rank low in customer service, quality, and selection.

_____ **4.** *Consumer Reports* offers information to help consumers make smart shopping decisions, especially for large and small appliances.
  (a) The information is included in the paragraph, but it's an example, not the main point.
  (b) This statement misrepresents the writer's idea.
  (c) The paragraph suggests this information, but it's off the subject.
  (d) The information states the writer's main point.

Labeling the sentences in this way should help you eliminate the obviously wrong choices and identify the correct one. Now place a check mark next to the sentence that represents the main idea. You should have marked the sentences as follows: 1 (b); 2 (d); 3 (a); 4 (c). So that makes number 2 the main idea.

Now do the same thing with the following paragraph:

> What's a food-loving entrepreneur to do? The recession has turned eating at home into a necessity. And opening a new restaurant, bakery, or pub requires a chunk of increasingly-hard-to-come-by capital. Enter the deliciously nimble food cart. In the past few years, more than 450 of these hyper-local, highly affordable eateries have sprung up in Portland, Oregon, bringing the sweet smell of commerce back to the streets. "Carts make it possible for people of modest means to eat out—usually more healthfully than at fast-food chain restaurants," reports **New Urban News** (Jan.-Feb. 2010). The carts are also easy on proprietors: Licenses cost $315, monthly rent averages $500, and they can be outfitted for as little as a few thousand dollars. Portland's carts are run by a mix of immigrants and culinary school graduates, and have fewer major health code violations per inspection than the area's restaurants do. The rapid proliferation also might finally settle the carts-versus-restaurants debate that keeps many cities from enacting vendor-friendly policies. "The commonly heard complaint is that . . . carts unfairly compete with brick-and-mortar restaurants," one Portlander told *New Urban News.* "If anything, the food carts seem to feed the Portland food buzz and create more consumer demand."
>
> —"Meals (and Deals) on Wheels." Originally published in *Utne Reader*, May/June 2010. Reprinted with permission. www.utne.com

Complete this exercise as you did before:

_____ **1.** The current recession means that people have to eat at home.

_____ **2.** Food carts have fewer health-code violations than restaurants.

_____ **3.** More cities should follow the example of Portland and allow food carts on their streets.

_____ **4.** The carts are cheap to operate, with licenses costing $315 and monthly rent $500.

_____ **5.** There are more than 450 food carts in Portland, which offer local, affordable food.

> **(a)** The information is included the paragraph, but it's a supporting detail.
>
> **(b)** The information is included in the paragraph, but it's a minor supporting detail and far too narrow to be the main idea.
>
> **(c)** The information states the writer's main point.
>
> **(d)** The information is not in the paragraph, though one might infer or conclude it.
>
> **(e)** The information is included in the paragraph, but it's too broad to be the main idea; food carts aren't mentioned.

And here are the answers: 1 (e); 2 (a); 3 (d); 4 (b); 5 (c)

CRITICAL THINKING EXERCISE

What might be the opposing view? Who might not be as favorable to the idea of food carts proliferating as this writer suggests? What might be two or three arguments against them?

IMPLIED MAIN IDEAS

Not all passages are as helpfully structured as those you have been working with. In the preceding selections, at least the main ideas are stated somewhere! However, some paragraphs present only the supporting details, which require you to determine the main idea yourself. In this type of paragraph, the main idea is *implied*—meaning that the supporting details *suggest* the main point without saying it directly. If you can't readily locate a main idea-sentence, ask yourself these two questions:

- What's the point of what I'm reading?
- What is the single most important idea that the writer wants me to come away with?

If you can come up with a single sentence—certainly no more than two—that answers these questions, then you will make significant gains in your reading. Read the next paragraph and, as before, answer the questions that follow. The passage is from an article called "Hello, My Name Is Unique" by Carlin Flora, originally published in *Psychology Today*. The subject is naming children. The word *iconoclastic* in sentence 3 means going against tradition or convention.[1]

(1) No one can predict whether a name will be consistent with a child's or a teen's view of herself. (2) The name could be ethnic, unique or white-bread, but if it doesn't reinforce her sense of self, she will probably be unhappy with it and may even feel alienated from parents or peers because of it. (3) An Annika with iconoclastic taste will be happy with her name, but a Tallullah who longs for a seat at the cheerleaders' table may feel that her name is too weird.

Which of the following best represents the main idea of the passage?

1. Unique or unusual names will reinforce a child's sense of self.
2. Weird names have become more popular in recent years.
3. A child may be unhappy with an unusual name if it doesn't reinforce her sense of self.
4. Parents should be careful when naming their children.

Which of the following would be the best title for this paragraph?

1. "One's Name and One's Sense of Self"
2. "Iconoclastic Names"
3. "New Fads in Naming Children"
4. "How Names Can Make Us Feel Alienated"

---

[1] From Greek, an *iconoclast* refers to a person who destroys traditional religious images and also to one who goes against tradition.

The answers are 3 and 1 respectively. In this paragraph the second part of the second sentence represents the writer's main idea. The first sentence simply introduces the subject but does not actually represent what the writer wants us to understand about the relationship between a child's name and his or her sense of self.

THESIS STATEMENTS IN ARTICLES AND ESSAYS

Articles and essays are both composed of individual paragraphs linked together in the same way a chain is linked together to produce a sustained piece of writing that may be a single page to 20 or more pages. Whatever the length, the writer of an article has in mind a focus or a point, which, like the main idea of a paragraph, may be stated or implied. This main idea is called the *thesis* or *thesis statement*. In your composition classes, you are probably familiar with the concept of a thesis. After all, your essay has to be about something. A writer may place the thesis near the beginning of the essay, in the middle, or at the end, but usually it comes somewhere near the beginning. In addition, a thesis might be two sentences, though rarely more than that.

To practice locating the thesis, here are the first four paragraphs from "Hello, My Name Is Unique," a passage from which you read earlier in this section. Three words that might be unfamiliar to you are defined here:

bard (paragraph 1)	a poet
idiosyncratic (paragraph 3)	unusual or peculiar to a particular individual
monikers (paragraph 4)	names

After you read these four paragraphs, underline the sentence that you think probably represents the thesis for the entire article.

1   Proper names are poetry in the raw, said the bard W. H. Auden. "Like all poetry, they are untranslatable." Mapping your name onto yourself is a tricky procedure indeed. We exist wholly independently of our name, yet they alone represent us on our birth certificates and gravestones.

2   Would a Rose by any other name be just as sweet-tempered? Does Orion feel cosmically special? Psychologists, parents and the world's Oceans, Zanes and Timothys are divided on the extent to which first names actually matter.

You Named Him *What?*

3   Today's parents seem to believe they can alter their child's destiny by picking the perfect—preferably idiosyncratic—name. (Destiny, incidentally, was the ninth most popular name for girls in New York City last year.) The current crop of preschoolers includes a few Uniques, with uncommonly named playmates like Kyston, Payton and Sawyer. From Dakota to Heaven, Integrity to Serenity, more babies are being named after places and states of mind. Names with alternative spellings are on the upswing, like Jaxon, Kassidy, Mikayla, Jazmine and Nevaeh (Heaven spelled backward), as are mix-and-match names such as Ashlynn and Rylan.

4   "For the first time in history, the top 50 names account for less than 50 percent of boys born each year, and for less than 40 percent of girls," says

Cleveland Kent Evans, professor of psychology at Bellevue University in Nebraska and author of *Unusual and Most Popular Baby Names.* Evans believes that our homogeneous strip-mall culture fosters the desire to nominally distinguish our children. He cites a boom in unique names dating to the late 1980s but says the taste for obscure monikers developed in the 1960s, when parents felt less obligated to keep certain names in the family.

Two possibilities exist for the thesis—the third sentence of paragraph 2 or the first sentence of paragraph 3. Here is a paraphrase of these two candidates for the thesis:

> 1. People disagree about the degree to which first names really matter. (paragraph 2)
> 2. Today's parents seem to think that they can influence a child's destiny by picking the perfect name, preferably an unusual one. (paragraph 3)

Which is the better choice? If you consider the details that follow the second example in the preceeding box, it appears that the writer, Carlin Flora, is going to explore the idea that parents are increasingly choosing idiosyncratic names. A careful reading of the entire selection, which you will do later in this book, confirms this. The writer is concerned with the impact of unusual names on our personalities. The writer mentions the fact that psychologists, parents, and people with unusual names disagree over the matter only as a lead-in to the thesis. Notice, too, that a caption used in the article, "Can Names Alter Our Self-Perception?" bears this out.

Exercise

This passage is the beginning of a chapter from a nonfiction book. Read it, and using one or more of the strategies discussed in this section, identify the thesis and write it in the space provided. (A *fedora*, mentioned in the first sentence, is a type of felt hat that was commonly worn by businessmen in the 1950s.)

A photograph first published in 1953 shows a throng of men in fedoras streaming onto the train platform in Park Forest, Illinois, with an accompanying caption that reads "5:57, back from the Loop." At the time, the photograph of similarly attired businessmen on a similar schedule returning from work pointed to a worrisome conformity. The picture ran in *Fortune* to accompany an unusually astute article by William H. Whyte, which he expanded into his landmark book about corporate conformity, *The Organization Man.*

Stand on the platform at Park Forest at 5:57 today, and not only are the fedoras gone, but so is the crush of workers streaming home. Many men—and now there are women, too—are pulling into Park Forest two or three hours later. And those who arrive at 5:57 are just as likely to have begun work at 7 a.m. as at 9 a.m. For many of Park Forest's residents, a ten-hour day seems as much the norm nowadays as an eight-hour day did in the 1950s. The 1953 photograph highlighted a haunting conformity, but at least those organization men were home in time to have dinner with the family or catch the last three innings of Johnny's Little League game.

For too many Americans, the conventional, comfortable forty-hour week has given way to the overloaded, overstressed sixty-hour week. If any aspect of the economic squeeze is hitting American workers across the board—white-collar and blue-collar, high-income and low-income, chief executives and janitors— it is the phenomenon of increased stress on the job, a combination of longer workweeks and having to toil harder and faster during one's hours at work.

Steven Greenhouse, *The Big Squeeze: Tough Times for the American Worker*

IDENTIFYING THE WRITER'S PURPOSE

Although he or she may not be aware of it when opening a new document on the computer screen, every writer has in mind some *purpose*, the intention or the reason he or she is going to the trouble of writing. The ancient Greeks taught that literature had three aims: to please, to instruct, and to persuade. What exactly did they mean?

THE WRITER'S PURPOSE IN CLASSICAL TERMS
• **To please:** to delight, entertain, amuse, give pleasure to, describe, paint a picture in words • **To instruct:** to teach, show, inform, examine, expose, analyze, criticize • **To persuade:** to convince, change one's mind, influence, argue, recommend, give advice to

Sometimes it is hard to see an exact distinction between "instructing" and "persuading" since the very act of "instructing" us about something that needs to be changed might also "convince" us of the need for that change. For example, in the passage about the mental abilities of various species of animals, the writer is clearly informing us (instructing), but there is also an implied or secondary purpose—to persuade us not only that these abilities exist but that they are marvelous in their own right. Maybe we humans aren't as distinctive as we think we are.

Another example of how a writer may have overlapping purposes can be seen in the Practice Essay by Dave Barry, "Tips for Women: How to Have a Relationship with a Guy." Barry humorously explores the difficulties men and women have talking to each other. Obviously, his purpose is, at least in part, to entertain. But what other purpose might he have? Because Barry pokes fun at men for their inability to commit to a relationship and at women for exhaustingly analyzing every little thing that happens between a man and a woman, his purpose seems more to instruct than to persuade. He is pointing out our differences, not trying to reform us or make us change our ways. Besides, what writer, discussing the age-old battle of the sexes, could ever accomplish that!

As you complete the exercises following the readings in Parts One through Four, the second question always asks you to choose the writer's purpose. In this case, choose the *primary* purpose and do not concern yourself with overlapping purposes.

1 DAVID SEDARIS
Hejira

Humorist David Sedaris is acclaimed for his two best-selling books, Me Talk Pretty One Day *(2001) and also* Dress Your Family in Corduroy and Denim *(2004), which was nominated for a Grammy award for Best Spoken Word Album and from which this selection is taken. His latest book is* Squirrel Seeks Chipmunk: A Modern Bestiary *(2010). The targets of Sedaris's humor, which some might describe as warped, are typically himself and his family.*

The title word hejira, *sometimes spelled* hegira, *has two meanings. In Arabic,* hejira *means "flight," referring to the prophet Mohammed's flight from Mecca to Medina in 622 A.D. that marks the beginning of the Muslim era. It refers now more generally to a flight to escape danger.*

Vocabulary Analysis

WORD PARTS

The prefix re- In paragraph 4, as Sedaris and his mother are driving to his sister's apartment, they listen to a *rebroadcast* of a radio call-in program. The prefix *re-* conveys the idea of a repeated action. Therefore, to *rebroadcast* means simply that a radio program is being aired a second time. However, not all words beginning with *re-* have this meaning: *Reconsider, reread, recalculate,* and *regenerate* do, but *register, regulate, residence,* and *rebuke* ("to scold") do not. To see how this works, strip away the prefix and see if the root can stand alone. If it can, then the prefix likely has the meaning discussed. *Broadcast* can stand alone, but *gister* and *buke,* for example, cannot.

DAVID SEDARIS

Hejira

1   IT WASN'T ANYTHING I had planned on, but at the age of twenty-two, after dropping out of my second college and traveling across the country a few times, I found myself back in Raleigh, living in my parents' basement. After six months spent waking at noon, getting high, and listening to the same Joni Mitchell record over and over again, I was called by my father into his den and told to get out. He was sitting very formally in a big, comfortable chair behind his desk, and I felt as though he were firing me from the job of being his son,

2   I'd been expecting this to happen, and it honestly didn't bother me all that much. The way I saw it, being kicked out of the house was just what I needed if I was ever going to get back on my feet. "Fine," I said, "I'll go. But one day you'll be sorry."

3   I had no idea what I meant by this. It just seemed like the sort of thing a person should say when he was being told to leave.

4   My sister Lisa had an apartment over by the university and said that I could come stay with her as long as I didn't bring my Joni Mitchell record. My mother offered to drive me over, and after a few bong hits I took her up on it. It was a fifteen-minute trip across town, and on the way we listened to the rebroadcast of a radio call-in show in which people phoned the host to describe the various birds gathered around their backyard feeders. Normally the show came on in the morning, and it seemed strange to listen to it at night. The birds in question had gone to bed hours ago and probably had no idea they were still being talked about. I chewed this over and wondered if anyone back at the house was talking about *me*. To the best of my knowledge, no one had ever tried to imitate my voice or describe the shape of my head, and it was depressing that I went unnoticed while a great many people seemed willing to drop everything for a cardinal.

5   My mother pulled up in front of my sister's apartment building, and when I opened the car door she started to cry; which worried me, as she normally didn't do things like that. It wasn't one of those "I'm going to miss you" things, but something sadder and more desperate than that. I wouldn't know it until months later, but my father had kicked me out of the house not because I was a bum but because I was gay. Our little talk was supposed to be one of those defining moments that shape a person's adult life, but he'd been so uncomfortable with the most important word that he'd left it out completely; saying only, "I think we both know why I'm doing this." I guess I could have pinned him down, I just hadn't seen the point. "Is it because I'm a failure? A drug addict? A sponge? Come on, Dad, just give me one good reason."

6   Who wants to say that?

7   My mother assumed that I knew the truth, and it tore her apart. Here was yet another defining moment, and again I missed it entirely. She cried until it sounded as if she were choking. "I'm sorry;" she said. "I'm sorry; I'm sorry, I'm sorry."

8   I figured that within a few weeks I'd have a job and some crummy little apartment. It didn't seem insurmountable, but my mother's tears made me

worry that finding these things might be a little harder than I thought. Did she honestly think I was that much of a loser?

9   "Really," I said, "I'll be fine."

10   The car light was on and I wondered what the passing drivers thought as they watched my mother sob. What kind of people did they think we were? Did they think she was one of those crybaby moms who fell apart every time someone chipped a coffee cup? Did they assume I'd said something to hurt her? Did they see us as just another crying mother and her stoned gay son, sitting in a station wagon and listening to a call-in show about birds, or did they imagine, for just one moment, that we might be special?

Exercises

Do not refer to the selection for Exercises A, B, and C unless your instructor directs you to do so.

A. DETERMINING THE MAIN IDEA AND PURPOSE

Choose the best answer.

_____ **1.** The main idea of the selection is that
   a. no one in the family was surprised when Sedaris's father asked him to move out.
   b. Sedaris spent most of his day in his parents' basement stoned and doing nothing.
   c. being asked to leave his parents' house because he was gay was a defining moment in Sedaris's life.
   d. Sedaris turned his life around and made something of himself after his father kicked him out of the house.

_____ **2.** The writer's purpose is to
   a. recount a painful but crucial turning point in his life.
   b. criticize his parents for their prejudice and lack of understanding.
   c. warn other parents of gay children about the wrong way to handle the situation.
   d. demonstrate the internal conflict he had over his sexual orientation.

B. COMPREHENDING MAIN IDEAS

Choose the correct answer for the multiple-choice items. Write the fill-in answers in the space provided using your own words.

_____ **1.** Sedaris moved back to his parents' house in Raleigh after
   a. dropping out of college twice and traveling around the country.
   b. finishing an army tour of duty.

      c. getting fired from yet another job.

      d. getting busted and sent to jail for drug possession.

2. Why did Sedaris think he was being asked to leave his parents' house?

_____

3. Why didn't Sedaris's father tell him what the real reason was for asking him to leave?

_____

_____ **4.** Sedaris describes his mother's reaction to his being asked to leave as

      a. unemotional, almost indifferent.

      b. sad, almost desperate.

      c. firm, unyielding.

      d. relieved and thankful.

_____ **5.** Sedaris decided that moving out wouldn't be so bad because he could

      a. return to school and finish his degree.

      b. get his life back on track and stop using drugs.

      c. finally gain the independence he needed.

      d. get a job and an apartment.

_____ **6.** Sedaris concludes that this encounter between himself and his mother in the car was in fact something

      a. special.

      b. very common.

      c. heartbreaking.

      d. pathetic.

COMPREHENSION SCORE

Score your answers for Exercises A and B as follows:

A. No. right _____ × 2 = _____

B. No. right _____ × 1 = _____

Total points from A and B _____ × 10 = _____ percent

C. SEQUENCING

These sentences from one paragraph in the selection have been scrambled. Read the sentences and choose the sequence that puts them back into logical order. Do not refer to the original selection.

1 He was sitting very formally in a big, comfortable chair behind his desk, and I felt as though he were firing me from the job of being his son. **2** After six months spent waking at noon, getting high, and listening to the same Joni Mitchell record over and over again, I was called by my father and told to get out. **3** It wasn't anything I had planned on, but at the age of twenty-two, after dropping out of my second college and traveling across the country a few times, I found myself back in Raleigh, living in my parents' basement.

_____ Which of the following represents the correct sequence for these sentences?
   a. 2, 1, 3
   b. 2, 3, 1
   c. 3, 2, 1
   d. Correct as written.

You may refer to the selection as you work through the remaining exercises.

D. INTERPRETING MEANING

Write your answers to these questions in your own words.

1. What are the two "defining moments" in the narrative? What does Sedaris mean by this phrase, and what does he say about them? _____

   _____

2. As Sedaris and his mother drive to his sister's apartment, they listen to a radio call-in program about identifying birds. Is Sedaris being humorous, ironic, merely irritable, or something else altogether when he wonders if anyone at home is talking about him, as the callers are talking about birds? Explain your answer. _____

3. Comment on the title of the selection. Why is it appropriate for the narrative Sedaris recounts? _____

E. UNDERSTANDING VOCABULARY AND IDIOMATIC EXPRESSIONS

Choose the best definition according to an analysis of word parts or the context.

_____ **1.** I *chewed this over* [paragraph 4]
   a. took a bite of something and chewed it
   b. worried about what to do next
   c. thought about the matter for a while
   d. realized what was really happening

_____ **2.** I could have *pinned him down* [5]
   a. wrestled him to the floor and not let him get up
   b. asked for a second chance
   c. started an argument
   d. asked him to be more precise

_____ **3.** Is it because I'm a failure? A drug addict? A *sponge*? [5]
   a. someone who lives off others' generosity
   b. someone who absorbs information readily
   c. someone who keeps a very clean house
   d. someone who takes drugs

_____ **4.** It didn't seem *insurmountable* [8]
  a. intelligent
  b. predictable
  c. impossible to overcome
  d. difficult to understand

F. TOPICS FOR DISCUSSION

1. In what ways is this narrative about communication, its difficulties and its failures?
2. How would you characterize the relationship between Sedaris's parents?

G. TOPICS FOR WRITING

1. Write a paragraph in which you evaluate the way that Sedaris and his father conducted the conversation between themselves. What went wrong? What would have been a better way?
2. Write a short narrative in which you recount an event that represented a defining moment in your life but that at the time you didn't realize its significance.

EXPLORE THE WEB

- An irreverent autobiography along with video clips and quotations is available at this site:

  www.literati.net/Sedaris

SHERMAN ALEXIE

Superman and Me

Sherman Alexie is a Native American writer who currently lives in Seattle. Born on the Spokane Indian Reservation, he had a difficult childhood, enduring a poor education and poverty and a reputation as an oddity. After college he became a writer. He is best known for two novels, The Lone Ranger and Tonto Fistfight in Heaven *(1994) and* The Absolutely True Diary of a Part-Time Indian *(2007), as well as writing the script for a major film,* Smoke Signals *(1998). Alexie is a founding board member of Longhouse Media, a nonprofit organization that teaches filmmaking skills to young Native Americans. This article was first published in* The Los Angeles Times; *it was also reprinted in* The Most Wonderful Books: Writers on Discovering the Pleasures of Reading.

Vocabulary Analysis

WORD PARTS

The prefix mono- The Greek prefix *mono-* means "one" or "single" and precedes many English words. When Alexie writes in paragraph 6 that his Indian classmates sang *monosyllabic* powwow songs, he means that they consisted of one-syllable words. Other words that begin with this prefix include *monotonous* (repetitiously dull); *monologue* (a long speech made by one person); and *monocle* (a small eyeglass for only one eye).

WORD FAMILIES

Clarity (paragraph 3) is a noun meaning the quality of being clear. Aside from the adjective *clear*, we also have *clearing, clearance, clarify,* and *clairvoyant*, which refers to the quality of being able to perceive objects or events not perceived by the senses. The root also appears in compound words like *clear-sighted* and *clear-eyed*.

Anthony Pidgeon/Redferns/Getty Images

SHERMAN ALEXIE

Superman and Me

1   I learned to read with a Superman comic book. Simple enough, I suppose. I cannot recall which particular Superman comic book I read, nor can I remember which villain he fought in that issue. I cannot remember the plot, nor the means by which I obtained the comic book. What I can remember is this: I was 3 years old, a Spokane Indian boy living with his family on the Spokane Indian Reservation in eastern Washington state. We were poor by most standards, but one of my parents usually managed to find some minimum-wage job or another, which made us middle-class by reservation standards. I had a brother and three sisters. We lived on a combination of irregular paychecks, hope, fear and government surplus food.

2   My father, who is one of the few Indians who went to Catholic school on purpose, was an avid reader of westerns, spy thrillers, murder mysteries, gangster epics, basketball player biographies and anything else he could find. He bought his books by the pound at Dutch's Pawn Shop, Goodwill, Salvation Army and Value Village. When he had extra money, he bought new novels at supermarkets, convenience stores and hospital gift shops. Our house was filled with books. They were stacked in crazy piles in the bathroom, bedrooms and living room. In a fit of unemployment-inspired creative energy, my father built a set of bookshelves and soon filled them with a random assortment of books about the Kennedy assassination, Watergate, the Vietnam War and the entire 23-book series of the Apache westerns. My father loved books, and since I loved my father with an aching devotion, I decided to love books as well.

3   I can remember picking up my father's books before I could read. The words themselves were mostly foreign, but I still remember the exact moment when I first understood, with a sudden clarity, the purpose of a paragraph. I didn't have the vocabulary to say "paragraph," but I realized that a paragraph was a fence that held words. The words inside a paragraph worked together for a common purpose. They had some specific reason for being inside the same fence.

This knowledge delighted me. I began to think of everything in terms of paragraphs. Our reservation was a small paragraph within the United States. My family's house was a paragraph, distinct from the other paragraphs of the LeBrets to the north, the Fords to our south and the Tribal School to the west. Inside our house, each family member existed as a separate paragraph but still had genetics and common experiences to link us. Now, using this logic, I can see my changed family as an essay of seven paragraphs: mother, father, older brother, the deceased sister, my younger twin sisters and our adopted little brother.

4   At the same time I was seeing the world in paragraphs, I also picked up that Superman comic book. Each panel, complete with picture, dialogue and narrative was a three-dimensional paragraph. In one panel, Superman breaks through a door. His suit is red, blue and yellow. The brown door shatters into many pieces. I look at the narrative above the picture. I cannot read the words, but I assume it tells me that "Superman is breaking down the door." Aloud, I pretend to read the words and say, "Superman is breaking down the door." Words, dialogue, also float out of Superman's mouth. Because he is breaking down the door, I assume he says, "I am breaking down the door." Once again, I pretend to read the words and say aloud, "I am breaking down the door." In this way, I learned to read.

5   This might be an interesting story all by itself. A little Indian boy teaches himself to read at an early age and advances quickly. He reads "Grapes of Wrath" in kindergarten when other children are struggling through "Dick and Jane." If he'd been anything but an Indian boy living on the reservation, he might have been called a prodigy. But he is an Indian boy living on the reservation and is simply an oddity. He grows into a man who often speaks of his childhood in the third-person, as if it will somehow dull the pain and make him sound more modest about his talents.

6   A smart Indian is a dangerous person, widely feared and ridiculed by Indians and non-Indians alike. I fought with my classmates on a daily basis. They wanted me to stay quiet when the non-Indian teacher asked for answers, for volunteers, for help. We were Indian children who were expected to be stupid. Most lived up to those expectations inside the classroom but subverted them on the outside. They struggled with basic reading in school but could remember how to sing a few dozen powwow songs. They were monosyllabic in front of their non-Indian teachers but could tell complicated stories and jokes at the dinner table. They submissively ducked their heads when confronted by a non-Indian adult but would slug it out with the Indian bully who was 10 years older. As Indian children, we were expected to fail in the non-Indian world. Those who failed were ceremonially accepted by other Indians and appropriately pitied by non-Indians.

7   I refused to fail. I was smart. I was arrogant. I was lucky. I read books late into the night, until I could barely keep my eyes open. I read books at recess, then during lunch, and in the few minutes left after I had finished my classroom assignments. I read books in the car when my family traveled to powwows or basketball games. In shopping malls, I ran to the bookstores and read bits and pieces of as many books as I could. I read the books my father brought home from the pawnshops and secondhand. I read the books I borrowed from the

library. I read the backs of cereal boxes. I read the newspaper. I read the bulletins posted on the walls of the school, the clinic, the tribal offices, the post office. I read junk mail. I read auto-repair manuals. I read magazines. I read anything that had words and paragraphs. I read with equal parts joy and desperation. I loved those books, but I also knew that love had only one purpose. I was trying to save my life.

8 Despite all the books I read, I am still surprised I became a writer. I was going to be a pediatrician. These days, I write novels, short stories, and poems. I visit schools and teach creative writing to Indian kids. In all my years in the reservation school system, I was never taught how to write poetry, short stories or novels. I was certainly never taught that Indians wrote poetry, short stories and novels. Writing was something beyond Indians. I cannot recall a single time that a guest teacher visited the reservation. There must have been visiting teachers. Who were they? Where are they now? Do they exist? I visit the schools as often as possible. The Indian kids crowd the classroom. Many are writing their own poems, short stories and novels. They have read my books. They have read many other books. They look at me with bright eyes and arrogant wonder. They are trying to save their lives. Then there are the sullen and already defeated Indian kids who sit in the back rows and ignore me with theatrical precision. The pages of their notebooks are empty. They carry neither pencil nor pen. They stare out the window. They refuse and resist. "Books," I say to them. "Books," I say. I throw my weight against their locked doors. The door holds. I am smart. I am arrogant. I am lucky. I am trying to save our lives.

Sherman Alexie, "Superman and Me," *The Los Angeles Times*, April 19, 1998. Copyright © 1998 Sherman Alexie. All rights reserved. Used by permission of Nancy Stauffer Associates.

Exercises

Do not refer to the selection for Exercises A, B, and C unless your instructor directs you to do so.

A. DETERMINING THE MAIN IDEA AND PURPOSE

Choose the best answer.

_____ 1. The main idea of the selection is that
　　　　a. education for Indian children needs to be improved.
　　　　b. reading for Alexie was not only a passion, but it also saved his life.
　　　　c. Alexie was heading for trouble in school until he learned to read.
　　　　d. it's unusual, or even odd, for a child to love to read as much as Alexie did.

_____ 2. The writer's purpose is to
　　　　a. describe what life is like for American Indian children on the reservation.
　　　　b. examine the influence his father had on his interests and character.

    c. argue that American education needs to be overhauled so that reading is stressed more.

    d. examine the impact of reading on his childhood and help Indian kids to save their own lives.

B. COMPREHENDING MAIN IDEAS

Choose the correct answer for the multiple-choice items. Write the fill-in answers in the space provided using your own words.

_____ **1.** Alexie writes that he learned to read
    a. at the age of three.
    b. in kindergarten.
    c. in first grade.
    d. at the age of 14.

2. The first thing that Alexie remembers reading was _____.

_____ **3.** Alexie began reading himself because
    a. he was a lonely child with few friends and a lot of time on his hands.
    b. his father loved to read, and since he loved his father a great deal, he decided to love reading, too.
    c. he had a teacher who loved reading and who inspired his students to do the same.
    d. he was curious about the world around him and thirsted for knowledge.

_____ **4.** Alexie realized at a young age the importance of paragraphs, which he compared to
    a. a building made with words.
    b. a box filled with words.
    c. a way to understand the world around him more clearly.
    d. a fence that held words.

5. What does Alexie say about smart Indians and the way they are perceived by Indians and non-Indians alike? _____

_____ **6.** When Alexie was in the reservation school system as a child
    a. his teachers recognized his talent and encouraged him to write.
    b. children were not taught to write poetry or stories because writing was considered to be beyond Indians.
    c. he remembers being excited and impressed by guest writers who came to the school to help the kids with their writing.
    d. the kids were encouraged to record their thoughts and feelings in journals and diaries.

COMPREHENSION SCORE

Score your answers for Exercises A and B as follows:

A. No. right _____ × 2 = _____

B. No. right _____ × 1 = _____

Total points from A and B _____ × 10 = _____ percent

C. SEQUENCING

These sentences from one paragraph in the selection have been scrambled. Read the sentences and choose the sequence that puts them back into logical order. Do not refer to the original selection.

1 But he is an Indian boy living on the reservation and is simply an oddity. **2** This might be an interesting story all by itself. **3** He reads "Grapes of Wrath" in kindergarten when other children are struggling through "Dick and Jane." **4** A little Indian boy teaches himself to read at an early age and advances quickly. **5** If he'd been anything but an Indian boy living on the reservation, he might have been called a prodigy.

_____ Which of the following represents the correct sequence for these sentences?

    a. 4, 5, 4, 1, 2
    b. 4, 3, 2, 1, 5
    c. 2, 4, 3, 5, 1
    d. Correct as written.

You may refer to the selection as you work through the remaining exercises.

D. INTERPRETING MEANING

Write your answers to these questions in your own words.

1. How exactly did Alexie teach himself to read? _____

_____

2. Read paragraph 5 again. Explain the behavior of Indian children in the classroom in the reservation school that Alexie attended. What was expected of them, and how did they behave? _____

_____

3. Read paragraph 7 again, paying careful attention to the way Alexie expresses the ideas expressed in the first four sentences and then in the sentences that follow. What interesting stylistic device does he use throughout the paragraph? What is the effect of this device? _____

_____

4. In the last paragraph Alexie writes, "I throw my weight against their locked doors." What is he referring to? _____

E. UNDERSTANDING VOCABULARY

Look through the paragraphs listed below and find a word that matches each definition. Refer to a dictionary if necessary. An example has been done for you.

Ex. arriving at unpredictable times [paragraph 1] _____ *irregular* _____

1. eager, enthusiastic [2] _____

2. not organized logically, haphazard [2] _____

3. words that tell a story [4] _____

4. a child with exceptional talents [5] _____

5. displaying silent resentment, bad humor [8] _____

F. USING VOCABULARY—VARIANT WORD FORMS

In parentheses before each sentence are some inflected forms of words from the selection. Study the context and the sentence. Then write the correct form in the space provided.

1. (*modesty, modest, modestly*) Alexie writes that in adulthood he referred to himself in the third person ("he") when describing his childhood and trying to sound _____ about his talents.

2. (*oddity, odd, oddly*) A child who lived on an Indian reservation and who loved to read as much as Alexie did was considered by the others to be simply _____.

3. (*submission, submit, submissive, submissively*) Defiant and sullen in class, Indian children learned to be _____ when confronted by a non-Indian adult.

4. (*clarity, clarify, clear, clearly*) Alexie remembers_____ the exact moment when he first understood the purpose of a paragraph.

5. (*subversion, subverted, subversive, subversively*) In school, Indian children learned to live up to their teachers' low expectations, but outside school they _____ them by being tough and very verbal.

G. TOPICS FOR DISCUSSION

1. What is the connection between the example that Alexie chooses from his first Superman comic book that illustrates how he learned to read and his experience teaching creative writing to Indian students today? What does Alexie consider to be the chief benefit of reading, for himself and for others as well?

2. Do you think that Alexie can get through to the "sullen and already defeated Indian kids who sit in the back row"? If so, how? What do you think has made these young Indians so resentful?

H. TOPICS FOR WRITING

1. Write a short narrative, following the model that Alexie uses, in which you explore your own first attempts to learn to read.
2. Write a short character profile of Alexie as he emerges in this essay. What kind of child was he? What kind of man is he now?

EXPLORE THE WEB

- On Sherman Alexie's official website you'll find information about his books and films, including clips of his readings, interviews, and a lot of other interesting topics.

  www.fallsapart.com.

3

JOE ABBOTT
To Kill a Hawk

Joe Abbott is a native of northern California's Humboldt County, the setting for the events that are described in this narrative retrospective. Before becoming a full-time reading teacher at Butte College in northern California, Abbott was actively involved with environmental groups, including the Año Nuevo Interpretive Association. (Año Nuevo, north of Santa Cruz, California, is home to a large population of elephant seals.) This article was first published in the Chico News and Review. *Abbott writes this about his piece: "I believe there are no issues more pressing than environmental concerns. In our confinement on this lonely and small planet we have to learn to live with the other species that share our existence, and must learn whether our purposes are altruistic or selfish—because it is increasingly apparent that our fates are inexorably connected. 'To Kill a Hawk' explains how I came to that belief."*

Vocabulary Analysis

WORD PARTS

ir-, irrevocable [paragraph 3] The prefix *-ir* is a variant of two more common prefixes that indicate negation, *un-* and *in-*. *Ir-* is used to make words beginning with the letter *r* negative, as in *irrevocable*, *irrational*, and *irresponsible*. *Irrevocable* is pronounced with the accent on the second syllable: ĭ-rĕv′ ə-kə-bəl Difficult words like this one are more accessible if you learn to break them down, like this:

> *ir-* ("not") + *voc* ("to call") + able (able to) = not able to be called back, not able to be reversed

WORD FAMILIES

cogn-, recognition [paragraph 14] When he saw the redtail hawk shot, Abbott experienced a shock of *recognition*, something that he had always known existed. The root of this noun is *cogn-*, from the Latin verb *cognoscere*, meaning "to know." Thus, when we recognize something, literally we know it again. Here are some other examples of words in this family:

cognitive   the mental process by which knowledge is acquired
cognizant   being aware, fully informed, conscious

precognition   knowing something before it happens
incognito   a person who does not want to be recognized

The title was undoubtedly chosen to echo the title of Harper Lee's Pulitzer-Prize winning novel of 1960, *To Kill a Mockingbird*, about racial inequality in the 1930s South.

JOE ABBOTT

To Kill a Hawk

1   So now we have revelation: ex-CIA agent claims Earth First! has engaged genetic scientists for development of a doomsday virus to rid the planet of pesky Homo sapiens infestation. It's an interesting story, although it would be more interesting to locate someone who believed anything these guys said anymore.

2   But the question of spook veracity aside, I recently spent an evening rereading (spiritual founder of Earth First!) Edward Abbey's *Desert Solitaire*. In the chapter "Serpents of Paradise," I came across an intriguing line: " . . . I'd rather kill a man than a snake," Abbey wrote. This struck a familiar tone for me, so I reached for something else I recently read, Robinson Jeffers' selected poems.

3   Sure enough, I found something in the poem "Hurt Hawks." Jeffers wrote: "I'd sooner, except for the penalties, kill a man than a hawk." A fine poem, as fine as Abbey's desert essays. But such a curious sentiment. As I compared these lines, they reminded me of something I'd forgotten, even though the thing forgotten was the kind of experience, an epiphany, really, that marks a person's life, a moment which designates an irrevocable turning point.

4   The epiphany was in part the result of something that happened the day before. It was summer of 1971, and a dozen friends and I had driven down the breathtakingly steep and tortuous road into Shelter Cove in southern Humboldt County to camp on the black sand beaches. We were pretty young then, and ill-prepared, and we quickly gobbled our meager food supplies. So I and a couple others went down into the cove to poach abalones among the rocks. The tide was ebbing and we didn't have to swim too much in the cold water, and since in those days abalone were a cinch to find before the season opened, we nabbed thirty in an hour or so.

5   Of course thirty abalone is meat enough for sixty people, not a dozen, and because we had no refrigeration and despite stuffing ourselves, gorging on the tasty butter-fried gastropods, most of the abalone went to waste. Since we had no way of preserving them, we buried the lot.

6   I had grown up a hunter and a fisherman, and I suppose I knew a little about the maintenance of fish or animal populations. I mean I'd killed for fun before without regret, yet when I left camp early the next morning I felt some remorse about those wasted abalones.

7   My girlfriend and I had just climbed above a coastal fog on the steep Shelter Cove road in her car, had almost reached the crest where the road forked for

the King's Range and Redway, when I noticed a big redtail puffed against the damp and chill of the morning. He was perched atop a huge roadside pine and, although I've always liked to watch hawks despite having shot a couple for no reason, I didn't slow or stop because I didn't want to disturb him. Perhaps I thought a hawk deserves a morning sunning to warm his hollow bones. More likely I identified with the predator.

8   But as we crested the mountain we came upon a red Dodge convertible (I've never forgotten) with two men in it, the passenger standing on his seat. He had a rifle scoped on the redtail.

9   I don't know why the moment touched me. To that point in my life I pretty much thought that whatever anybody else did to an animal was his own business. I stomped the brakes, the tires scrunching to a stop in the gravel. And for some reason I leaned on the horn—anything, to frighten the bird. For a moment it was almost as if I were the bird, that somehow our two fates were intertwined in a way I could not explain. It was like watching somebody hurt someone you love. I still can't explain the suddenness of it.

10   I pressed harder on the horn, but there was no sound. No, my girlfriend's horn hadn't worked for months. I had forgotten.

11   I don't know what the guy must have thought. Perhaps he believed I stopped so I'd not disturb his shot. For a long time (or maybe it seemed that way) the guy scoped the hawk while we just sat there, transfixed on the horrible inevitability of the moment. And then he fired.

12   Writing of such a moment, I realize that it perhaps inspires, even for the most sensitive persons, only a momentary disgust for the senseless act. One hawk of the thousands shot yearly. And this incident occurred so long ago.

13   But at that moment I experienced anger and sadness. Strange emotions for someone convinced that the beasts were on the planet so that humankind might hunt them down. The driver threw the convertible into gear and the two peeled away in a swirl of gravel and dust. I left the car idling in the dirt road and walked back to the cliff alongside the great pine. Looking down the bank I couldn't see the redtail. But I knew he'd been hit; grey fluff still drifted in the chill windless air.

14   Imagine the downy feathers hanging in air a few thousand feet above the ocean, above the steep tawny cliffs descending to the fog-shrouded beach where the abalones rotted in the black sand. Imagine me as I stood on the high cliff, stood looking for the big redtail, the bird no more to lift into the stiff afternoon wind off the ocean as the sun burned over the manzanita and pine-crested heights, the great mountains of the King's Range. Imagine behind my eyes something changing at that moment, a realization of the enormity not of the two men's sin but of my own; the recognition of something I had never suspected although it had ever been before me.

15   And then imagine how I could suddenly have seen those two men in that convertible disappear, heard their tires scramble in the pea gravel as the red convertible in one terrible moment hung in air over the long steep cliffs, heard the men's screams as the car plunged. . . .

16   Rather kill a man than a hawk or snake? I choose to kill none. Yet that morning long ago, for those few moments, without regret I could have heard that car

roll down those canyons. I could understand many things that are perhaps as ugly as the death of that redtail.

Exercises

Do not refer to the selection for Exercises A, B, and C unless your instructor directs you to do so.

A. DETERMINING THE MAIN IDEA AND PURPOSE

Choose the best answer.

_____ **1.** The main idea of the selection is that, for the writer, the death of the hawk meant
  a. the end of his adolescence and the beginning of adulthood.
  b. an epiphany or revelation that killing an animal for sport or fun is a senseless, stupid act.
  c. a recognition that human and animal lives are equally sacred.
  d. a much worse act than his and his friends' illegal poaching of abalone.

_____ **2.** The writer's purpose is to
  a. argue for stricter laws against poaching fish and game, especially of prized species like abalone.
  b. describe how beauty and cruelty are often intertwined in nature.
  c. relate a narrative to show the folly of youth and inexperience.
  d. describe an incident of cruelty and selfishness that forever transformed his thinking.

B. COMPREHENDING MAIN IDEAS

Choose the correct answer for the multiple-choice items. Write the fill-in answers in the space provided using your own words.

_____ **1.** At the beginning of the selection, Abbott refers to a poem by Robinson Jeffers called "Hurt Hawk," which contains the phrase,
  a. "I'd sooner kill a man than a hawk."
  b. "I'd rather kill a snake than a hawk."
  c. "I'd rather die than kill a hawk."
  d. "I'd sooner kill a hawk than a man."

_____ **2.** Abbott relates that the abalone along the Humboldt coast were easy to catch because
  a. they moved slowly and therefore were easy targets.
  b. they were brightly colored and therefore easy to spot.
  c. the season hadn't opened yet so they were plentiful.
  d. they came onto the beach to spawn.

3. Abbott and his friends had no way of preserving the extra abalone. What did they do with them? _____

_____ 4. Abbott writes that while he was growing up, he
   a. used to fish and hunt.
   b. was a vegetarian.
   c. believed that hunting and fishing were unethical.
   d. studied animal ecology and management of animal populations.

_____ 5. After watching the driver of the car taking aim to shoot the hawk, Abbott
   a. decided to report the man for illegal hunting.
   b. searched in vain for the bird in order to save it.
   c. felt as if his fate and the bird's fate were somehow intertwined.
   d. pushed the car with its occupants over the cliff.

6. What was the "shock of recognition" that Abbott experienced—the connection between their poaching abalone and the man's shooting of the redtail hawk? _____

COMPREHENSION SCORE

Score your answers for Exercises A and B as follows:

A. No. right _____ × 2 = _____

B. No. right _____ × 1 = _____

Total points from A and B _____ × 10 = _____ percent

C. SEQUENCING

These sentences from one paragraph in the selection have been scrambled. Read the sentences and choose the sequence that puts them back into logical order. Do not refer to the original selection.

1 One hawk of the thousands shot yearly. **2** And this incident occurred so long ago. **3** Writing of such a moment, I realize that it perhaps inspires, even for the most sensitive persons, only a momentary disgust for the senseless act.

_____ Which of the following represents the correct sequence for these sentences?
   a. 3, 2, 1
   b. 1, 3, 2
   c. 3, 1, 2
   d. Correct as written.

You may refer to the selection as you work through the remaining exercises.

D. DISTINGUISHING BETWEEN MAIN IDEAS AND SUPPORTING DETAILS

Label the following statements from the selection as follows: MI if it represents a *main idea* and SD if it represents a *supporting detail*.

_____ **1.** The epiphany that Abbott experienced was the result of the preceding day's poaching incident.

_____ **2.** The group camped on the black sand beaches and ate their meager food supply.

_____ **3.** The group poached 30 abalone they found among the rocks, but since they had no way to preserve those they didn't need, they buried them.

_____ **4.** Although Abbott had grown up hunting and fishing, he felt some degree of remorse for the wasted abalone.

E. INTERPRETING MEANING

Where appropriate, write your answers to these questions in your own words.

1. What is the connection between Edward Abbey's line in "Serpents of Paradise" and the line in Robinson Jeffers's poem (see paragraphs 2–3)? _____

_____

2. In paragraph 3, Abbott uses the word "epiphany" to describe the moment that changes his life. Consult a dictionary and then write a definition in your own words._____

3. What hint of a change occurs in Abbott's thinking in paragraph 6 as a result of the poaching incident? _____

4. Why was the sight of the man's scoping the redtail hawk and his subsequent shooting of it so terrible for the writer to witness? _____

_____

F. UNDERSTANDING VOCABULARY

Look through the paragraphs listed below and find a word that matches each definition. Refer to a dictionary if necessary. An example has been done for you.

Ex. Judgment Day [paragraph 1]   _____*doomsday*_____

1. truthfulness [2]   _____

2. unable to be reversed [3]   _____

3. twisting, winding, bending [4]   _____

4. stuffing with food, devouring greedily [5]   _____

5. motionless, with amazement, fear, terror [11]   _____

G. USING VOCABULARY

In parentheses before each sentence are some inflected forms of words from the selection. Study the context and the sentence. Then write the correct form in the space provided.

1. (*reveal, revelation, revelatory*) Abbott experienced an intense epiphany, a sudden _____ as he watched the man shoot the redtail hawk.

2. (*remorse, remorseful, remorsefully*) After the poaching incident, Abbott contemplated the significance of what he and his friends had done with _____.

3. (*prey, predator, predation, predatory*) Redtail hawks are birds of _____.

4. (*inevitable, inevitably, inevitability*) The worst part about watching the shooting of the hawk was that its death was _____.

5. (*inspire, inspiring, inspired, inspiration*) For the writer, the two incidents—poaching the abalone and the death of the hawk—were intertwined, _____ horror and disgust.

H. TOPICS FOR DISCUSSION

1. How would you characterize the tone (emotional feeling) of the two main parts of this narrative—the poaching of the abalone incident and the man's killing of the hawk?
2. Return to paragraphs 2 and 3. Comment on the use of the quotation from Robinson Jeffers' poem—"I'd rather kill a man than a snake." What are the implications of this quotation?
3. What is going through Abbott's mind as he watches the hawk's feathers floating in the air high above the ocean? What do these feathers signify to him?

I. TOPICS FOR WRITING

1. Write a narrative essay in which you explain the circumstances leading to an epiphany of your own.
2. Abbott seems to suggest that these intertwined experiences on that day on the Humboldt County coast changed his thinking about hunting and fishing. Write an essay in which you examine your own thoughts about hunting and fishing—for sport, not for a family's survival.

EXPLORE THE WEB

- What laws against poaching exist in your state? Is poaching a problem where you live? Read about this issue and its effect on your state's environment and animal population. Using Google or your favorite search engine, type in the following:
  - poaching laws, name of state (Example: poaching laws, Iowa)

School Days

Rose Castillo Guilbault was born in Mexico and later immigrated with her family to the United States, where they settled near King City, a small farming town in California's Salinas Valley, known as the lettuce capital of the world. Guilbault has had a varied journalistic career both in print and television. Currently, she is Vice President for Corporate Affairs for the California State Automobile Association as well as Vice-Chairman of the Commonwealth Club of California. This excerpt is from her recent book, Farmworker's Daughter: Growing Up Mexican in America (2005), *which recounts her memories of growing up in Nogales and King City, California, from a bicultural perspective.*

Vocabulary Analysis

WORD PARTS

This selection contains three useful word parts—two prefixes and one suffix. Prefixes and suffixes are parts of words that can't stand alone. A prefix is attached to the beginning of a root; it affects or changes the meaning of the root. A suffix, on the other hand, is attached to the end of a root and usually changes the word's grammatical part of speech, as you will see in these examples:

em- [paragraph 9] This prefix signifies "becoming" or "causing to be." Thus, the word *empowered* means "causing one to have power." Sometimes this prefix is spelled *en-*, depending on the first letter of the root word. You can easily determine the meaning of these words by just looking at the root following the prefix: *encourage, entrap, enliven, embitter.*

sub- [paragraph 45] The prefix *sub-* from the Latin means "under" and *conscious* means "aware." Therefore, one's *subconscious* is a partial sort of awareness because it is submerged below full consciousness. This prefix is easy to recognize in words like *submarine* ("under the ocean") or *subplot* ("a secondary plot"), but it is less easy to detect in other words. Look up the following four words in the dictionary and write their meanings in the space provided. If "under" is clearly suggested, write "yes" next to the definition. If not, write "no."

subterranean _____

subjugate _____

subordinate _____

subjective _____

ROSE GUILBAULT

School Days

1   I hated school. I hated leaving home every day. Home was safe, warm, and constant, without the conflicts I had to endure in the outside world. But I couldn't tell my mother that. She was so full of optimism.

2   "Oh, you're going to learn so many things. American schools are the best in the world! You'll be so smart because you'll know two languages." Her face shone with enthusiasm when she said these things, and I didn't want to dampen her spirits.

3   Her words suppressed my childish complaints. But even if I had dared share my feelings with her, I didn't yet have the vocabulary to explain the bigger issues that were the real source of pain, nor would I understand them myself for years to come. At six years of age, I lived in a world of confusion—the language, the kids, the culture spun around me like a vortex. Within one year I had moved away from family and the stability of a routine to a foreign country with a foreign language. Then we moved from town and our newly established relationships with friends and neighbors to an isolated farm where I had to readjust again and, now, school.

4   Each day presented challenges and I had to sort through them by myself. Even if I wanted to ask for help, what exactly would I ask for? Help me understand what the teacher is saying, or stop the kids from treating me like an oddball?

5   I intuitively knew that the person I leaned on for everything—my mother—would not be able to help me. She relied heavily on her own experiences as a basis of understanding the world, and just as the Wizard of Oz had nothing in his bag for Dorothy, she had nothing to smooth this assimilation for me. Once I stepped outside my door, I was all alone and had to fend for myself. The only thing I feared more than school was disappointing my mother, so I hid my anxieties.

6   Every morning, she walked me the full two miles to the school bus stop and stayed with me until the bus arrived. The boss's boys walked by themselves and stood on the opposite side of the road, not talking to us while we waited. It set the tone for a curious relationship. They weren't unfriendly, but neither were they forthcoming. Their whole family couldn't decide whether to treat us as subordinate employees or as neighbors.

7   I was glad to have my mother with me. Cattle roamed on one side of the road and the bulls liked to bellow and chase us along the fence. Their snorting and hoofing terrified me.

8   Leaving my mother and boarding the bus brought up still more fears. The big yellow bus was filled with high school kids who were to be dropped off first before we continued to the elementary school. The older kids laughed at me, and I couldn't understand most of what was being said. They'd often not let me sit next to them, stacking schoolbooks alongside empty seats when they saw me approach. I learned to automatically walk quickly to the back and sit by myself. I found all of this confusing and humiliating.

9   At school things were no better. The teacher's instructions would wash over me like a wave; I heard the sounds but didn't understand their purpose. But eventually, slowly and unexpectedly the English language revealed itself to me. Every new word and every new definition was like lifting a layer of film from my eyes, giving me clarity to see the world around me. Words empowered me and I pursued their secrets assiduously. At home all I had was an ancient English/Spanish dictionary my father had used to teach himself English, but its tiny print and archaic language did more to obscure meaning than shed light on it. I actually learned more from the grocery store–bought encyclopedias, which I read cover to cover one summer. By the end of first grade I was scholastically on track: I knew the alphabet, wrote in block print, and could read the "Dick and Jane" books. By second grade, my English was much improved. My interest in books also heightened with the acquisition of a library card, and it helped that the library was conveniently located across the street from San Lorenzo Elementary School. I loved the feel and smell of hardbound books at the library. I delighted in sitting quietly, trying to decipher the mysteries between their pages, mainly by interpreting the illustrations.

10   But for all my struggles in the classroom, my greatest challenges occurred on the playground. The girls talked about things I knew the words for but had no point of reference on. They talked about birthday parties with cake and games like pin the tail on the donkey and musical chairs, barbecues with hot dogs and root beer, and toys I'd never heard of.

11   One day Mona said we should bring our dolls to play with at recess. I wanted desperately to fit in, so I stuffed an old baby doll—the only doll I owned—into a paper bag.

12   "Why are you taking that paper bag to school?" my mother asked.

13   I knew she wouldn't understand why I'd want to take my doll, so I fibbed. "The teacher asked us to bring our dolls."

14   My mother raised an eyebrow but chose not to pursue the matter.

15   At recess, the other girls all pulled out their dolls. It made me want to laugh out loud—they'd all brought the very same one! I proudly pulled out my baby doll. Nobody had one like her!

16   "What is that?" Mona scrunched her nose at my doll. "Don't you have a Barbie?"

17   The other little girls twittered. What was a Barbie? I wondered. And why was my doll looked down on? I felt embarrassed and quickly stuffed my unworthy toy back into the paper bag. I would not be invited to play with them again. Nor would I be invited to Mona's or any of the other girls' birthday parties.

18   And that's why I hated school. Cultural gaffes were far more difficult to overcome than language gaps. I felt like an outsider, and I would not be able to shake that sense of alienation throughout my school years in King City.

19   My mother tried her best to be supportive. Surely she sensed my disaffection when I trudged home down the long road, looking weary from another day in the outside world.

20   "My teacher Mrs. Lewis doesn't like me," I confided once. "I'm always in trouble because she says I talk too much."

21   "Do you?" my mother asked gently.

22   "No. I just answer the girl next to me, but I get in trouble, not her."

23   The following week my mother insisted I take a tray of homemade enchiladas to Mrs. Lewis. I had to carry them on the school bus wrapped in a brown grocery bag. Even the high school kids couldn't hide their curiosity.

24   "What's in the bag?" they asked over and over.

25   I was mortified. What would they think if I told them I was taking food for my teacher? I'd seen some kids bring apples, but never an entree!

26   I refused to talk and huddled in the corner of the bus by myself, clutching my package.

27   "She's a retard," a high school boy said disgustedly. And that, mercifully, stopped the questions.

28   Once we reached the grammar school I nervously walked straight to my classroom, avoiding the playground. I arrived breathless. Anxious thoughts popped into my head. What if Mrs. Lewis was disgusted and threw the dish into the trash can. Or worse, acted superior and asked, "What is this? Does your family actually eat this?" I would not be able to bear it if Mrs. Lewis expressed any form of rejection toward my mother's offering. I would simply never go to school again!

29   "Why, what's this? It's not time to come in yet." Mrs. Lewis looked up from her desk when she heard me close the door.

30   "My mother sent you this." I thrust the package in front of me.

31   She put on the glasses that hung from a gold chain and often rested on her ample bosom, and strode toward me. Mrs. Lewis was plump but moved quickly.

32   She took the wrinkled package and unwrapped it carefully on her desk.

33   "Enchiladas!" she cried out. "I love enchiladas! How did your mother know?"

34   I shrugged happily. How *did* my mother know?

35   "Bless her heart," Mrs. Lewis clapped her hands together. "Homemade enchiladas!"

36   From that day I can honestly say I was treated differently. Mrs. Lewis was more patient and attentive after the gift.

37   But not all situations could be solved with homemade enchiladas. I wanted my mother to be a part of the classroom culture. I wanted her to be like the popular kids' mothers, to be a room mother so I would fit in with my classmates. But she couldn't because she didn't drive or speak English. Another teacher suggested she make cupcakes for classroom celebrations instead. I thought this presented a great opportunity to be accepted by the class. I had observed how kids whose mothers made cupcakes were given special stature by the others.

38   It didn't work out quite so easily, though.

39   "I don't know what a cupcake is," my mother said, perplexed.

40   "It's like a little cake. But it's in a wrapper," I tried to explain.

41   "I can make empanadas for your party. They're probably similar," she offered.

42   Now, I knew there was no similarity between empanadas and cupcakes other than their both being desserts, but my mother insisted I ask my teacher if she could bring them. I had a bad feeling about it, but I went ahead and asked anyway.

43   "Oh no, dear," Mrs. Steussy demurred. "The children only eat American things. Have her bring cupcakes."

44   Mama learned to make cupcakes by deciphering a recipe from her new Betty Crocker cookbook. The other mothers baked theirs in colored papers or pretty tinfoil cups and decorated them with candy and little umbrellas or flags or plastic figures identifying the occasion. If it was St. Patrick's Day, the cupcakes were green with little leprechauns on top. For St. Valentine's Day, white-frosted cupcakes would be decorated with red candy hearts and coordinated red foil cups.

45   But my mother's cupcakes never turned out like the other mothers'. Hers looked like pale muffins haphazardly spread with a glob of thin, runny white frosting (made from C&H confectioner's sugar and not Fluffy Frosting Mix). My classmates looked at the box lined with wax paper instead of colored tinfoil like the others and whispered "yuck." A knot formed in my throat and I silently swore I'd never ask my mother to make anything for class ever again. It was the beginning of a subconscious effort to keep my private life and school life separate. If the other kids didn't know about my home life, they would assume I was like them. I could be American at school just like everybody else. And as long as anyone who really mattered never came to my house—which was not difficult since we lived way out in the country—they'd never know the truth.

Rose Castillo Guilbault, "School Days" from *Farmworker's Daughter: Growing Up Mexican in America.* Copyright 2005. Reproduced with permission of Heyday Books in the format Textbook via Copyright Clearance Center.

Exercises

Do not refer to the selection for Exercises A, B, and C unless your instructor directs you to do so.

A. DETERMINING THE MAIN IDEA AND PURPOSE

Choose the best answer.

_____ 1.   The main idea of the selection is the writer's discovery that
   a. assimilation is much more than simply learning a new language and customs.
   b. she learned to assimilate at school but to keep her private life at home invisible and separate.

      c. humiliation and rejection were painful but necessary first steps on the road to becoming assimilated.

      d. her mother's encouragement and support helped her to endure the alienation she first experienced at school.

_____ **2.** The writer's purpose is to

      a. complain about the lack of support young immigrant children receive at school.

      b. suggest ways that immigrant children can successfully conquer their fears and sense of alienation.

      c. criticize her parents for not doing more to help her fit in better.

      d. relate her experiences and feelings of rejection, alienation, and accommodation as she tried in vain to become accepted.

B. COMPREHENDING MAIN IDEAS

Choose the correct answer for the multiple-choice items. Write the fill-in answers in the space provided using your own words.

_____ **1.** When Guilbault announced that she hated school, she said her mother expressed

      a. similar fears and uncertainties.

      b. optimism and encouragement.

      c. indifference and lack of interest.

      d. feelings of conflict and ambivalence.

_____ **2.** On the school bus, the high school students

      a. welcomed her and asked her to sit with them.

      b. moved their seats when they saw her get on the bus.

      c. laughed at her and refused to let her share their seats.

      d. helped her with her homework and taught her new English words.

_____ **3.** As she describes her status as a recent immigrant, Guilbault's greatest challenges lay

      a. in the classroom.

      b. at home, with her parents.

      c. on the school bus.

      d. on the playground.

_____ **4.** Guilbault's feelings of being an outsider, of being alienated were particularly reinforced

      a. when the other girls laughed at her doll.

      b. when the other children made fun of her English.

      c. at birthday parties where she didn't understand the games.

      d. when her teacher refused to give her extra help with her studies.

5. How did Mrs. Lewis, Guilbault's teacher, react to the gift of homemade enchiladas? _____

_____

6. What was the final humiliating experience for Guilbault that she describes in the reading? _____

_____

COMPREHENSION SCORE

Score your answers for Exercises A and B as follows:

A. No. right _____ × 2 = _____

B. No. right _____ × 1 = _____

Total points from A and B _____ × 10 _____ percent

C. SEQUENCING

These sentences from one paragraph in the selection have been scrambled. Read the sentences and choose the sequence that puts them back into logical order. Do not refer to the original selection.

1 The only thing I feared more than school was disappointing my mother, so I hid my anxieties. **2** She relied heavily on her own experiences as a basis of understanding the world, and just as the Wizard of Oz had nothing in his bag for Dorothy, she had nothing to smooth this assimilation for me. **3** I intuitively knew that the person I leaned on for everything—my mother—would not be able to help me. **4** Once I stepped outside my door, I was all alone and had to fend for myself.

_____ Which of the following represents the correct sequence for these sentences?
   a. 1, 3, 2, 4
   b. 3, 2, 4, 1
   c. 4, 3, 2, 1
   d. Correct as written

You may refer to the selection as you work through the remaining exercises.

D. LOCATING SUPPORTING DETAILS

For the main idea stated here, find details that support it: "Guilbault faced many unpleasant things when she boarded the school bus each day." [paragraph 8] The second and last ones have been done for you.

1. _____

2. She couldn't understand what the older kids were saying.

3. _____

4. _____

5. She sat by herself in the back of the bus.

E. UNDERSTANDING VOCABULARY

Choose the best definition according to an analysis of word parts or the context.

_____ **1.** I had to *fend* for myself [5]
   a. manage, do without help
   b. make a decision
   c. accept a difficult situation
   d. ask for help

_____ **2.** trying to *decipher* the mysteries [9; also 44]
   a. translate
   b. copy
   c. solve
   d. figure out

_____ **3.** I pursued their secrets *assiduously* [9]
   a. without interruption
   b. with great pleasure
   c. diligently, with persistence
   d. without much enthusiasm

_____ **4.** to *obscure* meaning [9]
   a. clarify, shed light on
   b. hide, conceal
   c. comprehend
   d. acquire

_____ **5.** cultural *gaffes* were far more difficult to overcome [18]
   a. clumsy mistakes
   b. humiliations
   c. misunderstandings
   d. customs, habits

_____ **6.** Mrs. Steussy *demurred* [43]
   a. whispered softly
   b. apologized
   c. demanded, ordered
   d. objected, protested

F. USING VOCABULARY—VARIANT WORD FORMS

In parentheses before each sentence are some inflected forms of words from the selection. Study the context and the sentence. Then write the correct form in the space provided.

1. (*intuition, intuitively*). From simple _____ Guilbault learned at an early age that she would have to rely only on herself, and not her mother, to become accepted.

2. (*stability, stable, stabilize*) Guilbault describes the difficulty she experienced moving from a _____ and secure environment to one of confusion and alienation.

3. (*anxiety, anxious, anxiously*) Guilbault was particularly _____ every morning when she boarded the school bus.

4. (*acquire, acquisition, acquisitive*) When she was able to _____ a library card, Guilbault turned to reading for both learning and comfort.

5. (*rely, reliance, reliable*) In her quest to fit in, Guilbault realized early that she had to learn self-_____

G. TOPICS FOR DISCUSSION

1. Guilbault feels an obvious conflict and ambivalence toward her mother and her supportive efforts. Comment on this conflict. Does Guilbault's realization that she has to go it alone in her quest to assimilate seem cruel or merely realistic?

2. Guilbault is now middle-aged, meaning that her account is set a generation ago. Do immigrant children today face the same cruelty and hostility that Guilbault describes? What cultural factors today suggest that acceptance might be easier?

H. TOPICS FOR WRITING

1. What makes assimilation for immigrants so difficult? Go through the selection again, making notes in the margin next to information that answers this question. Then write a short essay summarizing what Guilbault has to say about this problem.

2. If you have a friend, relative, or co-worker who has recently immigrated, interview him or her about the kinds of obstacles and problems the person encountered upon arrival. Then write a short essay discussing them. Include the measures the person took to overcome these difficulties.

EXPLORE THE WEB

*   It used to be said that America is a melting pot, a nation of immigrants. More recently, some cultural historians have begun to describe America as being more of a salad bowl, where each individual component (ethnic group) is part of a whole but retains its individual cultural traits. What questions are important to consider concerning immigration and assimilation? Begin with three websites to read various points of view.

*   Thomas M. Sipos, "A Nation of Assimilated Immigrants" *www.enterstageright.com/archive/articles/0605/0605immigrant.htm*

*   Russell Roberts, "Immigration and Assimilation"

*   Type in "Café Hayek" + immigration

*   Samuel P. Huntington, "Reconsidering Immigration: Is Mexico a Special Case?" *www.cis.org/articles/2000/back1100.html*

*   You can find a wealth of additional information by typing in "immigration" + "assimilation" in the search box of your favorite search engine.

5

COLBY BUZZELL

Johnny Get Your Textbook

Originally from San Francisco, Colby Buzzell joined the U.S. Army and was sent to Mosul, Iraq, for a one-year tour of duty as a machine gunner. Buzzell kept a blog during his Iraq tour, which became the basis of a 2005 book, My War: Killing Time in Iraq. *He is also the author of a second book,* Lost in America: A Dead-End Journey *(2011). This selection is a blog post, first published in September 2011 on the Veterans Administration website, the address for which is given in the Explore the Web section at the end.*

The title of this selection is a play on words. The phrase, "Johnny get your gun" was an expression commonly used to encourage young men to enlist in the military. In 1939 Dalton Trumbo published an antiwar novel, Johnny Got His Gun. *There are several songs with the title "Johnny Get Your Gun" sung by Metallica, Nausea, and other groups.*

You will notice two things: The style is informal, with occasional instances of incorrect capitalization and spelling, a grammar error or two, and a fair amount of slang. In addition, the exercises following this selection consist only of fill-in comprehension questions and two vocabulary exercises.

Vocabulary Analysis

WORD PARTS

The prefix pre- The prefix *pre-* means "before," and it is attached to dozens of English roots, for example, *predict*, *predetermine*, and *preread*. In paragraph 15, Buzzell uses the phrase *pre-pubescent teens*, referring to the period *before* puberty. In some cases, the meaning of the prefix *pre-* is somewhat obscured when it precedes a root. What do these words beginning with *pre-* mean? Of the six, for which two does the prefix have little or no connection with "before"?

prearrange	_____
precede	_____
precarious	_____
precursor	_____

premonition _____

pretense _____

WORD FAMILIES   **curriculum** Buzzell hopes to finish his two-year *curriculum* (see paragraph 29). A *curriculum* is a course of study. The root derives from the Latin verb, *currere*, to run. Other words in this family include *current*, *currency*, *course*, and *courier* (a messenger). The spicy Indian dish, *curry*, is not part of this family. That word derives from the Tamil *kari*.

COLBY BUZZELL

Johnny Get Your Textbook

1   With a half empty bottle of cheap wine in one hand (my third of the evening) and a DVD remote in the other, I sat on the sofa—eyes glazed over—numb. I was watching *Taxi Driver*, pressing the rewind button over and over again, replaying the same scene.

2   Wearing a Marine Corps shirt while doing pushups and sit-ups in his apartment, Travis Bickle narrates, "I gotta get in shape. Too much sitting has ruined my body. Too much abuse has gone on for too long. From now on there will be 50 pushups each morning, 50 pull ups. There will be no more pills, no more bad food, no more destroyers of my body. From now on there will be total organization. Every muscle must be tight."

3   I don't remember much after that. The next morning with bloodshot eyes raised at half staff, I stared at my beat-up reflection in the mirror. I looked like a retired punching bag—killing myself slowly every night was taking its toll. Not only that, when I took my shirt off, I looked pregnant. After splashing cold water on my face, I wondered how difficult the first day of sobriety was going to be. Somewhere in that drunken fog the night before I promised myself I was done drinking and I intended to keep that promise.

4   Our unofficial unit motto when we deployed to Iraq in 2003 was "Punish the Deserving," and shortly after we came back, I was discharged—like an expended 7.62 brass shell casing. From there, I guess you could say I was a functioning alcoholic. One of my inspirations for cleaning up was Sergeant Todd Vance. We served together in Iraq, and after getting out, he was a day laborer. He worked for minimum wage, laying brick all day, which he quit to attend community college courtesy of the GI Bill. After getting through that, Vance was accepted at a university—all while hitting the gym every day and becoming a competitive kick boxer. During all this time, I opted to self medicate.

5   What pains me now is the realization of how I've wasted away, perhaps the best years of my life, by drinking heavily with nothing to show for it. The first thing I had to do to quit drinking was to hate everything there was to hate about

it. I began to hate myself for drinking so much for so long, and to look with disgust at bars and those who wasted away inside them.

6   To help reinforce this, I would go to bars and order water, then I'd sit there and observe those totally inebriated, those who were like me—who drank heavily, all the way to last call. I watched how they acted and listened to their conversations. I couldn't do this initially. It took a couple months for me to be able to walk inside of a bar and walk out without any alcohol on my breath. My first goal was to lose all the pregnancy weight. I began to look at a beer as 150 calories, which meant I'd have to run a mile to burn it off. I don't like running more than I have to, so I skipped the beer.

7   After being a drunk seven days a week, I began waking every morning at sunrise to hit the gym. Conducting PT (Physical Training) and weapons maintenance (weightlifting) reminded me of my time in the Army—running around the airfield at Fort Lewis and lifting weights at the gym with guys in my platoon.

8   In three months I lost 30 pounds in empty calories and went from barely bench pressing to 275. With no roids.[1]

9   Next I targeted my mind. With happy hour over, it was time for Johnny to get his textbook.

10   The long string of students across from the Veterans Counseling Center at the City College of San Francisco stretched down the hallway and wrapped around the corner. I asked some girl what the line was for and she told me financial aid. After thanking her I walked right on by the have-nots. There was no need for me to wait with them since my college was paid for by Uncle Sam's GI Bill. All of it.

11   I asked my school's counselor what classes I would need to transfer into some fancy University of California school, like UC-Berkeley. He asked for my major, but I couldn't think of any. He said pick one. Silence filled his office as I sat there dumbly. He then asked what liked to do. I told him, "Writing."

12   Minutes later he drew up a two year plan for me so that I could someday transfer to a university. And then he told me to go to class, apply myself, and get good grades. Checks would arrive in the mail. Thanking him, I could instantaneously feel my spirits being lifted, and it's been a long while since I felt this good. My country was sending me a thank you card by taking care of me since, in a way, I took care of it eight years ago. I threw back on my sunglasses and thought to myself this is how life should be.

13   But that feeling was short lived. The first day on campus brought back flashbacks. Not of the war, but of high school and my first day of basic training where I was absolutely convinced that I had made the biggest mistake of my life. I found myself spending the majority of my free time asking god please: "Turn me into a bird so I can fly far, far away."

14   Making my way thru the Vaudeville on City College's main campus, young students—I'd imagine many from the older generations would write off as walking examples of the decline of western civilization—began to overrun my position. A brain cell deficient stoner asked if I had rolling papers, another welcomed me with a "yo dog" when trying to bum a cigarette, a girl passed by screaming into her cell phone about beating another girls ass, a burnout from the '60's was

---

[1] slang for "steroids"

yelling Bob Marley quotes thru a megaphone, and an Asian lady was finding her Zen by doing Tai Chi. To top it off, not far away was a tiny table set up by anti-war activists; no interest whatsoever shown at their lonely table, none whatsoever.

15   The VA hospital has me clinically diagnosed with PTSD[2] and none of this was making it any better. I felt like the old, un-hip creepy mid-thirties guy who somehow got dragged by his friends to Coachella[3] in a sea of pre-pubescent teens. In an effort to block this out of my head, I reminded myself of how my father—a Vietnam vet—remembers seeing Korean War Vets on his campus. He recalls them being a bit older, more mature, many with families to support, but being good students. This gave me hope.

16   Most students on campus, I imagine, are oblivious to Veteran students. To the untrained eye they blend in quite well in their civilian attire, but like sharks smelling blood in the water, other vets can do the same. There are little clues that only we can pick up on, such as: the way you carry yourself, language you use, the high and tight,[4] the dog tags, digital camo[5] back packs, a PT shirt or t-shirt with your old unit crest, or the green 550 cord bracelet.

17   Sprinkled within this mosh-pit of of students, I noticed other Veterans. I'm not talking just one or two, or even five or 10, but many, to the point where it literally felt like I was back on post again.

18   Everywhere I looked or turned I saw one, and they'd spot me. We'd exchange a subtle nod or even strike up the typical conversation most Vets have: What unit were you with? MOS? When were you over there? None would ask, what's it like over there? Or my personal favorite, did you kill anybody?

19   While smoking a post-U.S. History class cigarette outside of Cloud Hall, a voice curiously asked me if I was a Veteran. I looked up, he's about my age, from San Diego, Navy Vet, and worked in EOD (Explosive Ordinance Disposal). He talks with a laid back So-Cal[6] drawl as if he's maxing and relaxing back on the beach. He tells me that he was in the Middle East early on in the war around the same time I was. A job brought him up to the bay area and when he saw how much money he could receive by going back to school, he jumped on it. I asked him if he misses the military, and with a slight hint of regret he reminisces, "Oh yea, I thought it was going to be a career but. . ."

20   "What happened?"

21   "My second Tour."

22   Though I've only done one tour I nodded with understanding.

23   "I mean, I miss the professionalism of the military," he tells me, "I mean we're in that class, right, and I see homeboy sleeping on the fucking desk and if I was the teacher I would have kicked that desk and been like, get the fuck out! You don't want to be here? Fine, don't waste my time. You know, people all texting in class, and I'm just like what the hell is this, man?"

---

[2] The abbreviation representing the Post-Traumatic Stress Disorder
[3] The Coachella Music and Arts Festival in Indio, California, is a three-day event in the spring, offering a variety of music, including rock, hip hop, indie, and electronic.
[4] A common type of military haircut, like a buzz cut
[5] Short for "camouflage"—clothing with colorful blotches of greens and browns so that soldiers blend in with background vegetation
[6] Short for "Southern California"

24   Hearing this from him made me laugh out loud since I knew exactly what he was talking about. His advice to me, "Just don't give up, no matter how much bullshit you run into. So yea—that, and tenacity. You can accomplish anything if you try hard enough, you know?"

25   Academics have never been my strong suit. My final high school transcript has me rank at number 332 out of 344 students, which is nothing to brag about. But one of the many things I learned while serving in the Infantry are the phrases; "I can't" and, "I'm not good enough," or "I can't do it" don't exist. Especially while under fire.

26   I applied the lessons I learned while in the Army to my schooling. I hit the books hard my first semester and for the first time in my life, made the Dean's List. I fell in love I with my two U.S. history classes and spent hours in the library reading on my own—General MacArthur's landing at Inchon, General Sherman's "March To the Sea," and Patton in the Battle Of The Bulge.

27   For the first time since being out of the military, I now have a routine. I stay on this routine by forcing myself to stay focused and goal driven by immediately hitting the gym in the morning, and then taking Bart[7] to school. While waiting for BART at the Balboa station one morning, I ran into a guy from my math class who, like many asked me if I was an Iraq War veteran (he had spotted my camo backpack). I noticed he had one of these black and white Shemagh Arab scarves (in Iraq we called them "Haji Scarves") tied onto his rucksack. Due to their vogueness you can buy them at Urban Outfitters, I've seen too many hipsters rock them around their necks. Curious if there was any personal or sentimental meaning behind his scarf, he smiles and tells me it's his personal reminder to himself on what he's done, how he got here, and how he's able to be go back to school.

28   It's been awhile since I've hung out with my sister and when she saw me, she couldn't believe how different I looked, or the story of how when I was sifting through the numerous English department textbooks, I saw an article that I had written was now published in the Norton Reader.

29   I also told her, that for the first time since being back from Iraq, I felt like I was finally home. School has been somewhat therapeutic for me and I intend to finish that two year curriculum my counselor drew up for me.

30   During a pause in the conversation she brought up our mother, which cast a dark cloud over things since she passed away from cancer the year before. All she got to witness towards the end were the years I spent as a drunk.

31   "Mom always wanted you to quit drinking," my sister reminded me.

33   "And she always wanted you to go back to school."

34   It then hit me, since it didn't even occur to me before that, I was doing everything my mom always wanted me to do. I finally quit drinking and was going to school. Realizing this filled my heart with regret since I should've done all of this much sooner. My sister then added, "Mom would be proud."

35   Perhaps.

Colby Buzzell, "Johnny Get Your Textbook." Reprinted by permission of the author. Posted September 30, 2011 at http://www.blogs.va.gov/VAntage/4866/johnny-get-your-textbook

---

[7]BART—Bay Area Rapid Transit—is a five-county subway system

Exercises

You may refer to the selection while completing these exercises.

A. COMPREHENDING MAIN IDEAS

Write the answers for these questions in the space provided using your own words.

1. At the beginning of the selection, Buzzell keeps replaying a scene from the movie *Taxi Driver*. What is the main character, Travis Bickle, doing in this scene? _____

_____

2. Why was Buzzell so upset and pained about his drinking to "self-medicate"?

_____

3. How did Buzzell stop drinking? What measures did he take? _____

_____

4. When Buzzell's City College counselor asked him to choose a major, he finally came up with one, specifically _____ .

5. How did Buzzell finance his college education? _____

6. How did the veteran students on campus recognize each other so easily?

_____

7. What do Buzzell and the vet from San Diego think about their fellow students who either sleep or send text messages in class? _____

_____

8. After some initial discouragement, Buzzell did well in his college courses. How did he accomplish this? _____

_____

B. USING VOCABULARY

From the following list of vocabulary words, choose a word that fits in each blank according to both the grammatical structure of the sentence and context. Use each word in the list only once. Do not change the form of the word. (Note that there are three more words than sentences.)

deficient	sobriety	inebriated	oblivious
tenacity	therapeutic	opted	abused

Buzzell evidently _____ alcohol before he decided to change his life, because every night he became _____ drinking cheap wine. At City College, where he enrolled in classes, most of the students he encountered were _____ to the veteran students. Buzzell quickly learned that his _____ and hard work paid off, and after a while, school became _____ for him.

C. SMALL GROUP ACTIVITY—UNDERSTANDING SLANG/ IDIOMATIC EXPRESSIONS

Buzzell uses several informal and slang expressions. Consider these expressions in their context and then, working in small groups, try to determine their meaning. The paragraph number where each occurs is included. You might try the dictionary if you are unsure, or ask your instructor for help.

1. The next morning with bloodshot *eyes raised at half staff* [3]

   _____

2. killing myself slowly every night was *taking its toll* [3]

   _____

3. *hitting the gym* every day [4]

   _____

4. those who were like me—who drank heavily, all the way *to last call* [6]

   _____

5. with *happy hour* over [9]

   _____

6. I walked right by *the have-nots* [10]

   _____

7. sprinkled within this *mosh-pit* of students [17]

   _____

8. academics have never been *my strong suit* [25]

   _____

D. TOPICS FOR DISCUSSION

1. Why do you suppose Buzzell was so adrift after returning from his tour of duty in Iraq?
2. In what ways did his military experience serve him well when he returned to academic life?
3. Comment on the ideas expressed in paragraph 23. What are Buzzell and his fellow classmate suggesting about the teacher's handling of this behavior?

E. TOPICS FOR WRITING

1. Write a profile of Colby Buzzell as his character emerges in this blog post.
2. Write a profile of someone you know who turned his or her life around. What was the problem? What did the subject do to change?

EXPLORE THE WEB

- Here is the website where Buzzell's blog was first posted. You can read other blogs from veterans at the Veterans Administration website.

  www.blogs.va.gov/VAntage/4866/johnny-get-your-textbook

Cartoon For Analysis

- Roz Chast cartoon

© Roz Chast/The New Yorker Collection/www.cartoonbank.com

Study this cartoon. In a sentence of your own, state its main point.

_____

Does the cartoon pertain in any way to Buzzell's blog post? If so, how?

_____

What do you think the cartoonist's opinion of blogs is, judging from her drawing?

_____

6

JOHN BUSSEY
Old Hat for the New Normal

The Great Recession of 2008–2009 caused economic hardships for working-class and middle-class Americans, in particular because of persistent high unemployment and bank foreclosures. Even now, four years or more later, the repercussions are still evident. The Occupy Wall Street protest and its many offshoots expressed Americans' frustration with the direction the nation is heading in—the sobering statistic that 1 percent of the population is far richer than the other 99 percent. There is concern that the U.S. is becoming an oligarchy, meaning that the country might look like this: the wealthy few in control, a shrinking middle class, and a very large number of lower-class earners struggling to stay economically afloat with no hope of a brighter future. In short, we are on our way to becoming a nation of haves and have-nots.

The writer of this article, John Bussey, is executive business editor and assistant managing editor at The Wall Street Journal, *where it was published. The term "New Normal"—much in vogue during and after the Great Recession—refers to thriftiness that many Americans have adopted and a rejection of profligate or wasteful spending. In this article Bussey offers a twist on the subject of the new austerity.*

Vocabulary Analysis

WORD ENDINGS OR SUFFIXES— ADJECTIVES

English makes great use of suffixes, parts of words that attach to the end. (Prefixes are parts that attach to the beginnings.) Unlike prefixes, however, which usually affect the meaning of the root, suffixes, rather, indicate grammatical part of speech or function. From time to time in this book, we will address the subject of prefixes and suffixes. In this section, we will look at three common suffixes—*ent, ic,* and *ical,* which appear in these words from the selection; *prudent, emblematic, plastic, economic,* and *economical.* These suffixes all indicate that the words are adjectives, words that describe nouns, as is evident in these phrases: A *prudent* observation, an *emblematic* sign, an *economic* crisis, an *economical* purchase, and a *plastic* dish.

In the spaces provided, write three more adjectives, using each of the suffixes *ent*, *ic*, and *ical*.

_____   _____   _____

WORD HISTORY

bacchanal In paragraph 16 this phrase appears: "at the height of the nation's *bacchanal* in 2005." This word derives from the Roman and Greek god of wine, Bacchus (also referred to as Dionysius). The word *bacchanal* usually refers to excessive revelry and drunkenness, but in this context, Bussey is referring to our penchant for lavish spending before the Great Recession hit us with a sobering reality. He also refers to this spending as "blindingly profligate."

JOHN BUSSEY

Old Hat for the New Normal

1   I've been reading a lot about the "New Normal." And every time I see those words I think about shopping at Wal-Mart with my father, who turns 91 in March.

2   Dad was walking past a display of donuts selling for $2.50 a box. This is a man who likes nothing better than to save a nickel, who values duct tape above all else as a solution to home repair.

3   "Dad," I teased, "a box of fresh donuts for just $2.50! How can you pass up a deal like that?"

4   "That's nothing," he said. "Wait until tomorrow when they're a day old, they'll be a buck and a quarter."

5   For my father, and the generation or two that grew up with him, there's nothing new about the "new" normal. In fact, it's old hat.

6   What exactly does this latest buzz-phrase mean? It springs from the discovery that—big surprise!—we've been living beyond our means. Three years of economic crisis gave life to our new cliché, chastened as we now are to be more cost-conscious, more prudent. The term is all over newspapers, television and the blogosphere. Goodbye arugula, hello macaroni and cheese. It's the New Normal.

7   But, of course, it's nothing of the sort, as my father and millions of other Americans can attest. In fact, Dad is probably emblematic of a broad swath of America. He's never bought arugula. He is the regular old normal.

8   "You just have to be a teenager and go hungry," Dad begins. We were in his apartment in Florida, wrapping up leftover burritos in Wal-Mart-brand Great Value Plastic Wrap. "People don't realize how tough it was."

9   My father is from Minnesota and generally shies away from talking about himself, despite some of his remarkable achievements. He is, in a word, practical. Up on the shelf there's the bottle of Great Value Dishwashing Liquid, which, once Dad has finished diluting it, can last for months. There's Great Value Oatmeal and Great Value Cream of Mushroom Soup, too.

10   My father could afford a house on the beach but chose instead a modest apartment in a vast compound of buildings. His bedroom looks out over a lake, his kitchen over a parking lot. "It's perfect," he says, "it's all need. And it's conveniently located near the funeral home down the road." And then his favorite joke about his age: "What's not to like: I'm beating the actuarial tables."

11   Over the years, my brother and I replaced the creaky stove, retired the yellow shag carpet, and finally convinced Dad to accept a new easy chair. He still has the file folders from his days in World War II, which he now uses to hold his paper work.

12   For most of his youth, Dad sacked out in rooming houses, with family friends, or under the tarps of carnivals he worked. A bus driver and his wife once gave him shelter for $10 a week.

13   He rarely saw his mother. His father was a sweet man but was on the road much of the time. Two institutions anchored him: Marshall High School in Minneapolis, and the military. No matter how many flop houses he lived in, he always attended Marshall. And it was the military that finally gave him three squares a day.

14   That was all the boost he needed. He went to college, joined the National Guard, worked in Army intelligence, and then stayed in intelligence and also the Army reserves, eventually retiring as a full colonel. My father fought both the hot and cold wars. This kid who survived on carnival gigs during the Depression would measure the Communists at the construction of the Berlin Wall in 1961. He'd helicopter off the embassy roof in Saigon that last night in April 1975. He'd be on hand the first time the U.S. embassy in Tehran was stormed in February 1979.

15   And along the way he'd put three sons through college and cut checks for military charities, Boy's Town, and old friends like Aunt Lydia, not a legal aunt but someone who each year sent us jars of tomato juice she made from her garden, and who gave my father a place to sleep when he was a boy.

16   His story of lean beginnings and economical living is notable largely for how common it is in U.S. history, and how uncommon it seems to purveyors of the notion that a New Normal has gripped our innocent land, threatening our right to be spendthrifts. Personal saving as a percentage of disposable income has inched up to about 6% in the last several months, from a blindingly profligate 1.4% at the height of the nation's bacchanal in 2005. But it wasn't long ago—1982, in fact—that people were saving a more sturdy 10.9%.

17   True, my father has taken that statistic up much higher, where few would want to roam. But I look at him—and the decades of tenacity that he and others like him represent—and don't see much "new" in the latest read on normal.

18   I do wish, though, that he'd buy a new set of dishes. That's my plastic cereal bowl he's still using, from when I was in grade school.

19   "It's perfect," he says. "Works fine."

Exercises

Do not refer to the selection for Exercises A, B, and C unless your instructor directs you to do so.

A. DETERMINING THE MAIN IDEA AND PURPOSE

Choose the best answer.

_____ 1. The main idea of the selection is that
  a. Americans have only themselves to blame for their economic difficulties.
  b. the "new normal"—being thrifty and careful with money—of necessity has become the new standard of behavior for American consumers.
  c. when good times will return to the U.S. again, the "new normal" will be "old hat."
  d. the "new normal" is not new; earlier generations practiced thrift and didn't spend excessively.

_____ 2. The writer's purpose is to
  a. examine the causes of the Great Recession and show its effects on the nation.
  b. argue in favor of a return to higher savings and more careful spending.
  c. correct a common perception that the "new normal" isn't really new.
  d. tell his father's life story as a model for those readers who spend money recklessly.

B. COMPREHENDING MAIN IDEAS

Choose the best answer.

_____ 1. Bussey's father didn't buy the donuts on sale at Wal-Mart for $2.50 a box because
  a. he thinks donuts are unhealthy.
  b. he has diabetes and can't eat sweets.
  c. they would be half price if he waited until the next day.
  d. he doesn't like Wal-Mart's donuts.

_____ 2. For many Americans, the "new normal" has become a buzz-phrase, a catchy slogan, which to them means
  a. they have been spending way too much money and have changed their ways.
  b. we should return to earlier spending habits by paying cash rather than using credit cards.
  c. the term "normal" has lost its original meaning.
  d. we can never go back to our lavish spending habits again because it's apparent that the economy will be in trouble for years.

_____ **3.** Bussey's father doesn't live in a house on the beach because he
  a. prefers his modest apartment even though he could afford a better place.
  b. prefers to sleep on his friends' couches.
  c. can't afford it.
  d. likes the old place, filled with his favorite possessions and memories.

_____ **4.** Two institutions gave Bussey's father structure that was missing in his family, specifically, Marshall High School in Minneapolis and
  a. the college he attended.
  b. the military.
  c. his job as a traveling salesman.
  d. his job at a carnival.

_____ **5.** Bussey says that his father was a man of many accomplishments. Which one was not mentioned?
  a. helping Aunt Lydia financially, even though she wasn't really his aunt.
  b. making a bottle of Great Value Dishwashing Liquid last for months.
  c. putting three boys through college.
  d. liberating the American hostages in Tehran in 1979.

_____ **6.** Bussey offers some statistics to show how little Americans saved in 2005 compared with how much they saved in 1982. Which of the following pairs accurately represents these two savings rates?
  a. 1 percent in 2005 vs. 5 percent in 1982
  b. 1.9 percent in 2005 vs.10.9 percent in 1982
  c. 5 percent in 2005 vs. 7 percent in 1982
  d. 6 percent in 2005 vs. 10.9 percent in 1982

COMPREHENSION SCORE

Score your answers for Exercises A and B as follows:

A. No. right _____ × 2 = _____

B. No. right _____ × 1 = _____

Total points from A and B _____ × 10_____ percent

C. SEQUENCING

These sentences from one paragraph in the selection have been scrambled. Read the sentences and choose the sequence that puts them back into logical order. Do not refer to the original selection.

1 He is, in a word, practical. **2** There's Great Value Oatmeal and Great Value Cream of Mushroom Soup, too. **3** My father is from Minnesota and generally shies away from talking about himself, despite some remarkable achievements. **4** Up on the shelf there's the bottle of Great Value Dishwashing Liquid, which, once Dad has finished diluting it, can last for months.

_____ Which of the following represents the correct sequence for these sentences?
   a. 2, 3, 4, 1
   b. 3, 2, 3, 1
   c. 4, 2,3, 1
   d. 3, 1, 4, 2
   e. Correct as written.

You may refer to the selection as you work through the remaining exercises.

D. ANALYZING STRUCTURE AND INTERPRETING MEANING

Write your answers to these questions in your own words.

1. Locate the sentence that best represents the main idea of the article and write it in the space provided. _____

_____

2. Why does Bussey reject the current popular buzz-phrase the "new normal"? Besides the fact that they used to spend too much money, what specifically is his criticism of American consumers today? _____

_____

3. Explain what Bussey means at the end of paragraph 6 when he writes, "Goodbye arugula, hello macaroni and cheese." Why wouldn't Bussey's father have bought arugula? _____

_____

4. Why does Bussey tell the story of his father's beginnings and of his life?

_____

E. UNDERSTANDING VOCABULARY

Choose the best definition according to an analysis of word parts or the context.

_____ **1.**   *chastened* to be more cost-conscious [6]
         a. restrained, corrected by bad experience
         b. encouraged, prodded
         c. defeated, overcome
         d. characterized, typified
_____ **2.**   to be more *prudent* [6]
         a. realistic
         b. careful
         c. stingy
         d. sympathetic

_____ **3.** millions of other Americans can *attest* [7]
    a. complain about
    b. discover
    c. confirm
    d. be proud of

_____ **4.** our right to be *spendthrifts* [16]
    a. those who spend money recklessly or wastefully
    b. those who spend very little money, are exceedingly thrifty
    c. those who invest their money wisely
    d. those who are completely ignorant of how to manage money

_____ **5.** blindingly *profligate* [16]
    a. cautious, careful
    b. productive, prolific
    c. economical, thrifty
    d. reckless, wasteful

_____ **6.** the decades of *tenacity* [17]
    a. persistence, determination
    b. sacrifice, giving up important things
    c. a shared experience or memory
    d. discouragement, ruined hopes

F. SMALL GROUP ACTIVITY—UNDERSTANDING SLANG AND IDIOMATIC EXPRESSIONS

Bussey uses several informal and slang expressions. Consider these expressions in their context and then, working in small groups, try to determine their meaning. The paragraph number where each occurs is included. You might try the dictionary if you are unsure, or ask your instructor for help.

1. *old hat* for the new normal [title and paragraph 5] _____

2. this latest *buzz-phrase* [6] _____

3. *shies away from* talking about himself [9] _____

4. *What's not to like?* [10] _____

5. Dad *sacked out* in rooming houses [12] _____

6. no matter how many *flop houses* he lived in [13] _____

7. gave him *three squares* a day [13] _____

8. survived on carnival *gigs* [14] _____

G. TOPICS FOR DISCUSSION

1. Do you agree with Bussey's statement that the "new normal" shouldn't have come as a big surprise? What is another way that Bussey could have addressed this subject without using his father as an extended example? Would it have been as effective?

2. Discuss Bussey's father's early years—bunking down in flophouses, working at carnivals. What do you think this kind of life was like? Why did he live this way?

3. Comment on this excerpt from paragraph 16: "a New Normal has gripped our innocent land, threatening our right to be spendthrifts." What is Bussey's intention in writing this? What is his tone?

H. TOPICS FOR WRITING

1. Have your own spending habits changed as a result of the recent economic downturn? If so, what changes have you made? Write an essay in which you address your particular financial situation.

2. Write a short essay addressing the subject of why so many Americans have gotten into financial trouble by running up credit card bills that they can't pay off each month. Why is credit so alluring? What does our reliance on credit say about our values?

EXPLORE THE WEB

- The term "new normal" doesn't only refer to the new economic realities facing Americans today. Go to Google or to your favorite search engine and type in "new normal." See what comes up. What other areas of American life does this term now refer to?

Refining the Basics

Annotating, Paraphrasing, and Summarizing

The skills you will learn in Part Two follow directly from the work you did in Part One—finding main ideas and locating supporting details. The three skills you will learn here—annotating, paraphrasing, and summarizing—are extraordinarily useful not only for college students, but also for anyone who must understand, absorb, remember, and condense information from the printed page. The following diagram summarizes and defines them:

Annotating	A study and comprehension skill, which includes: Writing notes in the margin of a text, circling words you don't know, noting questions to ask, and otherwise interacting with the text
Paraphrasing	A comprehension and writing skill, which includes: Putting a writer's words into your own words without leaving anything important out, similar to translating
Summarizing	A comprehension and writing skill, which includes: Writing a passage that condenses a writer's ideas by identifying only the main points and omitting unimportant supporting details

What is the relationship among these three skills? Annotating is the first step both to good comprehension and to writing a successful summary; paraphrasing is a preliminary step necessary to produce a good summary. Finally, both paraphrasing and summarizing show you and your instructor how well you have understood what you read and how accurately you can convey the ideas in your own words.

ANNOTATING

College students often complain about having a bad memory because they claim not to remember a lot of what they read. But I think that the source of this problem lies elsewhere. The culprit may not be a bad memory, but *passive reading.* Rather than being actively involved with the material, a passive reader is an optimist. She reads the text once, hoping to get the full meaning without doing the hard work that good comprehension requires.

It's almost impossible for a reader—even a very experienced reader—to get the full meaning and to remember what's important after one only reading. (I am referring here specifically to your college reading assignments, where good comprehension is required, not to the kind of casual reading you do in popular magazines, in the daily paper, or online.) Nothing is more frustrating to a student than to complete an assigned essay for his English class and then to be forced to admit that he doesn't remember much of what he read.

Students whom I tutor each week tell me that they often don't understand much of what they read—a quite different problem from not remembering. When students tell me that they have read an essay three times and still don't get it, the more likely culprit is that they haven't bothered to look up unfamiliar vocabulary words. I always gently remind them that they could read an essay 50 times and, unless they know what the words on the page mean, they'll never get it. If this problem sounds familiar to you, now would be a good time to review the section at the beginning of the text on vocabulary improvement techniques.

As for the student who can't remember what he just read, he has wasted a lot of valuable time, requiring him to read the assignment again, and perhaps even a third time. It is much less likely that you will lose focus or that you will get distracted if you get into the habit of annotating the text. This means that while you read, you write notes in the margins.

You already have seen this process demonstrated in the introduction to Part One, where you identified main and supporting ideas. This next section explains and demonstrates the process of annotating in more detail. Throughout the text, you will have many opportunities to practice this skill, and your instructor may require you to practice annotating beyond the exercises in this book.

How to Annotate Annotating is sometimes called reading with a pencil in your hand. (And using a pencil is a good idea, so that you can erase your notes later, if you want to.) If you can't bear to mark up your text because you want to sell the book back after the course ends, then make a photocopy of the assignment. This will allow you to mark it up as much as you want.

Note, too, that annotating is not the same as marking the words with a yellow or pink highlighter. Many students rely on these markers as a study aid while they read their textbook assignments; reading instructors, however, generally discourage this practice. Such marks only tell you that the material will be important to learn—some day! As such, highlighting is a *passive* activity. And my students tell me that because they are uncertain what to highlight, they end up highlighting too much. Over-highlighting makes the pages look colorful to be sure, but it is not an efficient way to get and to retain the main points.

Careful annotating, in contrast, allows you both to read *actively* and to pull out the essential ideas at the same time. Here are some suggestions for good annotations. Study them before you continue on to study the models that follow.

TECHNIQUES FOR ANNOTATING	
Main ideas	Jot down little phrases in your own words, restating the main ideas.
Phrases or sentences that you don't understand	Put a question mark in the margin.
Vocabulary words that are unfamiliar to you	Circle them in the text.
Questions to ask in class	Write in the margin and mark with a clear symbol of your own devising.
Ideas that you disagree with	Write a star or some other symbol in the margin.

To illustrate this process, consider a brief excerpt from Selection 12 that appears in this section of the text, Virginia Morell's "Minds of Their Own," which discusses animal intelligence, cognition, and use of language. Read the passage first; then, study the annotations.

Dolphins—
social animals
Experiments in
Hawaii tested for
cognitive abilities
**Why are
dolphins called
"cosmopolitan"?

Louis Herman—
experimented to
see how complex
dolphin brains are
**What does he
mean by "flower"
in this sense?

Hand-and-arm
signals represented
basic grammar
Dolphins did
well, showed that
they understood
grammar

In the late 1960s a cognitive psychologist named Louis Herman began investigating the cognitive abilities of bottlenose dolphins. Like humans, dolphins are highly social and cosmopolitan, living in subpolar to tropical environments worldwide; they're highly vocal; and they have special sensory skills, such as echolocation. By the 1980s Herman's cognitive studies were focused on a group of four young dolphins—Akeakamai, Phoenix, Elele, and Hiapo—at the Kewalo Basin Marine Mammal Laboratory in Hawaii. The dolphins were curious and playful, and they transferred their sociability to Herman and his students.

"In our work with the dolphins, we had a guiding philosophy," Herman says, "that we could bring out the full flower of their intellect, just as educators try to bring out the full potential of a human child. Dolphins have these big, highly complex brains. My thought was, 'OK, so you have this pretty brain. Let's see what you can do with it.'"

To communicate with the dolphins, Herman and his team invented a hand- and arm-signal language, complete with a simple grammar. For instance, a pumping motion of the closed fists meant "hoop," and both arms extended overhead (as in jumping jacks) meant "ball." A "come here" gesture with a single arm told them to "fetch." Responding to the request "hoop, ball, fetch," Akeakamai would push the ball to the hoop. But if the word order was changed to "ball, hoop, fetch," she would carry the hoop to the ball. Over time she could interpret more grammatically complex requests, such as "right, basket, left, Frisbee, in," asking that she put the Frisbee on her left in the basket on her right. Reversing "left" and "right" in the instruction would reverse Akeakamai's actions. Akeakamai could complete such requests the first time they were made, showing a deep understanding of the grammar of the language.

Annotating Exercise In this exercise you are asked to annotate the five paragraphs that follow the preceding selection. Remember to keep your notes brief (don't write in complete sentences) and to circle unfamiliar words. In most cases, you will annotate to prepare to write an essay on a particular reading. For the purposes of this exercise, assume that you must write an essay explaining dolphin intelligence. Annotate for only this idea in the left margin.

"They're a very vocal species," Herman adds. "Our studies showed that they could imitate arbitrary sounds that we broadcast into their tank, an ability that may be tied to their own need to communicate. I'm not saying they have a dolphin language. But they are capable of understanding the novel instructions that we convey to them in a tutored language; their brains have that ability.

"There are many things they could do that people have always doubted about animals. For example, they correctly interpreted, on the very first occasion, gestured instructions given by a person displayed on a TV screen behind an underwater window. They recognized that television images were representations of the real world that could be acted on in the same way as in the re...

Th... *Does the dolphin (4) know what a prase is?* ...uctors too. If a trainer bent l... ...n on its back and lift its tail in... air. Although imitation was once... ...s a simpleminded skill, in rec... years, cognitive scientists... *Can dolphins (5)* ...t's extremely difficult, requi... *create their own* ...ther person's body and pose, ... *behavior?* ...sition—actions that imply...

"H... ...following a trainer's direct... ...le swam to the board... and, leaning to one side, gently... in on it, an untrained behav... The trainer, stretched her arms straight up... gnaling "Hooray!" and Elele... aped out, the air squeaking and clicking with delight.

"El... just love... to be right," Herman said. "And... e loved inventing things... made up a sign for 'create', which asked a dolphin to create its own behavior...

One fi... ...ord: Keep your annotations neat and ... You don't want to clutter up the margins with too many notes or with words that you can't read in a few weeks. Annotate only the main idea and important supporting details, not unimportant or reinforcing details.

PARAPHRASING

Next we turn to paraphrasing, a skill that I often use in both my reading and composition classes. Paraphrasing helps you to focus and to read accurately. As you will recall from the introduction to this section, *paraphrasing* means restating the writer's words in your own words. It is useful both to test comprehension and to clarify meaning. When you paraphrase, you need to go through the passage one sentence at a time, rewriting and changing the words into your own words as much as possible, without changing the meaning of the original. That's the hard part. Also, it is perfectly all right if your paraphrase turns out to be longer than the original. To write a successful paraphrase, consider the following suggestions:

TECHNIQUES FOR PARAPHRASING
• Substitute a synonym (a word that means the same) for a key word in the original.
• An exception to the above: Don't strain to find a synonym for major words. Call a dolphin a *dolphin*, not a marine cetacean mammal.
• Omit very unimportant ideas if your instructor allows this.
• Combine ideas when possible.
• Maintain the flavor and level of formality of the original passage.
• Do not inject your own ideas or opinions.

We will illustrate paraphrasing with some short passages and longer reading selections from Part One that you have already encountered. Study these samples of paraphrases of short excerpts.

We were Indian children who were expected to be stupid. Most lived up to those expectations inside the classroom but subverted them on the outside.

(Selection 2, Sherman Alexie, "Superman and Me")

Paraphrase Inside our classrooms, we Indian children acted as stupid as our teachers expected us to be, but outside the classroom we challenged this conception.

Here is a slightly more difficult example:

"It is curious that in English the word *blue* should represent depressing as well as transcendent things; that it should be the most holy hue and the color of pornography," wrote Victoria Finley in *Color: A Natural History of the Palette*.

(James Sullivan)

Paraphrase According to Victoria Finley in her book, *Color: A Natural History of the Palette*, it is strange that in English the word *blue* represents opposites—depression as well as things that transcend, holiness as well as pornography.

Paraphrasing Exercise—1 Here are two examples of sentences from short selections you have read, followed by three paraphrases. Choose the paraphrase that is the most accurate.

_____**1.** I once read an article whose author stated that racism is the only form of mental illness that is communicable. Clever but not entirely true. Racism in the U.S. is learned by us beginning at birth. (Leslie Marmon Silko)

    a. It's true that racism is a kind of mental illness, according to an article I read, which we learn growing up in the U.S.

    b. According to an article I read once, racism, unlike other mental illnesses, is communicable. Though this is a clever statement, it would be more accurate to say that we learn racism just by growing up in the U.S.

    c. Mental illnesses are communicable, as is racism, according to an article I read once. This is a clever statement, but it's not true because racism is something we are born with.

_____**2.** His story [his father's] of lean beginnings and economical living is notable largely for how common it is in U.S. history, and how uncommon it seems to purveyors of the notion that a New Normal has gripped our innocent land, threatening our right to be spendthrifts. (John Bussey)

    a. Growing up without a lot of material things and living frugally isn't new, as many people grew up in such circumstances throughout U.S. history, though those who want to sell us things think that it's something new and that a New Normal is threatening our right to squander money.

b. The New Normal is threatening our right to waste money on frivolous things, and those who want to sell us things are just following the example of those in U.S. history who learned to do without.

c. Throughout U.S. history, doing without and living frugally was a way of life, but you wouldn't know that from those who want to sell us things. The New Normal is threatening this tradition of thrifty living.

Paraphrasing Exercise—2 Now it's your turn. For each of the following passages, write your paraphrase in the spaces provided.

1. As a person of mixed ancestry growing up in the United States in the late 1950s, I knew all the cruel epithets that might be hurled at others; the knowledge was a sort of solace that I was not alone in my feelings of unease, of not quite belonging to the group that clearly mattered most in the United States.

(Leslie Marmon Silko)

_____

_____

_____

_____

2. For too many Americans, the conventional, comfortable forty-hour week has given way to the overloaded, overstressed sixty-hour week. If any aspect of the economic squeeze is hitting American workers across the board—white-collar and blue-collar, high-income and low-income, chief executives and janitors— it is the phenomenon of increased stress on the job, a combination of longer workweeks and having to toil harder and faster during one's hours at work.

(Steven Greenhouse)

_____

_____

_____

_____

_____

3. Intuitively I knew that the person I leaned on for everything—my mother— would not be able to help me. She relied heavily on her own experiences as a basis of understanding the world, and just as the Wizard of Oz had nothing in his bag for Dorothy, she had nothing to smooth this assimilation for me.

Once I stepped outside my door, I was all alone and had to fend for myself. The only thing I feared more than school was disappointing my mother, so I hid my anxieties.

(Rose Guilbault)

_____

_____

_____

_____

_____

_____

SUMMARIZING

Summarizing—the last skill—is the culmination of the other two skills: Before you can write a summary, you must first annotate the text; the summary-writing process requires you to paraphrase important points but also to eliminate minor supporting details. The point of writing a summary is to convey only the most important information, so you have to develop a feel for what to save and what to drop. This process sounds harder than it really is. When one paints a room, he or she has to spend more time preparing the surface than actually painting it. Writing a summary is the same. It just takes good preparation and practice.

First, study the following chart, which lists the techniques for summarizing. You may use them all, or you may decide that some work better than others. Before you begin, I suggest making a photocopy of the selection you are summarizing so that you can annotate it easily.

TECHNIQUES FOR SUMMARIZING

- Read the selection and circle unfamiliar words.
- Read the selection again, annotate it, and look up circled words.
- Underline important phrases and sentences and cross out unimportant material.
- Copy the notes from your margins onto a piece of paper or type them into a computer. Leave plenty of space between your notes from each paragraph.
- Review your notes. Add or delete information as needed.
- Rewrite the selection, condensing where you can. Substitute your own words for the writer's, where possible, and add transitions to show the relationship between ideas.
- Read through your summary and check for accuracy. Be sure you don't introduce your own ideas or opinions.

We begin with a short selection from the introduction to Part One, "Meals (and Deals) on Wheels." Some students find it helpful to cross out the relatively unimportant words and phrases in the original before they write a summary. I have done just that with this passage.

Original Passage

~~What's a food-loving entrepreneur to do?~~ The recession has turned eating at home into a necessity. And opening a new restaurant, bakery, or pub requires ~~a chunk of increasingly-hard-to-come-by~~ capital. ~~Enter the deliciously nimble~~ food cart. ~~In the past few years, more than~~ 450 ~~of these hyper-local, highly affordable~~ eateries ~~have sprung up in~~ Portland, Oregon, ~~bringing the sweet smell of commerce back to the streets~~.

Carts make it possible for people of modest means to eat out—usually more healthfully than at fast-food chain restaurants," ~~reports New Urban News (Jan.-Feb. 2010)~~. The carts are also easy on proprietors: ~~Licenses cost $315, monthly rent averages $500, and they can be outfitted for as little as a few thousand dollars. Portland's carts are run by a mix of immigrants and culinary school graduates, and have fewer major health code violations than the area's restaurants do.~~

~~The rapid proliferation also might finally settle the carts-versus-restaurants debate that keeps many cities from enacting vendor-friendly policies. "The commonly heard complaint is that . . . carts unfairly compete with brick-and-mortar restaurants," one Portlander told New Urban News. "If anything, the food carts seem to feed the Portland food buzz and~~ create more consumer demand." **(Length: 201 words)**

Summary

Portland, Oregon's food carts have had several advantages. People of modest means can eat out healthfully, and for the entrepreneurs, operating a food cart is a lot cheaper than opening a restaurant or bakery. Portland's 450 food carts are creating more consumer demand for healthy and affordable food. **(Length: 47 words)**

A good rule of thumb is that a summary should be about 25 percent of the original length. (Ask your instructor in case his or her requirements differ.) In the preceding sample, after some trimming from my first draft, I was able to condense the material to 47 words, just about a quarter of the original length. A summary assignment means that you have to let go of a lot of information in the original. Keep in mind that you are *summarizing*, not *paraphrasing*. You have to decide what to save and what to omit. This requires you to see the difference between main ideas and supporting details. Keep only what is absolutely essential to preserve the meaning and the flavor of the original.

Summarizing Exercises Here are two summarizing exercises. For each, write a summary of the suggested length. In the first one, I have crossed out the nonessential words and phrases. The second passage is a bit longer, and it is intact. Write your summary in the spaces provided beneath the passage. Do a word count to make sure that your summary is an appropriate length.[1]

> ~~"Think big-box stores and bargains are synonymous? Think again,"~~ declared a report on buying appliances ~~in the September 2005 issue of~~ *Consumer Reports*. "None of the major retailers outpriced the independents for ~~ranges, refrigerators, and other~~ large appliances, and only two were clear winners for small ones ~~such as grills and vacuums. What's more,~~ readers found Wal-Mart no cheaper than other stores overall, despite its low-price slogan." The report compared prices, service, selection, product quality, and checkout ease at independent appliance dealers, ~~Best Buy, Costco, Home Depot, Lowe's, Sears, Target, and Wal-Mart~~. Overall, the local stores outscored their big competitors by a significant margin. ~~Not only were they price-competitive— only Costco and Target beat them on price for small appliances and none of the chains did better on large appliances—~~but they offered a broader selection and better service. "Seventy-five percent of small-appliance buyers thought independent-store staffers were pleasant, informed, or helpful; five percent or fewer felt that way about Costco, Target or Wal-Mart workers," noted *Consumer Reports*. Wal-Mart ranked the lowest in terms of quality and selection; ~~40 percent of those who bought appliances at the chain had to settle for a different brand than they had planned to buy."~~ (Stacy Mitchell)

Length: 202 words

Suggested Length: 50 words

CRITICAL THINKING EXERCISE

Is it really true that big-box stores are more expensive than independent retailers when it comes to buying large or small appliances? The data in this passage comes from 2005, over seven years ago. Your task: Design a survey that would investigate the writer's claims. Do not actually compare prices between types of stores. Rather, show how you would go about proving or disproving Mitchell's claims.

[1]It's easy to count your words if you use Microsoft Word. First highlight your text. Then select "Word Count" from the "Tools" menu.

Original Passage

Monkeys in Zanzibar eat charcoal to neutralize toxins in their diet. ("A Briquette a Day," *Discover*)

The human population of Zanzibar, a Tanzanian island off the East African coast, doubles every 15 years or so. The island's red colobus monkeys, however, are dwindling as their habitats are destroyed for firewood and timber. But some monkeys have found a way to coexist with humans: they snack on charcoal.

Thomas Struhsaker, a zoologist at Duke University, has been studying the effects of selective logging on rain forest wildlife in eastern Africa. A Tanzanian biologist told him about the monkeys' charcoal habit in 1981. Over the years, as the human population grew, Struhsaker noticed that the monkeys ate more and more charcoal. "Each animal," he says, "eats about five grams a day."

The monkeys live in an area with almond, mango, and other exotic fruit trees. The leaves of these trees are rich in protein but also contain toxic compounds like tannic acids. Most animals avoid the leaves. But charcoal has a well-known ability to absorb toxins—it is

Summary

_____
_____
_____
_____
_____
_____
_____
_____
_____
_____
_____
_____
_____
_____
_____
_____
_____
_____
_____
_____
_____
_____
_____
_____
_____
_____
_____
_____
_____

used as a poison control agent, and in Europe people use it in liquid form as a digestive aid. When a monkey eats charcoal after chomping on leaves, its meal goes down a little easier. The charcoal selectively holds on to large tannic acid molecules, allowing them to pass through the body while smaller nutritious proteins are absorbed by the gut.

The monkeys snatch charcoal from kilns and also nibble on charred wood and tree stumps. Struhsaker isn't sure how they acquired the habit. "There must be a quick effect so they can learn by association," he says. Baby monkeys, at least, learn from imitating their mothers, and the mothers themselves may have learned from eating soil containing charcoal particles.

"These are pretty clever animals," says Struhsaker. "They've picked up a habit that allows them to exploit a resource to an extent that was not possible before." Despite this adaptation, red colobus populations are still shrinking in Zanzibar, even in nature reserves, where speeding cars take a large toll. "If they put the potholes back in the road, or built speed bumps, I think the reserve animals would be fine."

7 CAROLINE HWANG
The Good Daughter

After graduating from the University of Pennsylvania, Caroline Hwang completed an M.F.A. at New York University. Currently a magazine editor, Hwang's writing has appeared in Glamour, Self, YM, Redbook, *and* Newsweek, *where this article was first published.*

© John Smock

Vocabulary Analysis

WORD PARTS

The suffix –less and the prefix mis- The useful suffix *–less* conveys the meaning of "not having" or "without" to the word to which it is attached. In paragraph 6, Hwang writes that being able to say that she is Korean in other languages besides Korean strikes her as funny "in a *mirthless* sort of way." *Mirth* means "amusement" or "humor," so *mirthless* means "without humor." As we have seen before, suffixes usually indicate a grammatical part of speech, but *–less* is an example of a suffix that changes the meaning of the root.

Unlike most suffixes, prefixes usually add to or change the meaning of the root word. The prefix *mis-* means either "wrong" or "bad." When Hwang writes that she *mispronounced* her own name in Korean, she is describing an incorrect pronunciation. You can see this same meaning in the words *misspell, misunderstand,* and *misconceive.* Three words beginning with *mis-* where the prefix means "bad" are *misbehave, misconduct, misfortune.*

CAROLINE HWANG

The Good Daughter

1   The moment I walked into the dry-cleaning store, I knew the woman behind the counter was from Korea, like my parents. To show her that we shared a heritage, and possibly get a fellow countryman's discount, I tilted my head forward, in shy imitation of a traditional bow.

2   "Name?" she asked, not noticing my attempted obeisance.

3   "Hwang," I answered.

4   "Hwang? Are you Chinese?"

5   Her question caught me off-guard. I was used to hearing such queries from non-Asians who think Asians all look alike, but never from one of my own people. Of course, the only Koreans I knew were my parents and their friends, people who've never asked me where I came from, since they knew better than I.

6   I ransacked my mind for the Korean words that would tell her who I was. It's always struck me as funny (in a mirthless sort of way) that I can more readily say "I am Korean" in Spanish, German and even Latin than I can in the language of my ancestry. In the end, I told her in English.

7   The dry-cleaning woman squinted as though trying to see past the glare of my strangeness, repeating my surname under her breath. "Oh, Fxuang," she said, doubling over with laughter. "You don't know how to speak your name."

8   I flinched. Perhaps I was particularly sensitive at the time, having just dropped out of graduate school. I had torn up my map for the future, the one that said not only where I was going but who I was. My sense of identity was already disintegrating.

9   When I got home, I called my parents to ask why they had never bothered to correct me. "Big deal," my mother said, sounding more flippant than I knew she intended. (Like many people who learn English in a classroom, she uses idioms that don't always fit the occasion.) "So what if you can't pronounce your name? You are American," she said.

10   Though I didn't challenge her explanation, it left me unsatisfied. The fact is, my cultural identity is hardly that clear-cut.

11   My parents immigrated to this country 30 years ago, two years before I was born. They told me often, while I was growing up, that, if I wanted to, I could be president someday, that here my grasp would be as long as my reach.

12   To ensure that I reaped all the advantages of this country, my parents saw to it that I became fully assimilated. So, like any American of my generation, I whiled away my youth strolling malls and talking on the phone, rhapsodizing over Andrew McCarthy's blue eyes or analyzing the meaning of a certain upperclassman's offer of a ride to the Homecoming football game.

13   To my parents, I am all American, and the sacrifices they made in leaving Korea—including my mispronounced name—pale in comparison to the opportunities those sacrifices gave me. They do not see that I straddle two cultures, nor that I feel displaced in the only country I know. I identify with Americans, but Americans do not identify with me. I've never known what it's like to

belong to a community—neither one at large, nor of an extended family. I know more about Europe than the continent my ancestors unmistakably come from. I sometimes wonder, as I did that day in the dry cleaner's, if I would be a happier person had my parents stayed in Korea.

14   I first began to consider this thought around the time I decided to go to graduate school. It had been a compromise: my parents wanted me to go to law school; I wanted to skip the starched-collar track and be a writer—the hungrier the better. But after 20-some years of following their wishes and meeting all of their expectations, I couldn't bring myself to disobey or disappoint. A writing career is riskier than law, I remember thinking. If I'm a failure and my life is a washout, then what does that make my parents' lives? I know that many of my friends had to choose between pleasing their parents and being true to themselves. But for the children of immigrants, the choice seems more complicated, a happy outcome impossible. By making the biggest move of their lives for me, my parents indentured me to the largest debt imaginable—I owe them the fulfillment of their hopes for me.

15   It tore me up inside to suppress my dream, but I went to school for a Ph.D. in English literature, thinking I had found the perfect compromise. I would be able to write at least about books while pursuing a graduate degree. Predictably, it didn't work out. How could I labor for five years in a program I had no passion for? When I finally left school, my parents were disappointed, but since it wasn't what they wanted me to do, they weren't devastated. I, on the other hand, felt I was staring at the bottom of the abyss. I had seen the flaw in my life of halfwayness, in my planned life of compromises.

16   I hadn't thought about my love life, but I had a vague plan to make concessions there, too. Though they raised me as an American, my parents expect me to marry someone Korean and give them grandchildren who look like them. This didn't seem like such a huge request when I was 14, but now I don't know what I'm going to do. I've never been in love with someone I dated, or dated someone I loved. (Since I can't bring myself even to entertain the thought of marrying the non-Korean men I'm attracted to, I've been dating only those I know I can stay clearheaded about.) And as I near that age when the question of marriage stalks every relationship, I can't help but wonder if my parents' expectations are responsible for the lack of passion in my life.

17   My parents didn't want their daughter to be Korean, but they don't want her fully American, either. Children of immigrants are living paradoxes. We are the first generation and the last. We are in this country for its opportunities, yet filial duty binds us. When my parents boarded the plane, they knew they were embarking on a rough trip. I don't think they imagined the rocks in the path of their daughter who can't even pronounce her own name.

Exercises

Do not refer to the selection for Exercises A, B, and C unless your instructor directs you to do so.

A. DETERMINING THE MAIN IDEA AND PURPOSE

Choose the best answer.

_____ **1.**   The main idea of the selection is that
  a. children of immigrants find it impossible to assimilate completely.
  b. Hwang finds that deferring to her parents' wishes about remaining Korean has caused great psychological harm and anxiety.
  c. as a child of immigrants, Hwang is torn between her parents' dreams and her own.
  d. Hwang's decision to cut herself off from Korean culture and to adopt the habits and customs of her adopted culture has led to great conflict in her family.

_____ **2.**   The writer's purpose is to
  a. tell an amusing anecdote about how immigrants assimilate.
  b. examine the difficulties all immigrants face when moving to a new country.
  c. show how parental stubbornness about new cultural practices can lead to conflict.
  d. examine some of the personal conflicts and struggles she has had as a person straddling two cultures.

B. COMPREHENDING MAIN IDEAS

Choose the correct answer for the multiple-choice items. Write the fill-in answers in the space provided using your own words.

_____ **1.**   When the clerk at the dry cleaners heard how Hwang pronounced her surname, she
  a. laughed out loud.
  b. reprimanded her for her ignorance.
  c. corrected her pronunciation so she wouldn't make the mistake again.
  d. poked fun at Hwang and embarrassed her in front of the other customers.

_____ **2.**   What did the exchange with the dry cleaning clerk and later with her mother illustrate to Hwang? That
  a. she really was an American, so her mispronunciation didn't matter.
  b. her identity wasn't as clear-cut as her mother had suggested.
  c. she should study Korean so that she could learn more about her parents' culture.
  d. she was really unhappy living in the U.S. and wanted to get in touch more with her Korean heritage.

_____ **3.** When Hwang was growing up, her parents often told her that
   a. she could return to Korea whenever she wanted.
   b. she could choose whichever culture—Korean or American—she identified with the most.
   c. they wanted her to become fully assimilated and that she could even be president if she wanted to.
   d. she should try to resist the pressure to become Americanized.

4. Hwang's parents wanted her to go to school to study _____, while Hwang wanted to be a _____.

5. Apparently, Hwang dropped out of her graduate Ph.D. program in English because _____.

_____ **6.** Aside from her graduate school situation, what other area of her life is Hwang conflicted about in terms of pleasing her parents' expectations for her and following her own wishes?
   a. her choice of a career
   b. her choice of a future husband
   c. her decision to publish articles about her personal life
   d. her decision not to have children

COMPREHENSION SCORE

Score your answers for Exercises A and B as follows:

A. No. right _____ × 2 = _____

B. No. right _____ × 1 = _____

Total points from A and B _____ × 10 = _____ percent

C. SEQUENCING

These sentences from one paragraph in the selection may have been scrambled. Read the sentences and choose the sequence that puts them back into logical order. Do not refer to the original selection.

   1 I would be able to write at least about books while pursuing a graduate degree. **2** It tore me up to suppress my dream, but I went to school for a Ph.D. in English literature, thinking I had found the perfect compromise. **3** How could I labor for five years in a program I had no passion for? **4** Predictably, it didn't work out.

_____ Which of the following represents the correct sequence for these sentences?
   a. 1, 3, 2, 4
   b. 2, 1, 4, 3
   c. 2, 1, 3, 4
   d. 3, 1, 4, 2
   e. Correct as written.

You may refer to the selection as you work through the remaining exercises.

D. UNDERSTANDING VOCABULARY IN CONTEXT

Here are a few vocabulary words from the selection along with their definitions. Study these definitions carefully. Then write the appropriate word in each space provided according to the context, the way it is used. Note: You will use only three of the four words in each set.

queries	questions
surname	one's last name
disintegrated	fell apart
flinched	started or winced, as if in pain

1. Hwang was accustomed to people's _____ that attempted to determine what her ethnic background was. But when the dry cleaning clerk told her that she didn't know how to pronounce her own _____, she _____.

devastated	destroyed, overwhelmed with defeat
idioms	expressions in language whose meanings can't be discerned from the grammar
assimilated	absorbed into a larger cultural group
concessions	admissions or acknowledgements that something is true

2. Hwang's parents had encouraged her to become _____ ; however, because her parents weren't in favor of her graduate school course of study, they weren't _____ when she dropped out. In terms of choosing a husband, Hwang had unconsciously already decided to make some _____.

straddle	be on both sides of something
paradox	an apparent contradiction; a contradiction at least on the surface
obeisance	an attitude of deference, homage, or obedience
reap	obtain from effort and hard work

3. While children of immigrants _____ benefits from their dual experiences, it's also difficult for them because they have to _____ two different cultures. Hwang writes that as a daughter of Korean immigrants, she was a _____—on the one hand, bound to her parents by loyalty and love but on the other hand possessed by a new identity.

E. USING VOCABULARY—VARIANT WORD FORMS

Write the correct inflected form of the base word in each of the following sentences. Be sure to add the appropriate ending to fit the grammatical requirements of the sentence. Refer to your dictionary if necessary.

1. (*disintegrate*—use a noun). Hwang's sense of identity had already undergone a period of _____ after she had dropped out of graduate school.

2. (*mispronounced*—use a noun). Apparently, Hwang's _____ of her last name made it sound Chinese rather than Korean.

3. (*devastation*—use an adjective) Surprisingly, perhaps, Hwang's dropping out of graduate school wasn't as _____ either to her or to her parents as it might have been.

4. (*concession*—use a verb in the past tense) Although she hadn't thought out her plan carefully, Hwang _____ that marrying a Korean man might be a good idea.

F. ANNOTATING EXERCISE

For this exercise, assume that you are preparing to write an essay on this subject:

> Children of immigrants experience a two-sided conflict: On the one hand, they feel a sense of duty to please their parents for the sacrifices they made, but at the same time they want to fulfill their own dreams. How exactly did this conflict manifest itself in Hwang's life, and what choices did she make?

Go through the selection and locate any piece of information that supports this idea. Annotate each section by writing the main point in your own words in the left margin.

G. PARAPHRASING EXERCISE

Here are some sentences from the selection. Write a paraphrase of each passage in the space provided.

1. They do not see that I straddle two cultures, nor that I feel displaced in the only country I know. I identify with Americans, but Americans do not identify with me. I've never known what it's like to belong to a community—neither one at large, nor of an extended family.

   _____

   _____

   _____

2. By making the biggest move of their lives for me, my parents indentured me to the largest debt imaginable—I owe them the fulfillment of their hopes for me.

   _____

   _____

3. Children of immigrants are living paradoxes. We are in this country for its opportunities, yet filial duty binds us.

   _____

   _____

H. TOPICS FOR DISCUSSION

1. What is the specific conflict that Hwang experiences? Why are children of immigrants "living paradoxes"? What specifically is the problem?
2. Comment on the title of the selection, "The Good Daughter." Why is the title appropriate? What point of view does it convey?
3. How is Hwang's experience as the child of immigrant parents different from that of native-born children? Why were her attempts at compromise a failure?
4. Locate the figures of speech at the end of paragraphs 15 and 16. Explain their meaning.

I. TOPICS FOR WRITING

1. If a member of your family—perhaps a grandparent or one or both of your parents—immigrated to this country, conduct an interview, asking them to comment on the particular difficulties they encountered after arriving in this country. You can focus on subtopics like unfamiliar customs, difficulties with the language, encountering new food, or whatever else comes up in the conversation.
2. For Hwang, the encounter with the dry cleaning clerk was a revelation. In the same way, recount an experience that forced you to reconsider some previously held concept.
3. Write a brief profile of Caroline Hwang. What sort of person does she appear to be? What are the qualities of a good daughter? Does she exemplify them or not, and if so, how?

EXPLORE THE WEB

- If you type in Caroline Hwang + How I Write, you will find an article in which the writer describes how the *Newsweek* article that you just completed was the basis for her first novel, *In Full Bloom* (2003), the story of a young woman and her relationship with her immigrant mother.

8

STUDS TERKEL
Somebody Built the Pyramids

Louis "Studs" Terkel (1912–2008) was a writer, radio personality, and disk jockey, but he was best known as a social historian. Over the years Terkel published several books of taped interviews, among them Division Street: America *(1967), about his beloved city of Chicago;* Hard Times: An Oral History of the Great Depression in America *(1976); and* Working: People Talk About What They Do All Day and How They Feel About What They Do *(1974).*

Even though this selection was published over 35 years ago, the attitudes these workers display about their jobs resonate with modern workers, who if anything, experience even more stress, loss of identity, and lack of recognition than do the workers cited here. This essay was originally titled "Here Am I, a Worker" and appeared in Capitalism: The Moving Target. *Many of the workers interviewed in this piece appear in* Working, *cited above.*

Vocabulary Analysis

WORD PARTS

anti- [paragraph 14] Terkel writes that modern workers feel like *antiheroes*. The prefix *anti-* when attached to words in English means "against" or "in opposition to." You can see this meaning in common words like *antiwar*, *anti-American*, and *antislavery*. In the case of *antihero*, the word refers to a modern hero, one who lacks the qualities of a traditional hero. In the spaces below, write three more words that begin with this common prefix and their meanings.

_____

_____

_____

WORD FAMILIES

anonymous [paragraph 1] One of the common complaints of modern workers is that they feel *anonymous*, literally "having no name or identity." It comes from the Greek: *an-* ("without") + *nomen* ("name"). Other words in English with the root *nym* or *nomen* are *noun* (a grammatical term for a word that is the name of something), *synonym* (words with the same meaning), and *homonym* (words that sound the same but that have different spellings and meanings). What do these words mean? Check your dictionary if necessary.

antonym   _____

nominate   _____

nominal   _____

nom de plume _____

STUDS TERKEL

Somebody Built the Pyramids

1   In our society (it's the only one I've experienced, so I cannot speak for any other) the razor of necessity cuts close. You must make a buck to survive the day. You must work to make a buck. The job is often a chore, rarely a delight. No matter how demeaning the task, no matter how it dulls the senses or breaks the spirit, one *must* work or else. Lately there has been a questioning of this "work ethic," especially by the young. Strangely enough, it has touched off profound grievances in others, hitherto silent and anonymous.

2   Unexpected precincts are being heard from in a show of discontent by blue collar and white. Communiqués are alarming concerning absenteeism in auto plants. On the evening bus the tense, pinched faces of young file clerks and elderly secretaries tell us more than we care to know. On the expressways middle-management men pose without grace behind their wheels, as they flee city and job.

3   In all, there is more than a slight ache. And there dangles the impertinent question: Ought there not be another increment, earned though not yet received, to one's daily work—an acknowledgement of a man's *being?*

4   Steve Hamilton is a professional baseball player. At 37 he has come to the end of his career as a major-league pitcher. "I've never been a big star. I've done about as good as I can with the equipment I have. I played with Mickey Mantle and with Willie Mays. People always recognize them. But for someone to recognize me, it really made me feel good. I think everybody gets a kick out of feeling special."

5   Mike Fitzgerald was born the same year as Hamilton. He is a laborer in a steel mill. "I feel like the guys who built the pyramids. Somebody built 'em. Somebody built the Empire State Building, too. There's hard work behind it. I would like to see a building, say The Empire State, with a foot-wide strip from top to

bottom and the name of every bricklayer on it, the name of every electrician. So when a guy walked by, he could take his son and say, 'See, that's me over there on the 45th floor. I put that steel beam in.' Picasso can point to a painting. I think I've done harder work than Picasso, and what can I point to? Everybody should have something to point to."

6   Sharon Atkins is 24 years old. She's been to college and acridly observes: "The first myth that blew up in my face is that a college education will get you a worthwhile job." For the last two years she's been a receptionist at an advertising agency. "I didn't look at myself as 'just a dumb broad' at the front desk, who took phone calls and messages. I thought I was something else. The office taught me differently."

7   Among her contemporaries there is no such rejection; job and status have no meaning. Blue collar or white, teacher or cabbie, her friends judge her and themselves by their beingness. Nora Watson, a young journalist, recounts a party game, Who Are You? Older people respond with their job titles: "I'm a copy writer," "I'm an accountant." The young say, "I'm me, my name is so-and-so."

8   Harry Stallings, 27, is a spot welder on the assembly line at an auto plant. "They'll give better care to that machine than they will to you. If it breaks down, there's somebody out there to fix it right away. If I break down, I'm just pushed over to the other side till another man takes my place. The only thing the company has in mind is to keep that line running. A man would be more eager to do a better job if he were given proper respect and the time to do it."

9   You would think that Ralph Grayson, a 25-year-old black, has it made. He supervises twenty people in the audit department of a large bank. Yet he is singularly discontented. "You're like a foreman on an assembly line. Or like a technician sitting in a computer room watching the machinery. It's good for a person who enjoys that kind of job, who can dominate somebody else's life. I'm not too wrapped up in seeing a woman, 50 years old—white, incidentally—get thrown off her job because she can't cut it like the younger ones.

10   "I told management she was a kind and gentle person. They said 'We're not interested in your personal feelings. Document it up.' They look over my appraisal and say: 'We'll give her about five months to shape up or ship out.'"

11   The hunger persists, obstinately, for pride in a man's work. Conditions may be horrendous, tensions high, and humiliations frequent, yet Paul Dietch finds his small triumphs. He drives his own truck, interstate, as a steel hauler. "Every load is a challenge. I have problems in the morning with heartburn. I can't eat. Once I off-load, the pressure is gone. Then I can eat anything. I accomplished something."

12   Yolanda Leif graphically describes the trials of a waitress in a quality restaurant. They are compounded by her refusal to be demeaned. Yet pride in her skills helps her through the night. "When I put the plate down, you don't hear a sound. When I pick up a glass, I want it to be just right. When someone says, 'How come you're just a waitress?' I say, 'Don't you think you deserve being served by me?'"

13   Peggy Terry has her own sense of pride and beauty. Her jobs have varied with geography, climate, and the ever-felt pinch of circumstance. "What I hated worst was being a waitress, the way you're treated. One guy said, 'You don't

have to smile, I'm gonna give you a tip anyway.' I said, 'Keep it, I wasn't smiling for a tip.' Tipping should be done away with. It's like throwing a dog a bone. It makes you feel small."

14   Ballplayer. Laborer. Receptionist. Assembly-line worker. Truck driver. Bank official. Waitress. What with the computer and all manner of automation, add scores of hundreds of new occupations and, thus, new heroes and antiheroes to Walt Whitman's old anthem. The sound, though, is no longer melodious. The desperation is unquiet.

15   Perhaps Nora Watson has put her finger on it. She reflects on her father's work. He was a fundamentalist preacher, with whom she had been profoundly at odds.

16   "Whatever, he was, he was. It was his calling, his vocation. He saw himself as a core resource of the community. He liked his work, even though his family barely survived, because that was what he was supposed to be doing. His work was his life. He himself was not separate and apart from his calling. I think this is what all of us are looking for, a calling, not just a job. Most of us, like the assembly-line worker, have jobs that are too small for our spirit. Jobs are not big enough for people."

17   Does it take another, less competitive, less buck-oriented society to make one match the other?

From *Capitalism: The Moving Target*, ed. Leonard Silk. New York: Quadrangle/The New York Times Book Co., 1974, pp. 68-71. Appeared originally in *The New York Times*, March 19, 1973. Copyright © 1973 by Studs Terkel. Reprinted by permission of the Estate of Studs Terkel, c/o Donadio & Olson, Inc.

Exercises

Do not refer to the selection for Exercises A and B unless your instructor directs you to do so.

A. DETERMINING THE MAIN IDEA AND PURPOSE

Choose the best answer.

_____ **1.** The main idea of the selection is that
  a. working may be demeaning in today's competitive society.
  b. workers want more respect and recognition for their efforts.
  c. workers have rejected the traditional American work ethic.
  d. automation and computerization have disrupted the American workplace.

_____ **2.** The writer's purpose is to
  a. explain his own attitudes toward work and working.
  b. examine the attitudes and concerns of various workers toward their jobs.
  c. criticize American corporate leaders for providing poor treatment and pay.

    d. recommend ways that American workers can improve their working lives.

B. COMPREHENDING MAIN IDEAS

Choose the correct answer.

_____ **1.** Terkel states that for the workers he interviewed, a work ethic means that
    a. work builds character and makes us stronger.
    b. only those who work hard and endure unhappiness will be assured of rewards.
    c. one must know the difference between right and wrong and act accordingly.
    d. one must work no matter how demeaning the job is.

_____ **2.** As an example of worker discontent, Terkel offers a single example. Which one?
    a. the high number of people receiving unemployment compensation.
    b. the high number of people who frequently change jobs.
    c. the problem of absenteeism in auto plants.
    d. the extreme fatigue American workers suffer from.

_____ **3.** Terkel suggests that workers need "another increment," by which he means
    a. an acknowledgement of one's being.
    b. profit sharing and regular bonuses for a job well done.
    c. higher status and prestige.
    d. one's name on a plaque recognizing one's contribution to the finished product.

4. What was the hard lesson that Sharon Atkins, college graduate working as an ad agency receptionist, learned—the "myth that blew up" in her face?

_____

_____ **5.** What Ralph Grayson, the black supervisor in a bank, most dislikes about his job is
    a. having to monitor his workers to be sure they're doing their jobs.
    b. his employer's indifference to illness or other personal problems.
    c. having to evaluate and perhaps threaten to fire an older woman who isn't as productive as some of the younger workers.
    d. the laziness and inefficiency he must tolerate from the workers he supervises.

6. All of the workers whom Terkel quotes complain that their jobs fail them in one specific way. What complaint do they all make in common?

_____

COMPREHENSION SCORE

Score your answers for Exercises A and B as follows:

A. No. right _____ × 2 = _____

B. No. right _____ × 1 = _____

Total points from A and B _____ × 10 = _____ percent

C. LOCATING INFORMATION

Despite their complaints, it is evident that the workers Terkel interviewed show pride in their work and in doing a good job. For each of these people below, look through the paragraph cited and locate the specific information that reinforces this idea.

1. Mike Fitzgerald, steel mill laborer [paragraph 5] _____

   _____

   _____

2. Paul Dietch, truck driver [paragraph 11] _____

   _____

   _____

3. Yolanda Leif, waitress [paragraph 12] _____

   _____

   _____

D. INTERPRETING MEANING

Write your answers to these questions in your own words.

1. At the end of paragraph 1, Terkel writes that young workers in the 1970s were questioning their work ethic and making their grievances known, ending by saying that these grievances were "hitherto silent and anonymous." What does this phrase mean? _____

   _____

   _____

2. What does Mike Fitzgerald, the steel mill worker, mean when he says "I feel like the guys who built the pyramids. Somebody built 'em"? _____

   _____

   _____

   _____

3. Look again at paragraph 7. What difference does Terkel see in older workers and younger workers in the way they see themselves? _____

_____

_____

E. UNDERSTANDING VOCABULARY

Choose the best definition according to an analysis of word parts or the context.

_____ **1.** the *impertinent* question [paragraph 3]
  a. not displaying good manners, disrespectful
  b. irrelevant, not concerned with the subject
  c. unimportant, trivial
  d. unanswerable, debatable

_____ **2.** the hunger *persists* [11]
  a. increases, gets worse
  b. cannot be satisfied
  c. continues, endures
  d. needs to be documented

_____ **3.** the hunger persists, *obstinately* [11]
  a. unconsciously
  b. invisibly
  c. unfortunately
  d. stubbornly

_____ **4.** Leif *graphically* describes [12]
  a. reluctantly, hesitatingly
  b. boldly, courageously
  c. vividly, realistically
  d. angrily, showing a temper

_____ **5.** they are *compounded* [12]
  a. added to, made more important
  b. made less convincing
  c. demeaned, degraded
  d. mixed up, confused with

F. USING VOCABULARY

From the following list of vocabulary words, choose a word that fits in each blank according to both the grammatical structure of the sentence and the context. Use each word in the list only once. Do not change the form of the word. (Note that there are more words than blanks.)

acridly	demeaning	grievance	profound
anonymous	discontent	myth	whether

The most common _____ of these workers is that their jobs are _____, that their jobs are too small for their spirit. There is a feeling that their achievements are not recognized, _____ they are blue-collar workers or white-collar workers. The _____ seems to be especially _____ with workers who make a building or a monument that will last for hundreds of years but who still remain _____.

G. PARAPHRASING EXERCISE

Here are some sentences from the selection. Write a paraphrase of each passage in the space provided.

1. You must make a buck to survive the day. You must work to make a buck. The job is often a chore, rarely a delight. No matter how demeaning the task, no matter how it dulls the senses or breaks the spirit, one *must* work or else. Lately there has been a questioning of this "work ethic," especially by the young. Strangely enough, it has touched off profound grievances in others, hitherto silent and anonymous.

   _____

   _____

   _____

   _____

   _____

   _____

2. . . . there dangles the impertinent question: Ought there not be another incre- ment, earned though not yet received, in one's daily work—an acknowledge- ment of a man's *being*?

   _____

   _____

3. The hunger persists, obstinately, for pride in a man's work.

   _____

H. SUMMARIZING EXERCISE

Write a summary of the first excerpt in Exercise G above. Try to write no more than 25 words.

   _____

   _____

I. TOPICS FOR DISCUSSION

1. Is there any evidence that Terkel has preconceived ideas about work and attitudes toward work? In other words, do the ideas expressed by the work- ers he interviewed always match his ideas that work is demeaning and that among workers, "job and status have no meaning"? See in particular para- graphs 4–6.

2. Terkel's essay was published in the mid-1970s, nearly 40 years ago. Based on your firsthand knowledge and/or observation, do today's workers feel more fulfilled than those Terkel describes in this piece or do they exhibit the same discontent that he records?

3. If you were to play the party game, "Who Are You?" how would you identify yourself? How would your parents? Is the concept of self the same or different for these generations?

J. TOPICS FOR WRITING

1. In the conclusion, Terkel discusses the disconnect between our spirits and our jobs, ending with a rhetorical question, one asked for effect: "Does it take another, less competitive, less buck-oriented society to make one match the other?" Write a short essay in which you address this question and offer some suggestions to remedy the situation.

2. Terkel's essay is centered on the observation that 1970s workers felt a discontent in their lives, that their jobs didn't give them a sense of being. Interview several people whom you are acquainted with about their jobs and their feelings about the work they do. Present your findings in a short essay that you organize around a central impression. Use their ideas as support for this impression.

3. Write a short essay in which you describe your ideal job.

EXPLORE THE WEB

• In 2009 it was revealed that the FBI had kept extensive files going back as far as the 1940s on Studs Terkel. You can read about why the FBI was interested in keeping tabs on Terkel in an Associated Press article. In the search box of your favorite search engine, type in "Don Babwin" + "Studs Terkel" + "Nov. 26, 2009." You will find several links to Babwin's story.

• The pyramids of Egypt (including the Great Pyramid at Giza) are the last of the Seven Wonders of the Ancient World to survive. When Mike Fitzgerald laments that the names of the thousands of Egyptian slaves who built the pyramids are lost in history because no one commemorated their efforts, we might want to learn more about their history—how they were constructed, what they were used for, and so on. Do a search using your favorite search engine to locate pictures and information about these structures. Here is one site to get you started: http://touregypt.net/construction/

SHERRY TURKLE

The Nostalgia of the Young

Sherry Turkle is a professor of the social studies of science and technology at Massachu-setts Institute of Technology (MIT) and also a clinical psychologist. In her 2011 book, Alone Together: Why We Expect More from Technology and Less from Each Other, *Turkle explores the subject of technology and its effects on social interaction. In this excerpt, she examines the phenomenon of texting and its effects on communication between young people and between children and their parents.*

Vocabulary Analysis

WORD PREFIXES

bi- and other numerical prefixes English contains a large number of Latin and Greek prefixes referring to numbers. One of them is the prefix *bi-* meaning "two." The *biweekly* correspondence between two friends, then, means that the woman doing research in Thailand wrote to her friend in Chicago every two weeks. Other words that begin with the prefix *bi-* include *bifocals* (a type of glasses with two different lenses); *bisect* (to cut into two parts*)*; and *bisexual* (relating to both sexes).

Here are some other common Latin and Greek prefixes indicating number and some words illustrating them:

half	*semi-* (semisweet, semicircle); *hemi-* (hemisphere)
one	*uni-* (unicycle, unison, unicorn)
two	besides *bi-*, *duo-* (duet, dual)
three	*tri-* (tricycle, trimester, triplets, trident)

WORD PARTS

tele + graph Turkle writes, ironically as it turns out, that when she first encountered texting, she didn't think it would last because it was too *telegraphic*. The prefix *tele* means "distance" and the root *graphos* means "writing." Before the invention of the telephone, people used to communicate over long distances by wiring tele-grams. Besides the obvious words *television* and *telescope*, English contains a few other words with these word parts. Write the definitions of the following words in the space provided.

telepathy _____

teleconference_____

autobiography _____

graphology _____

SHERRY TURKLE

The Nostalgia of the Young

1   Cliff, a Silver Academy sophomore, talks about whether it will ever be possible to get back to what came "before texting." Cliff says that he gets so caught up in the back-and-forth of texting that he ends up wasting time in what he thinks are superficial communications "just to get back." I ask him about when, in his view, there might be less pressure for an immediate response. Cliff thinks of two: "Your class has a test. Or you lost your signal." Conspicuously absent—you are doing something else, thinking something else, with someone else.

2   We have seen young people walk the halls of their schools composing messages to online acquaintances they will never meet. We have seen them feeling more alive when connected, then disoriented and alone when they leave their screens. Some live more than half their waking hours in virtual places. But they also talk wistfully about letters, face-to-face meetings, and the privacy of pay phones. Tethered selves, they try to conjure a future different from the one they see coming by building on a past they never knew. In it, they have time alone, with nature, with each other, and with their families.

3   Texting is too seductive. It makes a promise that generates its own demand. The promise: the person you text will receive the message within seconds, and whether or not he or she is "free," the recipient will be able to see your text. The demand: when you receive a text, you will attend to it (during class, this might mean a glance down at a silenced phone) and respond as soon as possible. Cliff says that in his circle of friends, that means, "ten minutes, maximum."

    I will tell you how it is at this school. If something comes in on our phone and it's a text, you feel you have to respond. They obviously know you got it. With IM, you can claim you weren't at the computer or you lost your Internet connection and all that. But if it's a text, there's no way you didn't get it. Few people look down at their phone and then walk away from it. Few people do that. It really doesn't happen. . . . Texting is pressure. I don't always feel like communicating. Who says that we always have to be ready to communicate?

4   Indeed, who says? Listening to what young people miss may teach us what they need. They need attention.

ATTENTION

5   Teenagers know that when they communicate by instant message, they compete with many other windows on a computer screen. They know how little attention they are getting because they know how little they give to the instant messages they receive. One sophomore girl at Branscomb High School compares instant messaging to being on "cruise control" or "automatic pilot." Your attention is elsewhere. A Branscomb senior says, "Even if I give my full attention to the person I am IMing. . . they are not giving full attention to me." The first thing he does when he makes a call is to gauge whether the person on the other end "is there just for me." This is one advantage of a call. When you text or instant-message, you have no way to tell how much else is going on for the person writing you. He or she could also be on the phone, doing homework, watching TV, or in the midst of other online conversations.

6   Longed for here is the pleasure of full attention, coveted and rare. These teenagers grew up with parents who talked on their cell phones and scrolled through messages as they walked to the playground. Parents texted with one hand and pushed swings with the other. They glanced up at the jungle gym as they made calls. Teenagers describe childhoods with parents who were on their mobile devices while driving them to school or as the family watched Disney videos. A college freshman jokes that her father read her the Harry Potter novels, periodically interrupted by his BlackBerry. BlackBerries and laptops came on family vacations. Weekends in the country were cut short if there was no Internet service in the hotel. Lon, eighteen, says when that happened, his father "called it a day." He packed up the family and went home, back to a world of connections.

7   From the youngest ages, these teenagers have associated technology with shared attention. Phones, before they become an essential element in a child's own life, were the competition, one that children didn't necessarily feel they could best. And things are not so different in the teenage years. Nick, seventeen, says, "My parents text while we eat. I'm used to it. My dad says it is better than his having to be at the office. I say, 'Well, maybe it could just be a short meal.' But my mom, she wants long meals. To get a long meal with a lot of courses, she has to allow the BlackBerry." Things seem at a stalemate.

8   Children have always competed for their parents' attention, but this generation has experienced something new. Previously, children had to deal with parents being off with work, friends, or each other. Today, children contend with parents who are physically close, tantalizingly so, but mentally elsewhere. Hannah's description of how her mother doesn't look up from her BlackBerry to say hello when she picks her up at school highlights a painful contrast between the woman who goes to the trouble to fetch her daughter and the woman who cannot look up from her screen. Lon says he liked it better when his father had a desktop computer. It meant that he worked from a specific place. Now his father

sits next to him on the couch watching a football game but is on his BlackBerry as well. Because they are physically close, his father's turn to the BlackBerry seems particularly excluding.

9   Miguel, a Hadley senior, says that having his father scroll through his Black-Berry messages during television sports is "stressful" but adds "not the kind that really kills you. More the kind that always bothers you." Miguel says it is hard for him to ask his father to put the BlackBerry away because he himself texts when he is with his father in the car. "He has a son who texts, so why shouldn't he?" But when parents see their children checking their mobile devices and thus feel permission to use their own, the adults are discounting a crucial asymmetry. The multitasking teenagers are just that, teenagers. They want and need adult attention. They are willing to admit that they are often relieved when a parent asks them to put away the phone and sit down to talk. But for parents to make this request—and this no longer goes without saying—they have to put down their phones as well. Sometimes it is children (often in alliance with their mothers) who find a way to insist that dinner time be a time for talking—time away from the smartphone. But habits of shared attention die hard.

10   One high school senior recalls a time when his father used to sit next to him on the couch, reading. "He read for pleasure and didn't mind being inter-rupted." But when his father, a doctor, switched from books to his BlackBerry, things became less clear: "He could be playing a game or looking at a patient record, and you would never know. . . . He is in that same BlackBerry zone." It takes work to bring his father out of that zone. When he emerges, he needs time to refocus. "You might ask him a question and he'll say, 'Yeah, one second.' And then he'll finish typing his e-mail or whatever, he'll log off whatever, and he'll say, 'Yeah, I'm sorry, what did you say?'"

11   It is commonplace to hear children, from the age of eight through the teen years, describe the frustration of trying to get the attention of their multitasking parents. Now, these same children are insecure about having each other's atten-tion. At night, as they sit at computer screens, any messages sent or received share "mind space" with shopping, uploading photos, updating Facebook, watching videos, playing games, and doing homework. One high school senior describes evening "conversation" at his machine: "When I'm IMing, I can be talking to three different people at the same time and listening to music and also looking at a website." During the day, prime time for phone texting, communi-cations happen as teenagers are on their way from one thing to another. Teen-agers talk about what they are losing when they text: how someone stands, the tone of their voice, the expression on their face, "the things your eyes and ears tell you," as one eighteen-year-old puts it.

12   When I first encountered texting, I thought it too telegraphic to be much more than a way to check in. You could use it to confirm an appointment, settle on a restaurant, or say you were home safely. I was wrong. Texting has evolved into a space for confessions, breakups, and declarations of love. There is something to celebrate here: a new, exuberant space for friendship, a way to blow a virtual kiss. But there is a price. All matters—some delicate, some not—are crammed into a medium that quickly communicates a state but is not well suited for opening a dialogue about complexity of feeling. Texting—interrupted by bad

reception, incoming calls, and other text messages (not to mention the fact that it all goes on in the presence other people)—can compromise the intimacy it promises. There is a difference, says an eighteen-year-old boy, "between some-one laughing and someone *writing* that they're laughing." He says, "My friends are so used to giving their phones all the attention . . . they forget that people are still there to give attention to."

13   We met Robin, twenty-six, who works as a copywriter in a large and highly competitive advertising agency. She describes the demands of her job as "crush-ing." She has her BlackBerry with her at all times. She does not put it in her purse; she holds it. At meals, she sets it on the table near her, touching it fre-quently. At a business lunch, she explains that she needs to leave it on because her job requires her to be "on call" at all times. During lunch, she admits that there is more to the story. Her job certainly requires that she stay in touch. But now, whether or not she is waiting for a message from work, she becomes anx-ious without her BlackBerry. "If I'm not in touch, I feel almost dizzy. As though something is wrong, something terrible is wrong." The device has become a way to manage anxiety about her parents, her job, and her love life. Even if these don't go quite right, she says, "if I have the BlackBerry in control, I feel that at least everything isn't out of control." But something has gotten out of control. When Robin thinks of stress, she thinks of being without her BlackBerry. But she admits that she thinks of being with her BlackBerry as well.

14   Robin says that her need for the BlackBerry began with business e-mail, but now she uses it to spend many hours a day on Facebook. She makes no pretense that this is about "business." But Robin is no longer sure it is about pleasure. She describes being increasingly "annoyed" on Facebook. I ask her for an example—one of these moments of annoyance—and Robin begins to talk about her friend Joanne.

15   Robin and Joanne went to college together in Los Angeles. After graduating, Robin went to Chicago for a first job in publishing; Joanne stayed on the West Coast for graduate school in anthropology. Five years ago, Joanne's disserta-tion research took her to a village in Thailand. Joanne had e-mail access during her year in the village, and she wrote Robin long, detailed e-mails, five or six pages each. There was a letter every two weeks—a personal journal of Joanne's experience of Thai life. Robin describes them warmly—the letters were "elegant, detailed, poetic." Robin printed out the cherished letters; on occasion she still rereads them. Now Joanne is back in Thailand on a new project, but this time, she posts a biweekly journal to her Facebook page. There has been no falling out between the two women; Joanne has simply chosen a more "efficient" way to get her story out to all her friends. Robin still gets an occasional e-mail. But essen-tially, what was once a personal letter has turned into a blog.

16   Robin says she is ashamed of her reaction to Joanne's Facebook postings: "I was jealous of all of the other readers. They are not friends the way I am a friend." Robin understands Joanne's decision to "publish" her journal: "She is reaching more people this way. . . . Some can help in her career." But despite herself, Robin feels abandoned. The all-friend postings do not make her feel close to her friend.

17   After she tells this story, essentially about a personal loss, Robin adds a post-script that she describes as "not personal. I'm trying to make a general point."

She says that when Joanne wrote her letters, they were "from a real person to another real person." They were written to her, in all her particularity. Behind each letter was the history of their long friendship. The new letters on Facebook are generic. For a moment, Robin, the professional writer, allows herself a moment of judgment: "The journal is written to everyone and thus no one. It isn't as good." Robin misses receiving something that was just for her.

Exercises

Do not refer to the selection for Exercises A, B, and C unless your instructor directs you to do so.

A. DETERMINING THE MAIN IDEA AND PURPOSE

Choose the best answer.

_____ 1. The main idea of the selection is that
- **a.** texting has become an epidemic among young people, destroying their ability to communicate face-to-face and to experience empathy.
- **b.** constant texting deprives people—both teenagers and adults—the pleasure of full attention and a personal connection, to such an extent that young people express regret over a past they never knew.
- **c.** texting is an innovative form of communication that allows young people to stay in touch more closely than they could with the telephone.
- **d.** texting is a telegraphic method of communication suitable more for checking in than for saying anything meaningful.

_____ 2. The writer's purpose is to
- **a.** warn parents about the negative consequences of allowing their young children to own a cell phone.
- **b.** describe the various ways in which people communicate via cell phone and the ways doing so has changed us.
- **c.** examine some of the negative consequences that constant texting has brought about, both for young people and for adults.
- **d.** examine the good and bad points of texting in order to allow the reader to make up his or her own mind.

B. COMPREHENDING MAIN IDEAS

Choose the correct answer for the multiple-choice items. Write the fill-in answers in the space provided using your own words.

_____ **1.** How does Turkle characterize the relationship between young people and their cell phones? She says that young people are
   a. imprisoned.
   b. captivated.
   c. victimized.
   d. tethered.

_____ **2.** According to Turkle and at least one of the young people she interviewed, a major problem with texting or IMing is that
   a. the recipient may not want to answer the message right away, causing hurt feelings.
   b. the sender may not realize that the recipient is in class and therefore not available.
   c. there is no way to tell just how much attention the recipient is giving the message.
   d. young people no longer are capable of conversing with another person directly.

3. Concerning texting and scrolling through messages, young people evidently are copying the behavior of _____.

4. For one father, using his BlackBerry to check messages at the dinner table is acceptable because otherwise he _____

_____ **5.** According to Turkle, what is the most serious obstacle that cell phones present in the child-parent relationship, especially for children?
   a. the competition for attention that they feel they are being denied
   b. ruined family dinners, with everyone looking at their cell phones instead of talking
   c. the absence of joking around and creating shared memories
   d. the amount of money spent on technological gadgets that could well be spent on more useful things

_____ **6.** Robin and Joanne are old college friends. While Joanne did research in Thailand, she kept in touch with Robin by means of
   a. daily Facebook updates.
   b. instant messaging.
   c. texting on her BlackBerry.
   d. long letters sent every two weeks.

COMPREHENSION SCORE

Score your answers for Exercises A and B as follows:

A. No. right _____ × 2 = _____

B. No. right _____ × 1 = _____

Total points from A and B _____ × 10 = _____ percent

C. SEQUENCING

These sentences from one paragraph in the selection may have been scrambled. Read the sentences and choose the sequence that puts them back into logical order. Do not refer to the original selection.

1 It takes work to bring his father out of that zone. **2** One high school senior recalls a time when his father used to sit next to him on the couch, reading. **3** But when his father, a doctor, switched from books to his BlackBerry, things became less clear: "He could be playing a game or looking at a patient record, and you would never know . . . He is in that same BlackBerry zone." **4** When he emerges, he needs time to refocus. **5** "He read for pleasure and didn't mind being interrupted."

_____ Which of the following represents the correct sequence for these sentences?
a. 2, 5, 3, 1, 4
b. 2, 5, 4, 3, 1
c. 5, 2, 3, 4, 1
d. 1, 3, 2, 4, 5
e. Correct as written.

You may refer to the selection as you work through the remaining exercises.

D. LOCATING INFORMATION

In paragraphs 5–12, Turkle discusses the lack of attention that texting causes for both parents and young people. Locate three specific pieces of information that support this idea.

1. _____

2. _____

3. _____

E. LOCATING SUPPORTING DETAILS

For the main idea stated here from paragraph 9, find three relevant details that support it. Three supporting details have been done for you.

The relationship between parents and children is strained, and the need for attention isn't met when both parties are constantly texting in front of each other.

a. For Miguel, a high school senior, seeing his father scroll through his BlackBerry messages is "stressful" but "not the kind that really kills you."

b. _____

c. _____

d. Parents see their children texting, which gives them permission to text themselves; however, they don't realize that there is a "crucial asymmetry" in this situation.

e. _____

f. Children, sometimes allied with their mothers, are the ones who insist that dinnertime be for talking and that texting be prohibited.

F. UNDERSTANDING VOCABULARY

Look through each numbered paragraph in the following list and find a word that matches each definition. Refer to a dictionary if necessary. An example has been done for you.

Ex. a pleasurable longing for the past [title]   _nostalgia_

Extra credit point: One of the answers below is closely related to the answer in the example above. Hint: It's an adverb.

1.   existing only on the surface [paragraph 1]   _____

2.   a feeling of being disconnected, confused [2]   _____

3.   existing in the computer world but not in reality [2]   _____

4.   tied, fastened, restricted [2]   _____

5.   describing a feeling of wishful longing [2]   _____

6.   felt an excessive desire for something that belongs to another [6]   _____

7.   deadlock, a situation where no further action is possible [7]   _____

8.   beat, get the better of [7]   _____

9.   describing the feeling that something is greatly desired but just out of reach [8]   _____

10. false show, pretended reason or excuse [14]   _____

G. USING VOCABULARY—VARIANT WORD FORMS

In parentheses before each sentence are some inflected forms of words from the selection. Study the context and the sentence. Then write the correct form in the space provided.

1.   (_conspicuousness, conspicuous, conspicuously_) Turkle cites an observation made by Cliff, a high school student, who feels pressure to return a text message immediately. What he does not say, what is _____ in its absence, is that he might not respond because he's busy doing something else.

2. (*seduction, seduces, seductive, seductively*) Texting _____ us, Turkle says, because we accept the demand that a text message must be answered immediately.

3. (*exuberance, exuberant, exuberantly*) Turkle observes that our new _____ over sharing things via cell phones comes at a price.

4. (*complexity, complex, complexly*) Cell phones are not a good means of communicating _____ feelings.

5. (*anxiety, anxious, anxiously*) For Robin, who works at an ad agency, being without her BlackBerry makes her _____.

H. PARAPHRASING EXERCISE

Here are two excerpts from the selection, followed by three paraphrases. Choose the one that most accurately paraphrases the original.

_____ 1. Longed for here is the pleasure of full attention, coveted and rare.
   a. Full attention is a kind of pleasure, which is very rare these days.
   b. What children long for is the pleasure of someone paying full attention to them, but though they may desire this intensely, it doesn't happen very often.
   c. It is rare for children to pay full attention to something, even though they may say that they want this and that they find pleasure in it.

_____ 2. Children have always competed for their parents' attention, but this generation has experienced something new. Previously, children had to deal with parents being off with work, friends, or each other. Today, children contend with parents who are physically close, tantalizingly so, but mentally elsewhere.
   a. In terms of competing for their parents' attention, the current generation of children is experiencing a new phenomenon—parents who are physically present but whose minds are somewhere else.
   b. Today's generation of children has to compete for their parents' attention. Their parents are away at work or with friends and aren't around much to attend to their needs.
   c. It must be frustrating for children today to deal with parents who are in the same room but who aren't paying attention to them, unlike past generations of children, whose parents were more attentive to their needs.

3. Here is an excerpt for you to paraphrase:

Texting is too seductive. It makes a promise that generates its own demand. The promise: the person you text will receive the message within seconds, and whether or not he or she is "free," the recipient will be able to see your text. The demand: when you receive a text, you will attend to it (during class, this might mean a glance down at a silenced phone) and respond as soon as possible.

_____

_____

_____

_____

_____

I.   TOPICS FOR DISCUSSION

1. Does texting, in your opinion and in your experience, cause the serious negative consequences that Turkle outlines here? Has she stated her case fairly, or do you think she overstates the problem of lack of attention that texting from both parties brings about?

2. What situations have you observed that involved completely inappropriate texting or scrolling through messages?

3. Turkle offers one explanation for the seductive nature of texting in paragraph 3. What might be two or three other reasons for this seductive value?

4. What is the larger significance of texting for our society as a whole? What might be its longer-term effects, beyond those Turkle describes?

J.   TOPICS FOR WRITING

1. In "Johnny Get Your Textbook" by Colby Buzzell (see Selection 5 in Part One), he and his fellow veteran classmates at City College of San Francisco have observed students texting in class. If students' texting in the classroom is a problem at your college, write a proposal in which you explain a policy concerning the matter to be implemented campus-wide. Alternatively, write a proposal for some guidelines that a family might use to regulate cell phone use.

2. Write a rebuttal to Turkle's selection. That is, take the opposite stance and address the positive benefits that texting confers on both the sender and the recipient.

3. Just how addictive are cell phones, texting, and other forms of modern technology? In the search box of your favorite search engine, type in "Technology Withdrawal, Andrea Bennett." At the link you can read the results of a survey of young people aged 16–22 who said that they would give up their sense of smell if they could keep one technology item in their possession (a laptop or a cell phone topped the list). After reading the article, write an essay in which you explore the significance of the study's findings.

EXPLORE THE WEB

Sherry Turkle's book was well received when it was published in 2011. Find out what reviewers thought about the book by doing an online search. Two good sources would be _The New York Times_ and the _Washington Post_ websites.

10 ELIZABETH BERNSTEIN
How Facebook Ruins Friendships

Elizabeth Bernstein has been writing for The Wall Street Journal *for over ten years. Her topics have ranged from education to psychology to religion. Currently she writes stories about human relationships and interactions between family and friends, at home and at work. In this selection, Bernstein laments the changes Facebook has created in her friendships and evaluates this and other social media sites as a means of communicating with one's friends and family.*

Vocabulary Analysis

WORD ORIGINS

narcissism One person whom Bernstein interviewed for this article claims that constant posting on Facebook "is called narcissism" [paragraph 12]. In Greek mythology, Narcissus was a beautiful young man who was unable to love and who rejected everyone who developed romantic feelings for him. In one version of the myth, Nemesis, the goddess of revenge, decreed that Narcissus would fall in love with himself. One day, he leaned over a pool of water, saw his own reflection, and immediately fell in love with his own image. He lay next to the pool day after day, unable to take his gaze off his reflection. Eventually, he wasted away and died. The gods transformed his body into the flower we know today as narcissus. Today, the simple meaning of *narcissism* is self-love or self-admiration. The more complicated meaning is a psychological preoccupation with oneself often accompanied by a lack of empathy.

mecca In paragraph 21 Bernstein writes that "Facebook can also be a mecca for passive-aggressive behavior." The city of Mecca in Saudi Arabia is both the birthplace of Mohammed and the holiest city in Islam. Devout Muslims must make a pilgrimage to the city once in their lifetimes. When spelled with lowercase *m*, mecca refers to the center of an activity or interest, which is the definition that fits the context here.

ELIZABETH BERNSTEIN

How Facebook Ruins Friendships

1   Notice to my friends: I love you all dearly.

2   But I don't give a hoot that you are "having a busy Monday," your child "took 30 minutes to brush his teeth," your dog "just ate an ant trap" or you want to "save the piglets." And I really, really don't care which Addams Family member you most resemble. (I could have told you the answer before you took the quiz on Facebook.)

3   Here's where you and I went wrong: We took our friendship online. First we began communicating more by email than by phone. Then we switched to "instant messaging" or "texting." We "friended" each other on Facebook, and began communicating by "tweeting" our thoughts—in 140 characters or less—via Twitter.

4   All this online social networking was supposed to make us closer. And in some ways it has. Thanks to the Internet, many of us have gotten back in touch with friends from high school and college, shared old and new photos, and become better acquainted with some people we might never have grown close to offline.

5   Last year, when a friend of mine was hit by a car and went into a coma, his friends and family were able to easily and instantly share news of his medical progress—and send well wishes and support—thanks to a Web page his mom created for him.

6   But there's a danger here, too. If we're not careful, our online interactions can hurt our real-life relationships.

7   Like many people, I'm experiencing Facebook Fatigue. I'm tired of loved ones—you know who you are—who claim they are too busy to pick up the phone, or even write a decent email, yet spend hours on social-media sites, uploading photos of their children or parties, forwarding inane quizzes, posting quirky, sometimes nonsensical one-liners or tweeting their latest whereabouts. ("Anyone know a good restaurant in Berlin?")

8   One of the big problems is how we converse. Typing still leaves something to be desired as a communication tool; it lacks the nuances that can be expressed by body language and voice inflection. "Online, people can't see the yawn," says Patricia Wallace, a psychologist at Johns Hopkins University's Center for Talented Youth and author of "The Psychology of the Internet."

9   But let's face it, the problem is much greater than which tools we use to communicate. It's what we are actually saying that's really mucking up our relationships. "Oh my God, a college friend just updated her Facebook status to say that her 'teeth are itching for a flossing!'" shrieked a friend of mine recently. "That's gross. I don't want to hear about what's going on inside her mouth."

10   That prompted me to check my own Facebook page, only to find that three of my pals—none of whom know each other—had the exact same status update: "Zzzzzzz." They promptly put me to "zzzzzzz."

11   This brings us to our first dilemma: Amidst all this heightened chatter, we're not saying much that's interesting, folks. Rather, we're breaking a cardinal rule of companionship: Thou Shalt Not Bore Thy Friends.

12   "It's called narcissism," says Matt Brown, a 36-year-old business-development manager for a chain of hair salons and spas in Seattle. He's particularly annoyed by a friend who works at an auto dealership who tweets every time he sells a car, a married couple who bicker on Facebook's public walls and another couple so "mooshy-gooshy" they sit in the same room of their house posting love messages to each other for all to see. "Why is your life so frickin' important and entertaining that we need to know?" Mr. Brown says.

'I Just Ate a Frito Pie'

13   Gwen Jewett, for her part, is sick of meal status updates. "A few of my friends like to post several times a day about what they are eating: 'I just ate a Frito pie.' 'I am enjoying a double hot-fudge sundae at home tonight.' 'Just ate a whole pizza with sausage, peppers and double cheese,'" says the 49-year-old career coach in suburban Dallas. "My question is this: If we didn't call each other on the phone every time we ate before, why do we need the alerts now?"

14   For others, boredom isn't the biggest challenge of managing Internet relationships. Consider, for example, how people you know often seem different online—not just gussied up or more polished, but bolder, too, displaying sides of their personalities you have never seen before.

15   Alex Gilbert, 27, who works for a nonprofit in Houston that teaches creative writing to kids, is still puzzling over an old friend—"a particularly masculine-type dude"—who plays in a heavy-metal band and heads a motorcycle club yet posts videos on Facebook of "uber cute" kittens. "It's not fodder for your real-life conversation," Mr. Gilbert says. "We're not going to get together and talk about how cute kittens are."

16   James Hills discovered that a colleague is gay via Facebook, but he says that didn't bother him. It was after his friend joined groups that cater to hairy men, such as "Furball NYC," that he was left feeling awkward. "This is something I just didn't need to know," says Mr. Hills, who is 32 and president of a marketing firm in Elgin, III. "I'd feel the same way if it was a straight friend joining a leather-and-lace group."

17   And then there's jealousy. In all that information you're posting about your life—your vacation, your kids, your promotions at work, even that margarita you just drank—someone is bound to find something to envy. When it comes to relationships, such online revelations can make breaking up even harder to do.

18   "Facebook prolongs the period it takes to get over someone, because you have an open window into their life, whether you want to or not," says Yianni Garcia of New York, a consultant who helps companies use social media. "You see their updates, their pictures and their relationship status."

19   Mr. Garcia, 24, felt the sting of Facebook jealousy personally last spring, after he split up with his boyfriend. For a few weeks, he continued to visit his ex's Facebook page, scrutinizing his new friends. Then one day he discovered that his former boyfriend had blocked him from accessing his profile.

20   Why? "He said he'd only 'unfriended' me to protect himself, because if someone flirted with me he would feel jealous," Mr. Garcia says.

21   Facebook can also be a mecca for passive-aggressive behavior. "Suddenly, things you wouldn't say out loud in conversation are OK to say because you're sitting behind a computer screen," says Kimberly Kaye, 26, an arts writer in New

York. She was surprised when friends who had politely discussed health-care reform over dinner later grew much more antagonistic when they continued the argument online.

22   Just ask Heather White. She says her college roommate at the University of Georgia started an argument over text about who should clean their apartment. Ms. White, 22, who was home visiting her parents at the time, asked her friend to call her so they could discuss the issue. Her friend never did.

23   A few days later, Ms. White, who graduated in May, updated her Facebook status, commenting that her favorite country duo, Brooks & Dunn, just broke up. Almost immediately, her roommate responded, writing publicly on her wall: "Just like us." The two women have barely spoken since then.

Band-Aid Tactics

24   So what's the solution, short of "unfriending" or "unfollowing" everyone who annoys you? You can use the "hide" button on Facebook to stop getting your friends' status updates—they'll never know—or use TwitterSnooze, a Web site that allows you to temporarily suspend tweets from someone you follow. (Warning: They'll get a notice from Twitter when you begin reading their tweets again.)

25   But these are really just Band-Aid tactics. To improve our interactions, we need to change our conduct, not just cover it up. First, watch your own behavior, asking yourself before you post anything: "Is this something I'd want someone to tell me?" "Run it by that focus group of one," says Johns Hopkins's Dr. Wallace.

26   And positively reward others, responding only when they write something interesting, ignoring them when they are boring or obnoxious. (Commenting negatively will only start a very public war.)

27   If all that fails, you can always start a new group: "Get Facebook to Create an Eye-Roll Button Now!"

Exercises

You may refer to the selection to complete these exercises.

A. COMPREHENDING MAIN IDEAS

Write the answers for these questions in the space provided using your own words.

1. Bernstein cites several objections to Facebook concerning why it ruins friendships. List three points Bernstein makes to support these objections.

    a. _____

    b. _____

    c. _____

2. According to Bernstein, where did she and her friends "go wrong" in their friendships? What one step caused the whole situation to deteriorate?

_____

3. What significant feature does typing lack that face-to-face communication allows?

_____

4. Despite the "heightened chatter," what is wrong with a lot of Facebook postings?

_____

5. What is particularly damaging about Facebook when a couple breaks up?

_____

6. Why are actions like "unfriending," "unfollowing," or using the "hide" button merely "Band-Aid tactics"? What is Bernstein's recommendation for salvaging friendships in the Age of Facebook?

_____

B. UNDERSTANDING VOCABULARY IN CONTEXT

Here are a few vocabulary words from the selection along with their definitions. Study these definitions carefully. Then write the appropriate word in each space provided according to the context, the way it is used.

via	by means of
inane	lacking sense, empty
dilemma	a situation requiring a choice between two equally undesirable alternatives
nuances	slight differences in meaning or tone
cardinal	of primary importance

1. Facebook poses a classic example of a _____: A lot of what people post on their Facebook page is _____—what they are eating or photos of their pets . Thus the person breaks a _____ rule of friendship—Thou shalt not bore thy friends. Another problem is that when we communicate _____ Facebook, the information lacks the _____ that are expressed by one's voice and body language.

scrutinize	observe carefully, inspect with a critical eye
quirky	describing something unpredictable or peculiar
narcissism	excessive love of oneself
antagonistic	describing a contentious or unfriendly attitude
obnoxious	offensive, annoying, objectionable

2. Constantly posting information about oneself on Facebook can be construed as a form of _____. While the poster may see her submissions as _____ and amusing, one's friends might _____

them carefully and come away with a different impression. Bernstein also observes that people often become more _____ when debating controversial issues online than they would in a face-to-face situation. It's difficult to deal with an _____ "friend" who behaves in these ways, but there is one solution: Simply "unfriend" the person.

C. SMALL GROUP ACTIVITY—UNDERSTANDING SLANG AND IDIOMATIC EXPRESSIONS

Bernstein uses several informal idiomatic and slang expressions. Consider these expressions in their context and then, working in small groups, try to determine their meaning. The paragraph number where each occurs is included. You might try the dictionary if you are unsure, or ask your instructor for help.

1. *I don't give a hoot* [paragraph 2]   _____

2. But *let's face it* [9]   _____

3. *mucking up* our relationships [9]   _____

4. Why is your life so *frickin'* important? [12]   _____

5. not *gussied up* [14]   _____

6. a particularly masculine-type *dude* 15]   _____

7. he had *"unfriended"* me [20]   _____

8. just *Band-Aid tactics* [25]   _____

9. *run it by* that focus group of one [25]   _____

10. an *Eye-Roll Button* [27]   _____

D. TOPICS FOR DISCUSSION

1. Who is Bernstein's audience? How can you tell?
2. On balance, do you agree with Bernstein's observation about the damage Facebook causes friendships or do you think she is overstating the problem? Does she do an adequate job of supporting her observations?
3. Bernstein provides a refutation—admitting something positive about Facebook—early in the article. Locate this refutation. Can you think of other arguments in favor of Facebook that Bernstein might have included?
4. Irony is a stylistic device (and sometimes a device used in humor) in which the words suggest something different from what one might expect. The writer uses irony to highlight this incongruity. Consider paragraph 7 again, and explain why Bernstein's observations are ironic.
5. Read paragraph 13 again. Why does Facebook lend itself to inane postings about what people eat? As Bernstein says, "If we didn't call each other on the phone every time we ate before, why do we need the alerts now?" A good question to ask and one worth trying to answer.
6. What does it say about Americans when they prefer to discuss problems, for example, with who should clean the house, via Facebook rather than on the telephone or in person?

E. TOPICS FOR WRITING

1. Write a short essay in which you examine your own personal experience—whether good or bad or both—with using Facebook.
2. Discuss the concept of "unfriending" or "unfollowing" and its implications. Is this a plausible way to deal with annoying posts? Is there a better way to handle friends who bombard you with pictures of their kittens or updates on what they ate for dinner?

EXPLORE THE WEB

- Bernstein's recent *Journal* columns can be found at this website: www.topics .wsj.com/person/B/elizabeth-anne-bernstein/1260.

11

CHRIS ROSE
Hell and Back

Chris Rose is a native of Washington, D.C. After graduating from the University of Wisconsin, he joined the Washington Post *as a news clerk. In 1984 he moved to the New Orleans* Times-Picayune *to cover crime and politics. Throughout his career at the newspaper, he has also covered the culture and economics of New Orleans as well as the jazz and nightlife scene. After Hurricane Katrina in 2005, he began to cover the devastation that resulted from the storm, writing about his adopted city as it struggled to put itself back together. In 2006, Rose and several of his newspaper colleagues won the Pulitzer Prize for Public Service for their coverage of Katrina and its effects on the residents of the city. But the storm did more than destroy houses; it also affected the psyches of the inhabitants. In this selection from the* Times-Picayune, *Rose chronicles the depression that threatened to destroy him.*

Vocabulary Analysis

WORD PARTS

mal- [paragraphs 43, 44, and 61] Rose uses three words beginning with the prefix *mal-*, which means either "bad" or "ill." *Malevolence* (paragraph 43) means malicious or evil behavior (from *mal-* + *volens* ["to wish"]). Next, Rose refers to his depression as a *malady*, an illness (paragraph 44). Finally, *malaise* (paragraph 61) means a general feeling of unease or depression. Here are three more words beginning with this prefix:

malice	the desire to harm others, ill will
malign	to speak badly of others
malnutrition	poor nutrition

What do these two words mean? Consult a dictionary if you are unsure.

malignant	_____
malaria	_____

**WORD
FAMILIES**

sympathy, empathy [paragraphs 11 and 45] The words sympathy and empathy stem from the Latin root *-pathy* or *pathos*, meaning "emotions" or "feelings." When we experience sympathy, we literally feel the same feelings as another, from *sym-* ("same") and *-pathy*. *Empathy* means identification with another's feelings, but it is stronger than *sympathy* because it suggests that one has undergone the same experience. With sympathy, one simply understands the feelings another is experiencing without necessarily having experienced the same thing.

To complicate matters, from the Greek, the root *patho-* means "disease" or "suffering." Hence, a *pathologist* is one who studies the nature and causes of disease. Usually the context will indicate which meaning is intended.

CHRIS ROSE

Hell and Back

1   I pulled into the Shell station on Magazine Street, my car running on fumes. I turned off the motor. And then I just sat there.

2   There were other people pumping gas at the island I had pulled into and I didn't want them to see me, didn't want to see them, didn't want to nod hello, didn't want to interact in any fashion.

3   Outside the window, they looked like characters in a movie. But not my movie. I tried to wait them out, but others would follow, get out of their cars and pump and pay and drive off, always followed by more cars, more people. How can they do this, as if everything is normal, I wondered. Where do they go? What do they do?

4   It was early August, and two minutes in my car with the windows up and the air conditioner off was insufferable. I was trapped, in my car and in my head. So I drove off with an empty tank rather than face strangers at a gas station.

5   Before I continue, I should make a confession. For all of my adult life, I regarded depression and anxiety as pretty much a load of hooey. I never accorded any credibility to the idea that they are medical conditions. Nothing scientific about it. You get sick, get fired, fall in love, get laid, buy a new pair of shoes, join a gym, get religion, seasons change, whatever; you go with the flow, dust yourself off, get back in the game. I thought antidepressants were for desperate housewives and fragile poets.

6   I no longer feel that way. Not since I fell down the rabbit hole myself and enough hands reached down to pull me out. One of those hands belonged to a psychiatrist holding a prescription for antidepressants. I took it. And it changed my life. Maybe saved my life.

7   This is the story of one journey, my journey, to the edge of the post-Katrina abyss, and back again. It is a story with a happy ending—at least so far.

8   I had already stopped going to the grocery store weeks before the Shell station meltdown. I had made every excuse possible to avoid going to my office because I didn't want to see anyone, didn't want to engage in small talk, Hey, how's the family?

9   My hands shook. I had to look down when I walked down steps, holding the banister to keep steady. I was at risk every time I got behind the wheel of a car; I couldn't pay attention.

10   I lost 15 pounds, and it's safe to say I didn't have a lot to give. I stopped talking to Kelly, my wife. She loathed me, my silences, my distance, my inertia. I stopped walking my dog, so she hated me, too.

11   I stopped answering phone calls and e-mails. I maintained limited communication with my editors to keep my job at the New Orleans *Times-Picayune*, but I started missing deadlines anyway. My editors cut me slack. There's a lot of slack being cut in this town now. A lot of legroom, empathy, and forgiveness.

12   I tried to keep an open line of communication with my kids, but it was still slipping away. My two oldest, 7 and 5, began asking, "What are you looking at, Daddy?"

13   The thousand-yard stare. I couldn't shake it. Boring holes into the house behind my back yard. Daddy is a zombie. That was my movie: *Night of the Living Dead*. Followed by *Morning of the Living Dead*, followed by *Afternoon . . .*

14   My darkness first became visible during fall of 2005. As the days of covering Hurricane Katrina's aftermath turned into weeks, which turned into months, I began taking long walks, miles and miles, late at night, one arm pinned to my side, the other waving in stride.

15   I had crying jags and other "episodes." One day, while the city was still mostly abandoned, I passed out on the job, fell face first into a tree, snapped my glasses in half, gouged a hole in my forehead, and lay unconscious on the side of the road for an entire afternoon. You might think that would have been a wakeup call, but it wasn't. Instead, as I had with everything else that was happening to me, I wrote a column about it, trying to make it sound funny.

16   My wife and kids spent the last four months of 2005 at my parents' home in Maryland. Until Christmas I worked, and lived, completely alone. Even when my family finally returned, I spent the next months driving endlessly through bombed-out neighborhoods. I met legions of people who appeared to be dying from sadness, and I wrote about them.

17   I was receiving thousands of e-mails in reaction to my stories in the paper, and most of them were more accounts of death, destruction, and despondency by people from around south Louisiana. I am pretty sure I possess the largest archive of personal Katrina stories, little histories that would break your heart.

18   I guess they broke mine.

19   I never considered seeking treatment. I was afraid medication might alter my emotions to a point of insensitivity, lower my antenna to where I could no longer feel the acute grip that Katrina and the flood have on the city's psyche.

20   Talk about "embedded"[1] journalism; this was the real deal.

21   As time wore on, the toll at home worsened. I declined all dinner invitations that my wife wanted desperately to accept, something to get me out of the house, get my feet moving. I let the lawn and weeds overgrow and didn't pick up my dog's waste. I rarely shaved or bathed. I stayed in bed as long as I could, as often as I could.

22   I don't drink anymore, so the nightly self-narcolepsy that so many in this community employ was not an option. And I don't watch TV, so I developed an infinite capacity to just sit and stare. I'd noodle around on the piano, read weightless fiction, and reach for my kids, always, trying to hold them, touch them, kiss them. Tell them I was still here.

23   But I was disappearing fast, slogging through winter and spring and grinding to a halt by summer. I was a dead man walking. I had never been so scared in my life.

24   That summer, with the darkness clinging to me like humidity, my stories in the *Times-Picayune* moved from gray to brown to black. Readers wanted stories of hope, inspiration, and triumph, something to cling to; I gave them anger and sadness and gloom. They started e-mailing me, telling me I was bringing them down when they were already down enough.

25   This one, August 21, from a reader named Molly: "I recently became worried about you. I read your column and you seemed so sad. And not in a fakey-columnist kind of way."

26   This one, August 19, from Debbie Koppman: "I'm a big fan. But I gotta tell ya—I can't read your columns anymore. They are depressing. I wish you'd write about something positive."

27   There were scores of e-mails, maybe hundreds. I lost count. Most were kind, solicitous even; strangers invited me over for a warm meal. But this one, on August 14, from a reader named Johnny Culpepper, stuck out: "Your stories are played out, Rose. Why don't you just leave the city; you're not happy, you bitch and moan all the time. Just leave or pull the trigger and get it over with." I'm sure he didn't mean it literally, but truthfully, I thought it was funny. I showed it around to my wife and editors.

28   Three friends of mine had, in fact, killed themselves in the past year and I had wondered what that was like. I rejected it, but, for the first time, I understood why they did it. Hopeless, helpless, and unable to function. A mind shutting down and taking the body with it. A pain not physical but not of my comprehension, and always there, a buzzing fluorescent light. No way out, I thought. Except there was.

29   I don't need to replay the early days of trauma for you here. You know what I'm talking about. Whether you were in south Louisiana or somewhere far away, in a shelter or at your sister's house, whether you lost everything or nothing, you know what I mean.

---

[1]A reference to an earlier usage: During the American invasion of Iraq that begin in March 2003, dozens of print and television journalists were "embedded" with American troops, living with them and writing their experiences for the readers back home.

30   Maybe my case is more extreme because I immersed myself in the horror and became a full-time chronicler of sorrowful tales—an audience for other people's pain. There is no such thing as leaving it behind at the office when a whole city takes the dive.

31   Then again, my case is less extreme than that of the first responders, the doctors, nurses, and emergency medical technicians, and certainly anyone who got trapped in the Dome or the Convention Center or worse—in the water, in attics, and on rooftops. In some cases, stuck in trees.

32   I've got nothing on them. How the hell do they sleep at night?

33   None of it made sense. My personality has always been marked by insouciance and laughter, the seeking of adventure. I am the class clown, the life of the party, the bon vivant. I have always felt like I was more alert and alive than anyone in the room.

34   In the measure of how one made out in the storm, my life was cake. My house, my job, and my family were all fine. My career was gangbusters, all manner of awards and attention. A book with great reviews and stunning sales, full auditoriums everywhere I was invited to speak, appearances on television and radio, and the overwhelming support of readers who left gifts, flowers, and cards on my doorstep, thanking me for my stories.

35   I had become a star of a bizarre constellation. No doubt about it, disasters are great career moves for people in my line of work. So why the hell was I so miserable? This is the time of my life, I told myself. I am a success. I have done good things.

36   To no avail.

37   I changed the message on my phone to say: "This is Chris Rose. I am emotionally unavailable at the moment. Please leave a message." I thought this was hilarious. Most of my friends recognized it as a classic cry for help. My editor, my wife, my dad, my friends, and strangers on the street who recognized me from my picture in the paper had been telling me for a long time: You need to get help.

38   I didn't want help. I didn't want medicine. And I sure as hell didn't want to sit on a couch and tell some guy with glasses, a beard, and a degree from Dartmouth about my troubles.

39   Everybody's got troubles. I needed to stay the course, keep on writing, keep on telling the story of New Orleans. I needed to do what I had to do, the consequences be damned, and what I had to do was dig further and further into what has happened around here—to the people, my friends, my city, the region.

40   Lord, what an insufferable mess it all is. I'm not going to get better, I thought. I'm in too deep.

41   In his book *Darkness Visible: A Memoir of Madness*, which is the best literary guide to depression that I have found, William Styron recounts his descent into and recovery from depression. One of the biggest obstacles, he says, is the term itself, what he calls "a true wimp of a word."

42   He traces the medical use of the term to a Swiss psychiatrist named Adolf Meyer, who, Styron says, "had a tin ear for the finer rhythms of English and therefore was unaware of the semantic damage he had inflicted by offering 'depression' as a descriptive noun for such a dreadful and raging disease.

43   "Nonetheless, for over 75 years the word has slithered innocuously through the language like a slug, leaving little trace of its intrinsic malevolence and preventing, by its very insipidity, a general awareness of the horrible intensity of the disease when [it is] out of control."

44   He continues: "As one who has suffered from the malady in extremis yet returned to tell the tale, I would lobby for a truly arresting designation. 'Brainstorm,' for instance, has unfortunately been preempted to describe, somewhat jocularly, intellectual inspiration. But something along these lines is needed.

45   "Told that someone's mood disorder has evolved into a storm—a veritable howling tempest in the brain . . . even the uninformed layman might display sympathy rather than the standard reaction that 'depression' evokes, something akin to 'So what?' or 'You'll pull out of it' or 'We all have bad days.'"

46   Styron is a helluva writer. His words were my life. I was having one serious brainstorm. Hell, it was a brain hurricane, Category 5. But what happens when your despair starts bleeding over into the lives of those around you? What happens when you can't get out of your car at the gas station even when you're out of gas? (Man, talk about the perfect metaphor.)

47   Then last summer, a colleague of mine at the newspaper took a bad mix of medications and went on a violent driving spree, an episode that ended with his pleading with the cops who surrounded him with guns drawn to shoot him.

48   He had gone over the cliff. And I thought to myself: If I don't do something, I'm next.

49   The first visit to my psychiatrist, who asked not to be identified for this story, was August 15, 2006. I told him I had doubts about his ability to make me feel better. I pled guilty to skepticism. I'm no Tom Cruise[2]; psychiatry is fine, I thought. For other people.

50   My very first exchange with my doctor had a morbidly comic element to it. At least, I thought so. Approaching his office, I had noticed a dead cat in his yard. Freshly dead, with flies just beginning to gather around the eyes. My initial worry was that some kid who loves this cat might see it, so I said to him, "Before we start, do you know about the cat?"

51   Yes, he told me. It was being taken care of. Then he paused and said, "Well, you're still noticing the environment around you. That's a good sign."

52   The analyst in him had kicked in, but the patient in me was still resisting. In my lifelong habit of damping down serious discussions with sarcasm, I said to him: "Yeah, but what if the dead cat was the only thing I saw? What if I didn't see or hear the traffic or the trees or the birds or anything else?"

53   I crack myself up. I see dead things. Get it?

54   Yeah, neither did he.

55   We talked for an hour. He told me he wanted to talk to me three or four times before he made a diagnosis and prescribed any medication. When I came home from that first visit without a prescription, my wife was despondent and my editor enraged. To them, it was plain to see I needed something, anything, and fast.

---

[2] The actor Tom Cruise, a member of the Church of Scientology, made headlines when he denounced psychiatry treatments for depression on the *Oprah Winfrey Show*.

56   Unbeknownst to me, my wife immediately wrote a letter to my doctor, pleading with him to put me on something. Midway through my second session, I must have convinced him as well because he pulled out some samples of a drug called Cymbalta.

57   He said it could take a few weeks to kick in. Best case, four days. Its reaction time would depend on how much body fat I had; the more I had, the longer it would take. That was a good sign for me. By August, I had become a skeletal version of my pre-K self.

58   Before I left that second session, he told me to change the message on my phone, that "emotionally unavailable" thing. Not funny, he said.

59   I began taking Cymbalta on August 24, a Thursday. Since I had practically no body fat to speak of, the drug kicked in immediately. That whole weekend, I felt like I was in the throes of a drug rush: mildly euphoric, but also leery of what was happening inside me. I felt off balance. But I felt better, too. I told my wife this, but she was guarded. My long-standing gloom had cast such a pall over our relationship that she took a wait-and-see attitude.

60   By Monday, the dark curtain had lifted almost entirely. The despondence and incapacitation vanished, just like that, and I was who I used to be: energetic, sarcastic, playful, affectionate, and alive.

61   I started talking to Kelly about plans for the kids at school, extracurricular activities, weekend vacations. I had not realized until that moment that while I was stuck in my malaise, I had had no vision of the future whatsoever. It was almost like not living.

62   Kelly came around. We became husband and wife again. We became friends. It felt like a come-to-Jesus experience. It felt like a miracle. But it was just medicine, plain and simple.

63   I asked my doctor to tell me exactly what was wrong with me so I could explain it in this story. I still don't really understand it, the science of depression, the actions of synapses, transmitters, blockers, and stimulants. *The Diagnostic and Statistical Manual of Mental Disorders*, psychiatry's chief handbook, practically doubles in size every time it's reprinted, filled with newer and clearer clinical trials, research, and explanations.

64   But here's my doctor's take: The amount of cortisol, a hormone produced in response to chronic stress, increased to dangerous levels in my brain. The overproduction was blocking the transmission of serotonin and norepinephrine, neurotransmitters that mediate messages between nerves in the brain. This communication system is the basic source of all mood and behavior.

65   My brain was literally shorting out. The cells were not communicating properly. Chemical imbalances were dogging the work of my neurotransmitters, my electrical wiring. A real and true physiological deterioration had begun.

66   I had a disease. This I was willing to accept (grudgingly, since it ran against my lifelong philosophy of self-determination). I pressed my doctor: What is the difference between sad and depressed? How do you know when you've crossed over?

67   "Post-traumatic stress disorder is bandied about as a common diagnosis in this community, but I think that's probably not the case," he told me. "What people are suffering from here is what I call Katrina syndrome—marked by sleep disturbance, recent memory impairment, and increased irritability.

68   "Much of this is totally normal. . . . But when you have the thousand-yard stare, when your ability to function is impaired, then you have gone from 'discomfort' to 'pathologic.' If you don't feel like you can go anywhere or do anything—or sometimes, even move—then you are sick."

69   And that was me. And if that is you, let me offer some unsolicited advice, something that you've already been told a thousand times by people who love you, something you really ought to consider listening to this time: Get help.

70   I hate being dependent on a drug. Hate it more than I can say. But if the alternative is a proud stoicism in the face of sorrow accompanied by prolonged and unspeakable despair—well, I'll take dependence.

71   Today, I can take my kids to school in the morning and mingle effortlessly with the other parents. Crowds don't freak me out. I'm not tired all day, every day. I love going to the grocery store. I can pump gas. I notice the smell of night-blooming jasmine and I play with my kids and I clean up after my dog.

72   The only effect on my writing I have noticed is that the darkness lifted. I can still channel anger, humor, and irony, the three speeds I need on my editorial stick shift.

73   And I'm not the only one who senses the change. Everyone sees the difference, even readers. I'm not gaunt. I make eye contact. I can talk about the weather, the Saints, whatever. It doesn't have to be so dire, every word and motion.

74   Strange thing is this: I never cry anymore. Ever.

75   I cried every day from August 29, 2005, until August 24, 2006—360 days straight. And then I stopped. Maybe the extremes of emotion have been smoothed over, but, truthfully, I've shed enough tears for two lifetimes. Even at the Saints' *Monday Night Football* game, a moment that weeks earlier would have sent me reeling into spasms of open weeping, I held it together. A lump in my throat, to be sure, but no prostration anymore.

76   It's my movie now. I am part of the flow of humanity that clogs our streets and sidewalks, taking part in and being part of the community and its growth. I have clarity, and oh, what a vision it is.

77   I am not cured, not by any means. Clinical trials show Cymbalta has an 80 percent success rate after six months, and as I write this, I'm just two months in. I felt a backwards tilt recently—the long stare, the pacing, it crept in one weekend—and it scared me so badly that I went to my doctor and we agreed to increase the strength of my medication.

78   Before Katrina, I would have called somebody like me a wuss. Not to my face. But it's what I would have thought, this talk of mood swings and loss of control, all this psychobabble and hope-dope. What a load of crap. Get a grip, I would have said.

79   And that's exactly what I did, through a door that was hidden from me, but that I was finally able to see. I have a disease. Medicine saved me. I am living proof.

80   Emphasis on living.

Exercises

Do not refer to the selection for Exercises A, B, and C unless your instructor directs you to do so.

A. DETERMINING THE MAIN IDEA AND PURPOSE

Choose the best answer.

_____ 1. The main idea of the selection is that
   a. the writer's immersing himself in the sad stories resulting from Katrina led to a nearly crippling bout with depression.
   b. the instances of depression in New Orleans multiplied exponentially as a result of Katrina's devastation.
   c. for the writer, everyone else's troubles were more important than dealing with his own mental health.
   d. the writer believed that seeking treatment for depression only indicated a form of psychological weakness that he refused to give in to.

_____ 2. The writer's purpose is to
   a. compare his experiences with depression and recovery with those that other New Orleans residents endured as a result of Hurricane Katrina.
   b. describe a nightmarish journey, from his confrontation with depression to his gradual recovery.
   c. examine current psychological theories about the origin of depression.
   d. examine the experiences he and so many other Katrina victims underwent in the days following the hurricane.

B. COMPREHENDING MAIN IDEAS

Choose the correct answer.

_____ 1. One of the earliest manifestations of Rose's depression was his inability to
   a. complete his usual newspaper assignments.
   b. eat.
   c. sleep.
   d. interact with others.

_____ 2. Rather than engage in life's usual activities, Rose says that he essentially became
   a. darkness visible.
   b. a dead man walking.
   c. a television addict.
   d. bedridden.

_____ 3. As a result of his newspaper columns about the hurricane's aftermath, Rose received

    a. thousands of accounts of death and destruction from newspaper readers.

    b. a warning from his newspaper editors to make his stories more optimistic.

    c. hundreds of suggestions for how he could help himself recover.

    d. solace and relief that made him forget about his own troubles.

4. Rose rejected psychiatric help at first because

_____

_____ **5.** Rose quotes William Styron who says that the word *depression* does not do justice to the intensity of the disease and its effects on the sufferer. He says that a better term might be

    a. malevolence of the spirit.

    b. brainstorm.

    c. whirlwind.

    d. psychological abyss.

6. What ultimately saved Rose from his crippling affliction?

_____

COMPREHENSION SCORE

Score your answers for Exercises A and B as follows:

A. No. right _____ × 2 = _____

B. No. right _____ × 1 = _____

Total points from A and B _____ × 10 = _____ percent

C. SEQUENCING

These sentences from one paragraph in the selection may have been scrambled. Read the sentences and choose the sequence that puts them back into logical order. Do not refer to the original selection.

1 That summer, with the darkness clinging to me like humidity, my stories in the *Times-Picayune* moved from gray to brown to black. **2** Readers wanted stories of hope, inspiration, and triumph, something to cling to; I gave them anger and sadness and gloom. **3** They started e-mailing me, telling me I was bringing them down when they were already down enough.

_____ Which of the following represents the correct sequence for these sentences?

    a. 3, 2, 1

    b. 2, 3, 1

    c. 1, 3, 2

    d. Correct as written.

You may refer to the selection as you work through the remaining exercises.

D. IDENTIFYING SUPPORTING DETAILS

Place an X beside each statement that *directly* supports this main idea from the selection: Rose's depression manifested itself in some serious ways emotionally before he finally sought help from a psychiatrist.

1. _____ He stopped going to the grocery store and went to his office as little as possible.

2. _____ His hands shook, and he walked unsteadily.

3. _____ He tried to keep an open line of communication with his children.

4. _____ He developed a "thousand-yard stare."

5. _____ He read William Styron's account of his depression, *Darkness Visible.*

6. _____ He rarely shaved or bathed and stayed in bed as long as he could.

7. _____ He kept his sense of humor, even though it was dark.

8. _____ His stories were relentlessly gloomy and filled with anger and sadness.

E. UNDERSTANDING VOCABULARY

Choose the best definition according to an analysis of word parts or the context.

_____ 1. A lot of legroom, *empathy,* and forgiveness [paragraph 11]
   a. suffering
   b. identification with another's experience
   c. intense feeling of sorrow
   d. emotional distance or detachment

_____ 2. *legions* of people [16]
   a. multitudes, large numbers
   b. various groups or classes
   c. urban residents
   d. army soldiers

_____ 3. more accounts of death and *despondency* [17]
   a. destruction, damage
   b. flooding, deluge
   c. bravery, courage
   d. depression, dejection

_____ 4. the star of a *bizarre* constellation [35]
   a. brightly shining
   b. difficult to comprehend
   c. strange, odd
   d. crowded, overflowing

_____ 5. slithered *innocuously* [43]
   a. harmfully
   b. harmlessly

      c. quietly
      d. without notice

_____ **6.** to describe, somewhat *jocularly* [44]
      a. jokingly, humorously
      b. accurately, precisely
      c. colorfully, vividly
      d. critically, unsympathetically

F. USING VOCABULARY

From the following list of vocabulary words, choose a word that fits in each blank according to both the grammatical structure of the sentence and the context. Use each word in the list only once. Do not change the form of the word. (Note that there are more words than blanks.)

abyss	inertia	empathy	toll
bizarre	innocuously	solicitous	leery
euphoric	malaise	credibility	immersed

1. Rose writes that as he _____ himself in the sad stories from Katrina survivors, he descended into an _____ that he couldn't escape from.

2. His readers wrote him _____ letters, but the archive of sad stories had taken its _____ on him emotionally; he suffered from an _____ and from _____ a that he could not shake off.

3. _____ of psychiatrists, he placed no _____ in the idea that depression was a medical condition that could be cured by medication.

G. PARAPHRASING EXERCISE

Here are some sentences from the selection. Write a paraphrase of each passage in the space provided.

1. I never considered seeking treatment. I was afraid medication might alter my emotions to a point of insensitivity, lower my antenna to where I could no longer feel the acute grip that Katrina and the flood have on the city's psyche.

_____

_____

_____

2. Maybe my case is more extreme because I immersed myself in the horror and became a full-time chronicler of sorrowful tales—an audience for other people's pain. There is no such thing as leaving it behind at the office when a whole city takes the dive.

_____

_____

_____

H. SUMMARIZING EXERCISE

Write a summary of paragraphs 41–43 in the space below. The passage is approximately 150 words long, so your summary should be about 35 or 40 words.

_____

_____

_____

I.   TOPICS FOR DISCUSSION

1. Aside from his eventual decision to get help, what positive characteristics does Rose exhibit in his chronicle that seem to have helped him weather his depression without committing suicide?
2. Hurricane Katrina was a terrible natural disaster, one of the worst in American history. From what Rose writes, and from other sources, why did this particular natural disaster so strongly affect the nation's psyche?

J.   TOPICS FOR WRITING

1. If you have experience with someone suffering from depression, write a short chronicle tracing the person's bout with the illness—including symptoms, emotional and physical effects, and the ramifications of the disease on those around him or her.
2. Do some research on an illness or medical condition that has afflicted a member of your family. Use both print and online sources. Then write an essay summarizing the information you have gathered. Include a discussion of causes, symptoms, and treatment.

EXPLORE THE WEB

- Photographs of Hurricane Katrina's impact on New Orleans are widely available online. Go to Google, click on "images," and then type in "Katrina photographs."

- If you would like to learn more about depression—its symptoms, diagnosis, and treatment—do an online search or begin your study with this informative and authoritative website: www.nimh.nih.gov/health/topics/depression

IN THE BOOKSTORE

- Dave Eggers's 2009 nonfiction book, *Zeitoun*, is a readable account of what befell one New Orleans resident, a Syrian-American man who owned a painting contract company. Zeitoun sent his family out of the city when the order to evacuate came, but he decided to stay to help. What happened to him is chilling and harrowing.

12

VIRGINIA MORELL
Minds of Their Own

Alex, an African gray parrot; Betsy, a border collie; and Maya, a bottlenose dolphin—these diverse creatures demonstrate a remarkable facility for language, challenging the usual human claims of superiority in this regard. Virginia Morell is a science writer who writes frequently for National Geographic, *where this article was originally published. She is also the author of* Ancestral Passions: The Leakey Family *(1996).*

Vocabulary Analysis

WORD PARTS

-ize [digitized (paragraph 27); categorize (paragraph 37); synchronize (paragraph 81)] The suffix *-ize* is one of the most common verb endings in English. Its most common meaning is "to come to be" or "to make into" added to the root noun or adjective. Thus, *digitized* means "to make digital," *categorize* means "to put into categories," and *synchronize* means to "make something happen at the same time." To determine a meaning of a verb ending with *-ize*, simply drop off the ending and identify the meaning of the root. Here is an interesting word ending with the suffix *-ize*. What does it mean? Consult a dictionary if necessary.

bowdlerize _____

WORD FAMILIES

chron- [paragraph 81] As you saw in the preceding section, *synchronize* refers to several actions that occur at the same time. The root *chron-*, from Greek *khronos*, means "time." The prefix *syn-* means "same." Thus, when put together, the word means, literally "same" "time" "make." Other words containing the root *chron-* are *chronicle*, a record of the times; *chronological* (time order); and *chronometer* (a very precise type of watch).

Sometimes people develop a chronic cough. What does this mean? _____
_____

Another interesting word using the root *chron-* is *anachronism*. If you are unfamiliar with this word, look it up in the dictionary and write the definition in the space provided. Then come up with an example that fits this definition.

Definition   _____

Example   _____

Note: For Exercise D and E following the selection, you will be asked to distinguish between a fact and an opinion. A *fact* is a statement that can be verified or proved either by measurement, observation, or some other form of proof. An *opinion* represents someone's subjective interpretation and therefore can't be verified or proved.

VIRGINIA MORELL

Minds of Their Own

1   In 1977 Irene Pepperberg, a recent graduate of Harvard University, did something very bold. At a time when animals still were considered automatons, she set out to find what was on another creature's mind by talking to it. She brought a one-year-old African gray parrot she named Alex into her lab to teach him to reproduce the sounds of the English language. "I thought if he learned to communicate, I could ask him questions about how he sees the world."

2   When Pepperberg began her dialogue with Alex, who died last September at the age of 31, many scientists believed animals were incapable of any thought. They were simply machines, robots programmed to react to stimuli but lacking the ability to think or feel. Any pet owner would disagree. We see the love in our dogs' eyes and know that, of course, Spot has thoughts and emotions. But such claims remain highly controversial. Gut instinct is not science, and it is all too easy to project human thoughts and feelings onto another creature. How, then, does a scientist prove that an animal is capable of thinking—that it is able to acquire information about the world and act on it?

3   "That's why I started my studies with Alex," Pepperberg said. They were seated—she at her desk, he on top of his cage—in her lab, a windowless room about the size of a boxcar, at Brandeis University. Newspapers lined the floor; baskets of bright toys were stacked on the shelves. They were clearly a team—and because of their work, the notion that animals can think is no longer so fanciful.

4   Certain skills are considered key signs of higher mental abilities: good memory, a grasp of grammar and symbols, self-awareness, understanding others' motives, imitating others, and being creative. Bit by bit, in ingenious experiments, researchers have documented these talents in other species, gradually chipping away at what we thought made human beings distinctive while offering a glimpse of where our own abilities came from. Scrub jays know that other jays are thieves and that stashed food can spoil; sheep can recognize faces; chimpanzees use a variety of tools to probe termite mounds and even use weapons to hunt small mammals; dolphins can imitate human postures; the archerfish, which stuns insects with a sudden blast of water, can learn how to aim its squirt

simply by watching an experienced fish perform the task. And Alex the parrot turned out to be a surprisingly good talker.

5   Thirty years after the Alex studies began, Pepperberg and a changing collection of assistants were still giving him English lessons. The humans, along with two younger parrots, also served as Alex's flock, providing the social input all parrots crave. Like any flock, this one—as small as it was—had its share of drama. Alex dominated his fellow parrots, acted huffy at times around Pepperberg, tolerated the other female humans, and fell to pieces over a male assistant who dropped by for a visit. ("If you were a man," Pepperberg said, after noting Alex's aloofness toward me, "he'd be on your shoulder in a second, barfing cashews in your ear.")

6   Pepperberg bought Alex in a Chicago pet store. She let the store's assistant pick him out because she didn't want other scientists saying later that she'd deliberately chosen an especially smart bird for her work. Given that Alex's brain was the size of a shelled walnut, most researchers thought Pepperberg's interspecies communication study would be futile.

7   "Some people actually called me crazy for trying this," she said. "Scientists thought that chimpanzees were better subjects, although, of course, chimps can't speak."

8   Chimpanzees, bonobos, and gorillas have been taught to use sign language and symbols to communicate with us, often with impressive results. The bonobo Kanzi, for instance, carries his symbol-communication board with him so he can "talk" to his human researchers, and he has invented combinations of symbols to express his thoughts. Nevertheless, this is not the same thing as having an animal look up at you, open his mouth, and speak.

9   Pepperberg walked to the back of the room, where Alex sat on top of his cage preening his pearl gray feathers. He stopped at her approach and opened his beak.

10   "Want grape," Alex said.

11   "He hasn't had his breakfast yet," Pepperberg explained, "so he's a little put out."

12   Alex returned to preening, while an assistant prepared a bowl of grapes, green beans, apple and banana slices, and corn on the cob.

13   Under Pepperberg's patient tutelage, Alex learned how to use his vocal tract to imitate almost one hundred English words, including the sounds for all of these foods, although he calls an apple a "ban-erry."

14   "Apples taste a little bit like bananas to him, and they look a little bit like cherries, so Alex made up that word for them," Pepperberg said.

15   Alex could count to six and was learning the sounds for seven and eight.

16   "I'm sure he already knows both numbers," Pepperberg said. "He'll probably be able to count to ten, but he's still learning to say the words. It takes far more time to teach him certain sounds than I ever imagined."

17   After breakfast, Alex preened again, keeping an eye on the flock. Every so often, he leaned forward and opened his beak: "Ssse . . . won."

18   "That's good, Alex," Pepperberg said. "Seven. The number is seven."

19   "Ssse . . . won! Se . . . won!"

20   "He's practicing," she explained. "That's how he learns. He's thinking about how to say that word, how to use his vocal tract to make the correct sound."

21   It sounded a bit mad, the idea of a bird having lessons to practice, and willingly doing it. But after listening to and watching Alex, it was difficult to argue with Pepperberg's explanation for his behaviors. She wasn't handing him treats for the repetitious work or rapping him on the claws to make him say the sounds.

22   "He has to hear the words over and over before he can correctly imitate them," Pepperberg said, after pronouncing "seven" for Alex a good dozen times in a row. "I'm not trying to see if Alex can learn a human language," she added. "That's never been the point. My plan always was to use his imitative skills to get a better understanding of avian cognition."

23   In other words, because Alex was able to produce a close approximation of the sounds of some English words, Pepperberg could ask him questions about a bird's basic understanding of the world. She couldn't ask him what he was thinking about, but she could ask him about his knowledge of numbers, shapes, and colors. To demonstrate, Pepperberg carried Alex on her arm to a tall wooden perch in the middle of the room. She then retrieved a green key and a small green cup from a basket on a shelf. She held up the two items to Alex's eye.

24   "What's same?" she asked.

25   Without hesitation, Alex's beak opened: "Co-lor,"

26   "What's different?" Pepperberg asked.

27   "Shape," Alex said. His voice had the digitized sound of a cartoon character. Since parrots lack lips (another reason it was difficult for Alex to pronounce some sounds, such as *ba)*, the words seemed to come from the air around him, as if a ventriloquist were speaking. But the words—and what can only be called the thoughts—were entirely his.

28   For the next 20 minutes, Alex ran through his tests, distinguishing colors, shapes, sizes, and materials (wool versus wood versus metal). He did some simple arithmetic, such as counting the yellow toy blocks among a pile of mixed hues.

29   And, then, as if to offer final proof of the mind inside his bird's brain, Alex spoke up. "Talk clearly!" he commanded, when one of the younger birds Pepperberg was also teaching mispronounced the word green. "Talk clearly!"

30   "Don't be a smart aleck," Pepperberg said, shaking her head at him. "He knows all this, and he gets bored, so he interrupts the others, or he gives the wrong answer just to be obstinate. At this stage, he's like a teenage son; he's moody, and I'm never sure what he'll do."

31   "Wanna go tree," Alex said in a tiny voice.

32   Alex had lived his entire life in captivity, but he knew that beyond the lab's door, there was a hallway and a tall window framing a leafy elm tree. He liked to see the tree, so Pepperberg put her hand out for him to climb aboard. She walked him down the hall into the tree's green light.

33   "Good boy! Good birdie," Alex said, bobbing on her hand.

34   "Yes, you're a good boy. You're a good birdie." And she kissed his feathered head.

35   He was a good birdie until the end, and Pepperberg was happy to report th.
      when he died he had finally mastered "seven."

36   Many of Alex's cognitive skills, such as his ability to understand the concepts of
      same and different, are generally ascribed only to higher mammals, particularly
      primates. But parrots, like great apes (and humans), live a long time in complex
      societies. And like primates, these birds must keep track of the dynamics of
      changing relationships and environments.

37   "They need to be able to distinguish colors to know when a fruit is ripe or
      unripe," Pepperberg noted. "They need to categorize things—what's edible,
      what isn't—and to know the shapes of predators. And it helps to have a concept
      of numbers if you need to keep track of your flock, and to know who's single
      and who's paired up. For a long-lived bird, you can't do all of this with instinct;
      cognition must be involved."

38   Being able mentally to divide the world into simple abstract categories would
      seem a valuable skill for many organisms. Is that ability, then, part of the evolu-
      tionary drive that led to human intelligence?

39   Charles Darwin, who attempted to explain how human intelligence devel-
      oped, extended his theory of evolution to the human brain: Like the rest of our
      physiology, intelligence must have evolved from simpler organisms, since all
      animals face the same general challenges of life. They need to find mates, food,
      and a path through the woods, sea, or sky—tasks that Darwin argued require
      problem-solving and categorizing abilities. Indeed, Darwin went so far as to
      suggest that earthworms are cognitive beings because, based on his close obser-
      vations, they have to make judgments about the kinds of leafy matter they use
      to block their tunnels. He hadn't expected to find thinking invertebrates and
      remarked that the hint of earthworm intelligence "has surprised me more than
      anything else in regard to worms."

40   To Darwin, the earthworm discovery demonstrated that degrees of intelligence
      could be found throughout the animal kingdom. But the Darwinian approach
      to animal intelligence was cast aside in the early 20th century, when research-
      ers decided that field observations were simply "anecdotes," usually tainted by
      anthropomorphism. In an effort to be more rigorous, many embraced behavior-
      ism, which regarded animals as little more than machines, and focused their stud-
      ies on the laboratory white rat—since one "machine" would behave like any other.

41   But if animals are simply machines, how can the appearance of human intel-
      ligence be explained? Without Darwin's evolutionary perspective, the greater
      cognitive skills of people did not make sense biologically. Slowly the pendulum
      has swung away from the animal-as-machine model and back toward Darwin. A
      whole range of animal studies now suggest that the roots of cognition are deep,
      widespread, and highly malleable.

42   Just how easily new mental skills can evolve is perhaps best illustrated by
      dogs. Most owners talk to their dogs and expect them to understand. But this
      canine talent wasn't fully appreciated until a border collie named Rico appeared
      on a German TV game show in 2001. Rico knew the names of some 200 toys and
      acquired the names of new ones with ease.

43   Researchers at the Max Planck Institute for Evolutionary Anthropology in Leipzig heard about Rico and arranged a meeting with him and his owners. That led to a scientific report revealing Rico's uncanny language ability: He could learn and remember words as quickly as a toddler. Other scientists had shown that two-year-old-children—who acquire around ten new words a day—have an innate set of principles that guides this task. The ability is seen as one of the key building blocks in language acquisition. The Max Planck scientists suspect that the same principles guide Rico's word learning, and that the technique he uses for learning words is identical to that of humans.

44   To find more examples, the scientists read all the letters from hundreds of people claiming that their dogs had Rico's talent. In fact, only two—both border collies—had comparable skills. One of them—the researchers call her Betsy—has a vocabulary of more than 300 words.

45   "Even our closest relatives, the great apes, can't do what Betsy can do—hear a word only once or twice and know that the acoustic pattern stands for something," said Juliane Kaminski, a cognitive psychologist who worked with Rico and is now studying Betsy. She and her colleague Sebastian Tempelmann had come to Betsy's home in Vienna to give her a fresh battery of tests. Kaminski petted Betsy, while Tempelmann set up a video camera.

46   "Dogs' understanding of human forms of communication is something new that has evolved,"Kaminski said, "something that's developed in them because of their long association with humans." Although Kaminski has not yet tested wolves, she doubts they have this language skill. Maybe these collies are especially good at it because they're working dogs and highly motivated, and in their traditional herding jobs, they must listen very closely to their owners."

47   Scientists think that dogs were domesticated about 15,000 years ago, a relatively short time in which to evolve language skills. But how similar are these skills to those of humans? For abstract thinking, we employ symbols, letting one thing stand for another. Kaminski and Tempelmann were testing whether dogs can do this too.

48   Betsy's owner—whose pseudonym is Schaefer—summoned Betsy, who obediently stretched out at Schaefer's feet, eyes fixed on her face. Whenever Schaefer spoke, Betsy attentively cocked her head from side to side.

49   Kaminski handed Schaefer a stack of color photographs and asked her to choose one. Each image depicted a dog's toy against a white background—toys Betsy had never seen before. They weren't actual toys; they were only images of toys. Could Betsy connect a two-dimensional picture to a three-dimensional object?

50   Schaefer held up a picture of a fuzzy, rainbow-colored Frisbee and urged Betsy to find it. Betsy studied the photograph and Schaefer's face, then ran into the kitchen, where the Frisbee was placed among three other toys and photographs of each toy. Betsy brought either the Frisbee or the photograph of the Frisbee to Schaefer every time.

51   "It wouldn't have been wrong if she'd just brought the photograph," Kaminski said. "But I think Betsy can use a picture, without a name, to find an object. Still, it will take many more tests to prove this."

52   Even then, Kaminski is unsure that other scientists will ever accept her discovery because Betsy's abstract skill, as minor as it may seem to us, may tread all too closely to human thinking.

53   Still, we remain the inventive species. No other animal has built skyscrapers, written sonnets, or made a computer. Yet animal researchers say that creativity, like other forms of intelligence, did not simply spring from nothingness. It, too, has evolved.

54   "People were surprised to discover that chimpanzees make tools," said Alex Kacelnik, a behavioral ecologist at Oxford University, referring to the straws and sticks chimpanzees shape to pull termites from their nests. "But people also thought, 'Well, they share our ancestry—of course they're smart.' Now we're finding these kinds of exceptional behaviors in some species of birds. But we don't have a recently shared ancestry with birds. Their evolutionary history is very different; our last common ancestor with all birds was a reptile that lived over 300 million years ago.

55   "This is not trivial," Kacelnik continued. "It means that evolution can invent similar forms of advanced intelligence more than once—that it's not something reserved only for primates or mammals."

56   Kacelnik and his colleagues are studying one of these smart species, the New Caledonian crow, which lives in the forests of that Pacific island. New Caledonian crows are among the most skilled of tool-making and tool-using birds, forming probes and hooks from sticks and leaf stems to poke into the crowns of the palm trees, where fat grubs hide. Since these birds, like chimpanzees, make and use tools, researchers can look for similarities in the evolutionary processes that shaped their brains. Something about the environments of both species favored the evolution of tool-making neural powers.

57   But is their use of tools rigid and limited, or can they be inventive? Do they have what researchers call mental flexibility? Chimpanzees certainly do. In the wild, a chimpanzee may use four sticks of different sizes to extract the honey from a bee's nest. And in captivity, they can figure out how to position several boxes so they can retrieve a banana hanging from a rope.

58   Answering that question for New Caledonian crows—extremely shy birds—wasn't easy. Even after years of observing them in the wild, researchers couldn't determine if the birds' ability was innate, or if they learned to make and use their tools by watching one another. If it was a genetically inherited skill, could they, like the chimps, use their talent in different, creative ways?

59   To find out, Kacelnik and his students brought 23 crows of varying ages (all but one caught in the wild) to the aviary in his Oxford lab and let them mate. Four hatchlings were raised in captivity, and all were carefully kept away from the adults, so they had no opportunity to be taught about tools. Yet soon after they fledged, all picked up sticks to probe busily into cracks and shaped different materials into tools. "So we know that at least the bases of tool use are inherited," Kacelnik said. "And now the question is, what else can they do with tools?"

60   Plenty. In his office, Kacelnik played a video of a test he'd done with one of the wild-caught crows, Betty, who had died recently from an infection. In the film, Betty flies into a room. She's a glossy-black bird with a crow's bright, inquisitive

eyes, and she immediately spies the test before her: a glass tube with a tiny basket lodged in its center. The basket holds a bit of meat. The scientists had placed two pieces of wire in the room. One was bent into a hook, the other was straight. They figured Betty would choose the hook to lift the basket by its handle.

61 But experiments don't always go according to plan. Another crow had stolen the hook before Betty could find it. Betty is undeterred. She looks at the meat in the basket, then spots the straight piece of wire. She picks it up with her beak, pushes one end into a crack in the floor, and uses her beak to bend the other end into a hook. Thus armed, she lifts the basket out of the tube.

62 "This was the first time Betty had ever seen a piece of wire like this," Kacelnik said. "But she knew she could use it to make a hook and exactly where she needed to bend it to make the size she needed."

63 They gave Betty other tests, each requiring a slightly different solution, such as making a hook out of a flat piece of aluminum rather than a wire. Each time, Betty invented a new tool and solved the problem. "It means she had a mental representation of what it was she wanted to make. Now that," Kacelnik said, "is a major kind of cognitive sophistication."

64 This is the larger lesson of animal cognition research: It humbles us. We are not alone in our ability to invent or plan or to contemplate ourselves—or even to plot and lie.

65 Deceptive acts require a complicated form of thinking, since you must be able to attribute intentions to the other person and predict that person's behavior. One school of thought argues that human intelligence evolved partly because of the pressure of living in a complex society of calculating beings. Chimpanzees, orangutans, gorillas, and bonobos share this capacity with us. In the wild, primatologists have seen apes hide food from the alpha male or have sex behind his back.

66 Birds, too, can cheat. Laboratory studies show that western scrub jays can know another bird's intentions and act on that knowledge. A jay that has stolen food itself, for example, knows that if another jay watches it hide a nut, there's a chance the nut will be stolen. So the first jay will return to move the nut when the other jay is gone.

67 "It's some of the best evidence so far of experience projection in another species," said Nicky Clayton in her aviary lab at Cambridge University. "I would describe it as, 'I know that you know where I have hidden my stash of food, and if I were in your shoes I'd steal it, so I'm going to move my stash to a place you don't know about.'"

68 This study, by Clayton and her colleague Nathan Emery, is the first to show the kind of ecological pressures, such as the need to hide food for winter use, that would lead to the evolution of such mental abilities. Most provocatively, her research demonstrates that some birds possess what is often considered another uniquely human skill: the ability to recall a specific past event. Scrub jays, for example, seem to know how long ago they cached a particular kind of food, and they manage to retrieve it before it spoils.

69 Human cognitive psychologists call this kind of memory "episodic memory" and argue that it can exist only in a species that can mentally travel back in time. Despite Clayton's studies, some refuse to concede this ability to the jays. "Animals are stuck in time," explained Sara Shettleworth, a comparative psycholo-

gist at the University of Toronto in Canada, meaning that they don't distinguish among past, present, and future the way humans do. Since animals lack language, she said, they probably also lack "the extra layer of imagination and explanation" that provides the running mental narrative accompanying our actions.

70   Such skepticism is a challenge for Clayton. "We have good evidence that the jays remember the what, where, and when of specific caching events, which is the original definition of episodic memory. But now the goalposts have moved." It's a common complaint among animal researchers. Whenever they find a mental skill in a species that is reminiscent of a special human ability, the human cognition scientists change the definition. But the animal researchers may underestimate their power—it is their discoveries that compel the human side to shore up the divide.

71   "Sometimes the human cognitive psychologists can be so fixed on their definitions that they forget how fabulous these animal discoveries are," said Clive Wynne of the University of Florida, who has studied cognition in pigeons and marsupials. "We're glimpsing intelligence throughout the animal kingdom, which is what we should expect. It's a bush, not a single-trunk tree with a line leading only to us."

72   Some of the branches on that bush have led to such degrees of intelligence that we should blush for ever having thought any animal a mere machine.

73   In the late 1960s a cognitive psychologist named Louis Herman began investigating the cognitive abilities of bottlenose dolphins. Like humans, dolphins are highly social and cosmopolitan, living in subpolar to tropical environments worldwide; they're highly vocal; and they have special sensory skills, such as echolocation. By the 1980s Herman's cognitive studies were focused on a group of four young dolphins—Akeakamai, Phoenix, Elele, and Hiapo—at the Kewalo Basin Marine Mammal Laboratory in Hawaii. The dolphins were curious and playful, and they transferred their sociability to Herman and his students.

74   "In our work with the dolphins, we had a guiding philosophy," Herman says, "that we could bring out the full flower of their intellect, just as educators try to bring out the full potential of a human child. Dolphins have these big, highly complex brains. My thought was, 'OK, so you have this pretty brain. Let's see what you can do with it.'"

75   To communicate with the dolphins, Herman and his team invented a hand- and arm-signal language, complete with a simple grammar. For instance, a pumping motion of the closed fists meant "hoop," and both arms extended overhead (as in jumping jacks) meant "ball." A "come here" gesture with a single arm told them to "fetch." Responding to the request "hoop, ball, fetch," Akeakamai would push the ball to the hoop. But if the word order was changed to "ball, hoop, fetch," she would carry the hoop to the ball. Over time she could interpret more grammatically complex requests, such as "right, basket, left, Frisbee, in," asking that she put the Frisbee on her left in the basket on her right. Reversing "left" and "right" in the instruction would reverse Akeakamai's actions. Akeakamai could complete such requests the first time they were made, showing a deep understanding of the grammar of the language.

76   "They're a very vocal species," Herman adds. "Our studies showed that they could imitate arbitrary sounds that we broadcast into their tank, an ability that

may be tied to their own need to communicate. I'm not saying they have a dolphin language. But they are capable of understanding the novel instructions that we convey to them in a tutored language; their brains have that ability.

77   "There are many things they could do that people have always doubted about animals. For example, they correctly interpreted, on the very first occasion, gestured instructions given by a person displayed on a TV screen behind an underwater window. They recognized that television images were representations of the real world that could be acted on in the same way as in the real world."

78   They readily imitated motor behaviors of their instructors too. If a trainer bent backward and lifted a leg, the dolphin would turn on its back and lift its tail in the air. Although imitation was once regarded as a simpleminded skill, in recent years cognitive scientists have revealed that it's extremely difficult, requiring the imitator to form a mental image of the other person's body and pose, then adjust his own body parts into the same position—actions that imply an awareness of one's self.

79   "Here's Elele," Herman says, showing a film of her following a trainer's directions. "Surfboard, dorsal fin, touch." Instantly Elele swam to the board and, leaning to one side, gently laid her dorsal fin on it, an untrained behavior. The trainer stretched her arms straight up, signaling "Hooray!" and Elele leaped into the air, squeaking and clicking with delight.

80   "Elele just loved to be right," Herman said. "And she loved inventing things. We made up a sign for 'create,' which asked a dolphin to create its own behavior."

81   Dolphins often synchronize their movements in the wild, such as leaping and diving side by side, but scientists don't know what signal they use to stay so tightly coordinated. Herman thought he might be able to tease out the technique with his pupils. In the film, Akeakamai and Phoenix are asked to create a trick and do it together. The two dolphins swim away from the side of the pool, circle together underwater for about ten seconds, then leap out of the water, spinning clockwise on their long axis and squirting water from their mouths, every maneuver done at the same instant. "None of this was trained," Herman says, "and it looks to us absolutely mysterious. We don't know how they do it—or did it."

82   He never will. Akeakamai and Phoenix and the two others died accidentally four years ago. Through these dolphins, he made some of the most extraordinary breakthroughs ever in understanding another species' mind—a species that even Herman describes as "alien," given its aquatic life and the fact that dolphins and primates diverged millions of years ago. "That kind of cognitive convergence suggests there must be some similar pressures selecting for intellect," Herman said. "We don't share their biology or ecology. That leaves social similarities—the need to establish relationships and alliances superimposed on a lengthy period of maternal care and longevity—as the likely common driving force."

83   "I loved our dolphins," Herman says, "as I'm sure you love your pets. But it was more than that, more than the love you have for a pet. The dolphins were our colleagues. That's the only word that fits. They were our partners in this research, guiding us into all the capabilities of their minds. When they died, it was like losing our children."

84   Herman pulled a photograph from his file. In it, he is in the pool with Phoenix, who rests her head on his shoulder. He is smiling and reaching back to embrace

her. She is sleek and silvery with appealingly large eyes, and she looks to be smiling too, as dolphins always do. It's an image of love between two beings. In that pool, at least for that moment, there was clearly a meeting of the minds.

Virginia Morell, "Minds of Their Own," *National Geographic* (March 2008). Reprinted by permission of National Geographic Society.

Exercises

Do not refer to the selection for Exercises A, B, and C unless your instructor directs you to do so.

A. DETERMINING THE MAIN IDEA AND PURPOSE

Choose the best answer.

_____ **1.** The main idea of the selection is that
   a. scientists do not accept the concept that animals can think abstractly and use language intelligently; the animals in these studies have just been well trained.
   b. only humans are able to use true language; animals merely imitate sounds without understanding their meaning.
   c. current research on animals suggests that the roots of knowledge are deep and that limited forms of intelligence exist throughout the animal kingdom.
   d. current animal research has chipped away at the idea that human beings are the only creatures who are intelligent and who can use language.

_____ **2.** The writer's purpose is to
   a. offer reasons to support the proposal that more definitive research on animal intelligence needs to be conducted.
   b. summarize research on animal intelligence using illustrations from several species.
   c. convince the reader that animals are just as intelligent as human beings, if not more so.
   d. describe the controversy over experiments using animals.

B. COMPREHENDING MAIN IDEAS

Choose the correct answer.

_____ **1.** One significant problem facing researchers like Irene Pepperberg in her work with Alex, the African gray parrot, is that
   a. it's easy to project human thought and feelings onto creatures, making it necessary to devise research carefully.
   b. other scientists criticize these experiments, making it difficult to get the scientific community to take them seriously.

     c. funding for projects using animals is limited.

     d. animal-rights groups like PETA[1] object to research on animals.

_____ 2. Morell mentions five skills that are key signs of higher mental abilities, all of which are demonstrated in the animals cited in the articles. Which one was *not* mentioned?

     a. a grasp of grammar and symbols

     b. self-awareness

     c. the ability to reproduce human speech

     d. being creative

     e. understanding others' motives

     f. imitating others

3. What was the specific intention of Pepperberg's experiments with Alex, the African gray parrot?

_____

_____ 4. Remarkably, Alex could distinguish between

     a. sameness and difference between colors and shapes.

     b. consonants and vowels in spoken words.

     c. the humans and other parrots that make up his flock.

     d. quantities of objects.

5. Betsy, the border collie, has been studied for her language ability, specifically for her vocabulary of 300 words. What is another of Betsy's remarkable accomplishments?

_____

_____ 6. Scientists theorize that some birds have developed the mental ability to deceive, which probably stems from the

     a. competition for space in which to roam.

     b. innate tendency to be mischievous and to play games.

     c. need to compete with other deceptive creatures.

     d. need to hide food to get them through the winter.

COMPREHENSION SCORE

Score your answers for Exercises A and B as follows:

A. No. right _____ × 2 = _____

B. No. right _____ × 1 = _____

Total points from A and B _____ × 10 = _____ percent

C. SEQUENCING

These sentences from one paragraph in the selection may have been scrambled. Read the sentences and choose the sequence that puts them back into logical order. Do not refer to the original selection.

[1]People for the Ethical Treatment of Animals

1 Laboratory studies show that western scrub jays can know another bird's intentions and act on that knowledge. **2** So the first jay will return to move the nut when the other jay is gone. **3** Birds, too, can cheat. **4** A jay that has stolen food for itself, for example, knows that if another jay watches it hide a nut, there's a chance the nut will be stolen.

_____ Which of the following represents the correct sequence for these sentences?

    a. 1, 3, 4, 2
    b. 3, 4, 2, 1
    c. 3, 1, 4, 2
    d. Correct as written.

You may refer to the selection as you work through the remaining exercises.

D. DISTINGUISHING BETWEEN FACT AND OPINION—1

For each of the following paraphrased statements from the selection, write F if the statement represents a factual statement that can be verified or O if the statement represents the writer's or someone else's subjective interpretation. The first one is done for you.

1. ___F___ Charles Darwin, who attempted to explain how human intelligence developed, extended his theory of evolution to the human brain.

2. _____ Like the rest of our physiology, intelligence must have evolved from simpler organisms, since all animals face the same general challenges of life.

3. _____ They need to find mates, food, and a path through the woods, sea, or sky—tasks that Darwin argued require problem-solving and categorizing abilities.

4. _____ Indeed, Darwin went so far as to suggest that earthworms are cognitive beings because, based on his close observations, they have to make judgments about the kinds of leafy matter they use to block their tunnels.

5. _____ He hadn't expected to find thinking invertebrates and remarked that the hint of earthworm intelligence "has surprised me more than anything else in regard to worms."

E. DISTINGUISHING BETWEEN FACT AND OPINION—2

For each of the following paraphrased statements from the selection, write F if the statement represents a factual statement that can be verified or O if the statement represents the writer's or someone else's subjective interpretation.

1. _____ Dogs' understanding of human communication was a matter of evolution.

2. _____ Dogs' understanding of human communication developed because of their long association with humans.

3. _____   Wolves may not have the same language skills as dogs.

4. _____   Juliane Kaminski, a cognitive psychologist, has not yet tested wolves to determine their language capabilities.

5. _____   Border collies are especially good at understanding human language because they're working dogs.

6. _____   Herding breeds like border collies must listen carefully to their owners as they perform their traditional herding tasks.

F. INTERPRETING MEANING

Where appropriate, write your answers to these questions in your own words.

1. _____   Read paragraph 4 again. How is the main idea developed?
   a. a series of examples
   b. definitions of key terms
   c. a discussion of comparisons, or similar ideas
   d. classification into specific categories

2. Look at paragraph 6 again. Why didn't Irene Pepperberg herself pick out Alex at the pet store? _____

_____

_____

3. From the information presented in paragraphs 12–14, what is remarkable about the word that Alex used to describe an apple? _____

_____

4. What is the most important finding that emerged from the experiments with New Caledonian crows like Betty, as described in paragraphs 59–63?_____

_____

5. _____   Which of the following *best* represents the conclusion of the selection as a whole?
   a. "Gut instinct is not science, and it is all too easy to project human thoughts and feelings onto another creature." [paragraph 2]
   b. "Being able mentally to divide the world into simple abstract categories would seem a valuable skill for many organisms." [paragraph 38]
   c. "A whole range of animal studies now suggest that the roots of cognition are deep, widespread, and highly malleable." [paragraph 41]
   d. "This is the larger lesson of animal cognition research: It humbles us. We are not alone in our ability to invent or plan or to contemplate ourselves—or even to plot and lie." [paragraph 64]

G. UNDERSTANDING VOCABULARY

Look through each numbered paragraph in the following list and find a word that matches each definition. Refer to a dictionary if necessary. An example has been done for you.

Ex. unreal, existing only in the imagination
[paragraphs 2–3] _____ *fanciful* _____

1. marked by inventive skill and imagination [4]
_____

2. quality of being reserved or remote,
distant [5–6]
_____

3. the mental process of knowing, including
reasoning [22–23]
_____

4. spoiled, contaminated [39–40]
_____

5. capable of being shaped, formed, or
changed [40–41]
_____

6. unnaturally keen and perceptive; eerie [43]
_____

7. a false name, used to protect one's
identity [47–48]
_____

8. regard as arising from a certain cause [64–65]
_____

H. USING VOCABULARY—VARIANT WORD FORMS

Write the correct inflected form of the base word (in parentheses) in each of the following sentences. Be sure to add the appropriate ending to fit the grammatical requirements of the sentence. Refer to your dictionary if necessary.

1. (*category*—use a verb) Animals are intelligent because they _____ objects in the real world, such as food.

2. (*anthropology*—use another noun, plural in form) _____ in Leipzig, Germany, have studied Rico's amazing and unnerving ability to acquire language.

3. (*synchronize*—use a noun) One observation scientists have made about dolphin behavior is the _____ of their movements.

4. (*mispronunciation*—use a verb) Alex sometimes _____ words, which was understandable since parrots don't have lips, making some sounds difficult to produce.

5. (*demonstrate*—use an adverb) Having studied earthworms in some depth, Charles Darwin was able _____ to show degrees of intelligence in the animal world.

I. SUMMARIZING EXERCISE

Write a summary of paragraphs 38–41 in the space below. The passage is approximately 350 words long, so your summary should be about 75 words.

_____

_____

_____

_____

J. TOPICS FOR DISCUSSION

1. What is anthropomorphism? Have the scientists who conducted the various studies described in the selection guarded against this problem, and if so, how?
2. Why are some cognitive scientists so skeptical of animal researchers' findings about animal intelligence and animals' ability to use language?
3. Why are research experiments on crows, dolphins, parrots, and dogs like those described in this selection important? What myths and misconceptions have they overturned?

K. TOPICS FOR WRITING

1. Watch either of the two videos listed in Explore the Web on YouTube. Then write a short essay summarizing what you observed. Choosing either Alex or Skidboot, discuss his behavior as it reveals his cognitive skills.
2. If you have an animal of your own, write a short essay in which you assess your pet's intelligence, using examples from your own observation of its behavior. Show that the animal's behavior suggests the use of cognitive skills.

EXPLORE THE WEB

- Alex the African gray parrot died in 2007, but you can see this remarkable bird in action at many videos available on YouTube. Here is one:
- _www.youtube.com/watch?v=R6KvPN_Wt8I_
- Australian cattle dogs, also known as Queensland heelers, are an extremely intelligent breed of herding dogs. Watch a video of the amazing Skidboot, who was owned by a rancher named David Hartwig in Quinlan, Texas. After you watch the video, think about whether the dog is simply performing tricks or whether his actions suggest a higher intelligence. (Skidboot eventually went blind; he died in March 2007.)
- _www.youtube.com/watch?v=P2BfzUIBy9A_
- A great deal of information is available online about Alex's remarkable achievements and Irene Pepperberg's work with him. A good place to start is Wikipedia. Type in "Alex, African Gray Parrot."

13

OLIVIA WU

Alfresco Marriage Market

Olivia Wu is currently executive chef at Google (the Silicon Valley giant is known for the excellent and varied cuisine its employees receive as a benefit). She was formerly a staff reporter at the San Francisco Chronicle, *where this article first appeared, and she has also written for* Barron's. *In addition, she has operated a cooking school and a personal chef/catering service, published two books (*Stir-Fry Meals *and* Turning Fifty), *and she has reported extensively from China, writing both articles and blogs.*

Note: The word alfresco *in the title comes from Italian (though originally from Latin) and means "outdoors" or "in the open" [literally* al *("in") +* fresco *("in the fresh air")]. The word describes accurately the way some marriages are arranged in China, the subject of this selection.*

Vocabulary Analysis

WORD ROOTS

potential In paragraph 5, Wu describes how brokers come to People's Park in Shanghai to "negotiate *potential* partners for their subjects." This word in this context is an adjective meaning "having the possibility or the power." But *potential* can also be a noun, as you saw in the introductory section on improving your vocabulary, as in the sentence: "Jason has the *potential* to become a great basketball player." In this instance, *potential* refers to Jason's future capacity as a player. The root of *potential* is the Latin *potens* ("power"). You can see the same root in *potent*, *impotent*, and *potentate*, which refers to a monarch, one who dominates or who has power over others.

WORD PARTS

The Prefix mega- Wu refers to a *mega*-matchmaking event in March 2006 called the Liang-Zhu Mutual Marriage Fair. The prefix *mega-* literally means "one million" in Greek, but in English it means simply "very large." Walmart and Costco are *megastores*, computer power is measured in *megabytes*, and a *megalomaniac* describes a person who has delusions about his or her own importance.

Alfresco Marriage Market

1   — "Male, 26, 1980, Associate's Degree, 1.7 meters, realtor-manager, 2 homes (3-bedroom and 2-bedroom), 5,500 RMB."

2   "Wanted: Female, 1.6-meters, Associate's Degree, steady workplace in Pudong, kind-hearted, diligent at livelihood, 3,000 RMB."

3   The above is not an item in the personal classifieds, an online service, or some dating bulletin board. Instead, the message is handwritten in a faded felt-tip pen on a 9-by-11 white sheet of paper, protected by clear plastic and cradled in the lap of a middle-aged man.

4   It is an early Sunday morning at People's Park in Shanghai and a man (he refuses to give his name) is prepared for a long day of perching on the wall alongside a flower bed. He says he's the father of the 26-year-old described on his homemade poster.

5   He's one of some 50 brokers who congregate at the centrally located park for an informal marriage mart that materializes every fair-weather weekend. Clipped to shopping bags, taped to purses, laid on a low bush, pinned to a tree trunk, or just sitting in a lap, the signs are the springboard for the sign carriers to screen and negotiate potential partners for their subjects.

6   Despite the mix of modern and Confucian values, family is still the organizing principal and foundation of security in China, and marriage is its bedrock. To encourage marriage, or to get better prospects, the family (read, parents) itself becomes the search engine.

7   This kind of personals-info swapping via parents goes on in parks all over China, despite the fact that the young generation is computer savvy and dating-meeting services online are plenty busy. Called "xiang xing"—literally, "reciprocal relations" or "mutual marriage"—it is the arranged marriage of traditional China writ for the 21st century.

8   According to the China Census Bureau, the number of single adults in the country has exploded, from 1.7 million in 1982 to 16 million in 2002. Many of these are female white-collar workers and professionals, whose high education level means that their marriage choices are restricted—traditionally, they cannot marry below their educational level, income and job placement or position.

9   By some testaments, the in-the-park method works.

10   "It's my first time," says the father at People's Park. "My neighbor told me about it. He came and was successful. It took him six times coming here. His son had about 20 meetings with 20 girls before it worked," he said. The neighbor's son is going out with a girl and is headed toward marriage.

11   The first-timer's son knows what his father is doing, and supposedly is giving tacit consent to this activity. Besides, the son works seven days a week and is shy, the father says, adding, "We're desperate." (None of the people interviewed wanted their names used for this story.)

12   As he speaks, a 5-foot-tall, stoop-shouldered woman interrupts the conversation, jabbing with her elbow, grabbing the photograph of the son and peering

at it closely. She asks one question, drops the photo back on the first-timer's lap and walks away.

13   Next to the first-timer, a second man wearing a baseball cap pushes his sign forward. He brings out another, then another. He has six prospects, he says.

14   Someone in the crowd whispers that he is not reliable.

15   A little later, by 9:30 a.m., the signs are everywhere: one clipped with a clothespin to a shirt pocket, one weighed down by a Pepsi bottle.

16   A few advertise services: "A bridge to someone else," reads one.

17   Ningbo, a city of 5.4 million people about 80 miles south of Shanghai in Zhejiang province, held a mega-matchmaking event in March called the Liang-Zhu Xiang Xing Hui (Liang-Zhu Mutual Marriage Fair). The event was named after the mythical star-crossed lovers, Liang Shanbuo and Zhu Yingtai, whose parents prevented them from marrying. The pair died of grief, only to release themselves from their tomb as two butterflies. The Ningbo event's name would amount to calling a marriage mart the Romeo and Juliet Marriage Fair.

18   Call it tragic, or certainly ironic. Yet 80,000 participants went to that fair.

19   No thoughts of tragedy or irony entered the mind of one 69-year-old man this Sunday in People's Park. Sitting on a bench with his sign resting on his half-bared chest, shirt unbuttoned in the sweltering heat, he says the son he is trying to marry off is his last—"1976, Year of the Dragon, 1.74 meters," a computer engineer, 3,000 RMB ($375 monthly salary), seeking a female 2 to 3 years younger with an associate degree." From 3,000 RMB to 6,000 RMB is considered in the range of acceptable white-collar salaries.

20   "He's working. He only knows to go online to play games after work. What are you going to do with a kid like that?" he says to the other parents sitting around him.

21   Many of the parent brokers know each other from previous matchmaking marts. "Oh, that's a good system," says one middle-aged woman to another, about the way her compatriot has attached the sign to her purse.

22   The first round of poster reading often leads to a brief exchange of information. Then photographs might be shared. Then telephone numbers.

23   The game involves scoping out the parent and the remainder of the claims on the ad.

24   The most critical piece of information is education. An associate's degree (three years of college or university) or a bachelor's degree and above is always a point to advertise.

25   Equally important is the monthly salary requirement; usually the male salary is placed above the female salary. The firm for which a candidate works, if it is a foreign firm, is also usually placed high in an ad. If it is a female subject, the amount of mortgage left on a home is of critical importance.

26   It's all in a day's work for the parents, and they bring along an umbrella for shade, or a fan to keep cool, and perhaps a snack to fortify themselves in the middle of the day.

27   Some plan a full day's work, and sit until 6 p.m. The first-timer man has come in from the outskirts of Shanghai and will take a train back.

28   Some are less serious. The 69-year-old will give it a half day. "I'll sit till about 1 or 2 p.m., go to some restaurant to eat lunch, then go home after that."

29   What do the subjects, the bulk of whom are between 28 and 35, think of this? Absent from the milling, public swarm of warm bodies in the park, they share their views online.

30   "It makes me feel like I'm being sold the way they used to sell sons and daughters," a 28-year-old woman who calls herself Xiao V ("Little V") says on the Chinese language site, xinhuanet.com. "But I sympathize with my parents. What they do is pitiful, but I feel sorry for them. I don't want them to go; it's as if I have no ability to make my own friends. There is no trust."

31   Another young woman, Xiao Wei, answers on xinhuanet.com: "They won't say it to me, but they go out to do it. It's hard work; there's no face for them. It's more pressure than if they told me I should get married. I'd prefer it to be lighter, more natural. It will happen."

32   Another woman, 25, authors a blog she calls "Blind Date." She writes in Chinese, "My mother and father help match-make, but I find it very tiring when they find someone. We're two strangers. After we meet, we speak nonsense. Males are just looking for pretty face. And females are looking for money and position. It's too fake feeling."

33   Despite the fact that a park is the most public of all places, it's a type of black market and certain underground rules apply. Trust is not the basis of the encounter. This reporter and accompanying photographer eventually were shown they were not welcome. Some parents did not want their children's or their own faces and names to go beyond the local crowd. Children might not know their parents are pushing their prospects; the parents carry the shame of having non-marriageable kids. And, there is no guarantee of truth in advertising.

34   According to reports published by some wedding consulting companies that pay for marriage research, young Chinese are meeting and marrying through a mixture of traditional and some contemporary means: 20 percent through friends, 20 percent through matchmaking via family and friends, 15 percent at random, 10 percent on the Internet. The remainder meet through work, travel and professional matchmaking services.

35   The old ways are still relied upon. As singles search through electronic networks, their parents will use news from friends, relatives, neighbors and their own lively networks. The city park strategy may rank low or high, depending on experience.

36   Writes one unnamed single on the Web, "When I see my mother happy as I come home from work, I know she has found someone for me. I say to her, 'Last time it didn't work.' My mother then looks hurt and answers, 'Last time. Last time I found him in the park.' "

Exercises

Do not refer to the selection for Exercises A, B, and C unless your instructor directs you to do so.

A. DETERMINING THE MAIN IDEA AND PURPOSE

Choose the best answer.

_____ 1. The main idea of the selection is that
   a. it is difficult for young, single Chinese to find marriage partners because they work such long hours and have little leisure time.
   b. Chinese parents arrange marriages for their children, whether through using a traditional matchmaker or an online dating service.
   c. many Chinese parents have become the "search engines," seeking prospective marriage partners for their unmarried children at open-air marriage marts.
   d. the marriage rate in China has declined as the country has experienced huge economic growth.

_____ 2. The writer's purpose is to
   a. examine one parent's experience advertising for a marriage partner for his adult child.
   b. explain the various methods Chinese families use to find marriage partners.
   c. explain the family value system in China.
   d. examine the phenomenon of alfresco marriage markets.

B. COMPREHENDING MAIN IDEAS

Choose the correct answer for the multiple-choice items. Write the fill-in answers in the space provided using your own words.

_____ 1. According to Wu, the foundation and the primary organizing principle in Chinese society is
   a. the family.
   b. the Confucian value system.
   c. the Communist party.
   d. marriage.

_____ 2. Which of the following best describes the tradition among Chinese women in choosing a marriage partner?
   a. The family always makes the decision about whom their daughter will marry.
   b. She can marry anyone she wants, without respect to educational level or income.
   c. She must marry someone at the same educational, job, and income level.
   d. She must marry someone above her own educational, job, and income level.

_____ 3. Parents come to the outdoor marriage market for several reasons. Which one was not mentioned?
   a. An adult child might work very long hours and have little free time.
   b. An adult child might be too shy to socialize with a member of the opposite sex.
   c. An adult child might be divorced and therefore viewed as "damaged goods."
   d. An adult spends too much time playing online games and therefore doesn't socialize very well.

4. Of all the various pieces of information that parents exchange about prospective marriage partners, which two are the most critical?

_____

5. According to Wu, what is the one value or concept that is missing from the marriage market negotiations—the sharing of photos, the exchange of information, even the use of names and faces beyond the local crowd?

_____

_____ 6. What happened to Wu and to the photographer accompanying her at People's Park in Shanghai?
   a. They were made to feel unwelcome.
   b. They were told to leave.
   c. They were subject to searches of camera bags and purses.
   d. They were treated well by the parents who willingly told them their stories.

COMPREHENSION SCORE

Score your answers for Exercises A and B as follows:

A. No. right _____ × 2 = _____

B. No. right _____ × 1 = _____

Total points from A and B _____ × 10 = _____ percent

C. SEQUENCING

These sentences from one paragraph in the selection may have been scrambled. Read the sentences and choose the sequence that puts them back into logical order. Do not refer to the original selection.

1 The firm for which a candidate works, if it is a foreign firm, is also usually placed high in an ad. **2** Equally important is the monthly salary requirement; usually the male salary is placed above the female salary. **3** If it is a female subject, the amount of mortgage left on a home is of critical importance.

_____ Which of the following represents the correct sequence for these sentences?

a. 2, 1, 3
b. 3, 1, 2
c. 3, 2, 1
d. Correct as written.

You may refer to the selection as you work through the remaining exercises.

D. INTERPRETING MEANING

Write your answers to these questions in your own words.

1. What is the writer's attitude toward the subject of outdoor marriage markets? Does her opinion appear to be favorable, unfavorable, or neutral? How can you tell?

   _____

   _____

2. What does Wu mean at the end of paragraph 5 by the word "screen" in this quotation: "the signs are the springboard for the sign carriers to 'screen' potential partners"? _____

3. Look again at the second sentence of paragraph 6. When Wu writes, "the family (read, parents) itself becomes the search engine," what does "read, parents" mean?

   _____

4. Who has a harder time in China finding a marriage partner—a man or a woman? How do you know?

   _____

5. Ultimately, what does Wu say about the overall success of the outdoor city-park strategy?

   _____

E. UNDERSTANDING VOCABULARY

Look through each numbered paragraph in the following list and find a word that matches each definition. Refer to a dictionary if necessary. An example has been done for you.

Ex. hard-working, industrious [paragraphs 2–3]   _diligent_

1. gather, meet as a large group [4–5]   _____

2. sitting on top of something high [4–5]   _____

3. appears, happens [4–5]   _____

4. foundation, the very basis of something [5–6]   _____

5. potential clients or, here, marriage partners
   [6, 13, and 33]   _____

6. knowledgeable, having know-how [6–7]   _____

7. trading, exchanging [6–7]   _____

8. mutual, interchanged between two people [7–8]   _____

9. unspoken, but implied or understood [11–12]   _____

10. a person from one's own country, colleague
    [21–23]   _____

F. USING VOCABULARY—VARIANT WORD FORMS

Write the correct inflected form of the base word in each of the following sentences. Be sure to add the appropriate ending to fit the grammatical requirements of the sentence. Refer to your dictionary if necessary.

1. (*desperate*—use a noun). Some parents come to the open marriage market in the park out of a sense of _____ because their children have no time to look for a marriage partner.

2. (*reliable*—use a verb) Even though the marriage market is a new take on matchmaking, some families prefer to _____ on the old-fashioned way.

3. (*ironic*—use an adverb) _____, despite the tradition of arranged marriage and the new age of online dating sites, the open-air marriage market does have its successes.

4. (*mythical*—use a verb with an –*ed* ending) The Liang-Zhu Mutual Marriage Fair was named in honor of the Chinese version of Romeo and Juliet, _____ as star-crossed lovers.

5. (*fortification*—use a verb) Some parents bring snacks to _____ themselves.

6. (*strategy*—use an adjective) Having good pictures, a good salary, and a good education are of _____ importance in these parents' search for marriage partners.

G. SUMMARIZING EXERCISE

Write a summary of paragraph 6 using your own words. Try to write no more than 30 words.

_____

_____

_____

H. ANNOTATING EXERCISE

For this exercise, assume that you are preparing to write an essay on the reasons Chinese parents have become marriage brokers for their unmarried adult children. Annotate each section by writing the main point in your own words in the left margin.

I. TOPICS FOR DISCUSSION

1. Underlying Wu's article is the unstated assumption that Chinese society has changed in the past few years. Otherwise, a phenomenon like the alfresco marriage markets wouldn't exist. What sorts of social changes are suggested in the article?
2. Wu mentions the fact that there is a strong element of distrust at the marriage markets, offering support for this assertion in paragraph 33. Why do you suppose trust is lacking?
3. Would an institution like the outdoor marriage markets work in the U.S.? Why or why not? What would most young Americans say about their parents' negotiating and prospecting for a marriage partner?
4. Just how important are parents in the marriage-partner-selection process? To what extent does their influence depend on cultural norms? What is their position or influence in American culture? In other cultures represented by students in the class?
5. What, if any, advantages does the outdoor marketplace have over online dating services? What do the two methods have in common?

J. TOPICS FOR WRITING

1. Write an essay in which you contrast the Chinese and American methods of choosing marriage partners.
2. If you are familiar with a different culture, write an essay in which you contrast the way a marriage partner is chosen in this culture and in American culture.
3. How, apparently, do the young people mentioned in paragraphs 29–32 feel about their parents' efforts on their behalf to find a suitable marriage prospect? Write a paragraph summarizing their attitudes.

EXPLORE THE WEB

- Olivia Wu is well represented on the Web with various blogs and articles. You might find her articles reporting from China worth checking out.

PART THREE

Tackling More Challenging Prose

Making Inferences

Look carefully at this cartoon:

"I thought it was pretty good, for a book."

© David Sipress/The New Yorker Collection/www.cartoonbank.com

What can you conclude about the little boy from his remarks? The cartoonist does not tell us the boy's attitude toward books. He suggests or implies it, and from what he implies, we *infer*. This means that we draw a conclusion by reading into his remark—the boy probably prefers to play video games or watch television rather than read a book. Notice the comma before "for a book," which emphasizes the boy's usual lack of interest in reading books. You will practice making inferences like this with many of the readings in the next two parts of the text.

Let's say that on a cloudy winter day you are driving and you approach a narrow mountain road. Suddenly, you notice that all of the cars coming toward you have their headlights on, and you wonder why. One possibility is that the cars are part of a funeral procession. Another is that they are driving in an area in which headlights are required during the day (such as on narrow or windy roads or in daylight test zones) and that all the drivers forgot to turn off their lights. A third is that they have just emerged from dense fog. Which of these conclusions is accurate? (Any one of them could be true, of course, but one is *probably* more accurate than the other two.)

Usually the cars in a funeral procession have identifying signs on their windshields. And it would be unlikely that every single driver forgot to turn off the lights at the end of the narrow or windy section of road or at the end of a test zone. So the most likely possibility is that a patch of dense fog lies ahead. And, of course, if you reached that patch of fog as you proceed up the mountain, your inference would be confirmed.

What process is involved here? When you make an *inference*, you draw a conclusion from what is observed or said based on your past experience. You see this in the preceding example about drivers using their headlights. In reading, however, making inferences is a little different. It involves reading between the lines, to see what the writer *suggests* but does not directly or explicitly say. As you work through the inference exercises in this introduction and throughout the rest of the book, it's safer to stay within the confines of the passage rather than going outside it and using your own experience. This ensures good comprehension and reduces the chance of making inaccurate inferences or even wild speculations.

Let's look at a simple example from one of the readings you completed in Part Two, Olivia Wu, "Alfresco Marriage Market," in which she describes outdoor events throughout China where parents serve as marriage "search engines," seeking out suitable marriage partners for their unmarried adult children. Wu begins her article with two typical advertisements that parents post in public parks on Saturdays:

> "Male, 26, 1980, Associate's Degree, 1.7 meters, realtor-manager, 2 homes (3-bedroom and 2-bedroom), 5,500 RMB."
> "Wanted: Female, 1.6 meters, Associate's Degree, steady workplace in Pudong, kind-hearted, diligent at livelihood, 3,000 RMB."

Although Wu does not tell the reader what RMB stands for, we can infer that it is a monetary unit, in this case the salaries of these respective candidates. (In fact, RMB stands for Ren Min Bi, or the People's Money, also called the yuan.) We can go further and infer that these two numbers refer to the candidate's desired salary. Later on in the article Wu cites the figure 3,000 RMB, which is equivalent to a monthly salary of $375, thus confirming our original inference. But even without this information, we could infer its meaning without having to do an online search.

A little further along in the article, Wu writes:

> According to the China Census Bureau, the number of single adults in the country has exploded, from 1.7 million in 1982 to 16 million in 2002. Many of these are female white-collar workers and professionals, whose high education level means that their marriage choices are restricted— traditionally, they cannot marry below their educational level, income and job placement or position.

What is Wu suggesting about why the number of single adults in China has "exploded"? China's economy has experienced a boom in recent years, yet ironically, with increased employment opportunities, especially for women in white-collar and professional occupations, the result has been fewer opportunities for marriages. Unlike the U.S., where young people are often delaying marriage into their 30s, in China the tradition still holds that women cannot marry beneath their own level. So the increasing number of unmarried women is an unintended consequence of their economic gains.

Now let's look at a short magazine article. Titled "Don't Toss That Stapler," the unidentified writer describes a situation:

Indiana schoolteacher Lori Heiges was vexed to hear that a local business, in a fit of redecorating, tossed out its black staplers in favor of a maroon version—especially since her request for a single classroom stapler met with "maybe next year" from school officials. As state and federal budgets tighten, not only do schools struggle to keep the doors open but teachers end up paying for classroom supplies, writes Frank Gray in **The Journal Gazette** (Feb. 27, 2011). "This can add up when you have 180 students." The trashed staplers propelled Heiges to found Curriculum Opportunities and Resources for Educators (CORE). The volunteer-run store collects donated business supplies and sells them to teachers at deep discounts. "In a society where going green is all the rage," writes Gray, "CORE is an example of basic common sense." CORE disperses basics like scissors, folders, and crayons. It also finds unusual supplies from unusual sources: rolls of architectural drawing paper, pipe cleaners, and electronic timers. Even the local hospital is contributing to the cause by donating batteries from devices such as ventilators, which can be used only on a single patient. "The barely used batteries accumulate in buckets," Gray explains. "Now they're headed for area classrooms."

"Don't Toss That Stapler." Originally published in *Utne Reader*, September/October 2011. Reprinted with permission. www.utne.com

Based on the information in the passage, what inferences can you make? Why was Lori Heiges *vexed*, meaning annoyed or irritated, when she heard that a local business had thrown away all its black staplers? (Knowing the meaning of unfamiliar words is often crucial in making good inferences.) The passage suggests the reason, but doesn't say it directly: She was vexed because discarding these staplers was so wasteful, especially when she had requisitioned a single stapler for her classroom and was told to wait another year. A year to wait for a stapler! We can surely infer that her school district must be in really bad financial shape.

Second, what inference can you make about why a business would throw away black staplers and buy maroon ones? The writer says that there was a "fit of redecorating." What does this suggest? We can infer that the business owners wanted everything in the office to match a particular color scheme, including staplers. We can infer this because in our experience we know that redecorating usually means following a particular color scheme.

Is there anything else that we can infer from this passage? Again, the writer doesn't say this explicitly, but we might also infer that there is a great disparity or inequality between how companies and school districts spend money on supplies. There seems to be a disconnect here—the situation reflects a sad reality in today's economy. At a time when school districts around the country are struggling to educate the nation's students with shrinking budgets and declining revenue, this particular business is spending money on unnecessary things. One might also infer that at least this business is unaware of public schools' economic plight. The old black staplers were perfectly good, but it apparently didn't occur to anyone that someone else (i.e., teachers) could use them. This type of inference is broader, going beyond the scope of the passage, yet it seems safe enough to make given the information presented.

Many of my students find the inference questions in the text to be among the most challenging of the exercises, but they are really important to master if you want to be more than just an average reader. If you are able to see the implications in what a writer says, you can go far beyond merely understanding the simple surface meaning. Making inferences allows you to make connections between the writer's ideas that he or she may not have made, and to extend your understanding of the subject.

In the remainder of the text, you will encounter two kinds of inference questions. In the first type, you will be asked to evaluate inferential statements using this key: Y (Yes), N (No), or CT (Can't Tell). Study the explanation in the following box to see the differences between these answer choices:

LABELING INFERENCES

Y   A "yes" answer means that the inference is *probably* accurate. It states something that the writer's words actually imply or suggest.

N   A "no" answer means that the inference is *probably* inaccurate, either because it shows a misreading or a distortion of the writer's words, or because one part of the inference statement is accurate but another part is not, making the whole statement not accurate.

CT A "can't tell" answer means that *you can't be sure one way or the other* if the inference is logical or accurate. The writer does not mention anything that would allow you to draw such a conclusion, or the conclusion exists outside the selection in something else you have read or have other knowledge of. In other words, you "can't tell" from *this* particular passage.

Before we look at some sample inference questions, let us examine the difference between N and CT in more detail. Think about this statement:

Blue is a color, and north is a quality.

Is this an accurate statement? The first part is fine, but north is a direction, not a quality. It's the same with inferences. In a complicated inference containing two ideas, if one idea is accurate and the other is not, mark it N. CT, on the other hand, means just that—you simply can't tell. To return to our earlier headlight example, if only one car coming toward you has its headlights on, you wouldn't have enough information to make an inference. (Some people prefer to drive with their lights on during the day, especially on narrow, curvy roads, but this is not a generalization about all drivers that you can make from your driving experience.)

Following the explanation in the preceding box, label these inference questions from the passage above, "Don't Toss That Stapler":

_____ **1.**   Lori Heiges considered the company wasteful for getting rid of its black staplers.

_____ **2.**   Lori Heiges has been a long-time environmental activist.

_____ **3.**   Some teachers pay for their own classroom supplies because their school districts can't afford them; if they didn't, they would have to do without.

_____ **4.**   CORE has expanded to other states outside Indiana.

_____ **5.**   CORE accepts donated supplies which are, in turn, donated to local school districts.

Let's go through these inference questions one at a time.

- Question 1 should be marked Y. This is clearly suggested at the beginning of the passage by the word *vexed*, as you saw above.
- Question 2 should be marked CT. There is no evidence in the reading to suggest her interest in environmental issues.
- Question 3 should be marked Y based on the information implied in Frank Gray's quotation.
- Question 4 is clearly CT. The writer talks about CORE in Indiana but does not suggest that the idea has caught on elsewhere.
- Finally, question 5 should be marked N. Although the first part of the question is accurate, the second part is not. The items are not donated; they're sold at a discount. Thus, the entire inference is negated.

Here is another short passage from a reading you will encounter in Part Four—"The Bystander's Dilemma" by Marc Ian Barasch. In this paragraph the writer is describing the Greyston Bakery program, which a man named Bernie Glassman started in an attempt to give homeless people jobs and get them off the streets.

The business grew, eventually snagging a contract to make brownies for Ben and Jerry's Ice Cream. But it soon came smack up against the endemic problems of the neighborhood. People missed work because of drug problems. Batches of dough were ruined because employees lacked basic math skills to measure ingredients or the reading skills to decipher labels on cans.

Now consider these inferences. Mark them Y, N, or CT, as instructed above.

1. _____ Greyston Bakery was fortunate to get a contract from Ben & Jerry's.

2. _____ Lack of education is one reason that homeless people have trouble holding down jobs.

3. _____ The bakery workers' drug problems caused more problems than their lack of reading and math skills.

4. _____ The problems in the neighborhood where Greyston Bakery was located were temporary and could have easily been remedied with better funding and more social programs.

5. _____ The bakery never really got off the ground.

6. _____ Greyston Bakery eventually shut down.

Now compare your answers with these:

1. Y   **2.** Y   **3.** CT   **4.** N   **5.** N   **6.** CT

Here is an explanation of the answers:

- Question 1 should be marked Y. The verb "snagged" suggests that the contract with Ben & Jerry's was a positive development for the bakery.
- Similarly, question 2 is accurate because Barasch points to poor reading and math skills as two reasons that the bakery got into difficulty; its workers' inability to do simple math or to follow written instructions disrupted production.

- Question 3 is a good example of a statement that should be marked CT. Barasch does not indicate whether the workers' drug problems or their poor academic skills were equally to blame or whether one problem was worse than the other. We simply don't know because he doesn't provide any details.
- Question 4 is an inaccurate inference. The word "endemic" suggests that the drug and academic problems were prevalent and entrenched, therefore not easily solved.
- Question 5 stems from a misreading of the passage: The bakery must have been doing something right to get the initial contract to make brownies.
- And finally, question 6 is another example of a "can't tell" situation since Barasch does not reveal the bakery's fate. Perhaps changes were made and the bakery is doing just fine.

When doing the inference exercises, don't make wild guesses. Always return to the selection, read the appropriate passage again, and think about the writer's words and what they suggest. To help you work through the exercises and to strengthen your understanding of what you read, consider these suggestions:

HOW TO MAKE ACCURATE INFERENCES

- Look up the meanings of any unfamiliar words and consider the definitions in context.
- Think about the possibilities of interpretation by examining the writer's words and phrases.
- Look carefully at the way the statement is worded. Then return to the passage and locate the pertinent passage. Test the statement for accuracy.
- Remember that inferences are *statements of probability*, not facts. They proceed from facts, but they are not facts themselves.
- If you are in doubt about an answer, ask your instructor for help or for further clarification.

In order to make reliable inferences, you need to pay close attention to the passage. First, look up the meaning of any unfamiliar words. You can't interpret a passage accurately if you don't know what the writer is saying. For example, in the preceding passage, Barasch describes the neighborhood's problems as "endemic." Although you can probably get his general meaning without knowing the exact definition of "endemic," you might not make the connection between the bakery's troubles and these problems (drugs and poor educational skills). There is a big difference between temporary, easily solved problems and endemic ones that are entrenched and not easily solved.

If you are unsure about an answer, ask your instructor for help or for further clarification. If your college has a reading laboratory where tutoring is available, you might avail yourself of its services. Finally, remember that good readers may sometimes disagree over the answers because inferences are not always black and white. That's what makes them fun and challenging.

The second type of inference question is open-ended, requiring you to answer the question in your own words. For this final exercise, read the following article posted on the website of the *Chronicle of Higher Education* in December 2011. Open-ended inference questions follow it.

WASHINGTON D.C.—Many employers believe colleges aren't adequately preparing students for jobs, according to findings of a study presented here on Monday by the Accrediting Council for Independent Colleges and Schools.

The group surveyed more than 1,000 employers in various industries last month about whether job applicants possess the skills to thrive in the workplace. More than half of employers said finding qualified applicants is difficult, and just under half thought students should receive specific workplace training rather than a more broad-based education.

At a news conference announcing those findings, Rep. Virginia Foxx, the North Carolina Republican who is chairwoman of the U.S. House of Representatives higher-education subcommittee, urged institutions to heed employers' calls. "Colleges and universities are pandering to the students and giving them what they want, instead of what the employers want," she said. "I don't think you have to make a distinction between getting skills and getting an education. We need to do both."

According to the survey results, less than 10 percent of employers thought colleges did an "excellent" job of preparing students for work. Nearly 30 percent said finding the right applicant has grown harder in the past few years. On all hiring criteria included in the survey, such as adaptability and critical thinking, applicants were performing below employers' expectations.

Also on Monday, the accrediting council announced a Student Success Initiative to conduct further research and encourage colleges to focus on job training and placement.

Lacey Johnson, "Employers Say College Graduates Lack Job Skills,"
The Chronicle of Higher Education, www.chronicle.com, December 5, 2011.
Copyright 2011, The Chronicle of Higher Education. Reprinted with permission.

SMALL GROUP ACTIVITY—OPEN-ENDED INFERENCES

Working in groups of three or four, discuss these inference questions and then write your answers to the inference questions that follow in the space provided. If you are unsure about whether or not you can make an inference, write "can't tell because there's not enough information." Your instructor will compare the various groups' answers and evaluate them to check for accuracy.

1. According to the majority of businesses who responded to the survey, colleges and universities have the responsibility to train their students for jobs in the workplace. What is one reason that business owners might feel this way?

_____

2. According to the article, what specific skills are employers looking for? Are the two mentioned properly considered "skills"?

_____

3. Who is best suited to teach these—universities or employers?

_____

4. What are some skills that aren't mentioned that employers might be looking for?

_____

5. What does the word _pander_ in the third paragraph most likely mean? What do students want?

_____

6. Is the fact that Representative Virginia Foxx of South Carolina is a Republican of any significance?

_____

7. What do you think college and university faculty would say about the survey results?

_____

8. Whom does the accrediting council (mentioned at the beginning and again at the end) support in this discussion?

_____

As you might imagine, this article generated a lot of comments. You can read these for yourself by locating the article at _www.chronicle.com_. Type in the article title and scroll down to the bottom to see the readers' comments.

EXERCISE IN DISTINGUISHING BETWEEN FACT AND OPINION

A _fact_ is a statement that can be verified or proved either by measurement, observation, or some other form of proof. An _opinion_ represents someone's subjective interpretation and therefore can't be verified or proved. You have already seen one of these exercises in Part Two, and more are coming up in Parts Three and Four of the text. Practice with these assertions from the article you just read. Write F if the statement represents a factual statement that can be verified or O if the statement represents the writer's or someone else's subjective interpretation.

_____ 1. Many employers believe colleges aren't adequately preparing students for jobs.

_____ 2. Colleges aren't adequately preparing students for jobs.

_____ 3. The Accrediting Council for Independent Colleges and Schools surveyed more than 1,000 employers in various industries.

_____ 4. More than half of the employers surveyed think that finding qualified applicants is difficult.

_____ 5. Slightly less than half of the employers surveyed think that students should receive workplace training rather than a more broad-based education.

_____6. Colleges and universities are pandering to students by giving them what they want, according to Representative Virginia Foxx, a Republican from North Carolina.

_____7. Representative Foxx believes that colleges and universities can teach students skills and give them an education at the same time.

_____8. Based on two criteria—adaptability and critical thinking—applicants are performing below employers' expectations.

_____9. Finding the right applicant has been getting harder for employers in the past few years.

_____10. The accrediting council is encouraging colleges to focus on job training and placement.

Questions for Discussion

These questions involve further work in making inferences by asking you to respond to the various implications the article raises.

1. How well does the writer explain employers' concerns about college graduates who work for them? What other information might she have included?
2. Do you see anything illogical in this statement from paragraph 2: "just under half [of employers surveyed] thought students should receive specific workplace training rather than a more broad-based education"?
3. Have your own lower-division required college courses been geared toward a "broad-based education" or toward getting useful skills that you can employ in the workplace? Are you getting what you expected from them?
4. What *should* be the role of colleges and universities? Do you agree with Representative Virginia Foxx's assessment that "colleges and universities are pandering to the students and giving them what they want, instead of what the employers want"?
5. How likely is it that a college or university could adequately perform job training for its students? How worthwhile would that training likely be in a real corporation or business?

A final note: The inference-making process shows you the importance of reading carefully. In my experience both in teaching reading courses and, even more, in tutoring students one-on-one in reading, I have observed the wild flights of fancy students often indulge in. They read things into a passage that aren't there and the writer hasn't implied. These speculations result often in students completely misunderstanding what a writer says. Some other reasons for errors in reading are from inattention or poor concentration, lack of vocabulary, or unfamiliarity with the subject matter. But inferences remain the most difficult area requiring improvement. If you diligently apply the recommendations discussed in this introduction, it will also result in better, more accurate reading and a depth of understanding that superficial comprehension of only the main points cannot provide.

14 CARLA RIVERA
From Illiterate to Role Model

It has been estimated that 10 to 14 percent of the American population is functionally illiterate, depending on how that term is defined. The subject of this article is John Zickefoose and his struggle to learn to read at the age of 35. Carla Rivera, a graduate of UC Berkeley, covers education issues for The Los Angeles Times, *where this article was first published.*

Vocabulary Analysis

Three prefixes—*dys-*, *dis-*, and *il-* John Zickefoose suffered from both *dyslexia* and other *disabilities*. *Dys-* is a prefix originally of Greek origin. When attached to a root, it means "diseased," "difficult," or "bad." In the case of *dyslexia*, which refers to a specific type of reading disability, the Greek root *lexis* means "speech." Another common English word using this prefix is *dysfunction*. In contrast, the Latin prefix *dis-* means "absence of." *Dis-* has other meanings as well, so if you are unsure what a word beginning with this prefix means, check the dictionary.

Last, Rivera's subject is Zickefoose's *illiteracy*, meaning the inability to read [*il- + littera* ("letter"). The prefix *il-* means "not" and is a variant form of the two more common prefixes *un-* and *in-* which mean "not." In the case of *il-*, it is used to form the negative of words beginning with the letter "l," as in *illegal*, *illegitimate*, and *illogical*.

WORD PARTS

metamorphosis Used in paragraph 1, the word *metamorphosis* is of Greek origin. It can be broken down like this: *meta* ("change") + *morph* ("form") and means a transformation. *Metamorphosis* is the process that many insects like butterflies go through from the larval to the adult stages.

CARLA RIVERA

From Illiterate to Role Model

1   The metamorphosis is as quick as the turn of a page: John Zickefoose is a hyperactive goose, a laid-back bear, a monkey, a tiger. The children at the Corona Public Library squeal with laughter as the man whose name rhymes with Seuss becomes louder and more animated.

2   There was a time when reading the simple words of a picture book would have proved impossible for Zickefoose. He spent years in school overwhelmed with sadness that nothing came as easily to him as it did for others. He would become rowdy, preferring to be kicked out of class than to be called on by the teacher.

3   Zickefoose was functionally illiterate, unable to read a prescription label, his children's report cards or a menu. He was diagnosed as a young boy with dyslexia and attention deficit hyperactivity disorder and didn't learn to read and write until he was 35.

4   That's when everything changed. He became a poster boy for the Corona library's adult reading program, began to speak publicly about his own struggles and was named the library's literacy director. He founded a nonprofit youth organization.

5   And on Dec. 7, Zickefoose, 52, was sworn in as a member of the Corona-Norco Unified School District Board of Education.

6   For the boy who couldn't understand the words on his high school diploma, the journey to the school board was the culmination of a vow to do something meaningful in life and help prevent others from starting out as he did.

7   "I'll be able to bring, quite frankly, an unusual perspective of what it feels like to be in the classroom and be a failure," Zickefoose said. "I don't want any child to go through what I went through."

8   For years, even his wife wasn't aware of the severity of his limitations.

9   He would wish there was a magic pill he could take to make his disabilities disappear. The lowest point, he said, came when he couldn't understand his 7-year-old's homework assignments. When Shawn asked for help, Zickefoose sat with him at the kitchen table. But when Zickefoose looked at the textbook, all he saw were letters strung together that made no sense.

10   When he tried to fake his way through a bedtime story, his son would tell him, "No, Dad, that's not what it says." The little boy had no idea he was making him feel that he was failing as a father.

11   It was then that Zickefoose resolved to enroll in an adult literacy class at the Corona library. He was embarrassed and angry at himself. He had always been able to hide his illiteracy and wriggle out of uncomfortable situations. Now he believed there was no other option.

12   It didn't go well at first. Zickefoose insisted on starting with more complicated sentences and words than he was ready for, out of embarrassment. He wanted to cancel on his first day. This is stupid, he thought. He was incapable of learning.

13   But his tutor persuaded him to start with the basic building blocks of reading and writing. The one-on-one interaction was just what he needed.

14   Within six months, he was reading novels and nonfiction.

15   An estimated 30 million American adults can't read a newspaper or fill out a job application. Many have learning disabilities. Others are dropouts, victims of failing school systems. Some are immigrants with deficient English language skills who may also be illiterate in their native tongues.

16   But Zickefoose is also an anomaly. Only about 5% of adults who need services receive them, mainly because there is still so much shame attached to the condition, said David C. Harvey, president and chief executive of ProLiteracy, an international advocacy group. Zickefoose serves on the board of directors.

17   "John is a national role model because one of the most effective ways to break down that stigma is to have people who have had this problem talk about it," Harvey said. "He's a shining example of what can happen when someone gets services and puts those new skills to work."

18   Zickefoose was brought up in the Chicago suburb of Elmhurst, and his father and stepmother tried hard to help him. He blamed himself for his failures, not his teachers, whom he says were supportive and wanted him to succeed.

19   He went to specialists in Chicago who identified his problems in school but couldn't provide a solution.

20   "They have come so much further now in dealing with learning disabilities in a more efficient and productive manner," Zickefoose said. "Back then, they were good at diagnosing but they didn't have the tools to address it."

21   Once, in the fifth grade, he raised his hand to answer a question and was devastated when he got the answer wrong and a friend answered it correctly. Looking at a sign, a book or a newspaper was like being in a foreign country, confronted with a totally alien language, he said. Without the code, he couldn't master math or science or any other subject.

22   Still, he managed to scrape by with Ds and to graduate. Most states, in the late 1970s, did not require students to pass math and English tests to receive a diploma.

23   He got his driver's license in Illinois after taking the written part orally. He memorized such symbols as street signs and he had friends fill out job applications.

24   At 19, he bought a station wagon and moved to California, where his mother lived. He drove a truck for several years and then got a job restoring houses. He met Eileen, the woman who would become his wife. He managed to start his own restoration business, but that failed after a few years and he went to work for another company.

25   Eileen noticed that he always had a large wad of cash, not checks. He didn't have a bank account. "That would have taken skills to manage," she said recently.

26   He didn't think she really understood how serious his problems were. She thought he just didn't want to bother with paperwork or the bills. It was the only source of tension in their relationship. Once, Zickefoose tried to make her understand that he really couldn't read. "You don't get it, I can't do it," he told her.

27 Even now, she said, it's hard for her to believe his reading ability was so limited.

28 "He just seemed to do fine," she said. "He learned to compensate. If we went to a restaurant, he [already] knew what to order off a menu or he could tell by the pictures. When he couldn't, he would just order a hamburger."

29 "I was pretty good at faking it," Zickefoose said, "and it shows the depths of it that even with the woman I loved and cherished, I still felt I couldn't tell her."

30 During that time he hurt his back severely. But he continued working through the pain because he was terrified of being forced to find another job that might reveal his illiteracy.

31 "At that point I was 35, scared—panicked—and had no idea how I was going to get by."

32 He eventually had back surgery and went on disability. With Eileen's encouragement, he enrolled in the library's literacy program.

33 Mike Catellier had slipped and hurt his back while working as a store manager at a local supermarket. With time on his hands, he volunteered as a tutor at the Corona library. Zickefoose was the first adult with whom he worked.

34 There was an immediate bond: Both men were the same age, both married with children, and Catellier was facing back surgery.

35 "He was such a humble guy and so apologetic," recalled Catellier, now a Florida resident. "I think I convinced him not to be embarrassed and we got comfortable. He was very motivated. . . . He would meet me as often as I was able to come."

36 After so many years of torment, it turned out that Zickefoose was a quick study.

37 "John had stuff stored in his memory that I don't think he realized," Catellier said. "We started with first-grade books and basic vowel sounds, but we were able to move way faster through the material. He gives me credit, but it was really just me helping him focus on things, giving him strategies in finding books that he liked."

38 Zickefoose had always been interested in public speaking, and both he and Catellier joined Toastmasters. Zickefoose would dictate speeches and he and Catellier would work on concepts and words. As he improved, Zickefoose began writing himself.

39 He was still being tutored when he joined a book group at the library. He can't remember the first book he tackled. He remembers having to ask Catellier to help. But as the group discussed passages, he was overcome with a sense of accomplishment and well-being. Hey, check me out, he thought.

40 The experience was transforming. One of the first serious books he remembers reading is "Black Like Me," the true story of a white Texan who passed as black in the segregated south in the late 1950s. He was struck by the tale of living as an outcast.

41 "A new life sounds dramatic, but that's really how it was," he said. "Most people couldn't tell you when they learned to read, it just happened. But I can tell you exactly when the light bulb came on."

42 Now outreach coordinator at the library, Zickefoose appears to be straight-arrow, business-minded, even professorial. But his tie, with an imprint of the Looney Tunes' Tasmanian Devil, hints at a whimsical nature.

43   He formed UNITY (United Neighbors Involving Today's Youth) in 1996, and it has evolved into a coalition of 80 public and private agencies that have secured more than $17 million for the Corona-Norco school district. A generation of students know him as Mr. Z from his appearances at school assemblies where he preaches perseverance, using his own life as an example.

44   As a school board member, Zickefoose wants to prepare students earlier for college and a career and to pursue more outside funds for such school programs as arts and music.

45   "If a parent comes in with a child that is struggling, I feel like I can understand that at a very emotional level," Zickefoose said. "We want to find the positive qualities that a child has and enhance those."

46   No one is prouder of Zickefoose than his sons, Shawn, 24, a firefighter for the U.S. Forest Service in Redding, and Adam, 21, who will enter the Navy in February.

47   They were still young when Zickefoose began speaking publicly about his illiteracy, and they grew up hearing stories about how they had to help their father read.

48   Adam said his only surprise was learning how his dad was able to get through school. When Adam was growing up, his father was such a mainstay at the library that his friends thought he owned it. They thought he was cool.

49   "1 was never afraid to tell anybody," Adam said. "If anyone was having trouble reading, I'd tell them my dad couldn't even read his diploma."

Carla Rivera, "From Illiterate to Role Model," *Los Angeles Times*, January 5, 2011. Copyright © 2011 Los Angeles Times. Reprinted with permission.

Exercises

Do not refer to the selection for Exercises A, B, and C unless your instructor directs you to do so.

A. DETERMINING THE MAIN IDEA AND PURPOSE

Choose the best answer.

_____ **1.**   The main idea of the selection is that
   a. reading specialists are now better able to diagnose and remedy reading disabilities than they were in the past.
   b. to be functionally illiterate is to feel like an outcast in society.
   c. for John Zickefoose, learning to read was a transformative experience in his life.
   d. John Zickefoose's illiteracy made him unable to read his high school diploma, fill out job applications, or own a checking account.

_____ **2.**   The writer's purpose is to
   a. tell the story of John Zickefoose's journey from illiterate to role model and inspiration for other young people.

    b. explain the causes of illiteracy and how best to deal with the problem.

    c. tell John Zickefoose's life story.

    d. describe the difficult process of an adult's learning to read.

B. COMPREHENDING MAIN IDEAS

Choose the correct answer for the multiple-choice items. Write the fill-in answers in the space provided using your own words.

_____ **1.** Which two conditions was John Zickefoose diagnosed with as a child?
    a. hypertension and hyperactivity
    b. dyslexia and attention deficit hyperactivity disorder
    c. dyslexia and unruly behavior
    d. attention deficit hyperactivity disorder and autism

_____ **2.** According to Zickefoose, the lowest point in his life occurred when he
    a. was asked to give a speech that he couldn't read.
    b. received his high school diploma but couldn't read it.
    c. couldn't help with his 7-year-old son's homework assignment.
    d. didn't know how to read a restaurant menu in front of friends.

3. How and where specifically did John Zickefoose learn to read?

_____

_____ **4.** Who or what did Zickefoose blame for his past illiteracy?
    a. his parents, for not pushing hard enough or taking an interest in his education
    b. his teachers, for not pushing hard enough or working with him individually
    c. the reading specialists who diagnosed his condition but then didn't follow through with any further help
    d. himself

5. Why was Zickefoose allowed to graduate despite being unable to read? What system is in place that would prevent such a student from graduating now?

_____

_____ **6.** In Zickefoose's book club, the group read *Black Like Me*, the true story set in the 1950s of an experiment that describes the experience of a white man who passed as black in the Jim Crow South. This book appealed to him greatly because
    a. Zickefoose himself is black and so identified with the main character.
    b. it was the first book he had ever read cover to cover in his whole life.
    c. he identified with the main character, who was a social outcast.
    d. he learned about an important era in American history for the first time in his life.

COMPREHENSION SCORE

Score your answers for Exercises A and B as follows:

A. No. right _____ × 2 = _____

B. No. right _____ × 1 = _____

Total points from A and B _____ × 10 = _____ percent

C. SEQUENCING

These sentences from one paragraph in the selection may have been scrambled. Read the sentences and choose the sequence that puts them back into logical order. Do not refer to the original selection.

> **1** The lowest point, he said, came when he couldn't understand his 7-year-old's homework assignments. **2** He would wish there was a magic pill he could take to make his disabilities disappear. **3** But when Zickefoose looked at the textbook, all he saw were letters strung together that made no sense. **4** When Shawn asked for help, Zickefoose sat with him at the kitchen table.

_____ Which of the following represents the correct sequence for these sentences?
   a. 1, 3, 2, 4
   b. 2, 1, 4, 3
   c. 4, 3, 2, 1
   d. Correct as written.

You may refer to the selection as you work through the remaining exercises.

D. LOCATING INFORMATION

1. John Zickefoose was diagnosed as a child as having dyslexia, defined as difficulty in reading. Look again through the beginning paragraphs (1–10) and locate the information that explains a bit more specifically exactly what Zickefoose experienced when he tried to read.

   _____

2. Why was reading so difficult for John when he first started working with a tutor? What went wrong? (See paragraphs 11–15)

   _____

E. MAKING INFERENCES

For each of these statements write Y (yes) if the inference is an accurate one, N (no) if the inference is an inaccurate one, or CT (can't tell) if the writer does not give enough information to make an inference one way or another.

1. _____ Read paragraph 1 again. In this paragraph Zickefoose is probably reading a story to some children.

2. _____ John Zickefoose didn't learn to read as a child because he attended bad public schools.

3. _____ In paragraph 21, the writer implies that one doesn't need to know how to read well to do math or science.

4. _____ If students in the late 1970s had been required to pass a math and English test in order to graduate, Zickefoose probably wouldn't have received his diploma.

5. _____ If Zickefoose were a student today, his teachers probably would not have been able to help him any more than his teachers did in the late 1970s. Dyslexia remains essentially untreatable.

6. _____ Look at paragraph 24. Zickefoose's restoration business eventually failed because he couldn't read.

F. UNDERSTANDING VOCABULARY IN CONTEXT

Here are a few vocabulary words from the selection along with their definitions. Study these definitions carefully. Then write the appropriate word in each space provided according to the context, the way it is used. Note: You will use only four of the five words in each set.

metamorphosis	a transformation from one stage to another
anomaly	deviation from the normal, something irregular
perseverance	steady persistence, resolve, determination
outcast	someone who has been excluded from a group or society
stigma	mark of disgrace or shame

1. Despite being 35 when he learned to read, John was something of an _____ in another way. A lot of people who can't read suffer from the _____ and are ashamed to ask for help. In John's case, his _____ paid off. Learning to read allowed to overcome his perception of himself as an _____.

compensate	to make up for, counterbalance
culmination	the highest point or degree
whimsical	fanciful, quirky, capricious
mainstay	chief support, foundation, support
rowdy	disorderly, unruly, noisy

2. Like many children who can't read, John was _____ in class and later, as an adult, learned to _____ for his inability to read by ordering items from the pictures on a menu or asking friends to help him fill out job applications. But now, as a school board member, John has reached the _____ of his adult life. Learning to read has become a _____ in his life, truly a transformative experience.

G. USING VOCABULARY—VARIANT WORD FORMS

Write the correct inflected form of the base word in each of the following sentences. Be sure to add the appropriate ending to fit the grammatical requirements of the sentence. Refer to your dictionary if necessary.

1. (*severity*—use an adverb). There is no question that a person who is illiterate is _____ hampered in any developed society.

2. (*confrontation*—use a verb) Being _____ with written English was a difficult, embarrassing experience for John, like looking at a foreign language.

3. (*persuade*—use an adjective) John is now a role model for other young people struggling in school, and the fact that he himself conquered his illiteracy is surely a _____ message.

4. (*tense*—use a noun) The only source of _____ in John and Eileen's marriage was his lack of a bank account.

5. (*humble*—use a noun) John is not arrogant or boastful about his accomplishments. In fact, one friend says that he displays _____ in talking about his past.

6. (*limitation*—use a verb) John's illiteracy seriously _____ his options, though it took him years to realize he needed to do something about it.

H. SMALL GROUP ACTIVITY—UNDERSTANDING IDIOMATIC EXPRESSIONS

Rivera uses several informal and slang expressions. Consider these expressions in their context and then, working in small groups, try to determine their meaning. The paragraph number where each occurs is included. You might try the dictionary if you are unsure, or ask your instructor for help.

1. He became the *poster boy* [4]   _____

2. He would wish there was a *magic pill* [9]   _____

3. he tried to *fake his way through* [10]   _____

4. been able to *wriggle out of* uncomfortable situations [11]   _____

5. "You don't get it." [26]   _____

6. "I was pretty good at *faking it*." [29]   _____

7. Zickefoose was a *quick study* [36]   _____

8. Hey, *check me out.* [39]   _____

9. the *light bulb came on* [41]   _____

10. to be *straight-arrow*, business-minded [42]   _____

I. ANNOTATING EXERCISE

For this exercise, assume that you are preparing to write an essay on the problems that illiterate people face in our society. Go through the selection and locate any piece of information that supports this idea. Annotate each section by writing the main point in your own words in the left margin.

J. PARAPHRASING EXERCISE

Here is a passage from the selection, followed by three paraphrases. Choose the one that most accurately paraphrases the original passage.

_____ 1. For the boy who couldn't understand the words on his high school diploma, the journey to the school board was the culmination of a vow to do something meaningful in his life and help prevent others from starting out as he did.

   a. This journey was difficult: starting with not being able to read his high school diploma to learning to read and ending up a school board member made his family proud.

   b. Becoming a school board member was the final achievement in a long and difficult journey; having graduated from high school unable to read his own diploma, John turned his life around, promising not only to make something of himself but also to help others avoid the same fate.

   c. John made a vow that when he became a school board member, he would help others learn to read so that they could do something meaningful in their lives as he had done.

_____ 2. After so many years of torment, it turned out that Zickefoose was a quick study.

   a. Even though he learned quickly, John Zickefoose could never forget the agony he had experienced as an illiterate.

   b. Zickefoose studied hard because he wanted to learn to read as quickly as possible after so many years of torment.

   c. Despite the years of torment that he experienced, Zickefoose actually learned to read very quickly.

K. TOPICS FOR DISCUSSION

1. What is a functional illiterate? How does it differ from someone who is illiterate? Next, what does it mean to be "functionally literate" and how does it differ from being "functionally illiterate"?

2. It's obvious that Zickefoose slipped through the cracks, despite the fact that reading specialists diagnosed his condition. Do you think it's credible that Zickefoose blames himself for his illiteracy? What evidence does he provide to justify this statement?

3. What's missing in this article? What other information would you have liked to have about John Zickefoose's situation?

L. TOPICS FOR WRITING

1. Write a short essay in which you describe a typical day in the life of a functional illiterate going about the usual daily tasks.
2. Do you remember learning to read? If so, write a short essay in which you describe the process—who taught you, what you read, how you felt about the experience, whether you had good instruction or not.

EXPLORE THE WEB

-   The Literacy Information and Communication System (LINCS) is an agency devoted to matters relating to literacy research and resources. Here is the link:
    -   www.lincs.ed.gov
-   ProLiteracy is an international group whose mission is to promote literacy throughout the world. On their home page at the link below, you can click on "Ways to Get Involved" to find literacy programs in your area.
    -   www.literaryvolunteers.org

IN THE LIBRARY

-   *Black Like Me* (mentioned in paragraph 40) is a nonfiction book by John Howard Griffin, a journalist, published in 1961. Griffin undertook an experiment: He darkened his skin chemically and traveled around the South by bus—to Louisiana, Mississippi, Alabama, and Georgia—to see first-hand what it was like for African-Americans to live in a racially segregated culture.

15 JOHN SCHWARTZ
Extreme Makeover: Criminal Court Edition

John Schwartz is the National Legal Correspondent for the New York Times, *where this article was originally published. Schwartz attended the University of Texas at Austin; later he studied law and passed the bar, but he has never practiced law, preferring to write about legal issues. With Michael Osterholm, Schwartz is the author of a book* Living Terror, *which deals with the subject of biological terrorism. This article describes a legal conflict: whether a judge should have allowed John Ditullio, a neo-Nazi murder defendant, to have his tattoos cosmetically covered up at taxpayer expense before his trial for a double stabbing.*

Vocabulary Analysis

The prefix *neo-* The prefix *neo-* means "new or recent." In the case of *neo-Nazi*, the prefix is attached to Nazi to indicate a person who is now affiliated with or inspired by Nazism. (*Nazi* is short for National Socialist German Workers' Party, founded in Germany in 1919, the party in power during Adolf Hitler's regime.) *Neo-* precedes many English words, for example, *neonate* (newborn), *neophyte* (a beginning), and *neocon* (short for neo-conservative).

WORD ROOTS

survive Derived from Latin *super-* ("over") + *vivere* ("to live"), *survive* has a number of meanings in English: to remain alive, to carry on in difficult circumstances, to live longer than or to outlive. The root *vivere* can be found in other English words: *vivid* ("bright" or "distinctive'), *vivacious* ("lively" or "full of spirit"), *vivify* ("to give life to"), and *vivisection* ("the practice of doing medical research on live animals"). A related Latin root is the noun *vita*, meaning "life," which you can see in the words *vital*, *vitality*, and *vitamin*.

WORD ORIGINS

swastika, tattoos The swastika symbol (see paragraph 1) looks like this: ✦ Today it is remembered as a symbol of Nazi Germany. But Hitler only adopted the symbol; it is both ancient and universal. The word comes from *svastika*, a word in

Sanskrit (the classical language of India), meaning a sign of good luck. Today the symbol retains the power to inflame as it did in Nazi Germany. *Tattoo*, the practice of puncturing the skin and injecting colored dyes to form designs on the skin, derives from a Tahitian word, *tatu*, meaning "to prick."

JOHN SCHWARTZ

Extreme Makeover: Criminal Court Edition

1   CLEARWATER, Fla. — When John Ditullio goes on trial on Monday, jurors will not see the large swastika tattooed on his neck. Or the crude insult tattooed on the other side of his neck. Or any of the other markings he has acquired since being jailed on charges related to a double stabbing that wounded a woman and killed a teenager in 2006.

2   Mr. Ditullio's lawyer successfully argued that the tattoos could be distracting or prejudicial to the jurors, who under the law are supposed to consider only the facts presented to them. The case shows some of the challenges lawyers face when trying to get clients ready for trial—whether that means hitting the consignment shop for decent clothes for an impoverished client or telling wealthy clients to leave the bling at home.

3   "It's easier to give someone who looks like you a fair shake," said Bjorn E. Brunvand, Mr. Ditullio's lawyer.

4   The court approved the judicial equivalent of an extreme makeover, paying $125 a day for the services of a cosmetologist to cover up the tattoos that Mr. Ditullio has gotten since his arrest. This is Mr. Ditullio's second trial for the murder; the first, which also involved the services of a cosmetologist, ended last year in a mistrial. If convicted, he could face the death penalty.

5   "There's no doubt in my mind—without the makeup being used, there's no way a jury could look at John and judge him fairly," Mr. Brunvand said in an interview in his office here. "It's too frightening when you see him with the tattoos. It's a scary picture."

6   Hence the cosmetologist. Chele, the owner of the company performing the work, said the process takes about 45 minutes.

7   The first stage is a reddish layer to obscure the greenish tinge of the ink— "You cover a color with a color," she explained. Then comes Dermablend, a cosmetic aid that smoothes and obscures and is used to cover scars and pigmentation disorders like vitiligo. A flesh-toned layer is then sprayed on with an air gun, and finally, to avoid the porcelain-doll look that comes from an even-hued coat, a final color touchup intended to, as theatrical makeup artists say, "put blood back in."

8   The cosmetologist asked that she not be identified by her full name out of fear of reprisal and lost business. "We mostly do weddings," she said.

9   Colleen Quinn-Adams, a private investigator working on the case with Mr. Brunvand, said she had had to call 10 cosmetologists before finding one willing

to take on this particular client. "I would either get a long pause, and have to say, 'Are you still there?' or, 'I don't think we could handle that job.'"

10   While the move to pretty up a man accused of murder might seem bizarre, defense lawyers like Mr. Brunvand say they fight an uphill battle every day in court: though the law requires that juries see every defendant as innocent until proved guilty, they say, jurors are generally more likely to see someone who has been arrested as guilty.

11   Appearance is a big part of setting the right balance, said Anna M. Durbin, a lawyer in Ardmore, Pa., who has often run to used-clothing stores to find an alternative to the jail jumpsuit for clients without money or family. "You don't have a clean slate if you look like a perpetrator," she said.

12   Douglas Keene, a trial consultant in Austin, Tex., noted that making defendants look more like someone who is "kind of like me" does not come into play just in cases involving violence or poverty. "I counseled defendants during the Enron trial to remove $10,000 watches," he said.

13   The decision to cover Mr. Ditullio's tattoos could be more of a judgment call, Mr. Keene said. "People are wearing tattoos as a public statement of what's important to them," he said.

14   He recalled that Charles Manson carved a swastika on his forehead during his murder trial. "At what point does someone's decision to put a billboard on their forehead become something from which we have to protect them?" he asked.

15   Mr. Brunvand, who was appointed by the court, said inmates might tattoo themselves for many reasons: some may do so to project a more menacing appearance and to show affiliation with groups that might protect them.

16   Charlene Bricken, the mother of the young man Mr. Ditullio is accused of killing, Kristofer King, said she was outraged that the defendant would receive a court-approved makeover. "Did somebody tie him down while he was in jail and put these tattoos on him?" she asked angrily.

17   Ms. Bricken said that she had "no doubt" Mr. Ditullio was guilty—he sent a taunting Christmas card to the family from prison—and that the judge was "bending over backwards for the criminal."

18   Mr. Brunvand said the card Mr. Ditullio sent Ms. Bricken was "a terrible thing," but attributed it to "acting out in frustration" because of feelings that he had been falsely arrested and that "everybody had, in their minds, already convicted him."

19   He said he hoped to show that another member of a neo-Nazi group Mr. Ditullio had joined more closely resembled the initial description by the surviving victim of the attack and was the likely perpetrator. That person has left the state.

20   Mike Halkitis, the division director for the state attorney's office in New Port Richey, where the trial will be held, said that he fought the "absurd" request for a cosmetic cover-up last year, and that taxpayers should not have to pay for it.

21   While a richer defendant could pay for cosmetics or even tattoo removal, "the indigent defendant isn't entitled to the same defense an affluent defendant can get," he said. "That's case law."

22   Instead, Mr. Halkitis said, the judge could just as easily instruct the jury to ignore the tattoos in their consideration of the case. "We believe the jurors listen to judges' instructions," he said.

23   Mr. Halkitis suggested that the judge had ruled to allow the cosmetic assistance with an eye to higher courts in the event that Mr. Ditullio receives the ultimate penalty—"that there can't be a judge that overturns the death penalty on the basis that they should have whited the tattoos."

24   For Chele, the cosmetologist, the case has been a lesson in the justice system. "It's not about payment," she said. "It's about doing what's right to do this—to give this man a chance at a fair trial. We're not just doing this for John. We're doing this for justice, and our country."

Exercises

You may refer to the selection while you complete these exercises.

A. COMPREHENDING MAIN IDEAS

Write the answers for these questions in the space provided using your own words.

1. What is it about Ditullio's tattoos that, according to his defense attorney, would make them "distracting or prejudicial" to jurors?

    _____

2. What did Ditullio's makeover consist of, and who paid for it?

    _____

3. Why did ten cosmetologists turn down the job of working on John Ditullio? Why did "Chele," the cosmetologist who agreed to work on Ditullio, not want her full name used?

    _____

4. The law says that one is innocent until proven guilty. But in fact, jury members may believe something different. What is it?

    _____

5. Besides removing tattoos, what are two other examples Schwartz includes of changes defense attorneys have made in their clients' appearance before they go to court?

    _____

6. How did Charlene Bricken, the mother of one of the victims Ditullio is accused of killing, react when she learned that the judge approved a makeover for him? Why did she react this way?

    _____

7. What is another course mentioned that the judge could have taken instead of approving a cosmetic makeover with Ditullio?

_____

8. What was believed to be the ultimate reason that the judge allowed Ditullio to receive cosmetic "assistance"?

_____

B. MAKING INFERENCES

For each of these statements write Y (yes) if the inference is an accurate one, N (no) if the inference is an inaccurate one, or CT (can't tell) if the writer does not give enough information to make an inference one way or another.

1. _____   From paragraphs 1 and 15, we can infer that John Ditullio got his tattoos while serving time in prison.

2. _____   The cosmetic makeover that Ditullio received resulted in the complete removal of his tattoos. (See paragraph 7.)

3. _____   From paragraph 9 we can infer that the ten cosmetologists called to work on Ditullio's tattoos turned down the job because, like Chele, they were afraid of reprisals and lost business.

4. _____   A defendant's appearance is more important than the quality of the evidence presented by his or her defense attorney.

5. _____   A wealthy defendant could afford to pay for a cosmetic makeover, while an impoverished one couldn't. Therefore, to make things fair for everyone, the judge decided to authorize the expenditure and allow Ditullio to have the services of a cosmetologist.

6. _____   John Ditullio at first argued against having his tattoos covered up because he liked the menacing appearance they conveyed.

7. _____   The surviving victim identified the correct assailant, another member of Ditullio's neo-Nazi group, but since that person left town, the court had no choice but to bring Ditullio to trial for the crimes.

8. _____   According to what the writer implies in paragraph 22, the judge rejected the idea of instructing the jury to ignore the defendant's tattoos since he was concerned about a death penalty being overturned if the case were appealed to a higher court later.

9. _____   The cosmetic makeover worked, and John Ditullio was found innocent by the jury.

10. _____   The writer strongly suggests that the taxpayers should not have been charged for the cost of removing Ditullio's tattoos.

C. UNDERSTANDING VOCABULARY

Look through the paragraphs listed by number in brackets and find a word that matches each definition. Refer to a dictionary if necessary. An example has been done for you.

Ex. diverting, turning attention away from one's focus
[paragraphs 1–2]   *distracting*

1. poverty-stricken [1–2]   _____

2. makes indistinct, makes less noticeable [7]   _____

3. retaliation, inflicting injury in return for
   something [8–9]   _____

4. odd, strikingly strange [10–11]   _____

5. one who commits a crime [11 and 19]   _____

6. association, identification with a group [14–15]   _____

7. mocking, insulting in a contemptuous
   manner [17–18]   _____

8. needy, destitute, poor [21–22]   _____

9. wealthy, comfortable financially [21–22] _____

10. the greatest possible [23–24]   _____

D. USING VOCABULARY—VARIANT WORD FORMS

In parentheses before each sentence are some inflected forms of words from the selection. Study the context and the sentence. Then write the correct form in the space provided.

1. (*prejudice, prejudge, prejudicial, prejudicially*). John Ditullio's defense attorney believed that the jury would _____ his client if they saw his tattoos.

2. (*menace, menacing, menacingly*) Bjorn Brunvand, Ditullio's attorney, observes that prison inmates sometimes get tattoos to make themselves look more _____ .

3. (*falsification, falsify, false, falsely*) Inmates often believe that their accusers _____ evidence or that they have been _____ arrested by the police.

4. (*resemblance, resemble, resembling*) Brunvand, the defense attorney, argued in court that another person with a close _____ to Ditullio was the likely perpetrator.

5. (*absurdity*, *absurd*, *absurdly*) Mike Halkitis, who works for the state attorney's office, considered the request for a cosmetic cover-up an _____ that taxpayers should not have had to pay for.

6. (*ultimatum*, *ultimate*, *ultimately*) _____, the jury will have to decide on Ditullio's guilt or innocence after the trial ends.

E. PARAPHRASING EXERCISE

Here are some sentences from the selection. Write a paraphrase of each passage in the space provided.

1. While the move to pretty up a man accused of murder might seem bizarre, defense lawyers like Mr. Brunvand say they fight an uphill battle every day in court: though the law requires that juries see every defendant as innocent until proved guilty, they say, jurors are generally more likely to see someone who has been arrested as guilty.

   _____

   _____

   _____

2. "You don't have a clean slate if you look like a perpetrator."

   _____

3. "At what point does someone's decision to put a billboard on their forehead become something from which we have to protect them"?

   _____

   _____

F. TOPICS FOR DISCUSSION

1. Consider again the three statements in the paraphrasing exercise. Discuss the ramifications of each statement. On balance, what is your opinion about the judge's decision? Should Ditullio have been allowed to have his tattoos covered up to ensure that the jurors would treat him fairly, or should have he just had to live with his decision to get offensive, scary tattoos?

2. What is the writer's position on this issue? Is his purpose to favor one side or the other or to present both sides and to let the reader decide for himself or herself? How can you tell?

3. Why are tattoos so popular today?

4. If you have a job, what is your employer's policy regarding tattoos on employees? Do you find the policy fair and reasonable or not? Examine employers' right to regulate their employees' appearance.

G. TOPICS FOR WRITING

1. Write a short argumentative essay in which you take a stand on this issue and present your evidence to support it. You may use evidence from the article in support of your argument, but try to come up with your own reasons as well.
2. Write an essay in which you examine your reasons to get a tattoo or not to get one.

EXPLORE THE WEB

- Did the cosmetological work on John Ditullio's tattoos work in his favor? What did the jury find? Using Google, in the search box, type in "John Ditullio verdict, New York Times" to find the answer. In addition, several before and after photos of John Ditullio are available online. Again, type in "John Ditullio Photos," and you can judge for yourself.

16 "THE WAITER" Why Be a Waiter?

"The Waiter" is the online pseudonym (penname) of a New York waiter who wrote a blog titled WaiterRant for over four years, in which he wrote about his restaurant, his coworkers, and his customers—often including lengthy complaints about all three. In 2008 before starting his book tour to promote his book Waiter Rant, from which this selection is taken, "The Waiter" revealed his identity. His real name is Steve Dublanica, who has since quit being a waiter and has stopped contributing to his blog, though it is archived online. So far, he has refused to identify the New York restaurant where he worked, which he calls here "The Bistro," but it has been speculated that it's actually in New Jersey, not New York. Rumors persist.

Vocabulary Analysis

The prefix *ir-* In Selection 14, you were introduced to the prefix *il-*, variants of *un-* and *in-*, which are used to negate words. You will recall that *il-* negates words beginning with *l* like *illegitimate* or *illegal*. Similarly, *ir-* negates words beginning with *r*, as in the word *irregular* (paragraph 1). If you encounter a difficult and likely unfamiliar word like *irrevocable*, you can break it down like this:

ir- ("not") + *voc* ("to call") + *able* ("able to") = not able to be called back or reversed. The accent is on the second syllable. Other words beginning with *ir-* in this capacity are *irrational*, *irresponsible*, and *irreparable*. Despite its use in spoken language, there is no such word as *irregardless* in English. The correct word is *regardless*.

WORD PARTS

hyperbole, hyperbolic In paragraph 47, The Waiter writes, ". . . some waiters are *wasting* their lives. Too busy having fun and reveling in *hyperbolic* bitterness, these losers pretend they're above the fray of ordinary life. . ." The noun *hyperbole* is of Greek origin, and means "deliberate exaggeration for effect," as when you tell your friend that you want to stop and get a hamburger because you're "starving." The word is pronounced hī pûr' bə lē, with the accent on the second syllable. The adjective form, *hyperbolic*, is pronounced with the accent on the third syllable: hīpûr bŏl' ik. The word is formed from the Greek prefix *hyper-* meaning "excessive" and *ballein* ("to throw"). Other words beginning with *hyper-* are *hyperactive*, *hyperconscious*, and *hyperthyroidism*.

OTHER WORDS (FROM FOREIGN LANGUAGES) YOU NEED TO KNOW

tabula rasa [paragraph 22]	Latin for "blank slate," in this context referring to a person who is uninformed and inexperienced and who can therefore be more easily molded or trained
Byzantine [34]	An adjective usually describing a style of architecture associated with the Byzantine Empire. Here it refers to something extremely complicated and intricate.
c'est la vie [36]	French for "that's life" or "that's just the way things are"
bonhomie [48]	French for having a pleasant and genial disposition

"THE WAITER"

Why Be a Waiter?

1   Waiters depend on tips to survive. As you've read, it can be a fairly irregular source of income. You might think it's a miracle anyone wants to wait tables in the first place, but, trust me, there's usually never a shortage of applicants. Waiting tables is as addictive as crack cocaine.

2   It's the quiet zone between lunch and dinner service. I'm spread out in the back with an espresso and my copy of the *New York Times.* The staff's clustered around me, chattering away as they eat their midday meal. The door chimes. The sound of silverware scraping against plates comes to a halt. I look over the top of my paper, half expecting to see another adulterous couple skulking around the front door.

3   Standing in the doorway, however, is a fresh-faced kid no older than nineteen. He's not eating here. The staff breathes a sigh of relief. Lunch break uninterrupted, the noise of people eating refills the air.

4   "I'll bet he's looking for a job," Imelda says, digging into her pasta.

5   I sigh deeply. I had a busy morning and was enjoying my little moment of Zen. Annoyed, I fold my paper, place it on the table, and walk toward the front.

6   "Hi," the kid says, extending his hand. "Are you the manager?"

7   "I am," I acknowledge. I tell the kid my name and shake his hand.

8   "I'm looking for a job," the kid says. "Do you have any openings?"

9   "We do. Let me get you an application."

10   "Thanks."

11   I kneel down behind the hostess stand and rummage through the plastic filing cabinet where we keep the applications. Fluvio is terribly disorganized.

File pockets overflow with scores of forgotten résumés and applications. Fluvio doesn't look at 10 percent of applications people drop off. The secret to getting hired at The Bistro is catching Fluvio on the odd afternoon when he's actually here. If he likes you, you're hired.

12 I find an application and ask the young man to fill it out.

13 "You make good money here?" the kid asks, as he fills in the required fields.

14 "Depends on the day," I reply.

15 "Oh," the kid murmurs. "Which days are good money?"

16 "Fridays and Saturdays. We also have a strong Monday and Wednesday night."

17 "I'm available on weekends."

18 "We assign shifts based on seniority. It takes a while for new people to get to the really good shifts."

19 The kid looks crestfallen.

20 "But you never know," I say, trying to end the conversation on a light note. "I've got a waitress having a baby. Maybe something'll open up."

21 "Thanks," the kid replies. After a few minutes he stops writing and hands me the application

22 I skim over it. The kid's a student at a local college looking for extra money. He's worked summers at a deli but has no fine-dining experience. Sometimes not having experience is a plus. A newbie to the restaurant world's a tabula rasa that can be trained to do things just the way The Bistro wants them done. The downside's the amount of time you have to invest bringing the restaurant virgin up to speed. I've spent weeks training new servers, only to watch them throw in their apron to become professional yogis or Pilates teachers. That's a pain in the ass.

23 That's why we normally hire people with a couple of years under their belt. There's a downside to hiring experienced staff, of course—they often come in full of piss and vinegar and try to change the way things have been done for years. I'm not against reform or new ideas, but hotshots like that are usually after my job. They don't last long. Eventually they quit. Trust me, I have my ways. Fluvio isn't the only one who can act like a bastard.

24 "Okay," I say. "I'll give your application to the owner. If he's interested, he'll call you."

25 "Thanks," the kid says. "Any idea how long that'll be?"

26 I feel for the kid. He needs money, but he's not a good fit for The Bistro. It'd be cruel to hire him.

27 "If you don't hear from him in two weeks," I reply, hoping the kid reads between the lines, "then he's not interested."

28 The kid shows a flicker of disappointed understanding. "Thanks, sir," he says sheepishly.

29 "Good luck."

30 I watch the kid walk down the street. I feel bad for him, but I have to think about what's best for the restaurant. I keep my eye out for competent and quiet professionals, the smart waiters who keep their mouths shut and their eyes open. When jumping to another restaurant, these people don't rock the boat. They know patience is the key. Within months talent and good work ethics push

them to the top of the heap. Grateful managers feel compelled to award them with moneymaking shifts. If that doesn't happen, a professional waiter looks for greener pastures.

31   My espresso's gone cold. I head into the back to brew another one. As I listen to the steam press through the grounds, I wonder for the millionth time why anyone would want to become a waiter. The University of Chicago recently did a survey of twenty-seven thousand Americans about job satisfaction and happiness. Clergy and firefighters were at the top of the job-satisfaction list. Waiters were at the bottom. Considering the shit we put up with, that's no surprise. For me, that survey's findings are laden with personal irony. Like most little boys, I wanted to be a fireman when I grew up. When I got to college, I studied to be a priest. Now, at thirty-eight, I'm a waiter. I started out heading for the top of the list, only to end up on the bottom. Where did I go wrong?

32   People who become waiters fall into three distinct categories: people trying to become something else, people whose lives are falling apart, and people stuck somewhere in the middle. Tucked within those categories is a small and distinct subgroup, the professional servers, people who make waiting tables their life's work. I'll admit those three categories are kind of broad. Waiters often find themselves with one foot in one category and one in the other. I've personally been in all three categories simultaneously.

33   The first type of server is the one you're most accustomed to seeing. These are waiters who, when not fetching lemon for your water, are busy trying to become something *else.* They're going to college, pursuing dance careers, writing the great American novel, sculpting, drug dealing, modeling for pornographic Web sites, and, of course, *acting.* Lifelong waiterdom holds little appeal for these individuals. The only reason they're working in a restaurant is because the money and schedule allow them time to achieve their long-term goals.

34   Because university registrars take perverse pride in designing Byzantine class schedules that offer mandatory courses available only when Neptune's orbit intersects Pluto's during a leap year, students' academic calendars are notoriously chaotic. Since restaurant jobs have more flexibility in scheduling than other jobs, many waiters are college students. It's a natural fit; students take classes during the day, work in the evening, and party into the wee hours of the night. Sleep? You've got to be kidding me.

35   Money is also a big factor. There are few jobs outside waiting tables where workers can make so much money in such a short amount of time. A normal evening shift usually lasts eight hours. A good waiter working an upscale establishment can clear $200 a night, sometimes more. That's $25 an hour! Not all servers reach this level, of course, but even if they clear only $100 a night, that still works out to almost $13 an hour. That beats the hell out of working at the college bookstore or delivering pizza for minimum wage. Outside of drug dealing, dorm-room prostitution, and creating Web sites like MySpace, waiting tables provides the biggest financial bang for the least temporal buck.

36   After the students come the artistes—the endless procession of models, painters, writers, and actors—who struggle to make ends meet as they chase their *American Idol* dreams. I remember one waiter, an aspiring screenwriter, who shamelessly pitched his script to every unwilling customer he thought might get

him a shot at Hollywood. He had a brilliant idea, so it was tough to watch his zeal turn into measured optimism, devolve into cynicism, and finally ossify into "c'est la vie."

37   I've encountered a few "actors" along the way as well. One girl I worked with did foot-fetish films and cable TV porn on the side. She won't be winning any Academy Awards, but hey, you can't knock a girl for trying. It's small wonder why so many struggling actors wait tables—it's a great place to hone your thespian skills. You try selling "Chilean sea bass garnished with endive marmalade" with a straight face. Think of it as culinary method acting, complete with imperious Europeans screaming at you. All this talk about waiters and acting reminds me of that old joke.

38   "My son's an actor in New York."

39   "Really? What restaurant?"

40   That underscores the bitter reality many artists who wait tables struggle with on a daily basis. When asked what they "do," they usually reply, "I'm an actor," or "I'm a writer." For the first couple of years that's okay—but, after several years working in the restaurant biz, if the bulk of your income still comes from waiting tables, you're a waiter. Don't get me wrong. I admire people who struggle to pursue their artistic dreams, but when a guy claiming to be a writer has been a server for years and is still working on the draft of his first novel, he's living in the deluded zone.

41   Sometimes when aspiring photographers or sculptors realize they've been waiting tables for too long, that's the kick in the ass they need to get out there and hustle up their own luck. Many waiters, through effort and by dint of hard work, leave the restaurant behind to pursue their dream careers. Occasionally lightning strikes and a waiter goes from waiterhood to superstardom "overnight." My favorite story is of Erika Sunnegårdh, a forty-year-old aspiring opera singer who spent eighteen years waiting tables in the Bronx, hoping for her big break. Eighteen years is a *long* time to wait. Singing at funerals to keep her voice in shape, Erika was getting close to throwing in the towel. Having never appeared onstage in any opera *anywhere,* she tried out for a role in Beethoven's *Fidelio* at the Metropolitan Opera. Awed by the majesty of her voice, the producers asked her to understudy for the performer singing the title role. In classic Hollywood fashion, the star fell ill on the day the performance was being broadcast to 10 million radio listeners, and Erika stole the show. Now she's an opera star. I wish every aspiring singer and dancer I've met in the restaurant business could hit it big, but, as Simon Cowell mercilessly informs us every week, that can't always happen.

42   The next category of server, people who don't know what do with their lives, is the type of waiter I most closely identify with. It starts out innocently enough. You lose your job, have a nervous breakdown, get paroled, or have a midlife crisis, and you have no idea what to do next.

43   I think there are many waiters like me, sitting on life's fence and trying to figure out what they want to be when they grow up. Before age and limitations start creeping up on you, waiting can be a fun life. When you're in your early twenties, it's a blast, but then, when you're in your forties, it can be horrifying. I partly blame my predicament on that crack-cocaine quality of waiting

tables. Here, the schedule and easy money are important. Whereas with college students it's a means to an end, for the Hamlet waiter it's a narcotic, seductive influence. If you skip college and go into the restaurant business, the odds are good that you'll be making more than a college graduate for quite a while. I made more as a waiter than I ever did as a low-level flunky in corporate health care. After a few weeks of profitable shifts you begin to think, Hey, this isn't too bad. Of course, as time goes by, your friends' incomes will outstrip yours and leave you in the dust. Out of all my college-educated friends, I earn the least amount of money. Don't even talk to me about 401(k)s.

44   The schedule's also a biggie. If you're a night owl like me, you'll take to the restaurant business like a duck to water. I like getting up at eleven o'clock and going to bed at three. Night is my natural element. My synapses fire up when the moon's hanging in the sky. Since most people are off when I'm working and vice versa, there's never any line at the movies, and finding a parking spot at the mall's a snap. Waiters begin to pity nine-to-five wretches with their miserable traffic-filled commutes and weekends spent running errands. Living outside the normal flow of the workweek, waiters get to see how crazy American life can be. Of course, we can develop a smug sense of superiority about how we're somehow above it all. I certainly did.

45   Being on the outside of the mainstream, however, is fun only when you *choose* to be on the outside. When it's no longer a choice, when you wake up one day and realize that you have to wait tables to survive, the "waiter mystique" wears thin real fast. Most people who waited tables in college look back on their serving days with a twisted sense of nostalgia. That's because, in the back of their minds, they knew they were getting out. Longtime waiters who successfully escape to other professions look back on their time in the restaurant trenches the way shell-shocked vets look back on heavy combat. "Yeah, I met a few good men along the way—but I'd never want to go back."

46   Of course, some waiters do very well in this situation. My brother springs immediately to mind. He's been in the restaurant business since he was sixteen—almost twenty years. Along the way he's done it all. He's been a dishwasher, busboy, server, headwaiter, and manager. He's hired and fired people and gotten fired and hired himself. He's been punched, kicked, groped, insulted, and kissed.

47   My brother never planned on being in the restaurant business for so long. Like me, he's still trying to figure out what he wants to do when he grows up. Unlike me, however, he didn't wait to get on with his life as he tries to figure it out. It took several years, but he finished his college degree, got married, bought a house, and had a baby—all while being a waiter. This guy didn't sit around and cry "woe is me" and wait for the perfect situation to start his life. He threw himself into life's slipstream and ended up doing all right.

48   The sad truth is that some waiters are *wasting* their lives. Too busy having fun and reveling in hyperbolic bitterness, these losers pretend they're somehow above the fray of ordinary life, living a bonhomie existence that allows them to critique everyone's life choices but their own.

49   This appellation of loserdom doesn't apply to all waiters trying to figure out what they want to do. Many waiters, like my brother, are using the restaurant

business as a safe haven to venture out and build a life. Some waiters are just hiding. If you've worked in the restaurant business, you've seen the type of waiter I'm talking about. The ones who always talk about opening a restaurant, going back to school, starting a business, or touring Europe—only to spend year after year stuck in the same place. They're all talk.

50   There are a few rare individuals who make waiting tables a career. Usually hardy souls from parts of Europe where waiting is considered an honorable vocation (complete with formal schooling and internships), these servers are blessed with iron feet, steel legs, and an almost religious dedication to professionalism. The waiter I think of as the epitome of the career server is Wolfgang Zwiener, the former headwaiter at Peter Luger's steakhouse in Brooklyn. Zwiener came to New York from Bremen, Germany, after he completed a three-year apprenticeship. (Most waiters today train for three days and watch a sexual harassment video.) After a stint at Lüchow's on East Fourteenth Street in the early 1960s, Mr. Zwiener ended up at Peter Luger's, becoming the headwaiter in 1968. Over the decades, between all the double shifts and parties, he got married, had two sons, and, on a waiter's salary, put them both through college and bought a retirement home in Florida. It didn't hurt that almost all the tips were in cash.

51   After almost forty years at Luger's, Wolfgang decided to move up in the world. Instead of retiring, Wolfgang took his sons' advice and parlayed his lifetime of restaurant know-how into his own restaurant—Wolfgang's—the highly regarded steakhouse on Park Avenue. Since its grand opening in 2004, he's opened another location in the Tribeca section of Manhattan. I guess he's doing okay.

52   Over the years I met a few people like Zwiener, people who toiled for years at some of the fanciest restaurants in New York City and made a comfortable living for themselves and their families. These guys were dealt a hand, and they played it to the best of their ability. Waiters like these are the heroes of the profession, servers for whom hospitality, refinement, and good service are an almost priestly vocation. Deep down, I know I could never muster up the commitment to the restaurant business possessed by Zwiener and others like him. Compared to waiters of that caliber, I am but a humble amateur. But compared to the next group of waiters we're going to examine, I'm Michael Jordan.

53   Quite a few waiters have lives that are train wrecks. A famous chef once observed that the restaurant business is a haven for people who don't fit in anywhere else. That's true. The restaurant business can be like the French Foreign Legion—without the heavy weaponry. But think about it, if all these people don't fit in anywhere else, that usually means there's something *wrong* with them!

54   The restaurant business is a fluid and chaotic environment. Many hiring decisions are made under pressure. Managers need warm bodies to work the grill, wash dishes, chop onions, and bring food to the table. Owners often rely on instinct when hiring people, and references are rarely checked. With this kind of screening system fuckups can breed like cockroaches. Anyone who's ever worked in the restaurant industry has encountered results of these bad hires— the anxiety-producing drama queens, the falling-down drunks, the borderline

nymphomaniacs, the hardcore drug addicts, and the depressed guys who cry on every waitress's shoulder. These aren't just people with problems. Heck, we all have problems at some point. These individuals are so problematic they make working in a restaurant harder than it has to be. Over the years I've noticed wacko servers share some common characteristics.

- Divorced (usually twice, and they have *bad* relationships with their exes)
- DUI (multiple)
- No car (see above)
- Serious substance abuse problem (hence the DUI)
- Transient living situation (always crashing at friends' or strangers' houses, living out of cars, motels, or boarding homes)
- Show up to work dirty (why spend money on laundry when you can buy crack?)
- Always trying to borrow money; always owing coworkers money
- Never wanting to work the shifts they're scheduled—then crying because they're broke
- Always wanting to leave early
- Crying at work; nervous breakdowns in the walk-in fridge; bipolar behavior; nymphomania; subject to rages
- Talking to themselves (okay, I'll admit I've done that)
- Always whining and seeking sympathy; attention seeking
- And, for some reason, always have *bad teeth*

55   Don't worry, if you're a divorcée or you've had a DUI, you don't automatically qualify as a screw up. (I've needed two root canals since I've been a waiter!) Yet, if you've waited on tables, you've met servers who've had several of the above conditions operating simultaneously. There are servers out there who've worked every restaurant in the yellow pages, never stayed more than three months at any one place, and walk around looking like they're heavily medicated. Their résumés usually reflect a steady downward spiral in terms of job responsibility and income. These are the people you pray don't own guns.

56   Some managers and owners *love* hiring these kinds of people. Instead of trying to get them help or lending an understanding ear, they ruthlessly exploit them. Mentally ill or compromised people are vulnerable. People with drug problems, burned-out single moms, downsized tech workers struggling with depression, people with financial problems, or the average alcoholic are easy to manipulate. These are the waiters who won't complain when management steals from the tip-out, engages in discriminatory hiring practices, indulges in sexual harassment, or hurls sexist and racial invectives at the staff. Some restaurant managers go out of their way to hire messed-up people. Why? *Because they're easier to control.* If the staff's easy to control, then it's easier for management to rip them off to line their own pockets. Restaurant workers are basically disposable. Because waiters tend to be a self-involved lot, mentally ill coworkers often go unnoticed or ignored until they decompensate and can't perform. Since there's usually no health insurance in the restaurant industry, getting these people any kind of psychiatric help is expensive and well nigh impossible. When these workers flame out, they end up quitting or getting fired. If you start working at

a restaurant and discover that 80 percent of the people are beyond nuts, you're in a toxic work environment. Get out before you end up going crazy yourself.

56   The espresso machine finishes brewing my demitasse. I place it on a saucer and head back toward the front of the restaurant. As I sip my coffee I look out the front window and think about all the people I've worked with in the restaurant business. They're mostly faces not matching up to any names. Some of them worked in this business briefly and ended up doing something else. One of them died.

57   When people ask me what I do for a living, I tell them I'm a waiter. But I also want to tell them I'm a man who dreams of living a different life. My writing has been giving me hope that I'm a waiter working toward becoming something else. On my darkest days, however, I feel like a train-wreck personality that's going to stay in this business forever.

58   I sip my coffee and sigh. Maybe I should have been a fireman.

"Why Be a Waiter?" (pp. 119-30) from *Waiter Rant* by Steve Dublanica. Copyright © 2008 by Waiter Rant LLC. Reprinted by permission of HarperCollins Publishers.

Exercises

Do not refer to the selection for Exercises A, B, and C unless your instructor directs you to do so.

A. DETERMINING THE MAIN IDEA AND PURPOSE

Choose the best answer.

_____ 1.   The main idea of the selection is that
   a. being a waiter should be an honorable vocation, as it is in Europe.
   b. the writer classifies waiters into three groups, and despite the career's many advantages, few intend it to be a lifetime career.
   c. despite the good money earned in tips, working as a waiter is a stressful, often mind-numbing job that robs workers of their creativity and initiative.
   d. the restaurant business is a fluid and chaotic environment, which often leads to bad hiring decisions made under pressure.

_____ 2.   The writer's purpose is to
   a. explain why he became a waiter.
   b. classify restaurant waiters he has worked with and observed.
   c. persuade readers who aren't sure what to do with their lives to become waiters.
   d. complain about his fellow waiters for their poor work ethics and messed-up lives.

B. COMPREHENDING MAIN IDEAS

Choose the correct answer for the multiple-choice items. Write the fill-in answers in the space provided using your own words.

_____ **1.** The Waiter says that waiting on tables is addictive, humorously comparing it to
   a. alcohol.
   b. heroin.
   c. crack cocaine.
   d. cigarettes.

_____ **2.** When hiring a new waiter at a fine restaurant, most managers or owners prefer to hire
   a. people with emotional or psychological problems, even addiction problems, because they can be easily controlled.
   b. college students, because they need the money.
   c. aspiring actors, because they seldom get acting jobs and therefore are available for work.
   d. applicants with at least a couple of years experience because they know how things work and don't have to be trained in the basics.

_____ **3.** One way that professional waiters can succeed in the business is if they
   a. move around from restaurant to restaurant, getting more pay at each new place.
   b. keep their mouths shut and their eyes open and show a good work ethic.
   c. realize how lucky they are to have a job that has good hours and pays well, leaving them their days free to pursue their own interests.
   d. learn every aspect of running a restaurant, including waiting, so that eventually they can leave and open their own restaurant.

4. Two types of waiters mentioned were those trying to become something else and college students. What were two other types or classes the writer describes in detail?

_____

5. Why do waiters feel sorry for "nine-to-five wretches"—those who must work regular business hours?

_____

_____ **6.** The Waiter says that many waiters he has come into contact with have lives that are "train wrecks" displaying a variety of problems like multiple DUIs, drug problems, money problems, and a tendency to whine and complain. Yet some restaurant managers and owners like to hire applicants with these problems because

    a. they often have had the same problems in the past, and they know that being a waiter can help them overcome their problems.

    b. they feel sorry for them and want to help.

    c. they can't be choosy about whom they hire because so few people want the job.

    d. they find messed-up workers easier to control and to exploit.

COMPREHENSION SCORE

A. No. right _____ × 2 = _____

B. No. right _____ × 1 = _____

Total points from A and B _____ × 10 = _____ percent

C. SEQUENCING

These sentences from one paragraph in the selection may have been scrambled. Read the sentences and choose the sequence that puts them back into logical order. Do not refer to the original selection.

    1 People who become waiters fall into three distinct categories: people trying to become something else, people whose lives are falling apart, and people stuck somewhere in the middle. **2** Tucked within those categories is a small and distinct subgroup—the professional servers, people who make waiting tables their life's work. **3** I'll admit those three categories are kind of broad. **4** Waiter often find themselves with one foot in one category and one in the other. **5** I've personally been in all three categories simultaneously.

_____ Which of the following represents the correct sequence for these sentences?

    a. 4, 5, 1, 3, 2

    b. 1, 3, 2, 5, 4

    c. 3, 1, 2, 5 4

    d. Correct as written.

You may refer to the selection as you work through the remaining exercises.

D. MAKING INFERENCES

Write the answers to these inference questions in your own words.

1. What can you infer about this restaurant's environment or ambiance from the last sentence of paragraph 1?

_____

2. Read through the section from paragraph 6 to 26. Why didn't The Waiter hire the applicant? Why would it have been "cruel" to do so?

_____

3. According to a University of Chicago survey, being a waiter was at the bottom of the list of acceptable occupations in terms of job satisfaction. Yet being a waiter is a relatively popular occupation. How can you account for this discrepancy, according to what the writer implies?

_____

4. Read paragraphs 33–36 again. What do these three groups he describes have in common?

_____

5. Read paragraph 40 again in its entirety. Then consider the sentence where he writes, "after several years working in the restaurant biz, if the bulk of your income still comes from waiting tables, you're a waiter." What does he mean?

_____

6. In paragraph 45 the writer uses the term "waiter mystique." What does he mean by this term, and why does this mystique sometimes wear thin?

_____

7. In paragraph 53, The Waiter says this: "The restaurant business can be like the French Foreign Legion." In the context of this paragraph, what does he mean?

_____

8. What is it about the restaurant business that causes some managers and owners to make bad hires—hiring "fuckups" who cause trouble in the workplace and who "breed like cockroaches"? In what way is the restaurant business different from other businesses in terms of hiring requirements?

_____

E. DISTINGUISHING BETWEEN FACT AND OPINION

For each of the following statements from the selection, write F if the statement represents a factual statement that can be verified or O if the statement represents the writer's or someone else's subjective interpretation. The first two are done for you.

____**F**____ 1. Waiters depend on tips to survive.

____**O**____ 2. You might think it's a miracle anyone wants to wait tables in the first place.

_____ 3. Sometimes not having experience is a plus. A newbie to the restaurant world's a tabula rasa that can be trained to do things just the way The Bistro wants them done.

_____ 4. Since restaurant jobs have more flexibility in scheduling than other jobs, many waiters are college students.

_____5. I admire people who struggle to pursue their artistic dreams, but when a guy claiming to be a writer has been a server for years and is still working on the draft of his first novel, he's living in the deluded zone.

_____6. I think there are many waiters like me, sitting on life's fence and trying to figure out what they want to be when they grow up.

_____7. Waiters begin to pity nine-to-five wretches with their miserable traffic-filled commutes and weekends spent running errands.

_____8. The sad truth is that some waiters are *wasting* their lives.

_____9. Quite a few waiters have lives that are train wrecks. A famous chef once observed that the restaurant business is a haven for people who don't fit in anywhere else.

_____10. On my darkest days I feel like a train-wreck personality that's going to stay in this business forever.

F. UNDERSTANDING VOCABULARY

Look through the paragraphs listed by number in brackets and find a word that matches each definition. Refer to a dictionary if necessary. An example has been done for you.

Ex. dejected, dispirited [paragraphs 11–20] _____*crestfallen*_____

1. in an embarrassed or meek manner [26–30] _____

2. required, obligatory [33–34] _____

3. describing something known widely and unfavorably [33–34] _____

4. excessive devotion or enthusiasm [36–37] _____

5. describing acting or actors [36–37] _____

6. an attitude of jaded negativity, distrust, skepticism [36–37] _____

7. domineering, overbearing, especially in an arrogant manner [36–37] _____

8. a representative example of something [50] _____

9. susceptible to harm, defenseless, weak [56] _____

10. abusive language—plural form [56] _____

G. SMALL GROUP ACTIVITY—UNDERSTANDING SLANG AND IDIOMATIC WORDS AND EXPRESSIONS

Because this selection was originally a blog entry, The Waiter uses an unusually large number of informal and slang expressions. Consider these expressions in their context and then, working in small groups, try to determine their meaning. The paragraph number where each occurs is included. You might try the dictionary if you are unsure, or ask your instructor for help.

1. a *newbie* to the restaurant's world's a tabula rasa [22] _____

2. a couple of years experience *under their belt* [23] _____

3. they come in *full of piss and vinegar* [23] _____

4. *hotshots* like that are usually after my job [23] _____

5. these people don't *rock the boat* [30] _____

6. a professional waiter looks for *greener pastures* [30] _____

7. *you can't knock a girl for trying* [37] _____

8. working in the restaurant *biz* [40] _____

9. the *kick in the ass* they need [41] _____

10. *sitting on life's fence* [43] _____

11. the schedule's also a *biggie* [44] _____

12. these guys were *dealt a hand* [52] _____

13. I could never *muster up* the commitment [52] _____

14. a few waiters have lives that are *train wrecks* [53] _____

15. I've noticed *wacko* servers [54] _____

16. when these workers *flame out* [56] _____

H. ANNOTATING EXERCISE

For this exercise, assume that you are preparing to write an essay on why people become waiters. Go through the selection and locate any piece of information that supports this idea. Annotate each section by writing the main point in your own words in the left margin.

I. SUMMARIZING EXERCISE

Consider again paragraphs 32–43. Then summarize the three types of waiters that the writer describes in no more than 100 words.

_____

_____

_____

_____

J. TOPICS FOR DISCUSSION

1. If you have experience working in a restaurant, whether a fast-food or a fine-dining establishment or something in between, how accurate are The Waiter's observations about the three categories of waiters and their motivations to do this kind of work?

2. How would you describe the organization of this selection? The writer's writing style?

3. This selection was originally a blog posting, though it undoubtedly was revised to some extent. Are the idiomatic and slang expressions appropriate for his purpose or not?

K. TOPICS FOR WRITING

1. Write a short essay in which you examine the personality of The Waiter as it emerges in this selection. How would you characterize his disposition, his personality traits, his interests, and his goals for the future?

2. If you have experience working as a restaurant server, write a short essay in which you describe your own observations. You may write a comparison essay because your experience has been consistent with The Waiter's, or if your experience has been completely different, you can write a contrast essay.

3. Following the scheme The Waiter imposes on his material, write about three (or perhaps more) categories of workers at your current job. As the writer does here, describe the characteristics of each category, their motivation for doing the job, and their success at it.

EXPLORE THE WEB

- You can read four years' worth of The Waiter's blog at this address: *www. WaiterRant.net*.

17 STEVE STRIFFLER
Undercover in a Chicken Factory

This selection, reprinted from Utne Reader, *was adapted from an article originally published in* Labor History. *Steve Striffler was a graduate student in anthropology at the New School for Social Research when he went to Ecuador to study the country's struggle against United Fruit Company's monopoly over the growing of bananas. Now an associate professor in the anthropology department at the University of Arkansas in Fayetteville, Striffler has been studying the impact of globalization on labor, a theme which is addressed at the end of this article. Striffler spent two summers working in Arkansas poultry plants, which gave him material for his 2005 book* Chicken: The Dangerous Transformation of America's Favorite Food—*a look at "the triumph and tragedy of chicken," specifically delving into how chicken has become an unhealthy meat and how the poultry plants have changed the American South.*

Vocabulary Analysis

The prefix *trans-* Since Striffler uses three words beginning with the prefix *trans-*, this is a good place to study its meaning. The Latin word part *trans-* can be both a prefix and a word root, and it is the basis of a large number of English words. In the selection you will encounter *transport*s (paragraph 7), *transformed* (paragraph 8), and *transnational* (paragraph 46). As a prefix, *trans-* means "across." Therefore, *transport* means, literally, "to carry across." With the word *transform*, however, the meaning of "across" is lost, meaning instead "to change form." Finally, *transnational* describes the practice of people moving back and forth across the borders of nations, specifically here, from Mexico to the United States and back again. Other words beginning with *trans-* include *transcontinental*, *transmit*, *transcribe*, and *transitory*.

The prefix *mono-* You were already introduced to the prefix *mono-* in the selection by Sherman Alexie in Part One, but reviewing never hurts. The selection contains both the adverb *monotonously* (paragraph 11) and the noun *monotony* (paragraph

26). Striffler emphasizes the *monotony* of working in a chicken-processing plant. The Greek prefix *mono-* means "one" or "single," and *monotonous* means "having one tone," in other words, repetitively dull. Other words beginning with this prefix are *monarchy*, *monopoly*, *monologue*, *monotheism*, and *monochrome*.

STEVE STRIFFLER

Undercover in a Chicken Factory

1   Springdale, Arkansas, is an unremarkable working-class city at the center of the most productive poultry-producing region in the world. It is also home to the corporate headquarters of Tyson Foods. The company's Northwest Arkansas Job Center is a small building that resembles a government office. A sign in Spanish near the receptionist's desk says, "Do not leave children unattended." Another warns, "Thank you for your interest in our company, Tyson Foods, but please bring your own interpreter."

2   The receptionist seems surprised by my presence, "Sorry, hon, there are no openings for a mechanic." I assure her I'm not qualified to be a mechanic and that I want to work on a production line in one of the area's processing plants. She hands me a thick packet of forms and asks, "*You* want to work on the line?"

3   I can understand her confusion. The secretary and I are the only Americans, the only white folk, and the only English speakers in the room. Spanish predominates, but a couple in the corner converses in Lao and a threesome from the Marshall Islands in a Polynesian language. In less than two decades, the poultry industry has drawn the "workers of the world" to the American South, a region that saw few foreign immigrants during the 20th century. As I know from my research as an anthropologist, Latin Americans first arrived in northwest Arkansas in the late 1980s seeking these jobs. Today, about three-quarters of the workers in the plant are Latin American, with Southeast Asians and Marshallese accounting for many of the rest. Workers born in the United States are few and far between.

4   Tyson processes job applicants like it processes poultry. The emphasis is on quantity not quality. No one at the Job Center spends more than a minute looking at my application, and no single person takes the time to review it all. There are few pleasantries, but there is also no bullshit. I tell the interviewer I want a job at a processing plant, he makes a quick call, and five minutes later I have a job. Someone has already called my references, and I pass both the drug test and the physical. I'm Tyson material.

5   I arrive at the massive plant a few days later. At 3 p.m. sharp, the new recruits are escorted into a small classroom that contains a prominently displayed sign: "Democracies depend on the political participation of its citizens, but not in the workplace." Written in both English and Spanish, the message is clear in any language.

6   The nine (other) people in my orientation class are representative of the plant's second shift. Eight are Latin Americans, with six coming from Mexico and two from El Salvador. Six men, two women. As the younger men frequently

lament, women in the plant tend to be slightly older than the men. In this respect, Maria (early 40s) and Carmen (early 50s) are quite typical. The six men vary in age from their early 20s to their 60s. Jorge, in his mid-30s, has lived in California for the past 13 years, mostly working in a textile factory. Like Jorge, the Mexican workers often come from rural areas in the state of Guanajuato, spend time in California working in factories or picking fruit, then find their way to the promised land of Arkansas. Not only is everything in Arkansas much cheaper, but Tyson Foods pays around eight dollars an hour, offers insurance, and consistently provides 40 hours of work a week. Poultry processing is a tough way to achieve upward mobility, but that is precisely what these jobs represent for most immigrants.

Copyright © FoodCollection

7   After putting on our smocks, aprons, earplugs, hairnets, beard nets, and boots, we're given a tour. Most have killed chickens on farms, but nobody is prepared for the overwhelming sounds, sights, and smells that await us. It doesn't help that the tour begins in "live hanging" (*pollo vivo*). Carmen says what we all are thinking: "My God! (*¡Dios Mio!*) How can one work here?" The answer turns out to be simple. Live hanging pays a bit more and there is actually a waiting list for the job. Chickens are flooding into a dark and hot room at about 200 a minute. The smell is indescribable, suffocating, and absolutely unforgettable. Five or six workers grab the flailing chickens, hooking them by their feet to an overhead rail system that transports the birds throughout the plant. Blood, shit, and feathers are flying everywhere.

8   FORTUNATELY, I LAND a job on Saw Lines 1 and 2. It's not exactly pleasant, but it's a long way from live hanging. These "further" processing lines are at the heart of the revolution that has transformed the poultry industry and American diets over the past 25 years. Before then, most Americans bought chicken in one form: the whole bird. Today, Tyson produces thousands of "further processed/value-added" meat products. The poultry products include nuggets, patties, franks, pet food, and a range of parts in many shapes, sizes, textures, and flavors.

9   There are two identical processing lines where I work. Each takes a whole chicken, cuts it, marinates it, and breads it. With about 20 to 25 workers, each line processes what we've estimated to be about 80 birds a minute or 40,000

pounds of chicken a day. The lines are effectively divided into four sets of machinery: cut up, marinade, breading, and rebreading. Conveyer belts move the chicken from one section to the next. The birds are hung on the line, cut by rotating saws, injected with marinade (whose flavor changes depending on the day), and sent through a series of contraptions that lightly breads the parts. From there, the chicken is conveyed to another area to be cooked, packaged, and placed on tractor-trailers. Live birds enter the plant at one end; patties and nuggets depart from the other.

10   My coworkers are an interesting and diverse bunch. Of the 20 or so on the lines, two (excluding myself) are white Americans. Most white workers left the poultry plants during the region's economic boom in the 1990s, and those who remain tend to fall into two categories. An older group has been working at Tyson for more than 20 years, and they're hanging on to the benefits that seniority bestows. The few white workers who started more recently have few other options. Jane, for example, is well into her 60s. Factory work is all she knows. The language barrier keeps her from conversing with most of her coworkers, but she has a peculiar habit that endears her to nearly everyone. When the line stops, she often dances with an unsuspecting young man, embarrassing the victim but giving everyone else a much-needed laugh.

11   Most line workers are women, many in their 40s and 50s. In a plant where about two-thirds of the workers are male, this fact is telling. On-line jobs are the worst in the plant—monotonously, even dangerously, repetitive. These workers stand in the same place repeating the same motions for an entire shift. Women are concentrated in on-line jobs because they're excluded from all jobs that involve heavy lifting or running machinery. Mario, Alejandro, Roberto, Juan, Jeff, Carlo, and I come from all over the world, but in the plant we are "young" men who clean up waste, bring supplies, lift heavy objects, and operate hand carts and forklifts. As auxiliary workers, we do on-line work, but only intermittently.

12   I am to be the *harinero,* the breading operator, or as my 22-year-old supervisor Michael likes to call me, the little flour boy. Michael can't do the job himself and his instructions are simple: "Do what Roberto does." With five years on the job, Roberto can do every task on the line, fix the machines, and carry on a conversation at the same time. But he gives me formal training, which makes learning my new job a bit tricky. Roberto is neither friendly nor cool at first; and unlike virtually everyone else in the plant, he is unimpressed that I speak Spanish. We would eventually talk about everything from his wife's struggles at a nearby turkey plant to his kids' achievements at school. I would even visit his parents in Mexico. In the beginning, however, I just watch, hoping to gain his respect and learn enough to survive the first week.

13   I LEARN QUICKLY that "unskilled" labor requires immense skill. The job of *harinero* is extremely complicated. In a simple sense, the *harinero* empties 50-pound bags of flour all day. The work is backbreaking, but it takes less physical dexterity than many jobs on the line. At the same time, the job is multifaceted and cannot be quickly learned. The *harinero* constantly adjusts the breader and rebreader, monitors the marinade, turns the power on and off, and replaces old

flour with fresh flour. All this would be relatively manageable if the lines ran well. They never do.

14   Problems with the rebreader are the main reason the line shuts down. It is here, with Roberto, that my education as both *harinero* and worker begins. One of the first things I learn is that I'll be doing the job of two people. There have always been two *harineros,* one for each line. However, Michael, the supervisor, recently decided to run both lines with only one *harinero.* He is essentially doing what he has done, or will do, with virtually all the on-line jobs. Two workers, not three, hang chicken; two, not three or four, arrange parts; one, not two, checks the marinade levels. This downsizing has been going on throughout the plant. About six months earlier, a generation of supervisors who had mostly come up through the production lines were more or less forced from their jobs by a new set of plant managers. The new managers ordered the older supervisors to push the workers harder and harder. Knowing how hard work on the line could be, many supervisors refused by simply leaving the plant. The managers were then free to replace them with younger, college-educated supervisors like Michael.

15   Michael is a working-class kid clawing his way into the middle class. One of the first in his family to attend college, he just graduated from the University of Arkansas with a degree in poultry science. Supervisors start at under $30,000 a year. Although he "never imagined" earning that much right out of college, the trade-off is considerable. Michael arrives every day at 12:30 p.m. and never leaves before 3:30 a.m. Unlike the workers, of course, he enjoys a job with some variety, almost never gets his hands dirty, and can hope to move up the corporate ladder. At least in the short term, however, he's as consumed by the plant as the rest of us.

16   Nevertheless, Michael is the focus of our anger. Michael (guided by his bosses) oversees the downsizing. One reason he succeeds—besides the lack of a labor union and binding job descriptions—is that cutting workers on the line doesn't necessarily halt it. The fewer workers just have to work faster. But as Roberto pointed out, the breading operator is different. When the breading operator falls behind, the entire line stops. And Michael would soon be replacing two experienced *harineros,* Roberto and Alejandro, with a single trainee—me.

17   When Michael told them there would soon be only one *harinero,* Roberto and Alejandro used their seniority to find other positions. Michael posted the job but no one in the plant wanted it, Roberto says. "It was too much work. So he had to get a new guy who couldn't say no—someone like you."

18   Roberto is right, but he's being less than candid. Giving up the position *did* matter to him. Alejandro is more blunt: "I had eight years as *harinero.* I like the job. It's like family here. It doesn't mean anything to Michael. For him it's just a job and we're just Mexicans. He doesn't know anything anyway. I wanted to stay, but why? Fuck that! Twice as much work for the same salary. I did my job well. I have nothing to be ashamed of."

19   DURING MY FIRST weeks, the line keeps shutting down. Few of the problems are tied to me, but the entire process is slowed by the fact that there is only one real *harinero*—Roberto. The *harinero* has to fix everything, but the main problem is that the rebreader apparatus simply doesn't have enough power to circulate the flour while pushing the chicken along the belt. In short, when enough

flour flows through the valves to bread the chicken, the machine bogs down and the chicken piles up and falls on the floor. This results in loud shrieks from just about everyone. As breading operator, Roberto has to shut down the line and figure out which part of the rebreader isn't working.

20   The possible solutions to this problem shape an ongoing struggle between Michael, Roberto, and (now) me. First, the plant mechanics could feed enough power to the machine to handle both the chicken and the flour. This is clearly what Michael wants. Second, we could run less chicken, which, by reducing the weight on the belts, would allow the rebreader to operate properly at the current power level. This is simply unthinkable to Michael. His goal is to keep the line running at top speed and at full capacity all the time.

21   Roberto and I adopt two strategies to keep the rebreader running. First, we change the flour frequently. Fresh flour that's not yet wet and clumpy from the chicken circulates better. Michael, however, rejects this option because it costs more. Second, we try using only as much flour as the rebreader can support. But here again Michael insists that the rebreader can handle more (old) flour and that we're running it at levels that don't bread the chicken enough.

22   The difficulty for Roberto and me is that Michael is simply wrong. He passes by every hour and tells us to use more flour. He then leaves, and with remarkable precision the machine bogs down. We stop the line, clean up the mess, and lower the flour to a workable level. Michael then returns, calls for more flour, and the process begins again.

23   This uneasy and somewhat absurd tension continues all day. Only occasionally does Michael see the rebreader bog down because of his miscalculations. Roberto and I relish these moments. Roberto suddenly forgets how to fix the machine and simply watches as Michael frantically calls a mechanic on his walkietalkie. After talking to Michael and staring at the machine for 10 minutes, the mechanic swallows his pride and asks Roberto what the problem is. Roberto then looks at Michael, smiles at me, and fixes it.

24   Looking back, it's hard to explain why this petty struggle seemed so damn important. The irony, of course, is that it was in our interests to follow Michael's (uninformed) directions and let the line stop. It was a pain to keep fixing the machine, but we got paid the same whether it ran or not. Finally, the shutdowns benefited all the workers by giving them a break.

25   Why, then, were so many of us profoundly irritated when the lines stopped? Several factors were at work. The first was Michael's attempt to use not only fewer *harineros,* but fewer workers in general. It confirmed our collective perception: Michael's inexperience led to decisions that made our lives intolerable. They were also economically unsound. We believed we could run the lines better. Second, and most important, by concentrating decision making in his own hands, Michael removed the very thing—control over the labor process—that gave the *harinero* job its meaning. Finally, almost all the workers took great pride in jobs that likewise had been largely degraded.

26   Despite our protests, Michael forges ahead, and in my fourth week I begin running both lines. What he does not tell us, however, is that he has finally gotten the mechanics to boost the power. Roberto and I quickly discover that Michael has won. With more power, the rebreader almost never bogs down.

Running the lines no longer requires the expertise of someone like Roberto. But while the job demands less skill, it takes more work. I now fill the flour for two lines running at a faster pace. The intensity and monotony are almost unbearable. For the on-line workers the change is devastating. By the end of the week, Blanca, a Mexican woman in her 50s, is overwhelmed. She has been hanging chickens for too many years and her body can't keep up. Hoping to stay at Tyson until she retires, she quits within a week.

27 NOISE, SUPERVISION, and the job's intensity limit communication on the plant floor. The break room is a different situation. Twice a shift, for 30 minutes, workers watch Spanish-language television, eat and exchange food, complain, and relax. Supervisors almost never enter the room, and they're uncomfortable when they do. I was often the only American present. The few other Americans on the second shift almost always gathered in a smaller room where smoking is permitted and the TV is in English.

28 A telling moment occurred in the break room only three weeks after I arrived. Although I'd eventually tell my new friends that I was an anthropologist, no one knew at the time. However else they viewed me—as a strange gringo who spoke Spanish, as a *blanco* who was too stupid to get a good job, or as an inept breading operator—I wasn't yet seen as an anthropologist or professor.

29 After pushing us hard that day, Michael gave us free boxes of fried chicken to thank us. He'd do this half a dozen other times while I worked there, and it always got the same reaction. After looking at the chicken, we'd stare at each other until someone said something like this in Spanish: "Pure asshole. I am not going to eat this shit." For an awkward moment we'd glance at each other, look away, and pretend not to know what was going on. Then someone would say: "We can't throw away good food and we're all hungry. Let's eat this shit." And so we would, more pissed off than ever.

30 Michael's gesture was insulting for many reasons. First, he wasn't just giving us food; he was giving us chicken. Second, it didn't come close to making up for what the workers had just gone through on the plant floor. As paternalism, it was pathetic and transparent. (Why Michael didn't see this is a different question.) Finally, it was insulting because even as we hesitated we knew we'd eat the chicken.

31 As we chewed the chicken that day, we had the following exchange. No one directly mentioned Michael's gesture, as if all of us had agreed not to relive the humiliation.

32 *Roberto* welcomes me into the group: "Ai, Steve, you are almost Mexican. All you need is a Mexican wife to cook you some decent lunch and you would be Mexican."

33 *Alejandro*, also from Mexico, chimes in: "Yes, Steve is a Mexican. He speaks Spanish, eats with Mexicans, and he works like a Mexican. It's pure Mexicans here. We all eat chicken."

34 *Elisa*, three years on the job, kindly protests: "Ai . . . I'm not Mexican. I'm Salvadoran."

35 *Alejandro*, gently explaining: "Look, we're all Mexicans here [in the plant]. Screwed-over Mexicans." He points at Li, an older woman from Laos. "Look, even she is a Mexican. Pure."

36   We laugh as Li, who's too far away to hear, quietly devours a chicken wing.

37   *Ana*, catching on to Alejandro's point, finally agrees: "Yes, it's the truth. We are Mexicans here in the plant."

38   *I* ask, somewhat interested: "And outside the plant, in Springdale, Fayetteville, and Rogers? Are we all Mexicans outside?"

39   *Roberto* quickly responds: "Outside, we are all fucked. We're in Arkansas."

40   Everyone laughs.

41   *Alejandro,* more seriously, says to me: "Outside, you're a gringo. You are from here. Outside, we are Mexicans, but it is different. We're still screwed, but in a different way. We are foreigners. We don't belong. At least here in the plant we belong even if we are exploited. Outside, we live better than in Mexico, but we do not belong, we are not from here and keep to ourselves."

42   *I* then ask: "And in Mexico? Who are we in Mexico?"

43   *Roberto* says to me: "In Mexico, you are a gringo. You are a foreigner, but not like we are here in Arkansas. You are more like a tourist, treated well. We are not tourists here. We are treated more like outsiders. In Mexico, we are normal people, Mexicans, just like everyone else. But in Mexico there is no future. My children were all born here, they are Americans. They have a future. Now, when I return to Mexico I feel like a tourist. I have money, travel, visit people. Our future is here now."

44   *Alejandro* ends on a light note: "At least in Mexico the chicken has some fucking taste."

45   WHEN ALEJANDRO looks around at people from Mexico, El Salvador, Honduras, Vietnam, Laos, and the Marshall Islands, and says we are all Mexicans, he is making a statement about class. He is not confused by the bright lights of the postmodern world, or unclear where he is located, socially, racially, and geographically. Rather, he is playing with the label, using it almost as a synonym for worker. "Yes, we are all Mexicans here" is almost the same as, "Yes, we are all workers here." And not any kind of worker—but those who do what society sees as the worst work. Shit work. In this respect, Li, from Laos, is not singled out by accident. She is Mexican, one of us, because she does the same crap; because she eats Michael's chicken; and because she is Mexican to Tyson's management.

46   We've yet to appreciate the full impact of transnational migration, especially on people like my coworkers at the plant. In the process of crossing borders in search of opportunity, their experiences may be leading them to question the national loyalties that borders reinforce. As they work together, both immigrants and the native-born may be developing new identities that run counter to old notions of citizenship. And some of these new identities are grounded in class. Could it be that globalization internationalizes not only capital, but also workers? It's worth considering. Poultry plants are, after all, one of the places where workers of the world come together.

47   Such sites will not automatically unite this diverse working class any more than factories did in 19th-century England. But if we really want to understand the global migrations that are reshaping today's world, we need to look at culture not just in terms of ethnic rituals and customs. We also have to confront the realities of class. The Mexicans, Salvadorans, Vietnamese, and Americans at the plant

experience cultural differences every day when they exchange tortillas, tacos, rice, beans, and turkey sandwiches. But they also share—in different ways—the class experience of eating chicken that is as painful to swallow as it is to process.

"Undercover in a Chicken Factory," *Utne Reader*, January/February 2004. Adapted from Steve Striffler, "Inside a Poultry Processing Plant: An Ethnographic Portrait," *Labor History*, vol. 43, no. 3 (2002), pp. 305-313, reprinted by permission of the publisher (Taylor & Francis Ltd, http://www. tandf.co.uk/journals/).

Exercises

Do not refer to the selection for Exercises A, B, and C unless your instructor directs you to do so.

A. DETERMINING THE MAIN IDEA AND PURPOSE

Choose the best answer.

_____ **1.** The main idea of the selection is that
   a. immigrants from Mexico and Central America now predominate in America's poultry-processing plants.
   b. the writer's undercover job working in a poultry-processing plant allowed him to see what working conditions are like first-hand and to examine labor practices.
   c. American corporations like Tyson hire immigrant workers because they are usually unskilled, often don't speak the language, and are grateful for America's higher wages.
   d. the poultry-processing plants in the American South are essentially factories that have made processed chicken an unhealthy food to consume.

_____ **2.** The writer's purpose is to
   a. convince the reader to stop eating chicken because of the way these plants treat both the chickens and their workers.
   b. reveal the effects of corporate downsizing.
   c. offer several criticisms about globalization and its effect on transnational workers.
   d. write an expose of the atmosphere, working conditions, and attitudes toward employees in a poultry-processing plant.

B. COMPREHENDING MAIN IDEAS

Choose the correct answer for the multiple-choice items. Write the fill-in answers in the space provided using your own words.

_____ **1.** According to Striffler, about three-quarters of the workers at Tyson's plant in Arkansas come from
   a. the Marshall Islands.
   b. Latin America.
   c. Laos and other nations in Southeast Asia.
   d. small towns across the American South.

_____ **2.** For many immigrants, what does working in a poultry-processing plant represent, according to the article?

    a. a chance to learn English in the workplace without having to attend ESL classes.

    b. an opportunity to earn a decent living and to gain valuable experience.

    c. a way to gain upward mobility in American society.

    d. the only job they can get if they can't speak English well or if they don't have an education.

3. Despite the terrible smell and noise, why is a job in the "live hanging" section of the plant considered a desirable job, one that even has a waiting list?

_____

4. The concept of downsizing plays an important role in this selection. What is downsizing, and what has been its effect in the plant?

_____

_____ **5.** Whose fault is it that the breading machine continually breaks down?

    a. Roberto's, because he doesn't know how to work or fix the machine properly.

    b. The author's, because he's new and poorly trained.

    c. Michael's, because he's inexperienced and wants to speed up the production process no matter what its effect on the machinery.

    d. The machinery, because it's old and no longer in good working condition.

_____ **6.** Striffler concludes by discussing some effects of immigrants crossing the border to find work in another country. Which one was *not* mentioned?

    a. They may question their national loyalties that nations' borders used to reinforce.

    b. They develop new identities that are different from the old ideas about citizenship.

    c. Globalization not only affects economic capital, it affects workers' status as well.

    d. They may encounter a new identity grounded in class rather than in nationality.

    e. They feel gratitude that they can earn a decent living and are treated with respect.

COMPREHENSION SCORE

A. No. right _____ × 2 = _____

B. No. right _____ × 1 = _____

Total points from A and B _____ × 10 = _____ percent

C. SEQUENCING

These sentences from one paragraph in the selection may have been scrambled. Read the sentences and choose the sequence that puts them back into logical order. Do not refer to the original selection.

1 In a plant where about two-thirds of the workers are male, this fact is telling. **2** These workers stand in the same place repeating the same motions for an entire shift. **3** Most line workers are women, many in their 40s and 50s. **4** On-line jobs are the worst in the plant—monotonously, even dangerously, repetitive. **5** Women are concentrated in on-line jobs because they're excluded from all jobs that involve heavy lifting or running machinery.

_____ Which of the following represents the correct sequence for these sentences?
a. 3, 1, 4, 2, 5
b. 5, 2, 1, 3, 4
c. 2, 5, 1, 3, 4
d. 4, 2, 1, 5, 3
e. Correct as written.

You may refer to the selection as you work through the remaining exercises.

D. INTERPRETING MEANING

1. Write the sentence that represents the main idea of paragraph 9 in the space. Do the same thing for paragraph 10.

Paragraph 9:_____

Paragraph 10:_____

2. Explain the irony in the first sentence of paragraph 13.

_____

3. Why is there so much animosity toward Michael, the supervisor of the line where Striffler worked? What is Michael's background, and how does he perform his job?

_____

_____

4. In paragraph 45, what does Alejandro mean when he says to the assembled workers, who are from Mexico, El Salvador, Honduras, Vietnam, Laos, and the Marshall Islands, that "we're are all Mexicans"?

_____

5. Striffler concludes with this observation: "We also have to confront the realities of class. The Mexicans, Salvadorans, Vietnamese, and Americans at the plant experience cultural differences every day when they exchange tortillas, tacos, rice, beans, and turkey sandwiches. But they also share—in different

ways—the class experience of eating chicken that is as painful to swallow as it is to process." What does he mean?

_____

E. MAKING INFERENCES

Write the answers to these inference questions in your own words.

1. Read paragraph 2 again. Why did the receptionist assume Striffler was applying for a job as a mechanic?

_____

2. How can you tell, based on the information in paragraph 3, that the current influx of immigrant workers into the American South has been momentous?

_____

3. Explain the "message" conveyed from the sign described in paragraph 5.

_____

4. Look again at paragraph 8. What does the term "further processing" refer to? How has the production of chicken changed over the last 25 years?

_____

5. Michael, the *harinero* supervisor, receives a lot of attention in this selection, and it's clear that his inexperience makes the workers' jobs really difficult. From what Striffler suggests in paragraph 16, what is the primary reason that these workers can't complain about either Michael's interference or about their working conditions?

_____

6. Read paragraph 44 again. Why might chicken in Mexico taste better than the chicken Tyson produces?

_____

F. UNDERSTANDING VOCABULARY

Look through the paragraphs listed by number in brackets and find a word that matches each definition. Refer to a dictionary if necessary. An example has been done for you.

Ex. polite social exchanges, playful conversations
[paragraph 4]   *pleasantries*

1. complain about, express regret [6]   _____

2. the movement of people from one group or
   class to another [6]   _____

3. thrashing about wildly [7]   _____

4. confers, grants [10]   _____

5. describing something that starts and stops at intervals [11] _____

6. physical skill and grace, especially in the use of one's hands [13] _____

7. trivial, of little importance [23-24] _____

8. incompetent, bungling [27-28] _____

9. the practice of treating workers in a fatherly manner [29-30] _____

10. contrary to, in opposition [46] _____

G. USING VOCABULARY—VARIANT WORD FORMS

Write the correct inflected form of the base word in each of the following sentences. Be sure to add the appropriate ending to fit the grammatical requirements of the sentence. Refer to your dictionary if necessary.

1. (*transformed*—use a noun) Poultry plants that sprang up in the South in the last twenty years or so have resulted in a _____ in the American diet, in demographic patterns, and in labor practices.

2. (*blunt*—use an adverb) The Mexican workers speak _____ about their status as immigrants in the U.S. and the exploitation they endure.

3. (*absurd*—use a noun) There is an element of _____ in the tension between the workers and the supervisor, Michael, especially over the use of the breading machines.

4. (*miscalculation*—use a verb) When Michael _____, the breading machine stops working, and the assembly line comes to a halt.

5. (*humiliation*—use a verb) All of the workers felt that Michael had _____ them when he gave them a "gift" of chicken to eat during their break.

6. (*exploit*—use an adjective) There is no doubt that, based on Striffler's experience, that the company treats its employees in an _____ manner, especially as the result of downsizing.

H. SUMMARIZING EXERCISE

In the concluding three paragraphs (45–47) Striffler discusses the effects of globalization. Write a summary of these two paragraphs, keeping the length between 75 and 100 words.

_____

_____

_____

_____

I. TOPICS FOR DISCUSSION

1. Comment on the article's title. Why does Striffler use the word "factory," when the more common word is "plant" or "facility"? What does the word "factory" connote?

2. Examine Photo 3-3 on page 221 carefully. How would you describe the chicken nuggets as they are depicted?

3. Steve Striffler is an anthropologist. Why would an anthropologist be interested in studying how chickens are processed?

4. Striffler describes the line work as both monotonous and dangerous. He explains the monotony well, but not the danger. Why would such a job be dangerous?

5. Is Striffler being ironic when, in paragraph 6, he describes Arkansas as "the promised land"?

6. Comment on the workers' varied reactions to Michael's gift of fried chicken after working them hard during a shift. Are they being ungrateful or not?

7. What is the human element that you take away from this selection? If the job is so terrible and if workers are treated with such disdain, why do immigrants seek these jobs?

8. From what Striffler says, how have processing plants like Tyson's altered Americans' consumption of chicken? What do you think about the way the chickens are processed, according to Striffler's description?

J. TOPICS FOR WRITING

1. Striffler's book describes the change—for the worse, according to him—in the way chicken is produced in this country. Choose another subject on which you are familiar with an evident change for the worse in your lifetime. Describe the situation, explain the reason for the change, and examine its negative consequences.

2. Consider this quotation by 18th century politician and epicure Jean Anthelme Brillat-Savarin: "Tell me what you eat, and I will tell you who you are."" Write an essay in response to this quotation. Who are you?

EXPLORE THE WEB

- Striffler's article was published in 2004, and his book about the chicken industry was published in 2005. Have things changed since then? You can find a lot of information online about the social changes that chicken-processing plants have caused in Southern states like Arkansas (where the Tyson plant described here is located), Georgia, and Alabama, among others. If you go to Google or to your favorite search engine and type in the search box this string, you can locate more information: chicken processing plants, demographic changes.

18 MARTIN LINDSTROM
Selling Illusions of Cleanliness

This article was first published in The Wall Street Journal, *the nation's leading daily business newspaper. Recently, however, the paper has expanded its coverage and now includes coverage of technology, consumer issues, social trends, politics, and other topics of interest to the general reader. The writer of the article, Martin Lindstrom, is a marketing and branding consultant. The selection has been adapted from his new book* Brandwashed: Tricks Companies Use to Manipulate Our Minds and Persuade Us to Buy *(2011).*

Vocabulary Analysis

WORD ROOTS

phobia The Greek noun *phobia* refers to an unnatural fear of something. *Phobic* is the adjective form. In paragraph 13, Lindstrom uses the word *germophobic*, meaning a fear of germs. The word *phobia* can both stand by itself ("Susan has a *phobia* of spiders"), or it can be attached to many words in English to describe various persistent or abnormal psychological conditions. *Homophobia* is the fear of homosexuals, and *claustrophobia* is fear of confined spaces, from *claustrum* ("enclosed place") + phobia. What do these "phobia" words mean? Check a dictionary if you are unsure.

hydrophobia	_____
xenophobia	_____
agoraphobia	_____

MARTIN LINDSTROM

Selling Illusions of Cleanliness

1   As someone who's been on the frontlines of the branding wars, I've spent count-less hours with CEOs, advertising executives and marketing mavens at some of the biggest companies in the world. I've seen—and, honestly, been disturbed by—the full range of psychological tricks and schemes that some companies use to prey on our most deeply rooted fears, dreams and desires in order to per-suade us to buy their brands and products.

2   A key lesson: Fear sells. I recall a vintage early 20th century ad for lunchbox thermoses that bore an unforgettable tagline: "A Fly in the Milk May Mean a Baby in the Grave." Advertisers have since gotten more subtle in using fear to persuade us, but the underlying principle remains the same. The illusion of clean-liness or freshness is a particularly powerful persuader—and marketers know it.

3   To see all the tricks that marketers have for creating the appearance of fresh-ness, there's no better place to go than Whole Foods, the giant purveyor of natu-ral and organic edibles. As we enter Whole Foods, symbols—or what advertisers call "symbolics"—of freshness overwhelm us. The first thing you see is flow-ers—geraniums, daffodils, jonquils—among the freshest, most perishable objects on earth.

4   The prices for the flowers and other produce are scrawled in chalk on frag-ments of black slate, a tradition borrowed from outdoor markets in Europe. It's as if the farmer or grower had unloaded his produce (chalk and slate boards in hand), then hopped back in his flatbed truck and motored back to the country. But, in fact, while some of the flowers are purchased locally, many are bought centrally, and in-house Whole Foods artists produce the chalk boards.

5   These same tactics explain the coolers of chipped ice used by many supermar-ket chains. To our irrational, germ-fearing minds, tortillas, hot dogs and pickles must be fresher—and thus safer to eat—when they're sitting on a bed of ice, especially when the soda or juice perspires a little, a phenomenon the industry dubs "sweat" (the refrigerators in most juice and milk aisles are deliberately kept at the exact temperature needed for this "sweating" to occur).

6   Similarly, for years now, supermarkets have been sprinkling select vegetables with little dew drops of water. Why? Like ice displays, those drops serve as a symbol, albeit a bogus one, of freshness and purity. (That same dewy mist makes the vegetables rot more quickly than they would otherwise.)

7   In experiments on consumer behavior that I've carried out across the world, I often ask people to empty the contents of their fridge and freezer and then to rank and replace the items, one by one, depending on how "fresh" they perceive them to be.

8   What product consistently gets the highest ranking for freshness? Heinz ketchup. That's right, consumers consider bottled ketchup fresher than lettuce, tomatoes and onions. "Why Heinz?" I always ask, noting that the expiration date on the bottle isn't for another six months. "You're right," most reply after a moment. "I have no idea why I put that there."

9   So what's behind this bizarre impression? It's all in the way the ketchup is marketed. Even though it is made from tomato concentrate, Heinz plays up its "tomato-ness" and its deep red color—the shade of a right-off-the-vine beefsteak tomato.

10   Another powerful "symbolic" of purity and freshness? Fruit. In the juice world, it's a rule of thumb that the more fruit a manufacturer displays on the side of the juice carton, the greater its perceived freshness. Note the cascade of kiwis, oranges, mangoes and raspberries on most juice cartons.

11   Speaking of fruit, you may think a banana is just a banana, but it's not. Dole and other growers have made the creation of a banana into a mini-science. Sales records show that bananas with Pantone color 13-0858 (otherwise known as Vibrant Yellow) are less likely to sell than bananas with Pantone color 12-0752 (also called Buttercup), which is one grade warmer, visually, and seems to imply a riper, fresher fruit. So these companies plant bananas under conditions most likely to produce the "right" color.

12   Knowing that even the suggestion of fruit evokes powerful associations of health, freshness and cleanliness, brands across all categories have gone fruity on us, infusing everything from shampoos to bottled waters with pineapple, oranges, peaches, passion fruit and banana fragrances—engineered in a chemist's laboratory, of course. The same goes for baby soaps, nicotine chewing gum, lip balm, teas, vitamins, cosmetics and furniture polish. Mango-papaya conditioner, anyone? Orange-scented PineSol?

13   Will these products get your hair or your floors any cleaner than the regular versions? No. But the scent of fruit evokes strong associations of cleanliness for germophobic consumers. By now, our shampoos are so fruity that, instead of scrubbing with them, we're tempted to guzzle them down.

14   Shampoo companies also realize that the sheer volume of bubbles a shampoo generates can prompt thoughts of freshness and cleanliness—bubbles signal that the shampoo is strong and invigorating (just as the "sting" of an after-shave or the bubbles hitting our throat when we down sparkling water "inform" us that the product is fresh and uncontaminated). Some companies have gone so far as to create a chemical that accelerates the appearance and quality of bubbles, making bathers feel as though their hair is getting cleaner faster. I call this a "perceived justification symbol"—a moment designed to reassure us that we made the right purchase (and to ensure that we'll stay loyal to that product).

15   Finally, a fish story from Spain's Canary Islands: A friend of mine was once part of the crew that caught the day's supply of seafood for a harbor restaurant. Their catch was always transferred to a traditional fisherman's boat (the kind no one uses anymore). When customers arrived at the restaurant for lunch, the old boat would putter into the harbor and a grizzled old fisherman would deliver the fish, ostensibly reeled in just moments earlier. It was all staged, but the customers ate it up.

16   At the end of the day, we want to buy the illusions that the marketing world sells to us—hook, line and sinker. Which may be the scariest thing of all.

Exercises

You may refer to the selection while you complete these exercises.

A. COMPREHENDING MAIN IDEAS

Write the answers for these questions in the space provided using your own words.

1. Read paragraph 1 again. What is Lindstrom's attitude toward the psychological tricks and schemes companies use to persuade us to buy things? What words express that attitude?

   _____

2. In paragraph 2 Lindstrom begins with the sentence "A key lesson: Fear sells." Fear of what?

   _____

3. Explain the early 20th century advertising slogan, "A Fly in the Milk May Mean a Baby in the Grave."

   _____

4. Explain what Lindstrom means in paragraph 2 by the phrase "the illusion of cleanliness."

   _____

5. Why do supermarkets like Whole Foods (and, in fact, most markets) display cut flowers near the entrance to the store?

   _____

6. Why is it a bad idea for produce workers to spray vegetables with little drops of water?

   _____

7. What is it about Heinz ketchup that makes it rank near the top of the list for freshness in one's refrigerator? Why does he characterize this as a "bizarre impression"?

   _____

8. Why do bananas whose peel is the color of Buttercup (Pantone color 12-0752) sell better than bananas with peels the color of Vibrant Yellow (Pantone color 13-0858)?

   _____

9. Why are so many shampoos, hair conditioners, furniture polish, cosmetics, and so forth scented with fruit essences? Where do these fruit scents come from?

   _____

   _____

10. If a shampoo doesn't generate sufficient bubbles, what does the typical consumer think?

_____

B. INTERPRETING MEANING

1. Read the three introductory paragraphs again. Then write the sentence that
best represents the thesis statement in the space provided.

_____

_____

2. To what extent are the terms of thesis carried out in the selection as a whole?
Comment.

_____

3. What is a "perceived justification symbol"? See paragraph 14. What example
does Lindstrom provide to illustrate the concept?

_____

_____

4. Read the last two paragraphs again. Summarize the anecdote of the fishing
boat in the Canary Islands. What point is Lindstrom making here?

_____

_____

C. DISTINGUISHING BETWEEN FACT AND OPINION

For each of the following statements from the selection, write F if the statement
represents a factual statement that can be verified or O if the statement represents
the writer's or someone else's subjective interpretation.

_____1. I've seen and, honestly, been disturbed by—the full range of
psychological tricks and schemes that some companies use to prey
on our most deeply rooted fears, dreams and desires in order to
persuade us to buy their brands and products.

_____2. A key lesson: Fear sells.

_____3. The prices for the flowers and other produce are scrawled in chalk
on fragments of black slate, a tradition borrowed from outdoor
markets in Europe.

_____4. Like ice displays, those drops serve as a symbol, albeit a bogus one,
of freshness and purity.

_____5. In the juice world, it's a rule of thumb that the more fruit a
manufacturer displays on the side of the juice carton, the greater its
perceived freshness.

_____6. These companies plant bananas under conditions most likely to
produce the "right" color.

_____7.   Knowing that even the suggestion of fruit evokes powerful associations of health, freshness and cleanliness, brands across all categories have gone fruity on us, infusing everything from shampoos to bottled waters with pineapple, oranges. . . .

_____8.   The scent of fruit evokes strong associations of cleanliness for germophobic customers.

_____9.   Shampoo companies also realize that the sheer volume of bubbles a shampoo generates can prompt thoughts of freshness and cleanliness—bubbles signal that the shampoo is strong and invigorating. . . .

_____10.   By now, our shampoos are so fruity that, instead of scrubbing with them, we're tempted to guzzle them down.

D. UNDERSTANDING VOCABULARY IN CONTEXT

Here are a few vocabulary words from the selection along with their definitions. Study these definitions carefully. Then write the appropriate word in each space provided according to the context, the way it is used. Note: You will use only four of the five words in each set.

mavens	experts, those with special knowledge of a particular area
subtle	difficult to detect, not immediately obvious
bogus	fake, not genuine
accelerates	speeds, hastens
prey	exploit, make a profit at someone else's expense

1.   Advertisers and branding _____ have developed a whole constellation of manipulative tactics that _____ on our fear of germs. One example the writer cites is produce sprayed with little drops of water, which serve as a _____ symbol of freshness. In fact, spraying vegetables with water only _____ their decay.

implies	states indirectly, suggests
evoke	call forth, call to mind
ostensibly	apparently, but not actually
purveyors	those who sell something, especially food
albeit	although, however

2.   _____ of everything from shampoo to cleaning products know that fruit and fruit essences _____ freshness and cleanliness in consumers' minds. In the same way, consumers expect their shampoo to contain lots of bubbles, which _____ that the shampoo is doing its job. _____, branding is as important as the product itself.

E. TOPICS FOR DISCUSSION

1. Lindstrom is a branding consultant. What is branding? What do you think a branding consultant does?
2. In paragraph 2 Lindstrom quotes an early 20th century ad slogan, "A Fly in the Milk May Mean a Baby in the Grave." What might be a more subtle, early 21st century version of this message?
3. Do you agree with everything Lindstrom writes and with the accuracy of his examples? Is there anything in the selection that you find less than credible? Does he seem like a credible authority?
4. In exercise C above on distinguishing between fact and opinion, most of the answers should be marked "opinion." Does the presence of so many opinions affect the significance of what Lindstrom says? Does he do a sufficiently good job of supporting these opinions?
5. Have you yourself fallen prey to the "psychological tricks and schemes" that Lindstrom describes here? Was there anything in his selection that surprised you?
6. Does it seem odd that a marketing and branding consultant writes so critically of these persuasive and manipulative tactics? What's so bad about these practices? Why is Lindstrom "disturbed" by them?

F. TOPICS FOR WRITING

1. In your cupboard or closet, locate a product that you regularly use. Examine its branding with a critical eye. Then write a short essay in which you discuss any manipulative techniques that are evident in the packaging, design, or its contents.
2. What influences your buying habits? Choose a product that you buy regularly and write a short essay in which you explain the reasons that you buy this brand over another.
3. Go to your local supermarket and study the cartons of juice available in the refrigerated case. Does their packaging bear out what Lindstrom says? Alternatively, walk around your local supermarket and cast a critical eye over displays. If you identify any persuasive techniques aimed at influencing consumer behavior (especially appealing to the consumers' insistence on freshness and/or fear of germs), write about them.
4. Lindstrom's article is concerned with how food producers, advertisers, and purveyors prey on our fixation with cleanliness and freshness. An alternative assignment: Go to your favorite supermarket (preferably one owned by a large chain like Safeway, Whole Foods, Albertson's, or Kroger, because these tend to have more sophisticated marketing plans). As you walk around the store, take notes on the various other manipulative devices that your market uses to entice you to part with your money.

EXPLORE THE WEB

- Martin Lindstrom has a website with links to various articles. The address is *www.martinlindstrom.com*. For example, his site currently offers an article from *Time* that he wrote titled, "Why the Smell of Cinnamon Makes You Spend Money." In addition, if you type in the search box of Google this information: "Martin Lindstrom + Have You Been Brandwashed?," you can take his 10-question quiz to learn how susceptible you are to marketing techniques. You have to read the book to find the explanations for his answers. The website says that 80 percent of people who take the test score less than 4. That made me feel better, as I think I'm a savvy, careful shopper, and I scored 3. See how you do.

19 LAURENCE SHAMES
The Hunger for More

Before turning to writing as a full-time occupation in 1976, Laurence Shames worked as a taxi driver in New York City, as a lounge winger, furniture mover, shoe salesman, and other assorted random jobs. The author of 20 books, Shames was formerly the ethics columnist for Esquire. *Taken from the first chapter of his 1989 book,* The Hunger for More: Searching for Values in an Age of Greed, *this selection examines the American frontier and its influence on our tradition of materialism.*

Vocabulary Analysis

WORD PARTS

tri- *Tri-* is both a Greek and a Latin prefix, always indicating the numeral "three." Shames speaks of the American *trinity*—"frontier, opportunity, more"—in other words, ideas that Americans revere. (In traditional Christianity, the divine God is usually referred to as a trinity—God the father, God the Son, and God the Holy Spirit—three persons in one God.) Other words beginning with this prefix are *tricycle, triad, triplets, trio, trident,* and *trimester.*

What do these two words mean, and what is their etymology? Consult a dictionary if you are unsure.

tridentate _____

triumvirate _____

WORD FAMILIES

Speculate, speculative, speculators [paragraphs 1 and 3] Shames writes in the opening paragraph that Americans "have always been optimists, and optimists have always liked to *speculate.*" This verb and its relatives, *speculative* and *speculators,* all derive from the Latin word *specere* ("to watch," "to observe"). To *speculate,* in the sense that Shames uses the word, means to buy something risky with the idea that it may make a profit in the future. The root suggests here that one cannot "see" into the future, hence the risk. The connection with "watching" or "seeing" is more apparent in these words:

spectacle	a public performance, an object of interest (in other words, something worth looking at)
spectacular	describing an impressive or elaborate display (again, describing something worth looking at)
spectator	one who attends and sees a show or an event
spectacles	eyeglasses, enabling one to see clearly

LAWRENCE SHAMES

The Hunger for More

1   Americans have always been optimists, and optimists have always liked to speculate. In Texas in the 1880s, the speculative instrument of choice was towns, and there is no tale more American than this.

2   What people would do was buy up enormous tracts of parched and vacant land, lay out a Main Street, nail together some wooden sidewalks, and start slapping up buildings. One of these buildings would be called the Grand Hotel and would have a saloon complete with swinging doors. Another might be dubbed the New Academy or the Opera House. The developers would erect a flagpole and name a church, and once the workmen had packed up and moved on, the towns would be as empty as the sky.

3   But no matter. The speculators, next, would hire people to pass out handbills in the Eastern and Midwestern cities, tracts limning the advantages of relocation to "the Athens of the South" or "the new plains Jerusalem." When persuasion failed, the builders might resort to bribery, paying people's moving costs and giving them houses, in exchange for nothing but a pledge to stay until a certain census was taken or a certain inspection made. Once the nose-count was completed, people were free to move on, and there was in fact a contingent of folks who made their living by keeping a cabin on skids, and dragging it for pay from one town to another.

4   The speculators' idea, of course, was to lure the railroad. If one could create a convincing semblance of a town, the railroad might come through it, and a real town would develop, making the speculators staggeringly rich. By these devices a man named Sanborn once owned Amarillo.

5   But railroad tracks are narrow and the state of Texas is very, very wide. For every Wichita Falls or Lubbock there were a dozen College Mounds or Belchervilles, bleached, unpeopled burgs that receded quietly into the dust, taking with them large amounts of speculators' money.

6   Still, the speculators kept right on bucking the odds and depositing empty towns in the middle of nowhere. Why did they do it? Two reasons—reasons that might be said to summarize the central fact of American economic history and that go a fair way toward explaining what is perhaps the central strand of the national character.

7   The first reason was simply that the possible returns were so enormous as to partake of the surreal, to create a climate in which ordinary logic and prudence

did not seem to apply. In a boom like that of real estate when the railroad barreled through, long shots that might pay 100,000 to one seemed worth a bet.

8   The second reason, more pertinent here, is that there was a presumption that America would *keep on* booming—if not forever, then at least longer than it made sense to worry about. There would always be another gold rush, another Homestead Act, another oil strike. The next generation would always ferret out opportunities that would be still more lavish than any that had gone before. America *was* those opportunities. This was an article not just of faith, but of strategy. You banked on the next windfall, you staked your hopes and even your self-esteem on it; and this led to a national turn of mind that might usefully be thought of as the habit of more.

9   A century, maybe two centuries, before anyone had heard the term *baby boomer,* much less *yuppie,* the habit of more had been installed as the operative truth among the economically ambitious. The habit of more seemed to suggest that there was no such thing as getting wiped out in America. A fortune lost in Texas might be recouped in Colorado. Funds frittered away on grazing land where nothing grew might flood back in as silver. There was always a second chance, or always seemed to be, in this land where growth was destiny and where expansion and purpose were the same.

10   The key was the frontier, not just as a matter of acreage, but as idea. Vast, varied, rough as rocks, America was the place where one never quite came to the end. Ben Franklin explained it to Europe even before the Revolutionary War had finished: America offered new chances to those "who, in their own Countries, where all the Lands [were] fully occupied. . . could never [emerge] from the poor Condition wherein they were born."

11   So central was this awareness of vacant space and its link to economic promise, that Frederick Jackson Turner, the historian who set the tone for much of the twentieth century's understanding of the American past, would write that it was "not the constitution, but free land. . . [that] made the democratic type of society in America." Good laws mattered; an accountable government mattered; ingenuity and hard work mattered. But those things were, so to speak, an overlay on the natural, geographic America that was simply *there,* and whose vast and beckoning possibilities seemed to generate the ambition and the sometimes reckless liberty that would fill it. First and foremost, it was open space that provided "the freedom of the individual to rise under conditions of social mobility."

12   Open space generated not just ambition, but metaphor. As early as 1835, Tocqueville was extrapolating from the fact of America's emptiness to the observation that "no natural boundary seems to be set to the efforts of man." Nor was any limit placed on what he might accomplish, since, in that heyday of the Protestant ethic, a person's rewards were taken to be quite strictly proportionate to his labors.

13   Frontier; opportunity; more. This has been the American trinity from the very start. The frontier was the backdrop and also the raw material for the streak of economic booms. The booms became the goad and also the justification for the myriad gambles and for Americans' famous optimism. The optimism, in turn, shaped the schemes and visions that were sometimes noble, sometimes appalling, always bold. The frontier, as reality and as symbol, is what has shaped the American way of doing things and the American sense of what's worth doing.

14   But there has been one further corollary to the legacy of the frontier, with its promise of ever-expanding opportunities: given that the goal—a realistic goal for most of our history—was *more*. Americans have been somewhat backward in adopting values, hopes, ambitions that have to do with things *other than* more. In America, a sense of quality has lagged far behind a sense of scale. An ideal of contentment has yet to take root in soil traditionally more hospitable to an ideal of restless striving. The ethic of decency has been upstaged by the ethic of success. The concept of growth has been applied almost exclusively to things that can be measured, counted, weighed. And the hunger for those things that are unmeasurable but fine—the sorts of accomplishment that cannot be undone by circumstance or a shift in social fashion, the kind of serenity that cannot be shattered by tomorrow's headline—has gone largely unfulfilled, and even unacknowledged.

Exercises

Do not refer to the selection for Exercises A and B unless your instructor directs you to do so.

A. DETERMINING THE MAIN IDEA AND PURPOSE

Choose the best answer.

_____ **1.**   The main idea of the selection is that
   a. the American frontier, with its endless possibilities for opportunity and expansion, has shaped the country's national character.
   b. Americans are by nature an optimistic people who are willing to gamble and take bold risks.
   c. Americans believe in the Protestant ethic, the idea that one's rewards are proportionate to one's labors.
   d. American values are in the process of being redefined as the nation experiences diminished opportunities and declining natural resources.

_____ **2.**   With respect to the main idea concerning American cultural values and the American character, the writer's purpose is to
   a. criticize, even condemn, them.
   b. express regret for them.
   c. examine the historical and geographic conditions that gave rise to them.
   d. contrast them with older values and behavior patterns of earlier eras.

B. COMPREHENDING MAIN IDEAS

Choose the correct answer.

_____ **1.** Shames states that American optimism and speculation were demonstrated in the 1880s by the
   a. desire to escape the densely populated cities of the Midwest and the East.
   b. promise of easy money during the Gold Rush era.
   c. building of new towns in Texas.
   d. coming of the railroad to the American frontier.

_____ **2.** Ultimately, land speculators hoped to attract
   a. recent immigrants.
   b. cattle ranchers.
   c. railroads.
   d. gold prospectors.

_____ **3.** Shames writes that when speculators lost money, they did not mind too much because they presumed that
   a. the government would bail them out if they failed.
   b. they could always keep on moving west.
   c. the Homestead Act would be renewed every year.
   d. America would continue to experience booms.

_____ **4.** The crucial concept to explain the American belief in opportunity and expansion was the
   a. country's rich store of natural resources.
   b. frontier, with its unlimited space.
   c. American inclination for hard work.
   d. country's strong democratic system.

_____ **5.** Shames writes that, from the beginning, the American "trinity" has been
   a. ambition, wealth, and success.
   b. booms, gambles, and high risk.
   c. optimism, boldness, and social mobility.
   d. frontier, opportunity, and more.

_____ **6.** Shames concludes with the idea that, in America, "the concept of growth" has been applied almost exclusively to
   a. upward mobility.
   b. things that can be measured.
   c. the economy.
   d. personal accomplishments and achievements.

COMPREHENSION SCORE

A. No. right _____ × 2 = _____

B. No. right _____ × 1 = _____

Total points from A and B _____ × 10 = _____ percent

You may refer to the selection as you work through the remaining exercises.

C. DISTINGUISHING BETWEEN MAIN IDEAS AND SUPPORTING DETAILS

Label the following statements from the selection as follows: MI if it represents a *main idea* and SD if it represents a *supporting detail*.

1. _____ The speculators' idea, of course, was to lure the railroad.

2. _____ If one could create a convincing semblance of a town, the railroad might come through it, and a real town would develop, making the speculators staggeringly rich.

3. _____ By these devices a man named Sanborn once owned Amarillo.

4. _____ But railroad tracks are narrow and the state of Texas is very, very wide.

5. _____ For every Wichita Falls or Lubbock there were a dozen College Mounds or Belchervilles.

6. _____ These were bleached, unpeopled burgs that receded quietly into the dust, taking with them large amounts of speculators' money.

D. INTERPRETING MEANING

Where appropriate, write your answers for these questions in your own words.

1. In paragraph 2, Shames writes that the real estate speculators would "start slapping up buildings" in Texas. What does this phrase suggest about the quality of these buildings? _____

_____

2. _____ Read paragraph 9 again. A good title for this paragraph is
   a. "Nineteenth-Century Baby Boomers and Yuppies."
   b. "The Habit of More."
   c. "Second Chances."
   d. "Growth and Destiny."

3. In paragraph 12, Shames discusses the concept of the frontier as metaphor. What exactly does he mean? _____

_____

_____

4. _____ Which of the following sentences from the selection *best* states the main idea of the selection as a whole?
   a. "Americans have always been optimists, and optimists have always liked to speculate."
   b. "The next generation would always ferret out opportunities that would be still more lavish than any that had gone before."
   c. "Nor was any limit placed on what he might accomplish, since, in that heyday of the Protestant ethic, a person's rewards were taken to be quite strictly proportionate to his labors."

      d. "The frontier, as reality and as symbol, is what has shaped the American way of doing things and the American sense of what's worth doing."

E. MAKING INFERENCES

For each of these statements write Y (yes) if the inference is an accurate one, N (no) if the inference is an inaccurate one, or CT (can't tell) if the writer does not give enough information to make an inference one way or another. Be sure to return to the paragraph indicated before choosing your answer. In addition, write a brief explanation in support of your answer choice.

1. _____   Developers named buildings the Grand Hotel and the New Academy and named towns "the Athens of the South" or "the new plains Jerusalem" to make them sound more impressive than they really were. [paragraphs 2 and 3]

Explanation: _____

_____

2. _____   In the 1880s, the railroad companies would put a train through a Texas town only if the population was high enough to justify it. [paragraph 4]

Explanation: _____

_____

3. _____   The majority of real estate speculators made huge fortunes building towns in hopes of attracting the railroads. [paragraphs 6 and 7]

Explanation: _____

_____

4. _____   A prospector who lost a fortune in gold or silver or oil was almost always ruined financially. [paragraph 8]

Explanation: _____

_____

5. _____   The ambitions of today's yuppies and baby boomers can be directly traced back to the habit of more. [paragraph 9]

Explanation: _____

6. _____   If the United States were not so big geographically, it would not have developed such optimism in economic promise and expansion. [paragraphs 10–12]

Explanation: _____

_____

F. UNDERSTANDING VOCABULARY

Look through the paragraphs listed by number in brackets and find a word that matches each definition. Refer to a dictionary if necessary. An example has been done for you.

Ex. very dry, arid [paragraph 2] _____ *parched* _____

1. representative group [3] _____

2. outward appearance, barest trace [4] _____

3 small towns [5] _____

4. uncover or reveal by searching [8—two words] _____

5. regained, made up for [9] _____

6. squandered little by little, wasted [9] _____

7. period of greatest popularity or success [12] _____

8. stimulus, incentive [13] _____

9. causing consternation or dismay, terrible [13] _____

10. natural consequence or effect [14] _____

G. USING VOCABULARY—VARIANT WORD FORMS

In parentheses before each sentence are some inflected forms of words from the selection. Study the context and the sentence. Then write the correct form in the space provided

1. (*speculator, speculate, speculative*). In the 19th century Americans began to _____ on large tracts of empty land, hoping to attract not only new dwellers but also railroads.

2. (*optimism, optimistic, optimistically*) Shames traces our willingness to speculate on the unknown to the American tendency for _____

3. (*prudence, prudent, prudently*) During real estate booms like that of the 19th century, people don't always behave logically or _____

4. (*presumption, presume, presumable, presumably*) Americans followed the _____ that the boom would continue, that more oil and gold would be found.

5. (*surrealism, surreal, surrealistic, surrealistically*) Shames writes that there was a certain _____ quality to the land speculation on the American frontier.

6. (*hospitality, hospitable, hospitably*) The American ideal is more _____ to the idea of restless striving than it is to the ideal of contentment.

H. PARAPHRASING EXERCISE

Here are some sentences from the selection. Write a paraphrase of each passage in the space provided.

1. In America, a sense of quality has lagged far behind a sense of scale. An ideal of contentment has yet to take root in soil traditionally more hospitable to an ideal of restless striving.

   _____

   _____

   _____

2. The concept of growth has been applied almost exclusively to things that can be measured, counted, weighed. And the hunger for those things that are unmeasurable but fine—the sorts of accomplishments that cannot be undone by circumstance or a shift in social fashion, the kind of serenity that cannot be shattered by tomorrow's headline—has gone largely unfulfilled, and even unacknowledged.

   _____

   _____

   _____

I. LOCATING INFORMATION

Go through the article and locate any piece of information that supports this idea:

As a society, the United States is paying a price for our "hunger for more."

Identify the information by putting a star in the margin next to the sentence or by putting a bracket around the words.

J. TOPICS FOR DISCUSSION

1. Shames published the book from which this excerpt comes in 1989. How pertinent are his remarks in helping you understand these recent developments?

   - The Internet and technology boom of the late 1990s and the bursting of the technology bubble.
   - The speculative real estate bubble of the early 21st century, when homeowners were speculating that housing prices would continue to rise, followed by foreclosures and an economic recession.
   - The problem of rising consumer debt whereby consumers are overextended financially and unable to pay their credit card debt.

2. Shames strongly emphasizes the role of the frontier—with its symbolic and literal significance of unlimited land and unlimited opportunities. Based on your knowledge of American history and culture, what might be some other explanations that account for Americans' "hunger for more"?

K. TOPICS FOR WRITING

1. Write a paragraph or two as a personal response to this sentence from the selection: "The ethic of decency has been upstaged by the ethic of success."

2. To what extent do you accept Shames's thesis? What motivates you? Are you more committed to the typical "ideal of restless striving," as Shames calls it in his conclusion, or are you perhaps more committed to striving for an "ideal of contentment"? Ponder these two concepts and write an essay setting forth and examining your life as you are leading it now.

3. Do you use a credit card? Write an essay in which you examine your use of credit, your motivations, your buying behavior, your management of credit card debt, along with your reasons and any other information that seems pertinent to the discussion.

EXPLORE THE WEB

Shames mentions in paragraph 11 the contribution of Frederick Jackson Turner to our understanding of the American past. Turner specifically espoused the frontier theory in 1893, which declared that the vast American frontier was the single element that explained America's distinctive character and history. Turner's "frontier thesis" or "frontier theory" is available for you to peruse on the Internet. Using a search engine, type in "Frederick Jackson Turner, frontier theory" and you will be directed to several links.

20

VAL PLUMWOOD

Being Prey: Surviving a Crocodile Attack

Val Plumwood (1939–2008) was an Australian ecofeminist intellectual and a pioneer of environmental philosophy. She dedicated her career to what is sometimes described as ecological humanities, including work to preserve biodiversity and to control deforestation. Formerly Australian Research Council Fellow at the Australian National University, she also taught at North Carolina State University, the University of Montana, and the University of Sydney. The incident described in this narrative excerpt occurred in February 1985 near the city of Darwin in Kakadu National Park, located on the northern coast of Australia. The article was originally published in a different form in Travelers' Tales *(1999) and was included in* Best Science and Nature Writing 2001.

Vocabulary Analysis

WORD PARTS

The suffix –*ity* Five words in this selection illustrate this common noun suffix. (A prefix, you will remember, is a word part that comes at the beginning of a word that often indicates meaning. A suffix is a word part added to the end of a root, which makes the root into another part of speech. In other words, suffixes commonly indicate grammatical part of speech rather than convey meaning.) The noun suffix *-ity* is added to adjectives to form abstract nouns that express a state or condition. In paragraph 3, *timidity* means "the state of being timid," and in paragraph 10, *subjectivity* means "the condition of being subjective." The selection also contains the words *integrity*, *eternity*, and *capacities* (the latter is the plural spelling)

WORD FAMILIES

Aquatic [paragraph 2] Plumwood writes that "the crocodile was a symbol of the power and integrity of this place and the incredible richness of its *aquatic* habitats." *Aqua* can refer both to the color blue-green (like the sea), or simply to water.

Other examples of words in the family using this root are *aquaplane*, *aquarium*, *aqueous* (an adjective meaning "watery"), and *aqueduct*, (a system for transporting water, from *aqua ducere* ["to lead"])

**TWO
OTHER
IMPOR-
TANT
WORDS**

Aboriginal and indigenous [paragraphs 2 and 5] *Aboriginal*, when capitalized, refers to the *indigenous* or original inhabitants of Australia. When written in lower case, *aboriginal* refers to any original inhabitants of a particular region, for example, the Ainu of Japan or the Indians of North and South America. Both words are of Latin origin: *Aboriginal* comes from the prefix *ab-* + *origine* ("beginning"), and *indigenous* derives from the Latin root *indigina*, "a native."

VAL PLUMWOOD

Being Prey: Surviving a Crocodile Attack

1   In the early wet season, Kakadu's paperbark wetlands are especially stunning, as the water lilies weave white, pink, and blue patterns of dreamlike beauty over the shining thunderclouds reflected in their still waters. Yesterday, the water lilies and the wonderful bird life had enticed me into a joyous afternoon's idyll as I ventured onto the East Alligator Lagoon for the first time in a canoe lent by the park service. "You can play about on the backwaters," the ranger had said, "but don't go onto the main river channel. The current's too swift, and if you get into trouble, there are the crocodiles. Lots of them along the river!" I followed his advice and glutted myself on the magical beauty and bird life of the lily lagoons, untroubled by crocodiles.

2   Today, I wanted to repeat that experience despite the drizzle beginning to fall as I neared the canoe launch site. I set off on a day trip in search of an Aboriginal rock art site across the lagoon and up a side channel. The drizzle turned to a warm rain within a few hours, and the magic was lost. The birds were invisible, the water lilies were sparser, and the lagoon seemed even a little menacing. I noticed now how low the 14-foot canoe sat in the water, just a few inches of fiberglass between me and the great saurians[1], close relatives of the ancient dinosaurs. Not long ago, saltwater crocodiles were considered endangered, as virtually all mature animals in Australia's north were shot by commercial hunters. But after a decade and more of protection, they are now the most plentiful of the large animals of Kakadu National Park. I was actively involved in preserving such places, and for me, the crocodile was a symbol of the power and integrity of this place and the incredible richness of its aquatic habitats.

3   After hours of searching the maze of shallow channels in the swamp, I had not found the clear channel leading to the rock art site, as shown on the ranger's sketch map. When I pulled my canoe over in driving rain to a rock outcrop for a hasty, sodden lunch, I experienced the unfamiliar sensation of being watched.

---

[1] Saurians refers to Sauria, the suborder of reptiles including lizards, crocodiles, and alligators. The Greek root is sauros or "lizard." (Ed.)

Having never been one for timidity, in philosophy or in life, I decided, rather than return defeated to my sticky trailer, to explore a clear, deep channel closer to the river I had traveled along the previous day.

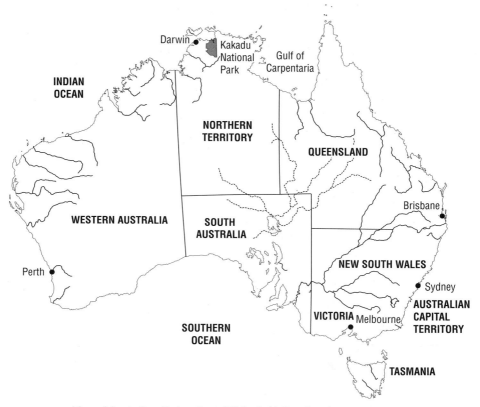

Map of Australia with location of Kakadu National park

4   The rain and wind grew more severe, and several times I pulled over to tip water from the canoe. The channel soon developed steep mud banks and snags. Farther on, the channel opened up and was eventually blocked by a large sandy bar. I pushed the canoe toward the bank, looking around carefully before getting out in the shallows and pulling the canoe up. I would be safe from crocodiles in the canoe—I had been told—but swimming and standing or wading at the water's edge were dangerous. Edges are one of the crocodile's favorite food-capturing places. I saw nothing, but the feeling of unease that had been with me all day intensified.

5   The rain eased temporarily, and I crossed a sandbar to see more of this puzzling place. As I crested a gentle dune, I was shocked to glimpse the muddy waters of the East Alligator River gliding silently only 100 yards away. The channel had led me back to the main river. Nothing stirred along the riverbank, but a great tumble of escarpment cliffs up on the other side caught my attention. One especially striking rock formation—a single large rock balanced precari-

ously on a much smaller one—held my gaze. As I looked, my whispering sense of unease turned into a shout of danger. The strange formation put me sharply in mind of two things: of the indigenous Gagadgu owners of Kakadu, whose advice about coming here I had not sought, and of the precariousness of my own life, of human lives. As a solitary specimen of a major prey species of the saltwater crocodile, I was standing in one of the most dangerous places on earth.

6   I turned back with a feeling of relief. I had not found the rock paintings, I rationalized, but it was too late to look for them. The strange rock formation presented itself instead as a telos[2] of the day, and now I could go, home to trailer comfort.

7   As I pulled the canoe out into the main current, the rain and wind started up again. I had not gone more than five or ten minutes down the channel when, rounding a bend, I saw in midstream what looked like a floating stick—one I did not recall passing on my way up. As the current moved me toward it, the stick developed eyes. A crocodile! It did not look like a large one. I was close to it now but was not especially afraid; an encounter would add interest to the day.

8   Although I was paddling to miss the crocodile, our paths were strangely convergent. I knew it would be close, but I was totally unprepared for the great blow when it struck the canoe. Again it struck, again and again, now from behind, shuddering the flimsy craft. As I paddled furiously, the blows continued. The unheard of was happening; the canoe was under attack! For the first time, it came to me fully that I was prey. I realized I had to get out of the canoe or risk being capsized.

9   The bank now presented a high, steep face of slippery mud. The only obvious avenue of escape was a paperbark tree near the muddy bank wall. I made the split-second decision to leap into its lower branches and climb to safety. I steered to the tree and stood up to jump. At the same instant, the crocodile rushed up alongside the canoe, and its beautiful, flecked golden eyes looked straight into mine. Perhaps I could bluff it, drive it away, as I had read of British tiger hunters doing. I waved my arms and shouted, "Go away!" (We're British here.) The golden eyes glinted with interest. I tensed for the jump and leapt. Before my foot even tripped the first branch, I had a blurred, incredulous vision of great toothed jaws bursting from the water. Then I was seized between the legs in a red-hot pincer grip and whirled into the suffocating wet darkness.

10   Our final thoughts during near-death experiences can tell us much about our frameworks of subjectivity. A framework capable of sustaining action and purpose must, I think, view the world "from the inside," structured to sustain the concept of a continuing, narrative self; we remake the world in that way as our own, investing it with meaning, reconceiving it as sane, survivable, amenable to hope and resolution. The lack of fit between this subject-centered version and reality comes into play in extreme moments. In its final, frantic attempts to protect itself from the knowledge that threatens the narrative framework, the mind can instantaneously fabricate terminal doubt of extravagant proportions: *This is not really happening. This is a nightmare from which I will soon awake.* This desperate

---

[2] Telos is a word of Greek origin meaning "the end result of a goal-oriented process." The word also appears in paragraph 22 on page 257. (Ed.)

delusion split apart as I hit the water. In that flash, I glimpsed the world for the first time "from the outside," as a world no longer my own, an unrecognizable bleak landscape composed of raw necessity, indifferent to my life or death.

11   Few of those who have experienced the crocodile's death roll have lived to describe it. It is, essentially, an experience beyond words of total terror. The crocodile's breathing and heart metabolism are not suited to prolonged struggle, so the roll is an intense burst of power designed to overcome the victim's resistance quickly. The crocodile then holds the feebly struggling prey underwater until it drowns. The roll was a centrifuge of boiling blackness that lasted for an eternity, beyond endurance, but when I seemed all but finished, the rolling suddenly stopped. My feet touched bottom, my head broke the surface, and coughing, I sucked at air, amazed to be alive. The crocodile still had me in its pincer grip between the legs. I had just begun to weep for the prospects of my mangled body when the crocodile pitched me suddenly into a second death roll.

12   When the whirling terror stopped again I surfaced again, still in the crocodile's grip next to a stout branch of a large sandpaper fig growing in the water. I grabbed the branch, vowing to let the crocodile tear me apart rather than throw me again into that spinning, suffocating hell. For the first time I realized that the crocodile was growling, as if angry. I braced myself for another roll, but then its jaws simply relaxed; I was free. I gripped the branch and pulled away, dodging around the back of the fig tree to avoid the forbidding mud bank, and tried once more to climb into the paperbark tree.

13   As in the repetition of a nightmare, the horror of my first escape attempt was repeated. As I leapt into the same branch, the crocodile seized me again, this time around the upper left thigh, and pulled me under. Like the others, the third death roll stopped, and we came up next to the sandpaper fig branch again. I was growing weaker, but I could see the crocodile taking a long time to kill me this way. I prayed for a quick finish and decided to provoke it by attacking it with my hands. Feeling back behind me along the head, I encountered two lumps. Thinking I had the eye sockets, I jabbed my thumbs into them with all my might. They slid into warm, unresisting holes (which may have been the ears, or perhaps the nostrils), and the crocodile did not so much as flinch. In despair, I grabbed the branch again. And once again, after a time, I felt the crocodile jaws relax, and I pulled free.

14   I knew I had to break the pattern; up the slippery mud bank was the only way. I scrabbled for a grip, then slid back toward the waiting jaws. The second time I almost made it before again sliding back, braking my slide by grabbing a tuft of grass. I hung there, exhausted. *I can't make it*, I thought. *It'll just have to come and get me.* The grass tuft began to give away. Flailing to keep from sliding farther, I jammed my fingers into the mud. This was the clue I needed to survive. I used this method and the last of my strength to climb up the bank and reach the top. I was alive!

15   Escaping the crocodile was not the end of my struggle to survive. I was alone, severely injured, and many miles from help. During the attack, the pain from the injuries had not fully registered. As I took my first urgent steps, I knew something was wrong with my leg. I did not wait to inspect the damage but took off away from the crocodile toward the ranger station.

16   After putting more distance between me and the crocodile, I stopped and realized for the first time how serious my wounds were. I did not remove my clothing to see the damage to the groin area inflicted by the first hold. What I could see was bad enough. The left thigh hung open, with bits of fat, tendon, and muscle showing, and a sick, numb feeling suffused my entire body. I tore up some clothing to bind the wounds and made a tourniquet for my bleeding thigh, then staggered on, still elated from my escape. I went some distance before realizing with a sinking heart that I had crossed the swamp above the ranger station in the canoe and could not get back without it.

17   I would have to hope for a search party, but I could maximize my chances by moving downstream toward the swamp edge, almost two miles away. I struggled on, through driving rain, shouting for mercy from the sky, apologizing to the angry crocodile, repenting to this place for my intrusion. I came to a flooded tributary and made a long upstream detour looking for a safe place to cross.

18   My considerable bush[3] experience served me well, keeping me on course (navigating was second nature). After several hours, I began to black out and had to crawl the final distance to the swamp's edge. I lay there in the gathering dusk to await what would come. I did not expect a search party until the following day, and I doubted I could last the night.

19   The rain and wind stopped with the onset of darkness, and it grew perfectly still. Dingoes[4] howled, and clouds of mosquitoes whined around my body. I hoped to pass out soon, but consciousness persisted. There were loud swirling noises in the water, and I knew I was easy meat for another crocodile. After what seemed like a long time, I heard the distant sound of a motor and saw a light moving on the swamp's far side. Thinking it was a boat, I rose up on my elbow and called for help. I thought I heard a faint reply, but then the motor grew fainter and the lights went away. I was as devastated as any castaway who signals desperately to a passing ship and is not seen.

20   The lights had not come from a boat. Passing my trailer, the ranger noticed there was no light inside it. He had driven to the canoe launch site on a motorized trike and realized I had not returned. He had heard my faint call for help, and after some time, a rescue craft appeared. As I began my 13-hour journey to Darwin Hospital, my rescuers discussed going upriver the next day to shoot a crocodile. I spoke strongly against this plan: I was the intruder, and no good purpose could be served by random revenge. The water around the spot where I had been lying was full of crocodiles. That spot was under six feet of water the next morning, flooded by the rains signaling the start of the wet season.

21   In the end I was found in time and survived against many odds. A similar combination of good fortune and human care enabled me to overcome a leg infection that threatened amputation or worse. I probably have Paddy Pallin's incredibly tough walking shorts to thank for the fact that the groin injuries were not as severe as the leg injuries. I am very lucky that I can still walk well and have lost few of my previous capacities. The wonder of being alive after being held—quite literally—in the jaws of death has never entirely left me. For the

---

[3] "Bush" here refers to the Australian bush, the vast area of the country that is not settled. (Ed.)
[4] Dingoes are wild dogs native to Australia. (Ed.)

first year, the experience of existence as an unexpected blessing cast a golden glow over my life, despite the injuries and the pain. The glow has slowly faded, but some of that new gratitude for life endures, even if I remain unsure whom I should thank. The gift of gratitude came from the searing flash of near-death knowledge, a glimpse "from the outside" of the alien, incomprehensible world in which the narrative of self has ended.

22   . . . [T]he story of the crocodile encounter now has, for me, a significance quite the opposite of that conveyed in the master/monster narrative. It is a humbling and cautionary tale about our relationship with the earth, about the need to acknowledge our own animality and ecological vulnerability. I learned many lessons from the event, one of which is to know better when to turn back and to be more open to the sorts of warnings I had ignored that day. As on the day itself, so even more to me now, the telos of these events lies in the strange rock formation, which symbolized so well the lessons about the vulnerability of humankind I had to learn, lessons largely lost to the technological culture that now dominates the earth. In my work as a philosopher, I see more and more reason to stress our failure to perceive this vulnerability, to realize how misguided we are to view ourselves as masters of a tamed and malleable nature. . . .

Val Plumwood, "Being Prey," *Terra Nova: Nature & Culture,* Summer 1996. Copyright © 1996 by Val Plumwood. Reprinted by permission of the author. In *The Ultimate Journey: Inspiring Stories of Living & Dying,* ed. James O'Reilly, Sean O'Reilly, and Richard Sterling (San Francisco: Travelers' Tales, 2000).

Exercises

Do not refer to the selection for Exercises A, B, and C unless your instructor directs you to do so.

A. DETERMINING THE MAIN IDEA AND PURPOSE

Choose the best answer.

_____ **1.**   The main idea of the selection is that
  a. surviving a near-death crocodile attack gave the writer a glimpse into an incomprehensible part of nature and of human life.
  b. crocodiles are fiercely dangerous creatures who prey on humans who venture into their waters.
  c. the writer's experience in the Australian bush was useful when she encountered a crocodile.
  d. in confronting her crocodile attacker, the writer learned that human endurance and the will to triumph can conquer every peril in nature.

_____ **2.**   The writer's purpose is to
  a. describe an exotic location in a faraway place.
  b. tell a frightening story that gave the writer a new perspective on life.
  c. present an account of the writer's experience as a naturalist.
  d. observe and describe a powerful creature in its own environment.

B. COMPREHENDING MAIN IDEAS

Choose the correct answer for the multiple-choice items. Write the fill-in answers in the space provided using your own words.
Choose the correct answer.

_____ 1.   Before the writer set off in a canoe to explore, the park ranger at Kakadu National Park told her not to
a. venture into the main river channel.
b. stay out in the water too long.
c. climb onto the channel's muddy banks.
d. be afraid of the park's crocodiles.

_____ 2.   When the writer crossed the sandbar to see the place from a closer view, she initially felt both
a. wonder and delight.
b. unease and fear of danger.
c. anxiety and panic.
d. curiosity and a desire to see more.

3.   When the writer first encountered the crocodile, what did it resemble to her?

_____

_____ 4.   Plumwood writes that, when faced with danger, it is human nature to
a. alter reality by doubting that the danger is real.
b. feel terrified by the reality of the situation.
c. feel intimately connected to the reality of the situation.
d. adopt a purely objective point of view.

5.   After the crocodile attacked the first two times, how was Plumwood finally able to escape the crocodile's grasp?

_____

_____ 6.   As a result of her near-death experience, Plumwood
a. decided to investigate potential dangers before setting off on such an adventure again.
b. promised to seek the advice of experts before starting off on a dangerous journey.
c. sustained lifelong crippling serious injuries to her leg.
d. felt gratitude for the gift of life.

COMPREHENSION SCORE

A. No. right _____ × 2 = _____

B. No. right _____ × 1 = _____

Total points from A and B _____ × 10 = _____ percent

C. SEQUENCING

These sentences from one paragraph in the selection may have been scrambled. Read the sentences and choose the sequence that puts them back into logical order. Do not refer to the original selection.

1 I did not wait to inspect the damage but took off away from the crocodile toward the ranger station. **2** Escaping the crocodile was not the end of my struggle to survive. **3** As I took my first urgent steps, I knew something was wrong with my leg. **4** During the attack, the pain from the injuries had not fully registered. **5** I was alone, severely injured, and many miles from help.

_____ Which of the following represents the correct sequence for these sentences?
    a. 4, 3, 1, 5, 2
    b. 5, 3, 4, 1, 2
    c. 2, 5, 4, 3, 1
    d. 3, 5, 2, 4, 1
    e. Correct as written.

You may refer to the selection as you work through the remaining exercises.

D. IDENTIFYING SUPPORTING DETAILS

Place an X in the space for each sentence from the selection that _directly_ supports this main idea: "Few of those who have experienced the crocodile's death roll have lived to describe it."

1. _____ It is, essentially, an experience beyond words of total terror.

2. _____ The crocodile's breathing and heart metabolism aren't suited to prolonged struggle.

3. _____ The roll is an intense burst of power designed to overcome the victim's resistance quickly.

4. _____ The crocodile then holds the feebly struggling prey underwater until it drowns.

5. _____ I prayed for a quick finish and decided to provoke it by attacking it with my hands.

6. _____ After putting more distance between me and the crocodile, I stopped and realized for the first time how serious my wounds were.

E. MAKING INFERENCES

For each of these statements write Y (yes) if the inference is an accurate one, N (no) if the inference is an inaccurate one, and CT (can't tell) if the writer does not give you enough information to make an inference one way or another.

1. _____ Plumwood was an experienced canoeist. [article as a whole]

2. _____ The writer got into trouble and encountered crocodiles because the ranger's sketch of the waterways was wrong. [paragraph 3]

3. _____ If Plumwood had asked the Aboriginal Gagadgu owners of Kakadu Park for advice, they would undoubtedly have told her not to venture into the waterways in a canoe. [paragraph 5]

4. _____ When Plumwood awaited "what would come" after the attack, she is referring to certain death. [paragraph 18]

5. _____ Apart from the fact that Plumwood didn't want the crocodile that attacked her killed, the particular crocodile would have been difficult to identify. [paragraph 20]

F. INTERPRETING MEANING

Where appropriate, write your answers for these questions in your own words.

1. _____ Which of the following sentences from the selection *best* represents the main idea?
   a. "As a solitary specimen of a major prey species of the saltwater crocodile, I was standing in one of the most dangerous places on earth."
   b. "Our final thoughts during near-death experiences can tell us much about our frameworks of subjectivity."
   c. "I struggled on, through driving rain, shouting for mercy from the sky, apologizing to the angry crocodile, repenting to this place for my intrusion."
   d. "The gift of gratitude came from the searing flash of near-death knowledge, a glimpse 'from the outside' of the alien, incomprehensible world in which the narrative of self has ended."

2. The first part of the essay establishes a mood that strongly contrasts with the mood after the attack. What contrasts in emotion are suggested?

   _____ and _____

3. Paragraph 10 is quite difficult. Study it carefully and also read the last sentence of the selection, which repeats the same idea. To help you, first what do the words "inside" and "outside" refer to in the phrases "from the inside" and "from the outside"? _____

   _____

   _____

4. _____ A good title for paragraph 11 would be
   a. "Experiencing Total Terror."
   b. "Why Crocodiles Kill."
   c. "An Unbelievable Experience."
   d. "Crocodile Behavior."

5. Look through paragraphs 11 and 12 again. List three phrases that convey the intense violence of the crocodile's attack. _____

_____

_____

G. UNDERSTANDING VOCABULARY

Look through the paragraphs listed by number in brackets and find a word that matches each definition. Refer to a dictionary if necessary. An example has been done for you.

Ex. threatening, frightening [paragraph 2]   *menacing*

1. the state of being whole and unimpaired [2]   _____

2. natural environments, surroundings [2]   _____

3. an intricate network, a labyrinth [3]   _____

4. soggy, full of water [3]   _____

5. referring to native inhabitants [5]:   _____

6. not inclined to believe [9]   _____

7. agreeable, open to [10]   _____

8. make up, invent [10]   _____

9. gloomy, offering little hope [10]   _____

10. overwhelmed, nearly destroyed [19]   _____

H. PARAPHRASING EXERCISE

Here are the last four sentences of paragraph 21, followed by three paraphrases. Choose the one that most accurately paraphrases the original passage.

_____ 1.   The wonder of being alive after being held—quite literally—in the jaws of death has never entirely left me. For the first year, the experience of existence as an unexpected blessing cast a golden glow over my life, despite the injuries and the pain. The glow has slowly faded, but some of that new gratitude for life endures, even if I remain unsure whom I should thank. The gift of gratitude came from the searing flash of near-death knowledge, a glimpse "from the outside" of the alien, incomprehensible world in which the narrative of self has ended.

      a. I am grateful to God for saving me. Having been so close to the jaws of death has given me a new perspective on life. I have had to endure pain from my injuries, but even though that pain is now receding, I realize that the knowledge of an alien world that I gained from this experience has made me a better, less self-centered person.

b. In the time since I nearly died from being in the crocodile's jaws, I have not forgotten the wonder of life. Although I my injuries were painful, just being alive made everything seem to glow. The glow has lessened to some extent, but I am still grateful. I saw "from the outside" the strange and inexplicable world that was so different from the world of myself.

c. The gift of gratitude that I feel from my near-death experience has brought a blessing to my life that I never would have dreamed of before. The pain from the injuries has been intense, but that pain has also shown me that being alive is the most precious thing in the world. One can gain this experience, however, only from being caught, literally, in the jaws of death.

I. SUMMARIZING EXERCISE

1. Write a sentence summarizing paragraph 10._____

_____

_____

_____

2. Write a sentence summarizing paragraph 21._____

_____

_____

J. TOPICS FOR DISCUSSION

1. Go to a good unabridged dictionary, in the library if necessary, and look up the meaning of the Greek word *hubris*. To what extent do Plumwood's actions reflect this concept?

2. What are some devices that the writer uses to maintain interest and to create suspense and terror in the reader?

K. TOPICS FOR WRITING

1. Write a short narrative in which you describe an experience where you felt, as Plumwood did, "total terror." It does not have to be an incident as harrowing as a crocodile attack, but everyone has felt intense fear at one time or another.

2. What kind of person did Val Plumwood reveal herself to be from the description of her near-death experience in Australia? Write a character sketch in which you discuss her traits, being sure to provide evidence from the narrative to support your characterizations.

EXPLORE THE WEB

- End the confusion over the difference between crocodiles and alligators by checking one or more website. Using Google or your favorite search engine, type in "alligators and crocodiles, differences" in the search box. You will find several relevant sites.

- Information as well as photographs of Kakadu National Park are available online. Begin by typing in this address: *www.environment.gov.au/parks/kakadu*. Or type in "Kakadu National Park, Australia."

PART FOUR

Mastering Reading about Complex Ideas

In order to comprehend nonfiction (including textbooks), you'll need the ability to recognize two important features of this kind of writing: patterns of development and transitional elements.

Patterns of Development

The patterns of development and their functions are listed here:

PATTERNS OF DEVELOPMENT				
List of Facts or Details	Examples	Reason—Cause and Effect	Description of a Process	Contrast
Includes factual details to support the main idea.	Uses specific instances of something more general to support the main idea.	Offers reasons (shows causes and effects) that explain why as support for the main idea.	Explains the steps one needs to follow to support the main idea.	Sets two subjects side by side and examines their differences to support the main idea.

Let's say that you are wrestling with a big decision that you must make about your future. You know that you are interested in helping people, and you come up with a list of careers where such an interest would be required for someone to succeed and be happy. On a sheet of paper you note the following: nurse, doctor, teacher, charity worker, mental health worker, social worker. What you have done is provide *examples,* specific instances of careers that involve helping others.

Now you have another decision: Should you apply to the four-year state university 50 miles away or should you study for the first two years at your local community college and then transfer? Again, you write down the good and bad aspects of both institutions and analyze their differences. Now you're *contrasting.* And when a friend asks you why you want to become, say, a social worker, you come up with some *reasons* that the field of social work appeals to you.

These logical processes, which we do all the time in our daily lives, are also present in writing. Called *patterns of development*, they refer to the internal logic of a passage, the way the writer gets his or her ideas across, the pattern that the writer imposes on his or her material. The choice of the appropriate pattern of development depends on the subject. But your starting point, as the reader, is to recognize that these patterns of development pertain to our thought processes. When looked at this way, you can see that you are already familiar with them. In this introduction we will examine each briefly and illustrate them with some short passages. Studying these patterns will help you keep on track as you read and allow you to follow the writer's thinking process.

LIST OF FACTS OR DETAILS

The pattern of *listing facts* or *listing details* is perhaps the simplest one to recognize. Following the main idea, each supporting sentence presents factual evidence to support the main assertion. Consider this passage from Selection 12 by Virginia Morell. You may recall the discussion of Betsy, the border collie, who has an amazing grasp of language. In a sidebar to the article (not reprinted in the selection), Morell supports the main idea that Betsy has an unusually large vocabulary.

Vincent J. Musi/Aurora Photos, Inc.

How much thought goes on behind those eyes? A lot, in this case. Six-year-old "Betsy" can put names to objects faster than a great ape, and her vocabulary is at 340 words and counting. Her smarts showed up early: At ten weeks she would sit on command and was soon picking up on names of items and rushing to retrieve them—ball, rope, paper, box, keys, and dozens more. She now knows at least 15 people by name, and in scientific tests she's proved skilled at linking photographs with the objects they represent. Says her owner, "She's a dog in a human [pack]. We're learning her language, and she's learning ours."

—Virginia Morell, "Minds of Their Own," *National Geographic*

EXAMPLES

An *example* is a specific instance of something more general. As you saw earlier, nursing and social work are examples of fields involving helping people. Consider this paragraph about the Ohlone Indians, who inhabited parts of Northern

California hundreds of years ago. Malcolm Margolin begins with the statement that, in comparison to Europeans, Ohlones seemed lazy. (You can tell that the writer is challenging this observation because he puts the word *laziness* in quotation marks.) The examples have been briefly annotated for you in the margin. Note that the first example is preceded with the helpful transitional phrase, "for example," and the next three little examples follow logically from that connector.

Main idea: Episodic harvesting explains "laziness"

Examples: deer hunting—arduous

Acorn, seed, and salmon harvests— hard work but for short periods

No crops to cultivate, animals to tend, ditches to dig

The episodic character of the harvesting also helps explain another much noted Ohlone characteristic: their so-called "laziness." For them hard work came only in spurts. Deer hunting, for example, was an arduous pursuit that demanded fasting, abstinence, great physical strength, and single-mindedness of purpose. The acorn harvest, the seed harvest, and the salmon harvest also involved considerable work for short periods of time. But when the work was over, there was little else to do. Unlike agricultural people, the Ohlones had no fields to plow, seeds to plant, crops to cultivate, weeds to pull, domestic animals to care for, or irrigation ditches to dig or maintain. So at the end of a harvest they often gave themselves over to "entire indolence," as one visitor described it—a habit that infuriated the Europeans who assumed that laziness was sinful and that hard work was not just a virtue for a God-given condition of human life.

—Malcolm Margolin, *The Ohlone Way*

REASONS—CAUSE AND EFFECT

The cause-effect relationship indicates the *reasons* that explain an effect, which can be a situation, a problem, a trend, in other words, what caused it to occur. In writing, this pattern answers the question "why"? Every effect (every situation, every problem, every trend) has at least one cause or reason to explain it—and often multiple causes.

First, you need to learn to identify which is the cause and which is the effect. Let's examine one example:

Vinh passed his English class because he studied hard every day and got help from a tutor.

The *effect* is that Vinh passed his class, and the *reasons* or *causes* are that he studied hard and went to a tutor. The word *because* helps you distinguish between the two elements. But not all cause-effect passages are so easily identified. Let's practice with two more examples.

The first one is by Paco Underhill, a consultant whose specialty is the design of American malls.

(1) Today's malls do a dismal job of signaling us as to what goes on inside. (2) This is mainly because of the disconnect that exists at their very core. (3) Malls house retailing, but they are not owned, developed, or built by retailers. (Paco Underhill, *Call of the Mall*)

Study the logical connection between the sentences and then label them, identifying cause and effect next to each sentence number.

Sentence 1: _____

Sentence 2: _____

Sentence 3: _____

You should have marked the sentences like this: Sentence 1—effect; sentences 2 and 3—cause.

Now consider a second excerpt. This one is by Malcolm Gladwell, in which he describes the impact of the social media revolution:

> (1) The world, we are told is in the midst of a revolution. (2) The new tools of social media have reinvented social activism. (3) With Facebook and Twitter and the like, the traditional relationship between political authority and popular will has been upended, making it easier for the powerless to collaborate, coordinate, and give voice to their concerns. (Malcolm Gladwell, "Small Change," *The New Yorker*)

Label the sentences as you did before.

Sentence 1: _____

Sentence 2: _____

Sentence 3: _____

You should have labeled the first sentence *cause* and the other two sentences *effect*.

DESCRIPTION OF A PROCESS

If you wanted to make an omelet for your Sunday morning breakfast, you could follow a cookbook recipe or you could follow your instincts. Either way, you would go through a *process,* a series of steps that, if followed in order, would produce something edible. First you would crack three eggs into a bowl and beat them. Then you would heat a little butter in your pan. Next, you would grate some cheese and chop some onions, add the eggs to the pan, and so forth. Writers use the process pattern for two primary purposes: (1) to show how to do something, for example, how to make an omelet, how to change a flat tire, or how to burn CDs; or (2) to show how something occurred, for example, how glaciers formed during the Ice Age or how a surfer tackles a big wave.

In this illustrative paragraph, Sophie Petit-Zerman discusses the phenomenon of laughter and answers this question: "Is it true that laughing can make us healthier?" Each step in the process is numbered to help you follow the discussion:

> [Laughter is] undoubtedly the best medicine. For one thing it's exercise. (1) It activates the cardiovascular system, so heart rate and blood pressure increase, (2) then the arteries dilate, causing blood pressure to fall again. (3) Repeated short, strong contractions of the chest muscles, diaphragm, and abdomen increase blood flow into our internal organs, and forced respiration—the *ha! ha!*—makes sure that this blood is well oxygenated. (4) Muscle tension

decreases, and indeed (5) we may temporarily lose control of our limbs, as in the expression "weak with laughter."

—Sophie Petit-Zerman, "No Laughing Matter," *Discover*

CONTRAST

How does a Honda differ from a Toyota? How are high school English classes different from college English courses? What are the major differences between the two sports websites espn.com and sportsline.com? When a writer sets two subjects side by side and examines their differences, he or she is using the *contrast* pattern. In this example, Bruno Bettelheim explores the main idea stated in the first sentence by contrasting fairy tales and dreams. Again, study the annotations:

Differences
between fairy tales
& dreams

Open vs. disguised
wish fulfillment

Relief of pressure
and happy ending
vs. lack of solution
for inner pressures

There are, of course, very significant differences between fairy tales and dreams. For example, in dreams more often than not the wish fulfillment is disguised, while in fairy tales much of it is openly expressed. To a considerable degree, dreams are the result of inner pressures which have found no relief, of problems which beset a person to which he knows no solution and to which the dream finds none. The fairy tale does the opposite: it projects the relief of all pressures and not only offers ways to solve problems but promises that a "happy" solution will be found.

—Bruno Bettelheim, *The Uses of Enchantment: The Meaning and Importance of Fairy Tales*

EXERCISE IN IDENTIFYING PATTERNS OF DEVELOPMENT

Here are a few short passages. Read them carefully, and then write the pattern of development that each represents in the first space. To refresh your memory, the answer choices are listed again:

- List of facts or details
- Examples
- Reason—cause and effect
- Description of a process
- Contrast

To make the exercise more challenging, write the sentence that represents the main idea in the second space provided. If no particular sentence seems to represent the main idea, write your own main-idea sentence.

A.

As was true of games before the digital age, there's a remarkable array of video games. Chess and bowling aren't very similar, but we intuitively understand that both are games. Likewise, video games encompass everything from simple online puzzles to simulated football games and professional wrestling matches to the "God game," in which the player adopts an omniscient view to influence the development of entire societies. In The Sims, the best-selling PC game of all time, players control the lives of individual humans as they go about their mundane lives. (It may sound unappealing, but The Sims comes from a long tradition. It is, in effect, another way to play house.) New genres frequently emerge. A "music" genre has arisen in response to the popularity of Dance Dance Revolution, a game in which players must move their feet in time to music on different areas of a dance pad.

—Chris Suellentrop, "Playing with Our Heads," *Utne Reader*

Pattern of development: _____

Main idea: _____

_____

B.

Popcorn

Why does popcorn pop? No one seems to have investigated the problem in much detail, and so what follows is the current educated guess. Recall that starch grains are embedded in a protein matrix, and that this matrix is probably stronger in popcorn than in other types because its protein-to-starch ratio is higher. When the kernel is heated in hot oil, the small amount of moisture it contains partly gelatinizes the starch grains; this happens at around 150°F (66°C). Then, as the kernel temperature reaches the boiling point, the water vaporizes and expands rapidly in volume. The hard protein matrix holds until the pressure becomes too great, at which point the kernel bursts open and the endosperm expands in volume on account of the sudden pressure drop. At the same time, the already cooked starch granules are dried out as the water vapor escapes, and the endosperm texture becomes light and crisp. If, however, popcorn is cooked in a covered pan that offers no escape for the water vapor, the spongy endosperm will absorb it again, and chewy, tough popcorn is the result.

Popcorn pops well only when it falls within the narrow range of 11 to 14% moisture content, to which the better brands are adjusted before being packed in air-tight containers.

—Harold McGee, *On Food and Cooking: The Science and Lore of the Kitchen*

Pattern of development: _____

Main idea: _____

_____

C.

The platforms of social media are built around weak ties. Twitter is a way of following (or being followed by) people you may never have met. Facebook is a tool for efficiently managing your acquaintances, for keeping up with the people you would not otherwise be able to stay in touch with. That's why you can have a thousand "friends" on Facebook, as you never could in real life.

—Malcolm Gladwell, "Small Change," *The New Yorker*

Pattern of development: _____

Main idea: _____

_____

D.

One characteristic that seems to distinguish small cats from big cats is the manner of eating. A small cat typically crouches over its food, all four feet neatly on the ground, in the familiar posture of a domestic cat eating from a dish. A big cat, on the other hand, typically lies down to eat and holds its food with its front paws. A small cat often begins eating at the head or neck of its victim, while a big cat usually starts at the haunch or belly. Even so, the form of eating has more to do with the size of the food than with the size of the cat—a tiger given a small piece of meat does not normally lie down for it but simply laps it up off the ground in passing or crouches directly above it, housecat style. Or if such a bit of meat is tossed to him, the tiger may catch it with a snap of his small front teeth—his incisor teeth—and then push the morsel into his mouth with the back of his wrist or with the side of his paw.

—Elizabeth Marshall Thomas, *The Tribe of Tiger*

Pattern of development: _____

Main idea: _____

_____

E.

Note: This paragraph refers to the Occupy Wall Street protests that took place in New York City during the summer and fall of 2011.

Because any kind of amplified sound is forbidden, bullhorns included, the meetings are conducted in an ingenious way. A speaker says a few words, then pauses; the audience repeats them, loudly and in unison; the speaker says a few more; the chorus repeats; and so on. If the group is unusually large, the repetitions radiate out, like a mountain echo.

The listeners register their reactions silently, with their hands. Four fingers up, palms outward: Yay! Four fingers down, palms inward: Boo! Both hands rolling: Wrap it up! Clenched fists crossed at the wrists: No way, José! There's something oddly moving about a crowd of smartphone-addicted, computer-savvy people cooperating to create such an utterly low-tech, strikingly human, curiously tribal means of amplification—a literal loudspeaker.

—Hendrik Hertzberg, "A Walk in the Park," *The New Yorker*

Pattern of development: _____

Main idea: _____

_____

F.

Next time you're at a mall, instead of going directly inside, stroll around the perimeter of the place. It will be one of the more joyless promenades you'll ever make. You'll be very alone out there, on a narrow strip of sidewalk, assuming it has a sidewalk—many malls don't—with maybe a security guard or two to keep you company. (They'll be watching you closely, since someone who walks around at all is, by definition, an odd character.) There will almost certainly be shrubbery, neatly clipped, but it's greenery of the most generic kind. Nobody thought you'd ever look too closely at it. Its only job is to be green.

—Paco Underhill, _Call of the Mall_

Pattern of development: _____

Main idea: _____

_____

G.

The writer, a linguist and an anthropologist, studied the Pirahã, a tribe of Indians who live in the Amazonian jungle of Brazil.

Pirahã houses reveal important distinctions between their culture and ours. When I think of Pirahã houses, I am often reminded of Henry David Thoreau's suggestion in _Walden_ that all a person really needs is a large box that he can carry around to protect himself from the elements. The Pirahãs don't need walls for defense, because the village is the defense—every member of the village will come to the aid of every other member. They don't need houses to display wealth, because all Pirahãs are equal in wealth. They don't need houses for privacy, because privacy is not a strong value—though if privacy is needed for sex, relieving oneself, or anything else, the entire jungle is around, or one can leave the village in a canoe. Houses don't need heating or cooling, because the jungle provides a nearly perfect climate for lightly clothed human bodies. Houses are just a place to sleep with moderate protection from the rain and sun. They are places to keep one's dogs and the few belongings that a family has. Each house is a rectangle formed by three rows of three poles each, with the center row higher to allow for the roof to be raised in the middle.

—Daniel L. Everett, _Don't Sleep, There Are Snakes_

Pattern of development: _____

Main idea: _____

_____

H.

Many bright people are really in the dark about vegetable life. Biology teachers face kids in classrooms who may not even believe in the metamorphosis of bud to flower to fruit and seed, but rather, some continuum of pansies becoming petunias becoming chrysanthemums; that's the only reality they witness as landscapers come to campuses and city parks and surreptitiously yank out one flower before it fades from its prime, replacing it with another. (My biology-professor brother pointed this out to me.) The same disconnection from natural processes may be at the heart of our country's shift away from believing in evolution. In the past, principles of natural selection and change over time made sense to kids who'd watched it all unfold. Whether or not they knew the terms, farm families understood the processes well enough to imitate them: culling, selecting, and improving their herds and crops. For modern kids who intuitively believe in the spontaneous generation of fruits and vegetables in the produce section, trying to get their minds around the slow speciation of the plant kingdom may be a stretch

—Barbara Kingsolver, *Animal, Vegetable, Miracle*

Pattern of development: _____

Main idea: _____

_____

Transitional Elements

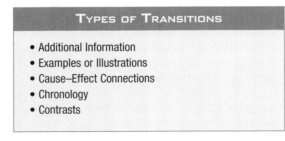

TYPES OF TRANSITIONS

- Additional Information
- Examples or Illustrations
- Cause–Effect Connections
- Chronology
- Contrasts

Transitions or *transitional elements* make the logical relationships between ideas clear. They are sometimes called *markers*, because they "mark" the place where a writer shifts ideas or indicates a particular logical connection. In this way, they serve as a bridge between ideas, helping us follow the writer's thinking, keeping us on track, and showing us where a shift—sometimes a very subtle shift—in thought begins. As you will see, transitions can be either single words or phrases. And sometimes an entire paragraph may be used in this way, pointing back to the preceding paragraph and at the same time pointing ahead to the next idea in the chain of ideas.

Some writers use lots of transitions; others use none at all. But when they are present, they are useful. Contrary to what some students have been taught, transitions do not necessarily come at the beginning of sentences. They can appear in the middle of sentences or even at the end. By studying a number of examples, you will quickly become proficient at locating transitions. The most common types of transitional elements follow. Each is illustrated by a passage from a reading in Parts One through Three that you may have already read.

TRANSITIONS THAT INDICATE ADDITIONAL INFORMATION IS COMING

These transitions are most commonly used in the first two patterns: listing facts and details and offering examples. Here are some examples:

and
next
first, second. . .
besides
in the same way
in addition
further
furthermore
moreover
also

EXAMPLES FROM THE READINGS

- All this online social networking was supposed to make us closer. *And* in some ways it has.

  —Elizabeth Bernstein, "How Facebook Ruins Friendships"

- Shampoo companies *also* realize that the sheer volume of bubbles a shampoo generates can prompt thoughts of freshness and cleanliness.

  —Martin Lindstrom, "Selling Illusions of Cleanliness"

TRANSITIONS THAT INTRODUCE EXAMPLES OR ILLUSTRATIONS

These transitions signal that a writer is going to give an example or illustration to reinforce a more general idea. Here are some examples:

for example
for instance
to illustrate
such as
as a case in point
consider the following
namely

> **EXAMPLES FROM THE READINGS**
>
> • Dolphins often synchronize their movements in the wild, *such as* leaping and diving side by side, but scientists don't know what signal they use to stay so tightly coordinated.
>
> —Virginia Morell, "Minds of Their Own"
>
> • The few white workers who started more recently have few other options. Jane, *for example*, is well into her 60s. Factory work is all she knows.
>
> —Steve Striffler, "Undercover in a Chicken Factory"

TRANSITIONS THAT SHOW CAUSE–EFFECT CONNECTIONS

Although not as common, a few transitional elements signal a cause–effect relationship. Interestingly, there are few transitional or connector words that indicate *cause*. The writer can show cause only by using words like *because* or *since* or *given* or *for* (in the sense of "because") or by writing a phrase like *that being the case* or *one reason for*, or something similar. There are, however, a few transitions that indicate *effect* or *result*:

as a result
consequently
therefore
thus
then
hence

> **EXAMPLES FROM THE READINGS**
>
> • Some restaurant managers go out of their way to hire messed-up people. Why? *Because* they're easier to control. If the staff's easy to control, then it's easier for management to rip them off to line their own pockets.
>
> —The Waiter, "Why Be a Waiter?"
>
> • New Caledonian crows are among the most skilled of tool-making and tool-using birds, forming probes and hooks from sticks and leaf stems to poke into the crowns of the palm trees, where fat grubs hide. *Since* these birds, like chimpanzees, make and use tools, researchers can look for similarities in the evolutionary processes that shaped their brains.
>
> —Virginia Morell, "Minds of Their Own"

TRANSITIONS THAT SHOW CHRONOLOGICAL ORDER OR TIME PROGRESSION

This group of transitions is most evident in the process pattern or in narrative writing. Writers use them to ensure a logical progression of steps or a sequence of events. Study these examples:

then
meanwhile
later
eventually
after a few days
next
in 2009

EXAMPLES FROM THE READINGS

- These "further" processing lines are at the heart of the revolution that has transformed the poultry industry and American diets over the past 25 years. *Before then*, most Americans bought chicken in one form: the whole bird. *Today*, Tyson produces thousands of "further processed/value-added" meat products.

    —Steve Striffler, "Undercover in a Chicken Processing Factory"

- The bank *now* presented a high, steep face of slippery mud. The only obvious avenue of escape was a paperbark tree near the muddy bank wall. I made the split-second decision to leap into its lower branches and climb to safety. I steered to the tree and stood up to jump. *At the same instant*, the crocodile rushed up alongside the canoe, and its beautiful, flecked golden eyes looked straight into mine.

    —Val Plumwood, "Being Prey: Surviving a Crocodile Attack"

TRANSITIONS THAT SHOW CONTRAST

This last group of transitions helps keep the reader on track when the writer is moving back and forth between two subjects to show the differences between them. Consider these examples:

but
yet
still
however
nevertheless
nonetheless
on the other hand
in contrast
instead
whereas

EXAMPLES FROM THE READINGS

- *Despite* the mix of modern and Confucian values, family is still the organizing principal and foundation of security in China, and marriage is its bedrock.

  —Olivia Wu, "Alfresco Marriage Market"

- When I finally left school, my parents were disappointed, *but* since it wasn't what they wanted me to do, they weren't devastated. I, *on the other hand*, felt I was staring at the bottom of the abyss.

  —Caroline Hwang, "The Good Daughter"

- When Alejandro looks around at people from Mexico, El Salvador, Honduras, Vietnam, Laos, and the Marshall Islands, and says we are all Mexicans, he is making a statement about class. He is not confused by the bright lights of the postmodern world, *or* unclear where he is located, socially, racially, and geographically. *Rather*, he is playing with the label, using it almost as a synonym for worker.

  —Steve Striffler, "Undercover in a Chicken Factory"

- Being on the outside of the mainstream, *however*, is fun only when you choose to be on the outside.

  —The Waiter, "Why Be a Waiter"?

EXERCISE IN IDENTIFYING TRANSITIONS

Here are two passages for you to practice with, one easy, the other a bit more difficult. As you read, underline the transitions. Then in the spaces provided, write the transitional element (a word or phrase) and indicate its function.

A.

Children have always competed for their parents' attention, but this generation has experienced something new. Previously, children had to deal with parents being off with work, friends, or each other. Today, children contend with parents who are physically close, tantalizingly so, but mentally elsewhere.

—Sherry Turkle, "The Nostalgia of the Young"

1. Transition: _____   Function: _____
2. Transition: _____   Function: _____
3. Transition: _____   Function: _____

B.

(1) Most high schools in the United States offer abundant options and only minimal requirements. (2) Students may choose easy courses, unaware of the disadvantages, because no one informs them that harder courses pay off

in college preparation. (3) As a result, far too many students' high school coursework is poorly coordinated with college standards. (4) In contrast, Japan and Finland, which produce some of the highest-achieving students in the world, have well-integrated curricula based on consistent standards across schools, and between high schools and university entrance exams. (5) In the United States, school reform movements often point to the creation of "high standards" or "college-ready standards" as important components in improving student achievement and degree completion. (6) But these many disjointed reform movements are not coordinated, and they have not led to coordination between high schools and colleges.

—James E. Rosenbaum and Kelly Iwanaga Becker,
"The Early College Challenge," *American Educator*

1. Transition: _____   Function: _____
2. Transition: _____   Function: _____
3. Transition: _____   Function: _____
4. Transition: _____   Function: _____

Some Final Considerations

As mentioned earlier, a writer is under no obligation to use transitional elements to make your reading easier. When a writer doesn't use transitions, how can you maintain focus, keep on track, and follow what the writer is saying? As stated frequently in this text, reading with a pencil in your hand—actively annotating—can help a lot. Actively thinking about the connections between ideas can help as well. To illustrate this process, consider this short excerpt from Tim Guest's 2007 book, *Second Lives: A Journey though Virtual Worlds*, which focuses on the origin of Second Life, a virtual world website. The passage has only four transitions, which are underlined. However, there are numerous logical patterns embedded in the sentences, which I have noted in the left margin.

chronological—
establishes time

contrast

detail

time (next step in
the narrative)

more details

time progression

contrast

cause–effect

example

<u>By June 1999</u>—after putting himself through college with the profits from his own software company—Philip decided that what he wanted wasn't the ability to change the real world, <u>but</u> to conquer it and replace it with something better: a virtual world with no barrier between thought and action. He left his position as chief technology officer of RealNetworks, which had bought out his video streaming software, and joined forces with an old colleague to form Linden Lab. Their vision was a renovation of Philip's childhood dream: a world where people could build whatever they liked, and become whoever they wanted.

Right from the beginning of online worlds, the players were quicker than the developers to recognize the possibilities in their new virtual lives. The designers of EverQuest were stunned when they discovered players were getting married online. In The Sims Online, you can combine objects, but not create new ones, and the residents worked hard to overcome this limitation.

another example

cause–effect

In one case, a group of Sims residents decided they wanted a piano, so they built one out of a desk and chairs, with cigars for piano keys.

Of course, we don't really read this way; that is, it seems tedious to label ideas. Still, it does show the process, and with practice, I hope that for you the process of seeing the logical connections between a writer's thoughts becomes so automatic that you no longer have to concentrate so much on them as you read. It takes practice and experience to achieve this confidence, but it's a very worthwhile goal.

21

DEBRA J. DICKERSON
Raising Cain

Debra J. Dickerson writes on race relations and racial identity. A graduate of Harvard Law School, Dickerson started her writing career when she published "Who Shot Johnny?" in The New Republic *(1996), in which she describes a drive-by shooting that left her nephew paralyzed. Since then, she has published her work in various publications—*The Washington Post, The New York Times Magazine, The Village Voice, Salon, *and* Mother Jones, *where she currently blogs. "Raising Cain" was first published on the online site* Salon.com. *In it, she talks about her feelings of ambivalence when she learned she was pregnant with a boy. As an African-American feminist, Dickerson is concerned about the very real problems American black males face in the United States, and she worried about how she could raise her son to be a caring, compassionate person without being, as she says, "a hypocrite or a castrator."*

Vocabulary Analysis

WORD
PARTS
The prefix *a-* The Greek prefix *a-* is attached to several English roots to indicate an absence or lack of something. In paragraph 15, Dickerson uses the phrase "*amorphous* future." *Amorphous* means lacking a shape, from *a-* ("without") + *morph* ("shape" or "form"). Other words beginning with *a-* are *apolitical* (having no interest in politics), *amoral* (having no sense of morality), *apathy* (having no feeling, indifferent), and *agnostic* (one who does not know if God exists).

DEBRA J. DICKERSON

Raising Cain

1   Dec. 11, 2006 When I was pregnant with my first child, who is now 5, I was ecstatic to learn he was a boy. This was odd, since I did not much like those of the male gender. Little boys even less, because I'd seen the center-of-the-universe process by which they become men.

2   I might have been equally happy to learn he was a girl (as I was with my second, who is 3). I was just plain happy to know more, anything, about this mysterious new presence that was dismantling my carefully constructed life. Yet, from the beginning, I wondered how I would reconcile my feminism with raising a son. How could I do it without becoming either a castrating mother straight out of O'Neill[1] or an ovo-hypocrite[2] who talks woman power but raises her own precious boy to be no more enlightened, and no less entitled, than any Promise Keeper?[3]

3   Black people always demand that I focus only on the holy calling of raising a black man, period. But it seems to me that if I get the manhood part right, the black part will take care of itself. If he earns my respect by becoming a moral, hardworking, courageous humanist who shoulders his responsibilities, he can be as "incognegro" as Wayne Brady.[4] Race schmace:[5] His blackness is his to define. My dilemma is raising a man when he's the only one of his gender to whom I give the benefit of the doubt.

4.   I should explain: When I say I don't like little boys, I mean that, before I had kids, all children annoyed me, albeit boys in particular because of their penchant for a mayhem that left obedient little girls ignored. When I was growing up in the inner city, children were the A-No. 1 way to ruin your life and guarantee that you'd be broke and tied to one loser or the other for the rest of your life. Once I was grown, and single till 40, children became the whining pests who kept my friends from being able to carry on a conversation for more than five minutes or who kept insisting that I exclaim over their crayon scrawls and stuttered nonsense.

5   While my own childhood was wonderful in some ways, it was so much grimmer than that of the privileged children I've encountered as an adult that I found myself resenting them both their freedom to be children and the unceasing

---

[1]Eugene O'Neill (1888–1953) was an American playwright best known for *Mourning Becomes Electra* and *Long Day's Journey into Night*. He won the Nobel Prize for literature in 1936. (Ed.)

[2]*Ovo-* is the Latin root for "egg." (Ed.)

[3]A Christian organization based in Denver, Colorado, that seeks to help men take responsibility for their families by fulfilling seven promises. (See the website at the end of the Exercises.) In 1997 the Promise Keepers held a march in Washington, DC, at which it was estimated that one million men, many of them African-American men, attended. (Ed.)

[4]*Incognegro* is a blend of *incognito* ("unknown") + the Spanish word for black. Wayne Brady is a television talk-show host, actor, and comedian. Dickerson means that Wayne Brady is not culturally black, in other words, he is post-racial, like Barack Obama. (Ed.)

[5]"Race schmace" is an example of a Yiddish expression in which one says a word and then repeats it, but this time changing the first consonant to "sch." The phrase thus dismisses the idea. (Ed.)

stream of nurturing adult attention they received. Poor kids have to fend more for themselves emotionally; it makes us strong but it also makes us sad.

6   Putting the mourning of my own childhood aside, I just mean to say that children primarily meant to me that I'd always be taking care of someone, a fate too many women accept as given. When you grow up a poor black girl in a huge family you spend your life caring for the whole world. Children, I knew, meant that I'd be a human mop and short-order cook forever (see Katherine Newman's "A Different Shade of Gray" for an excellent, if depressing, look at how most inner-city grandmothers never get to retire, since they have to pick up every-body's slack). I wasn't always sure I'd escape poverty but I was damn sure I could escape parenthood.

7   So having children, while always a leap of faith, was especially hard for me because I knew there was a strong chance that the same fear of losing control that led me out of poverty might well keep me from surrendering myself to those walking little need-bags. Here's what I mean: for decades, I was the living embodiment of delayed gratification. I had something like a phobia of indulging myself, as people from my background understandably did with sloth, crime or drugs. The first time it ever occurred to me to lie down with a nasty cold was my first year of law school. I actually stared, appalled at what I was thinking, at the bed in my dorm room like a thief looking at an open bank teller's drawer. I was 33. That was also the year I took my first aspirin. I was afraid that if I weak-ened for even one moment the downhill slide might never stop.

8   The poor have no backup system, and I worried where such self-indulgence might lead. And what are children but the ultimate self-indulgence, the perfect monkey wrench thrown into even the most together woman's life? I knew women who kept their children at arm's length and it broke even *my* heart. At 41, I was less afraid of miscarriage or birth defects than of being a cold, distant mom too neurotic to surrender to her own babies. But when I found myself constantly stroking the same spot on the right side of my belly as my son grew, exulting in every blurry ultrasound of his huge head and tiny little spine, I was pitifully grate-ful. Thank God, my fears about not being able to love him were easily squashed.

9   Two kids later, I know my fears about kids being the perfect trap were justi-fied because I have completely "mommed out." Though even before I conceived I told anyone who would listen that I was going to hire a nanny and get right back to my work and travel, now I get teary because my daughter insists on dressing herself and my son no longer accepts being called Boo Boo. ("That's not my name, Mom.") Now that he's past the androgynous baby stage my dilemma is how to be true to my feminist principles and true to my son's needs. In my community, it is often noted that black mothers raise their daughters but merely love their sons. How do I raise them both?

10   My unapologetic, "bite me" feminism was formed as I grew up in the fun-damentalist Christian black working class, where I was supposed to be seen working and not heard questioning. I'm still pissed off about it. However much racism a black man encountered in the outside world, he always had his women folk to come home to and lord over, however benignly he might choose to do so. When my handyman, truck-driving father returned from a grueling day's work, he filled his time as he chose. I have few memories of my mother when

she wasn't still in her pink waitress uniform cooking, cleaning, doing laundry or tending to one of her six kids until long past my bedtime. As soon as each girl was old enough to reach the stove, we joined her on the bucket brigade while my brother idled. I was raised to be such a rough-knuckled chambermaid, I thought the hospital corners and tongue lashings of Basic Training and Officer Training School were a respite.

11   When I was 16 and he was 12, my brother and I had the same curfew. My father actually punished him the few times he helped us girls, so we didn't have the heart to keep making him help. When we feminists go on about institutional-ized sexism, this is what we mean; thanks, Dad, for making me complicit in my own subjugation. There's nothing lower than a black woman who keeps a dirty house or neglects her kids (except a lesbian), but a happily unemployed black man shuffling between his mama's, his big mama's and his latest girl-friend's house? It's hard out there for a brother. Spending 12 years in the military, where the black men worked just as hard to keep the women in their place as did Mr. Charlie, sealed the feminist deal.

12   So what to do with this son of mine? How to love him? How to *raise* him? How to mold him into a manly man but not a bruiser? And most of all, how not to interpret his every troubling move (e.g., refusing to wait to be called on, hit-ting a classmate who was uninterested in being his girlfriend, torturing his little sister) as a harbinger of a male chauvinist pig in the making?

13   But, adding another princess costume to my daughter's cache the other day, it occurred to me that I *was* a hypocrite, just not the kind I had so feared. I have no doubt that indulging (OK, creating) my daughter's Cinderella fascination is but one, far from definitive layer in her development as a woman. With something like evil satisfaction this summer, I feigned deafness when her princess regalia repeatedly got caught in her trike's wheels. When I finally came to help, I told her, "Princesses sit on thrones, honey. They can't ride bikes. So I think you'll have to choose either the ball gown or the bike." She chose the ball gown and we sat on the porch together while her brother NASCAR'd up and down on his bike. I wasn't the least bit concerned. "We got nothing but time," I thought hap-pily as I watched her watch her brother's freedom.

14   So why no patience with, or confidence in, my son?

15   I see now that it's my anger, however justified, and not my feminism, that clouds this particular issue. There's no inherent difference between either my daughter or my son's interrupting class, hitting classmates, abusing the weak. The problem is my having read gender in, making it worse for a boy, my boy, any boy, to do those things. If I stay focused in the now and in transcendent principles—pacifism except in self-defense or in protection of others, good citi-zenship, empathy, tolerance, fairness, responsibility—I can stay focused on my kids' actual needs and not their amorphous future potential to be either victim or victimizer. My goal is to raise two feminists too smart and too honest to either accept or perpetuate gender-based unfairness. Now I have a story to tell them about how easy it is to fall into those traps.

Debra J. Dickerson, "Raising Cain," Salon.com, December 11, 2006. The article first appeared in Salon.com, at http://www.salon.com. An online version remains in the Salon archives. Reprinted with permission.

Exercises

Do not refer to the selection for Exercises A and B unless your instructor directs you to do so.

A. DETERMINING THE MAIN IDEA AND PURPOSE

Choose the best answer.

_____ **1.** The main idea of the selection is that the writer
   a. experienced a very different childhood growing up in the inner city than the more privileged children she has observed.
   b. wrestled with the problems of how to raise her son in such a way that he would become a good man without being a chauvinist brute.
   c. experienced a conflict about how to raise her son and daughter because she had different expectations for their futures.
   d. enthusiastically accepted the role of mother even though it disrupted her career.

_____ **2.** The writer's purpose is to
   a. recommend strategies for coping with the various problems all mothers face.
   b. argue for a gender-free course of action when raising children of both sexes.
   c. examine the conflicts and ambivalent feelings she had about how to raise a black boy to become a man.
   d. challenge others in the African-American community to change their lax child-rearing practices with regard to raising boys.

B. COMPREHENDING MAIN IDEAS

Choose the correct answer for the multiple-choice items. Write the fill-in answers in the space provided using your own words.

_____ **1.** Dickerson faced a conflict in dealing with her son, namely, the conflict between her desire to raise her son to be a moral and hard-working black man and
   a. her family's expectations for him.
   b. his own desires and personality traits.
   c. the pressures of his peers who might not share her values.
   d. her feminist ideals.

_____ **2.** The writer states that before she had children she generally didn't like children. Which of the following does she not mention as a reason for this feeling?
   a. Children require an unlimited supply of energy, and the writer doubted that she was up to the task.

    b. Little girls are taught to be obedient and are generally ignored while little boys are allowed to get away with creating turmoil or with being idle.

    c. Children disrupt one's career plans.

    d. Other people's children are whining pests whose every word and every drawing is a work of art.

    e. Children require constant attention from their mothers, thus assuring women a life of constant drudgery.

3. Dickerson describes several aspects of her own childhood, and she comes to a conclusion about children who grow up in a large family in a poor community. What is it? _____

_____ **4.** The writer cites an often-repeated concept about raising children in the black community, namely that black mothers

    a. merely love their daughters but raise their sons.

    b. raise their sons but merely love their daughters.

    c. raise their daughters but merely love their sons.

    d. raise their sons and daughters with equal expectations.

_____ **5.** Dickerson says that in the working-class family she grew up in,

    a. her brother worked just as hard around the house as his sisters.

    b. her younger brother was treated very differently from her and her sisters, in particular because he was not expected to help.

    c. everybody pitched in to do household chores according to a chart.

    d. both parents indulged all the children and asked them to do only minor chores.

6. At the end of the article, Dickerson realizes that, despite all her worrying, she really needs to focus on one thing, namely

_____

COMPREHENSION SCORE

Score your answers for Exercises A and B as follows:

A. No. right _____ × 2 = _____

B. No. right _____ × 1 = _____

Total points from A and B _____ × 10 = _____ percent

You may refer to the selection as you work through the remaining exercises.

C. LOCATING INFORMATION

Locate the specific information that reinforces each idea from the selection. Paragraph numbers are provided for you.

1. What is Dickerson's specific complaint about the way black boys are raised in the African-American community? [paragraphs 1–2] _____

_____

_____

2. Why didn't Dickerson indulge herself, even going so far as never to take an aspirin for a headache before she was in law school? [paragraph 7]

   _____

   _____

3. According to Dickerson, who in the family is responsible for subjugating women, for institutionalized sexism? [paragraphs 10–11] _____

   _____

   _____

4. In what way was basic training and officer training school different from the discipline Dickerson underwent at home? [paragraphs 10–11] _____

   _____

   _____

D. UNDERSTANDING STRUCTURE

Follow the directions for each section that follows. Review the introductory discussion of patterns of development if necessary.

1. Read paragraph 2 again and locate the single transitional word. Write it in the first space. Then decide which pattern of development the paragraph represents and write it in the second space.

   _____   _____

2. What pattern of development is used in paragraph 4?

   _____

3. Here are four types of logical relationships: contrast—showing the differences between two things; reasons—showing why something exists; process—showing steps in chronological order; examples—showing specific illustrations of something. Which one is implied in paragraph 5?

   _____

4. Read paragraphs 7 and 10 again. Then decide which pattern of development the paragraph represents. _____

E. UNDERSTANDING VOCABULARY

Look through the paragraphs listed by number in brackets and find a word that matches each definition. Refer to a dictionary if necessary. An example has been done for you.

Ex. emasculating, depriving of masculinity
[paragraphs 2–3]   _____ _castrating_ _____

1. although, even though [3–4]   _____

2. state of disorder, causing chaos or destruction [3–4]　　　　　　　　　　　_____

3. inclination, liking for [3–4]　　　　　　_____

4. attempt or manage without help [5–6]　　_____

5. short interval of rest or relief [10]　　　_____

6. physically demanding, exhausting [10]　　_____

7. something that indicates or foreshadows what is to come [11–12]　　　　　_____

8. associated with wrongdoing, participating in a bad tradition [11–12]　　_____

9. pretended [13]　　　　　　　　　　　_____

10. cause to continue, prolong the existence of [15]　_____

F. USING VOCABULARY—VARIANT WORD FORMS

Write the correct inflected form of the base word (in parentheses) in each of the following sentences. Be sure to add the appropriate ending to fit the grammatical requirements of the sentence. Refer to your dictionary if necessary.

1. (*ecstatic*—use a noun) When Dickerson discovered that she was pregnant with a boy, she experienced the same _____ that most women feel.

2. (*reconciliation*—use a verb) For Dickerson, the hardest part about raising a boy is the need to _____ the dilemma between adhering to her feminist ideals and raising a boy.

3. (*hypocrite*—use an adjective) Women who raise boys, especially if they are feminists, often feel _____ because they are torn between sticking to their feminist ideals and spoiling their sons.

4. (*sloth*—use an adjective) The writer claims that for many African-Americans who were raised in poverty, self-indulgence means living a _____ life or getting involved with crime or drugs.

5. (*subjugation*—use a verb) Dickerson blames her father who, like many black men, _____ their women by not making the same demands on their sons as they do on their daughters.

6. (*transcendent*—use a verb) Dickerson concludes that certain principles— pacifism, responsibility, and fairness—_____ all gender issues.

G. SMALL GROUP ACTIVITY—UNDERSTANDING SLANG WORDS AND EXPRESSIONS

Dickerson uses several informal and slang expressions. Consider these expressions in their context and then, working in small groups, try to determine their meaning. The paragraph number where each occurs is included. If you are unsure, ask your instructor or other classmates for help.

1. children were the *A-No. 1 way* to ruin your life [paragraph 4] _____

   _____

2. Children, I knew, meant that I'd be a *human mop and short-order cook* [6]

   _____

3. keep me from surrendering myself to those walking little *need-bags* [7]

   _____

4. Children [are] . . . the perfect *monkey wrench* thrown into even the most together woman's life [8] _____

   _____

5. I have completely *"mommed out"* [9] _____

   _____

6. My unapologetic, *"bite me"* feminism [10] _____

   _____

7. we joined her on *the bucket brigade* [10] _____

   _____

8. *tongue lashings* of Basic Training [10] _____

   _____

9. a harbinger of a *male chauvinist pig* in the making [12] _____

   _____

10. while her brother *NASCAR'd* up and down on his bike [13] _____

   _____

H. PARAPHRASING EXERCISE

Here is a passage from the selection, followed by three paraphrases. Choose the one that most accurately paraphrases the original passage.

_____ The poor have no backup system, and I worried where such self-indulgence might lead. And what are children but the ultimate self-indulgence, the perfect monkey wrench thrown into even the most together woman's life?

   a. If you are poor, you have no resources to fall back on when things go wrong. I worried that having children was only a matter of an unnecessary selfish pleasure, one that had the possibility of interfering with even the most organized mother's life.

   b. For poor people, having children is a last resource, which makes their lives both more fulfilled and more difficult. Though some say that having children is just another form of self-indulgence, children are, in fact, the perfect way to make a woman more organized and willing to sacrifice.

   c. Poor people have a tough time when they have children because they have to be even more organized than parents with money. Those who are not poor, who are on the outside, may consider having children a supreme example of self-indulgence, but having children also leads to more committed, responsible, and organized parenting.

I. TOPICS FOR DISCUSSION

1. Think about Dickerson's attitude (point of view) in this essay. Does she seem angry, realistic, hostile, clear-thinking, or something altogether different?

2. Are Dickerson's concerns about how to raise her son (as opposed to how to raise her daughter) a result of her feminism, of the specific characteristics of the African-American community, or of the concerns of all parents who wrestle with expectations for their children?

3. Dickerson's assessment and explanation of the divergence in the way black boys and black girls are raised is rather harsh. As she writes, "It's hard out there for a brother." Yet there might be other reasons—besides parental indulgence—to explain why "sloth, crime or drugs" have exercised so much of a pull in poor communities. Discuss other points of view that are contrary to her thinking.

4. What are the origins of Dickerson's feminism as they are revealed throughout the selection? Has having two children changed her thinking? If so, how?

G. TOPICS FOR WRITING

1. Write a rebuttal to Dickerson's essay, in which you offer different explanations and counterarguments for her ideas.

2. Dickerson emphasizes that the hard work African-American women do, especially in poor households, is a tradition that starts in childhood. As she says, "When you grow up a poor black girl in a huge family you spend your life caring for the whole world." How different is the situation for girls from another ethnic or economic group that you are familiar with? Write a short essay in which you address the role of a young girl in a family you are familiar with.

3. If you have a sibling or siblings of the opposite sex, were you raised differently from them? If so, how? What were your parents' expectations? disciplinary measures? curfew rules? requirements for performing household chores? Write an essay in which you examine these areas with respect to your upbringing and that of your siblings.

EXPLORE THE WEB

- Debra Dickerson's blog posts for Mother Jones can be accessed at this link: www.motherjones.com/authors/debra-j-dickerson
- You can read the article online that started Dickerson's writing career, "Who Shot Johnny?" by typing in the writer's name and the title in the search box of your favorite search engine.

22 TAMARA LUSH
Living Inside a Virtual World

Tamara Lush is an Associated Press reporter who covers events and issues in Florida. This article, first published in the San Jose Mercury News *and reprinted on the Huffington Post website (as well as on other websites), describes the experience of Ryan Van Cleave, an English professor whose marathon sessions playing World of Warcraft almost destroyed him and his family. Lush details the psychological changes that his compulsive playing brought about, including a discussion of whether or not such compulsive playing is truly an addiction.*

Vocabulary Analysis

WORD ROOTS

transport In Selection 17, "Undercover in a Chicken Factory," you studied the prefix *trans-*, meaning "across." In this selection, we will look at the word's root. Lush writes in paragraph 2 that Ryan Van Cleave "was mentally and emotionally *transported* to another world" when he played World of Warcraft. The root *portare* comes from Latin and means "to carry." Thus to *transport* means, literally, "to carry across from one place or state to another." Other verbs in English with this root include *import* (literally, "to carry in"), *export* ("to carry out"), *deport* ("to carry away"), and *report* ("to carry back"). What do these two words mean?

portable _____

portage _____

TAMARA LUSH

Living Inside a Virtual World

Chris O'Meara / AP Images

1   SARASOTA, Fla.—At the height of what he calls his addiction, Ryan Van Cleave would stand in the grocery store checkout line with his milk and bread and baby food for his little girls and for a split second think he was living inside a video game.

2   It sounds crazy, but it's true: Something would catch his attention out of the corner of his eye—maybe another shopper would make a sudden move for a Hershey bar—and he was mentally and emotionally transported to another world.

3   World of Warcraft, to be exact.

4   It was his favorite video game, the one he played every night, every day, sometimes all weekend. The sudden movement in the store triggered a response similar to when he was in front of the computer screen, battling dragons and monsters for up to 60 hours a week. Van Cleave's heart pounded. His breathing quickened.

5   But then the thirtysomething family man would catch his breath and come back to reality. Sort of.

6   World of Warcraft began to crowd out everything in Van Cleave's world. His wife. His children. His job as a university English professor.

7   Before teaching class or late at night while his family slept, he'd squeeze in time at the computer screen, playing. He'd often eat meals at the computer— microwave burritos, energy drinks, Hot Pockets, foods that required only one hand, leaving the other free to work the keyboard and the mouse.

8   Living inside World of Warcraft seemed preferable to the drudgery of everyday life. Especially when the life involved fighting with his wife about how much time he spent on the computer.

9   "Playing 'World of Warcraft' makes me feel godlike," Van Cleave wrote. "I have ultimate control and can do what I want with few real repercussions. The real world makes me feel impotent . . . a computer malfunction, a sobbing child, a suddenly dead cell phone battery—the littlest hitch in daily living feels profoundly disempowering."

10   Despite thoughts like this, despite the dissociative episodes in supermarkets, he did not think he had a problem IRL—gamerspeak for In Real Life. But he did, and a reckoning was coming.

—

11   Van Cleave grew up in suburban Chicago. He was adopted, which he said always made him feel like an outsider in his own home and in the world. As a kid, he was more interested in guitars and computers.

12   In high school, each year brought more exciting games with better graphics, but his parents didn't see a problem because all teen boys seemed to play video games. And their son also played guitar in a band, so video games weren't the only thing in his life.

13   Same with college. "Gaming 15–20 hours a week in college is no big deal," said Van Cleave, who graduated from Northern Illinois University with a degree in English. "The problem occurred after that, when I got into the real world."

14   He earned a master's degree and a PhD in creative writing at Florida State, was named a poetry fellow at the University of Wisconsin-Madison, and found a teaching job at the University of Wisconsin-Green Bay. Then in the fall of 2003, he was offered a tenure-track position at Clemson University in South Carolina—his dream job.

15   His wife, Victoria, became pregnant for the first time; the baby was unplanned and Van Cleave admitted being shocked at the idea of becoming a father. He and his wife were late for her first ultrasound because Van Cleave was playing Madden Football, a sports game.

16   It was around this time that World of Warcraft entered his life.

17   Van Cleave ended up playing one entire weekend, stealing away to the computer while his family was sleeping or while his parents, who were visiting, played with his baby daughter.

18   Victoria used one word to describe her feelings: "disgusted."

19   She felt abandoned. "I couldn't believe that someone could choose a virtual family over a real one."

20   One reason Van Cleave was so captivated: It offered different perspectives. Previously, most games Van Cleave played were seen from a bird's eye view, looking down at the action. In WoW, a player can zoom, pan and look at a scene exactly how a human does in real life.

21   Three years into his job at Clemson, Van Cleave's life began to fall apart. His four dogs died, one after another from various causes. His wife was pregnant again. Then Van Cleave began to get the impression that other faculty disliked him and wanted him gone. But he didn't try to repair the rifts, instead channeling his anxieties into WoW, a virtual world he could control.

22   "All that tethered me to anything meaningful during this time was WoW, which I clung to for dear life," he wrote.

23   For millions who play, the lure of games like WoW is hard to resist.

24   Players create an "avatar," or online character, who operates within a startlingly detailed storyline and graphics. Playing makes the gamer feel like the star of a really awesome sci-fi movie.

25   While in-game, characters form "guilds," or teams, and go on "quests" to find items, conquer lands or achieve new levels. They occasionally fight with other players or guilds, slay zombies, clash with evil elves or kill monsters. Players talk to each other in the game via headsets and often form intense friendships.

26   "People play those games often in a desire to meet their social needs," said Hilarie Cash, a Washington state therapist who runs a six-bed inpatient program for Internet and video game addicts. "There's a sense of friendship and self-esteem you develop with your teammates, you can compete and be cooperative. It really feels as though it meets your social needs."

27   Unlike other games, WoW didn't end. It went on and on, with characters roaming through different realms and meeting new people along the way. When Van Cleave had reached the apex of one world and hit the maximum points a character could possess, there were always other characters to create and more loot to amass. Meanwhile, the game makers offered expansions every year, which meant new worlds to explore, new levels to achieve.

28   "There was always something better and cooler," he said. "You can never have enough in-game money, enough armor, enough support. You've got to keep up with the virtual Joneses."

29   The maker of World of Warcraft, Blizzard Entertainment, declined to comment when contacted by The Associated Press.

30   In the past five years, news stories have described people suffering exhaustion after playing a game for 50 hours straight, of teens killing their parents after having games taken away, and of parents neglecting infants while mesmerized by the online world.

31   Yet not all authorities believe the games are addictive.

32   "I do not believe that the concept of 'addiction' is useful; it only describes strong temptations; it does not explain strong temptations. What makes the temptation so strong? The memory of past pleasant experiences with the behavior that we are talking about—in this case videogames," wrote Jackson Toby, a professor emeritus of sociology at Rutgers University, in an email to The Associated Press. "I don't believe that someone can be addicted to videogames."

33   The American Psychiatric Association will not list video game addiction as a mental disorder in the 2012 edition of the Diagnostic and Statistical Manual of Mental Disorders. However, the APA said there is a possibility that a group of reward-seeking behavioral disorders—including video game addiction and Internet addiction—will be included in an appendix of DSM-5 to "encourage further study."

34   Van Cleave and others insist video game addiction is similar to gambling addiction.

35   By the time his second baby was born in 2007, Van Cleave was playing some 60 hours a week.

36   A few months later, Clemson didn't renew his contract and said he would not achieve tenure. He was hired for a one-year fellowship at George Washington University, teaching one class, but that meant he had more time for gaming while the stress of finding a long-term, full-time job ratcheted up.

37   He spent money on gaming and bought two new computers so he could see better game graphics.

38   In 2007, Van Cleave had three different World of Warcraft accounts (each at a cost of $14.95 a month). A secret Paypal account paid for two of the accounts so his wife wouldn't hound him about the cost.

39   He spent $224 in real money to buy fake gold, so he could get an in-game "epic-level sword" and some "top-tier armor" for his avatar.

40   Changes in Van Cleave's personality began to appear. Among those who noticed was his best friend from high school, Rob Opitz, who lived in another state but played "World of Warcraft" with him for years.

41   "When things in IRL—in real life—would interrupt what was going on in the game, he would get very loud very quickly about those things," Opitz recalled. "During that time, it's kind of like everything was completely over the top. It wasn't that he was a little mad, he was in a full-blown rage."

42   Van Cleave was about to hit bottom.

—

43   It was Dec. 31, 2007. Van Cleave was halfway through his yearlong fellowship at George Washington University. Yet there he was, standing on the Arlington Memorial Bridge. He was thinking about jumping into the icy water.

44   He had been gaming for 18 hours straight and wasn't feeling well. He had told his wife that he was going to buy cough drops for his sore throat. But his misery was not just physical.

45   "My kids hate me. My wife is threatening (again) to leave me," Van Cleave would write in his book. "I haven't written anything in countless months. I have no prospects for the next academic year. And I am perpetually exhausted from skipping sleep so I can play more Warcraft."

46   That night marked the first time Van Cleave realized he had a problem.

47   The self-examination pulled him back from the bridge railing. He went home and deleted the game from his computer.

48   For the next week, his stomach and head hurt and he was drenched in sweat—like an addict withdrawing from drugs.

49   Staying away from WoW was difficult, but he didn't re-install the game.

50   And he started rebuilding—In Real Life.

51   Said his wife: "I didn't believe him. I had heard it all before and had no confidence that he would stop."

52   Van Cleave worked on his professional life. He freelanced, wrote poems and young adult books. He wrote the tell-all about his addiction, titled "Unplugged" and published last year.

53   He set his sights on a job, sending out 182 resumes.

54   In 2010, he was hired as an English professor at the Ringling School of Art and Design in Sarasota. Van Cleave and his family bought a beige stucco home in a quiet subdivision.

55   It's an irony in Van Cleave's new, game-free life that Ringling is one of the nation's top schools for video game designers.

56   He knows his students spend much of their lives online, and he worries about them. "I don't think video games are evil," said Van Cleave. "That's not what I'm saying at all. I think games are fine if they are part of a balanced life."

57   Last semester, he had two students in class who talked about WoW non-stop. It made Van Cleave anxious.

58   Over the past year, he has talked about out-of-control gaming to various mental health groups.

59   But even now, four years after he stopped gaming, Van Cleave thinks about World of Warcraft.

60   Then there are his dreams.

61   In them, he is playing one of his former characters, running through the virtual world. When he wakes, sweating and out of breath, he always has the same impulse: to rush to the computer and log into the game.

Tamara Lush, "Living Inside a Virtual World," *San Jose Mercury News,* August 28, 2011. Used with permission of The Associated Press. Copyright © 2011. All rights reserved.

Exercises

You may refer to the selection while you complete these exercises except for Exercise B.

A. COMPREHENDING MAIN IDEAS

Write the answers for these questions in the space provided using your own words.

1. Identify two psychological effects that Ryan Van Cleave experienced from long hours of playing World of Warcraft.

_____

_____

2. Van Cleave is quoted as saying that playing World of Warcraft made him feel "godlike" and that the real world made him feel "impotent." What does he mean?

_____

_____

3. The initials "IRL" stand for "In Real Life." What IRL problems did Van Cleave have?

_____

_____

4. How did Van Cleave's wife, Victoria, respond to her husband's marathon playing sessions?

_____

5. The writer says that games that use avatars, like World of Warcraft, serve a particular psychological function for players. What is it?

_____

6. What is it about World of Warcraft and the way it works that made it so addictive for Van Cleave? Why couldn't he stop playing?

_____

7. How did World of Warcraft affect Van Cleave's academic career?

_____

8. What finally brought Van Cleave to the edge, to the realization that he had hit bottom? How did he stop playing?

_____

_____

B. SEQUENCING

These sentences from one paragraph in the selection may have been scrambled. Read the sentences and choose the sequence that puts them back into logical order. Do not refer to the original selection.

1 Unlike other games, WoW didn't end. **2** Meanwhile, the game makers offered expansions every year, which meant new worlds to explore, new levels to achieve. **3** When Van Cleave had reached the apex of one world and hit the maximum points a character could possess, there were always other characters to create and more loot to amass. **4** It went on and on, with characters roaming through different realms and meeting new people along the way.

_____ Which of the following represents the correct sequence for these sentences?
a. 1, 3, 2, 4
b. 1, 4, 3, 2
c. 3, 1, 2, 4
d. 2, 4, 1, 3
e. Correct as written.

C. DISTINGUISHING BETWEEN FACT AND OPINION

For each of the following statements from the selection, write F if the statement represents a factual statement that can be verified or O if the statement represents the writer's or someone else's subjective interpretation.

_____1. "Playing World of Warcraft makes me feel godlike," Van Cleave wrote.

_____2. "Gaming 15–20 hours a week in college is no big deal," said Van Cleave.

_____3.   Previously, most games Van Cleave played were seen from a bird's eye view, looking down at the action. In WoW, a player can zoom, pan, and look at a scene exactly how a human does in real life.

_____4.   For millions who play, the lure is hard to resist.

_____5.   "I do not believe that the concept of 'addiction' is useful; it only describes strong temptations. What makes the temptation so strong? The memory of past pleasant experiences with the behavior that we are talking about—in this case videogames," wrote Jackson Toby, a professor emeritus of sociology at Rutgers University, in an email to The Associated Press. "I don't believe that someone can be addicted to videogames."

_____6.   Van Cleave and others insist video game addiction is similar to gambling addiction.

_____7.   "I don't think video games are evil," said Van Cleave. "That's not what I'm saying at all. I think games are fine if they are part of a balanced life."

_____8.   But even now, four years after he stopped gaming, Van Cleave thinks about World of Warcraft.

D. UNDERSTANDING VOCABULARY IN CONTEXT

Here are a few vocabulary words from the selection along with their definitions. Study these definitions carefully. Then write the appropriate word in each space provided according to the context, the way it is used. Note: You will use only four of the five words in each set.

disempowering	depriving of power or influence
drudgery	tedious or unpleasant work
virtual	simulated, carried on by means of a computer
trigger	set off, initiate, cause to occur
impotent	lacking power or energy, helpless

1. The smallest action in the real world could _____ a psychological response in Van Cleave. Playing for 50 or 60 hours at a time left him feeling _____ and unable to cope with reality. Living inside a _____ world was preferable to the _____ of everyday life.

malfunction	faulty or improper functioning
repercussions	indirect effects or results, stemming from an action
reckoning	a settlement of accounts, a final time of judgment
rifts	breaks in otherwise friendly relationships
tethered	tied, attached, secured

2. Before Van Cleave finally admitted that he had a serious problem on his day of _____, the _____ of his addiction were overwhelming, both in terms of his career and his family. He could not repair the _____ between himself and his colleagues at

Clemson University. He couldn't deal with little problems like a computer _____ or a crying child.

apex	the highest point
perpetually	lasting for a long time
hitch	a small problem or difficulty
mesmerized	in a hypnotic state, enthralled, spellbound
captivated	attracted, fascinated

3.   _____ exhausted from not sleeping and eating only junk food, Van Cleave was transported to another state. His experience playing World of Warcraft went way beyond being merely _____ by the game; he was operating in a near-_____ state. His only goal was to reach the _____ of one world and then move on to the next level.

E. ANNOTATING EXERCISE

For this exercise, go through the selection and locate any piece of information that refers to the psychological effects of excessive video-game playing. Annotate by writing the main points in your own words in the left margin.

F. TOPICS FOR DISCUSSION

1.   What is it about games like World of Warcraft that makes them so absorbing, if not addictive?
2.   Lush mentions "dissociative episodes" in paragraph 10. What does she mean by this term?
3.   There apparently is some disagreement about whether or not video game addiction really exists. Comment on the quality of evidence that Lush presents on this matter, in particular the evidence in paragraphs 32 and 33, in particular Jackson Toby's comment about "strong temptations." Do you find this explanation convincing or not? What information in the article contradicts the expert testimony cited?
4.   What is ironic about the fact that a man like Ryan Van Cleave became so lost in World of Warcraft? Why does he make an unlikely subject for this topic?
5.   In the concluding paragraphs, Van Cleave reveals that he feels "anxious" when two of his students at the Ringling School of Art and Design "talk about WoW nonstop." Should he intervene and tell them about his experience, or not? Explain your thinking.

G. TOPICS FOR WRITING

1.   Write a short essay in which you discuss the concept of video game addiction in comparison with addiction to a substance like cigarettes, alcohol, or a drug like cocaine. What do the two types of addiction have in common? How are they different?
2.   Should video games carry a warning that excessive playing can lead to antisocial behavior or to addiction? Write a short essay addressing the pros and cons of this proposal.

3. If you are familiar with a person who spends far too much time playing video games or even just being online, write a profile of the person. How has the time spent at the computer affected his or her social life, academic life, career, or relationships with family members?

EXPLORE THE WEB

- If you are interested in the topic, find more information about video game addiction online. In the search box of your favorite search engine, type in "video game addiction" + "information."

- How was Ryan Van Cleave's 2010 book received? Locate reviews of his memoir by typing in the search box the writer's name + the title (*Unplugged: My Journey into the Dark World of Video Game Addiction*) + reviews.

DAN ARIELY

The Problem of Procrastination and Self-Control

This selection comes from Dan Ariely's 2008 book, Predictably Irrational, *in which he addresses the issue of consumer behavior and our growing consumerism. Ariely is the Alfred P. Sloan Professor of Behavioral Economics at MIT and a visiting professor at Duke University. He also writes for the popular media, including* The New York Times, *the* Washington Post, Scientific American, *and* The Wall Street Journal. *Ariely's most recent book is* The Honest Truth about Dishonesty *(2012). This selection is subtitled, "Why We Can't Make Ourselves Do What We Want to Do."*

Vocabulary Analysis

WORD PARTS

The root *dict-* Ariely explains a research study he conducted with his MIT students to test their self-control and adherence to deadlines for submitting three papers during the semester. For the third group of students, he imposed a *dictatorial treatment* (see paragraph 20), meaning that he *dictated* three absolute deadlines for submission. To *dictate* means "to impose a command on another person" and *dictatorial* means "commanding" or "authoritarian." Both words stem from the Latin verb *dicere* ("to tell"), and it is the basis of a large number of words in English, among them to *predict* (to tell beforehand), *diction* (choice of words in speaking or writing), *contradict* (to speak against), *benediction* (good saying, a blessing), and *verdict* (what a jury or judge says about the disposition of a court case).

DAN ARIELY

The Problem of Procrastination and Self-Control

1   Onto the American scene, populated by big homes, big cars, and big-screen plasma televisions, comes another big phenomenon: the biggest decline in the personal savings rate since the Great Depression.

2   Go back 25 years, and double-digit savings rates were the norm. As recently as 1994 the savings rate was nearly five percent. But by 2006 the savings rate had fallen below zero—to negative one percent. Americans were not only not saving; they were spending more than they earned. Europeans do a lot better—they save an average of 20 percent. Japan's rate is 25 percent. China's is 50 percent. So what's up with America?

3   I suppose one answer is that Americans have succumbed to rampant consumerism. Go back to a home built before we had to have everything, for instance, and check out the size of the closets. Our house in Cambridge, Massachusetts, for example, was built in 1890. It has no closets whatsoever. Houses in the 1940s had closets barely big enough to stand in. The closet of the 1970s was a bit larger, perhaps deep enough for a fondue pot, a box of eight-track tapes, and a few disco dresses. But the closet of today is a different breed. "Walk-in closet" means that you can literally walk in for quite a distance. And no matter how deep these closets are, Americans have found ways to fill them right up to the closet door.

4   Another answer—the other half of the problem—is the recent explosion in consumer credit. The average American family now has six credit cards (in 2005 alone, Americans received 6 billion direct-mail solicitations for credit cards). Frighteningly, the average family debt on these cards is about $9,000; and seven in 10 households borrow on credit cards to cover such basic living expenses as food, utilities, and clothing.

5   So wouldn't it just be wiser if Americans learned to save, as in the old days, and as the rest of the world does, by diverting some cash to the cookie jar, and delaying some purchases until we can really afford them? Why can't we save part of our paychecks, as we know we should? Why can't we resist those new purchases? Why can't we exert some good old-fashioned self-control?

6   The road to hell, they say, is paved with good intentions. And most of us know what that's all about. We promise to save for retirement, but we spend the money on a vacation. We vow to diet, but we surrender to the allure of the dessert cart. We promise to have our cholesterol checked regularly, and then we cancel our appointment.

7   How much do we lose when our fleeting impulses deflect us from our long-term goals? How much is our health affected by those missed appointments and our lack of exercise? How much is our wealth reduced when we forget our vow to save more and consume less? Why do we lose the fight against procrastination so frequently?

8   IN CHAPTER 5 we discussed how emotions grab hold of us and make us view the world from a different perspective. Procrastination (from the Latin *pro,* meaning *for;* and *cras,* meaning *tomorrow*) is rooted in the same kind of problem. When we promise to save our money, we are in a cool state. When we promise to exercise and watch our diet, again we're cool. But then the lava flow of hot emotion comes rushing in: just when we promise to save, we see a new car, a mountain bike, or a pair of shoes that we must have. Just when we plan to exercise regularly, we find a reason to sit all day in front of the television. And as for the diet? I'll take that slice of chocolate cake and begin the diet in earnest tomorrow. Giving up on our long-term goals for immediate gratification, my friends, is procrastination.

9   As a university professor, I'm all too familiar with procrastination. At the beginning of every semester my students make heroic promises to themselves—vowing to read their assignments on time, submit their papers on time, and in general, stay on top of things. And every semester I've watched as temptation takes them out on a date, over to the student union for a meeting, and off on a ski trip in the mountains—while their workload falls farther and farther behind. In the end, they wind up impressing me, not with their punctuality, but with their creativity—inventing stories, excuses, and family tragedies to explain their tardiness. (Why do family tragedies generally occur during the last two weeks of the semester?)

10   After I'd been teaching at MIT for a few years, my colleague Klaus Werten-broch (a professor at INSEAD, a business school with campuses in France and Singapore) and I decided to work up a few studies that might get to the root of the problem, and just maybe offer a fix for this common human weakness. Our guinea pigs this time would be the delightful students in my class on consumer behavior.

11   As they settled into their chairs that first morning, full of anticipation (and, no doubt, with resolutions to stay on top of their class assignments), the students listened to me review the syllabus for the course. There would be three main papers over the 12-week semester, I explained. Together, these papers would constitute much of their final grade.

12   "And what are the deadlines?" asked one of them, waving his hand from the back. I smiled. "You can hand in the papers at any time before the end of the semester," I replied. "It's entirely up to you." The students looked back blankly.

13   "Here's the deal," I explained. "By the end of the week, you must commit to a deadline date for each paper. Once you set your deadlines, they can't be changed." Late papers, I added, would be penalized at the rate of one percent off the grade for each day late. The students could always turn in their papers before their deadlines without penalty, of course, but since I wouldn't be reading any of them until the end of the semester, there would be no particular advantage in terms of grades for doing so.

14   In other words, the ball was in their court. Would they have the self-control to play the game?

15   "But Professor Ariely," asked Gaurav, a clever master's student with a charming Indian accent, "given these instructions and incentives, wouldn't it make sense for us to select the last date possible?"

16   "You can do that," I replied. "If you find that it makes sense, by all means do it."

17   Under these conditions, what would you have done?

I promise to submit paper 1 on week _____

I promise to submit paper 2 on week _____

I promise to submit paper 3 on week _____

18   What deadlines did the students pick for themselves? A perfectly rational student would follow Gaurav's advice and set all the deadlines for the last day of class—after all, it was always possible to submit papers earlier without a penalty, so why take a chance and select an earlier deadline than needed? Delaying the deadlines to the end was clearly the best decision if students were perfectly

rational. But what if the students are not rational? What if they succumb to temptation and are prone to procrastination? What if they realize their weakness? If the students are not rational, and they know it, they could use the deadlines to force themselves to behave better. They could set early deadlines and by doing so force themselves to start working on the projects earlier in the semester.

19   What did my students do? They used the scheduling tool I provided them with and spaced the timing of their papers across the whole semester. This is fine and good, as it suggests that the students realize their problems with procrastination and that if given the right opportunities they try to control themselves—but the main question is whether the tool was indeed helpful in improving their grades. To find out about this, we had to conduct other variations of the same experiments in other classes and compare the quality of papers across the different conditions (classes).

20   Now that I had Gaurav and his classmates choosing their individual deadlines, I went to my other two classes—with markedly different deals. In the second class, I told the students that they would have no deadlines at all during the semester. They merely needed to submit their papers by the end of the last class. They could turn the papers in early, of course, but there was no grade benefit to doing so. I suppose they should have been happy: I had given them complete flexibility and freedom of choice. Not only that, but they also had the lowest risk of being penalized for missing an intermediate deadline.

21   The third class received what might be called a dictatorial treatment: I dictated three deadlines for the three papers, set at the fourth, eighth, and twelfth weeks. These were my marching orders, and they left no room for choice or flexibility.

22   Of these three classes, which do you think achieved the best final grades? Was it Gaurav and his classmates, who had some flexibility? Or the second class, which had a single deadline at the end, and thus complete flexibility? Or the third class, which had its deadlines dictated from above, and therefore had no flexibility? Which class do you predict did worst?

23   When the semester was over, Jose Silva, the teaching assistant for the classes (himself an expert on procrastination and currently a professor at the University of California at Berkeley), returned the papers to the students. We could at last compare the grades across the three different deadline conditions. We found that the students in the class with the three firm deadlines got the best grades; the class in which I set no deadlines at all (except for the final deadline) had the worst grades; and the class in which Gaurav and his classmates were allowed to choose their own three deadlines (but with penalties for failing to meet them) finished in the middle, in terms of their grades for the three papers and their final grade.

24   What do these results suggest? First, that students do procrastinate (big news); and second, that tightly restricting their freedom (equally spaced deadlines, imposed from above) is the best cure for procrastination. But the biggest revelation is that simply offering the students a tool by which they could precommit to deadlines helped them achieve better grades.

25   What this finding implies is that the students generally understood their problem with procrastination and took action to fight it when they were given

the opportunity to do so, achieving relative success in improving their grades. But why were the grades in the self-imposed deadlines condition not as good as the grades in the dictatorial (externally imposed) deadlines condition? My feeling is this: not everyone understands their tendency to procrastinate, and even those who do recognize their tendency to procrastinate may not understand their problem completely. Yes, people may set deadlines for themselves, but not necessarily the deadlines that are best for getting the best performance.

26   When I looked at the deadlines set by the students in Gaurav's class, this was indeed the case. Although the vast majority of the students in this class spaced their deadlines substantially (and got grades that were as good as those earned by students in the dictatorial condition), some did not space their deadlines much, and a few did not space their deadlines at all. These students who did not space their deadlines sufficiently pulled the average grades of this class down. Without properly spaced deadlines—deadlines that would have forced the students to start working on their papers earlier in the semester—the final work was generally rushed and poorly written (even without the extra penalty of one percent off the grade for each day of delay).

27   Interestingly, these results suggest that although almost everyone has problems with procrastination, those who recognize and admit their weakness are in a better position to utilize available tools for precommitment and by doing so, help themselves overcome it.

Exercises

You may refer to the selection while you complete these exercises except for Exercise B.

A. COMPREHENDING MAIN IDEAS

Write the answers for these questions in the space provided using your own words.

1. Ariely cites the size of closets in American homes as an example of "rampant consumerism." Compared to houses built a century ago, how have our closets changed?

_____

2. According to Ariely, why don't we save money for retirement, start that diet we've been meaning to start, or begin an exercise program we've been meaning to begin? Why do we "lose the fight against procrastination"?

_____

3. The word *procrastination* comes from two Latin word parts, *pro-* and *cras-*. What do these two word parts mean?

_____

4. As a university professor, Ariely has observed student behavior for many years. What behavior in his students does he describe, from the beginning of the semester to the end?

   _____

5. Ariely and his colleague, Klaus Wertenbroch, designed a research study using students in Ariely's consumer behavior course. The second group had no particular deadlines for the three required papers and only had to turn them in by the end of the last class. The third group received the "dictatorial treatment," meaning that they had three fixed deadlines during the term for submitting papers. What were the submission requirements for the first group of students?

   _____

6. Of the three groups of students, which group received the best grades on their papers?

   _____

7. What does Ariely conclude from this study? Which is the best cure for students' habitual procrastination?

   _____

8. What was the most noticeable problem with the group of students who were allowed to choose their own deadlines? What mistake did they make, and what was the result?

   _____

   _____

B. SEQUENCING

These sentences from one paragraph in the selection may have been scrambled. Read the sentences and choose the sequence that puts them back into logical order. Do not refer to the original selection.

   1 To find out about this, we had to conduct other variations of the same experiment in other classes and compare the quality of papers across the different conditions (classes). **2** What did my students do? **3** This is fine and good, as it suggests that students realize their problems with procrastination and that if given the right opportunities they try to control themselves—but the main question is whether the tool was indeed helpful in improving their grades. **4** They used the scheduling tool I provided them with and spaced the timing of their papers across the whole semester.

   _____ Which of the following represents the correct sequence for these
            sentences?
            a. 1, 2, 4, 3
            b. 2, 4, 3, 1
            c. 2, 4, 1, 3
            d. 4, 3, 1, 2
            e. Correct as written.

C. UNDERSTANDING STRUCTURE AND MEANING

Answer the following questions by writing your answer in the space provided.

1. Read paragraph 2 again. What is the pattern of development used?

    _____

2. What two patterns of development are used in paragraph 3?

    _____

3. Explain the meaning of the first sentence of paragraph 6: "The road to hell is paved with good intentions."

    _____

4. Read paragraph 8 again. What, according to Ariely, is the chief obstacle to our good intentions not to procrastinate?

    _____

5. What pattern of development is most evident in paragraph 9?

    _____

6. Read paragraph 18 again. What was the rational behavior that the students in the first group exhibited?

    _____

7. Look again at the beginning of paragraph 24. Ariely writes: "What do these results suggest? First, that students do procrastinate (big news). . . ." How would you describe the tone reflected in the parenthetical remark "big news"?

    _____

8. Again, in paragraph 24 Ariely refers to offering students a "tool" that would help them? What tool is he referring to?

    _____

D. USING VOCABULARY IN CONTEXT

From the following list of vocabulary words, choose a word that fits in each blank according to both the grammatical structure of the sentence and the context. Use each word in the list only once. Do not change the form of the word. (Note that there are more words than sentences.)

precommit	gratification	succumb	rational
revelation	dictated	flexibility	utilize
phenomenon	exert	penalized	rampant

Ariely believes that one reason Americans procrastinate is our _____ consumerism and desire for immediate _____. We easily

_____ to temptation and act against a more _____ approach to acquiring things. Further, the study that Ariely and his colleague conducted produced a _____. When Ariely _____ the exact dates for submitting papers spread throughout the semester, allowing for no _____, the results were improved grades. He concluded that students are aware that they procrastinate; therefore, giving them an opportunity to _____ to reasonable deadlines properly spaced throughout the term would help them overcome the temptation.

E. SUMMARIZING EXERCISE

Summarize the research study that Ariely conducted with his MIT students described in paragraphs 11–27. Try to write no more than 250–300 words.

F. TOPICS FOR DISCUSSION

1. Is procrastination a problem in your everyday life (diet, exercise, saving money) or in your academic life? If so, have you established any coping measures, and if so, what are they?
2. How much credibility is there in Ariely's premise—that rampant consumerism and the desire for immediate gratification are responsible not only for our inability to save and our tendency to run up our credit cards bills, but also deflect us from our long-term goals and may even affect our health?
3. What is the connection between consumerism—buying things on credit that we can't readily afford—and procrastination?
4. Comment on the study that Ariely conducted. Do you agree with his assessments and conclusions? Can you think of a variable that might have been included in the study? Why did Ariely say that he wouldn't be reading any of the students' papers until the end of the term? How might that have influenced the outcome of the study?
5. Ariely concludes that, at least based on this study, the group with the three fixed deadlines performed the best. Why do you suppose this result occurred? Do you see any contradiction in the results of the study—improved grades for those with the "dictatorial" schedule—and his remarks in paragraph 9?

F. TOPICS FOR WRITING

1. Based on Ariely's selection and on your own observation and experience, what is the best system that college instructors should follow for submitting papers throughout the term? What works best for you? Choose the method and write a short essay defending it, using your own experience if appropriate.
2. Ariely uses the example of consumer debt and the size of American closets as evidence of our rampant consumerism. What are some other examples? Write an essay in which you address the idea of consumerism, using your own examples as evidence. Include a discussion of whether or not consumerism is as damaging as Ariely suggests.

EXPLORE THE WEB

- Help is out there online! The first link below, from the Writing Center of the University of North Carolina at Chapel Hill, gives sound advice on overcoming the tendency to put things off.

  writingcenter.unc.edu/resources/handouts-demos/. . ./procrastination

- Next is a funny video clip from YouTube, "Procrastination Help with Ellen DeGeneres." She doesn't offer any advice, but she does make enormous fun of her own procrastinating tendencies. Go to www.youtube.com and type in the title cited.

24 CARLIN FLORA
Hello, My Name Is Unique

Formerly a senior editor and writer for Psychology Today, *where this article was first published, Carlin Florin has degrees from the University of Michigan and the Columbia University Graduate School of Journalism. Her current project is writing a book on how friends influence our lives. Does one's name alter one's self-perception? This is the question Flora raises in this article. Parents are increasingly giving their children distinctive names based on the assumption that such names can influence a child's destiny. The original article included a sidebar with dozens of names in alphabetical order from the Class of 2022 (that is, children born in 2004). Among them are Atom, Chianti, Desperate, Gator, Jaguar, Maverick, Poppy, Reality, Skyy, Sy'rai, Tookie, Unique, and Xerox, to cite just a few.*

Vocabulary Analysis

WORD FAMILIES

The Greek prefix *homo-* The adjective *homogeneous* is formed from the Greek prefix *homo-* ("same") and *genos* ("kind"). The adjective thus describes people who are alike in their characteristics, whether by virtue of their age, interests, gender, political preferences, or some other characteristic. Other words beginning with this prefix are *homonym,* words that have the same sound but different meanings (like *cash* and *cache,* or *sew, sow,* and *so)* and *homosexuality,* a sexual preference for a person of the same sex. But be careful not to confuse the Greek prefix with the Latin one, which, unfortunately, may be spelled the same. In Latin *homo* means "man," as in *homicide* or *homo sapiens.*

In your dictionary, look up the word *homophonic.* What does it mean? What are the word parts? Does the prefix *homo-* come from Latin or Greek?

homophonic _____

idiosyncratic [paragraph 3] The adjective *idiosyncratic* and the noun *idiosyncrasy* also derive from Greek word parts, and though there are only a few words in English beginning with *idio-,* they form an interesting group. The prefix *idio-* means "own" or "private." An *idiosyncrasy* is a characteristic that is peculiar to a particular person or group. For example, Pierre, the husband of my friend Therese, will not allow onions in their house. The eighteenth-century German writer Friedrich Schiller kept a bag of rotting green apples in his desk drawer because he thought that the smell inspired him to write. These are idiosyncrasies. Three other words in this family are these:

idiom	an expression peculiar to a particular language
idiot	a foolish or stupid person, now offensive, from Greek *idiotes* ("a private person")
idiopathic	describing a disease with no particular cause, in other words, a disease peculiar to a particular individual

CARLIN FLORA

Hello, My Name Is Unique

1   Proper names are poetry in the raw, said the bard W. H. Auden. "Like all poetry, they are untranslatable." Mapping your name onto yourself is a tricky procedure indeed. We exist wholly independently of our names, yet they alone represent us on our birth certificates and gravestones.

2   Would a Rose by any other name be just as sweet-tempered? Does Orion feel cosmically special? Psychologists, parents and the world's Oceans, Zanes and Timothys are divided on the extent to which first names actually matter.

YOU NAMED HIM WHAT?

3   Today's parents seem to believe they can alter their child's destiny by picking the perfect—preferably idiosyncratic—name. (Destiny, incidentally, was the ninth most popular name for girls in New York City last year.) The current crop of preschoolers includes a few Uniques, with uncommonly named playmates like Kyston, Payton and Sawyer. From Dakota to Heaven, Integrity to Serenity, more babies are being named after places and states of mind. Names with alternative spellings are on the upswing, like Jaxon, Kassidy, Mikayla, Jazmine and Nevaeh (Heaven spelled backward), as are mix-and-match names such as Ashlynn and Rylan.

4   "For the first time in history, the top 50 names account for less than 50 percent of boys born each year, and for less than 40 percent of girls," says Cleveland Kent Evans, professor of psychology at Bellevue University in Nebraska and author of *Unusual & Most Popular Baby Names*. Evans believes that our homogeneous strip-mall culture fosters the desire to nominally distinguish our children. He cites a boom in unique names dating to the late 1980s but says the taste for obscure monikers developed in the 1960s, when parents felt less obligated to keep certain names in the family.

5   "It's really hard to name a kid," says Jill Bass, 35, who is expecting her second child. "It reflects what kind of person you are." She and her husband, Carl Vogel, 37, are struggling to find a name that is unique but not too trendy. "We don't want to go the Jake, Zak and Tyler route," says Bass. "It will sound like one of those year-2000 names. We don't want to sound as though we were trying so hard."

6   Distinguishing a child in just the right way is the first task parents feel charged with. Accordingly, parents-to-be increasingly track the popularity of names on the Social Security Administration's Web site and canvass the cottage industry of baby-name books. About 50 such books were published between 1990 and 1996. Since 1997, more than 100 new books have been published.

7   New parents rattle off diminutives and acronyms as if reciting scales. "I wanted a truly awesome, convertible name that could collapse into a normal name. Something like Charles Henry Underhill Grisham Sernovitz, because CHUGS would be a great college nickname," says Andy Sernovitz, 33, whose son Charles Darwin Grisham Sernovitz was born last November. Darwin was a nod to mom Julie Grisham's science-writing vocation.

8   Today, children are christened in honor of sports teams, political parties, vacation spots and food cravings. Adam Orr, a die-hard Cubs fan, wanted to name his first child Clark Addison or Addison Clark, the names of the streets that form the intersection at Chicago's Wrigley Field. Alas, he and his wife, Annisa, are expecting a daughter this spring. Records of kids named Espn tell of parents with a more general love of sports. Christie Brinkley reportedly named her youngest child Sailor as a tribute to a favorite pastime. Jamie Oliver, the British culinary star, christened his child Poppy Honey, not nearly so unfortunate a name as that of a poor soul dubbed Gouda.

9   Increasingly, children are also named for prized possessions. In 2000, birth certificates revealed that there were 298 Armanis, 269 Chanels, 49 Canons, 6 Timberlands, 5 Jaguars and 353 girls named Lexus in the U.S. The trend is not surprising: In an era in which children are viewed as accessories, such names telegraph our desire for creative, social or material success. It would be ironic if young Jaguar or Lexus grew up to drive a Honda Accord.

10   While a name may be a palimpsest for parental aspirations (hence the concerns of savvy parents that they not appear to be striving too hard), a name also reflects high hopes for the child himself. Choosing an uncommon name is perceived as an opportunity to give your child a leg up in life, signaling to the world that he or she is different. In *Snobbery*, cultural critic Joseph Epstein argues that a child named Luc or Catesby seems poised for greater achievements than selling car insurance.

AM I REALLY A JORDAN?

11   The announcements are in the mail; a religious ceremony may seal the decision. The name is chosen, and it is a word that will become so familiar that the child's brain will pull it out of white noise. It is the first word she will learn to write. But what are the consequences of a particular name for self-image?

12   They're not earth-shattering, according to a study by psychologist Martin Ford, an assistant dean at George Mason University in Virginia. Ford found no correlation between the popularity or social desirability of a given name and academic or social achievement. "This doesn't mean that a name would never have any effect on a child's development," he explains. "But it does suggest that the probability of a positive effect is as large as that of a negative effect. It also suggests that a name is unlikely to be a significant factor in most children's development."

13   Children and teens either struggle to stand apart or try desperately to fit in. A singular name eases the former pursuit but thwarts the latter. If parents give a child an offbeat name, speculates Lewis Lipsitt, professor emeritus of psychology at Brown University, "they are probably outliers willing to buck convention, and that [parental trait] will have a greater effect on their child than does the name."

14   A name may occasionally trigger expectations that are difficult to meet because a child lacks the appropriate talent or temperament. "If your parents are great musicians, and they name you Yehudi, there could be a sense that you cannot live up to your name," Lipsitt says. Likewise, a naturally shy child may cringe when he is introduced as Attila.

15   No one can predict whether a name will be consistent with a child's or a teen's view of herself. The name could be ethnic, unique or white-bread, but if it doesn't reinforce her sense of self, she will probably be unhappy with it and may even feel alienated from parents or peers because of it. An Annika with iconoclastic taste will be happy with her name, but a Tallullah who longs for a seat at the cheerleaders' table may feel that her name is too weird.

16   A child's attitude toward his name is a gauge of self-esteem, says psychologist Ron Taffel, author of *Nurturing Good Children Now.* "If self-esteem is low, even a David or Jenny could hate their name—as a reflection of how they feel about themselves."

17   By the time most people reach adulthood, they have made peace with their name or changed it. And, as parents of Dax and Skyy will be gratified to learn, young adults today report that they feel buoyed by an unorthodox appellation.

18   "It's interesting knowing that very few people have your name," says Cabot Norton, 35. "It's a point of pride to say, 'I've never met another Cabot.'"

19   Says Maren Connary, 29, "I had a rebellious nature that I felt was justified by my name. If I'd been named Mary, I think I'd be more conformist."

20   "I hated my name when I was a kid," Wven (pronounced *you-vin*) Villegas, 29, says. "I stood out for all the wrong reasons. But I decided that if my name wasn't the same as everyone else's, then I wouldn't be the same, either. Now I love my name so much that I had it tattooed on my right arm."

21   Parents may be further empowered to christen their children idiosyncratically given that names aren't the rich source for taunts they once were. "Kids today are used to a variety of names, so it is almost too simple for them to make fun of each other for that," says Taffel. "Cruelty is more sophisticated now."

22   The experiences of children of mixed ethnic and racial backgrounds shed light on the power of names to determine identity. If such children are insecure or confused about their origins, the role of their name becomes more important. Donna Jackson Nakazawa, author of *Does Anybody Else Look Like Me?,* advises

parents of biracial or multi-ethnic children to choose a name that represents both branches of the family tree, or at least a nickname that does so. Nakazawa's nine-year-old son is Christian Jackson Nakazawa; his nickname is Chrischan, which means "dear beloved child" in Japanese.

23 Nakazawa cites the cautionary tale of a young woman who was adopted from China by a white American couple who gave her a Chinese-sounding name. As a teenager, the girl began researching her heritage and discovered her name was not, in fact, Chinese. She was devastated.

24 Cleveland Evans believes the personal story behind a name can serve as an anchor. In most cases, Evans says, people are only at a disadvantage if there is no story attached to their name. "It doesn't matter what the story is, as long as it is more complex than, 'We just liked the name.'" A name connected to previous generations can feel like your ancestors' arms wrapped warmly around you.

25 Not everyone agrees that the rationale behind a name is crucial. Misia Landau, a narratologist and science writer at Harvard Medical School, argues that the "story" of a name doesn't necessarily drive personal narratives, because of the myriad factors at play. "Providing a child with a name is incredibly variable." says Landau. "And I don't think people today say, 'Your namesake would never have acted that way.'"

BUT YOU DON'T LOOK LIKE A MARTHA!

26 There are names you probably don't think about at all—the equivalent of a black suit. And there are busy purple scarves of names, names that cannot be ignored, that must be reckoned with. "People are always going to ask me why I am named Cabot," Norton says. "And they are probably going to assume I am an East Coast WASP,[1] whereas I'm actually a North Florida atheist."

27 Names produce piquant impressions: Olaf sounds oafish to non-Scandinavians. Shirley is perky. A ballerina named Bertha doesn't sound as compelling as one named Anastasia. But are certain names better suited to some people than to others, and can a name change overhaul one's self-image?

28 Michael Mercer, an industrial psychologist and co-author of *Spontaneous Optimism,* recalls a former co-worker who had interpersonal and legal problems: "She changed her name to Honore, and it was her way of mutating from someone who goofed things up to someone who is honorable."

29 Norma Sofía Marsano, 28, had always been a Norma but decided to go by her middle name when she left Kentucky to attend college in Michigan. "I felt that Norma held me back. Sofía sounds fun and cute, whereas Norma sounds like an ugly-girl's name. I liked myself more when I started going by Sofía."

30 A name change may influence how we perceive ourselves and others because of racial, class or geographical stereotypes. Our "Anastasia" file may include adjectives like *attractive, graceful* and *vaguely Slavic*—descriptors that fit our conception of a ballerina but not a Bertha.

31 Author Bruce Lansky has capitalized on these implicit associations with *The Baby Name Survey Book: What People Think About Your Baby's Name.* Lansky

---

[1]An acronym for white Anglo-Saxon Protestant (Ed.)

compiled 100,000 impressions of 1,700 names, promising to help parents pick a name with positive connotations. Readers learn that Vanna is considered dumb, Jacqueline is elegant and Jacob, the number-one baby name for boys, is "a highly religious man who is old-fashioned and quiet."

32   Lansky's "namesakes" (Vanna White, Jackie O., Jacob in the Old Testament) are achingly transparent. And such associations hold only until we meet another Vanna, according to psychologist Kenneth Steele, who found that a name attached to a "real" person, or even a photograph, will transcend stereotypes. Steele exposed a group of subjects to a set of names previously judged to be socially desirable (Jon, Joshua, Gregory) or undesirable (Oswald, Myron, Reginald). A second group of subjects viewed these names accompanied by photographs. The addition of the photos erased the good or bad impression left by the name alone.

33   To what degree, then, does a name elicit racial or ethnic bias? Marianne Bertrand, a professor of economics at the University of Chicago, created resumes with names that are considered conspicuously white (such as Brendan) or black (such as Jamal) and found that regardless of credentials, resumes with white sounding names generated twice as many callbacks. But this doesn't mean that conspicuously "black" names, like Lashonda or Tremayne, are themselves liabilities: The employers in Bertrand's study might have discriminated against a black applicant regardless of his name. Roland Fryer, a professor of economics at Harvard University, found that a black Molly and a black Lakeisha with similar socioeconomic backgrounds fared equally well.

34   Whether people swoon over—or even disdain—our name is beyond our control. Ultimately, self-esteem and the esteem of the world dictate the degree to which we hold our name dear. Like our vocation or hometown, we tout our name as a distinguishing mark if it "fits." If it doesn't, we might say that, like an inaccurate horoscope, we don't believe in that stuff anyway. We'll change our name, disregard it or consider it just a synonym for *me*.

Exercises

Do not refer to the selection for Exercises A, B, and C unless your instructor directs you to do so.

A. DETERMINING THE MAIN IDEA AND PURPOSE

Choose the best answer.

_____   1.   The main idea of the selection is that
   a. many parents today believe that choosing an idiosyncratic or unusual name for their child can change his or her destiny.
   b. psychologists have determined that one's name influences a person's self-image and the kind of person he or she becomes.

     c. parents should be careful when naming their child, since weird names can follow a child for life and cause embarrassment and teasing from others.

     d. since the 1960s parents have sought to rebel against tradition by abandoning the long-time practice of conferring family names on their children.

_____ **2.** The writer's purpose is to

     a. list some unusual names and explain what they reveal about people.

     b. warn parents not to give their children unusual names that will haunt them for the rest of their lives.

     c. trace the history of naming practices in the United States.

     d. examine some theories about the effects of giving children unusual or idiosyncratic names.

B. COMPREHENDING MAIN IDEAS

Choose the correct answer.

_____ **1.** Flora mentions several categories of contemporary names and naming practices. Which of the following was not mentioned?

     a. Names for places and states of mind, like Dakota, Serenity, or Ocean.

     b. Reversing names traditionally associated with the opposite gender, for example, naming a girl Stephen or a boy Louise.

     c. Names with alternative spellings, like Jazmine, Kassidy, or Nevaeh (Heaven spelled backward).

     d. Names associated with sports teams or food, like Sailor, Poppy Honey, or Gouda.

     e. Names associated with prized possessions, like Jaguar, Timberland, or Armani.

_____ **2.** According to a theory espoused by psychology professor Cleveland Kent Evans, giving children unusual names may be the result of

     a. the need to outdo other parents by choosing ever more distinctive names.

     b. the acknowledgement that a name really does affect a child's destiny.

     c. a reaction against our homogeneous"strip-mall" culture.

     d. the lack of tradition in American culture.

3. When parents name a child Armani, Chanel, Lexus, or Canon, what does the writer say is their motivation? What do they regard their children as being?

_____

_____ **4.** Psychologist Martin Ford, who has studied the correlation between names and academic and social achievement, concluded that

     a. a name positively affects a child's self-esteem and achievement.

    b. more study is needed before a clear pattern of effects becomes evident.

    c. a name is unlikely to be a significant factor in a child's development.

    d. the current generation of children has been seriously damaged by having such singular names.

5. What advice does Donna Jackson Nakazawa, author of *Does Anybody Else Look Like Me?*, give to parents who are naming a child of mixed race or mixed ethnicity?

_____

_____ 6. Certain names may influence how we perceive ourselves and others because they reflect

    a. our unconscious feelings about real people who share those names.

    b. impressions created by the media.

    c. our unfulfilled desires and ambitions.

    d. racial, class, or geographical stereotypes.

COMPREHENSION SCORE

Score your answers for Exercises A and B as follows:

A. No. right _____ × 2 = _____

B. No. right _____ × 1 = _____

Total points from A and B _____ × 10 = _____ percent

C. SEQUENCING

These sentences from one paragraph in the selection may have been scrambled. Read the sentences and choose the sequence that puts them back into logical order. Do not refer to the original selection.

1 About 50 such books were published between 1990 and 1996. **2** Accordingly, parents-to-be increasingly track the popularity of names on the Social Security Administration's Web site and canvas the cottage industry of baby-name books. **3** Distinguishing a child in just the right way is the first task parents feel charged with. **4** Since 1997, more than 100 new books have been published.

_____ Which of the following represents the correct sequence for these sentences?

    a. 3, 2, 1, 4

    b. 1, 2, 4, 3

    c. 3, 1, 4, 2

    d. Correct as written.

You may refer to the selection as you work through the remaining exercises.

D. DISTINGUISHING BETWEEN MAIN IDEAS AND SUPPORTING DETAILS

Label the following sentences from two paragraphs in the selection as follows: MI if it represents a *main idea* and SD if it represents a *supporting detail*.

_____ 1.   Children and teens either struggle to stand apart or try desperately to fit in.

_____ 2.   A singular name eases the former pursuit but thwarts the latter.

_____ 3.   If parents give a child an offbeat name, speculates Lewis Lipsitt, professor emeritus of psychology at Brown University, "they are probably outliers willing to buck convention, and that [parental trait] will have a greater effect on their child than does the name."

_____ 4.   A name may occasionally trigger expectations that are difficult to meet because a child lacks the appropriate talent or temperament.

_____ 5.   "If your parents are great musicians, and they name you Yehudi, there could be a sense that you cannot live up to your name," Lipsitt says.

_____ 6.   Likewise, a naturally shy child may cringe when he is introduced as Attila.

E. IDENTIFYING PATTERNS OF DEVELOPMENT

Read again the paragraphs listed below. Then write the pattern of development each passage uses. Here are your answer choices:

list of facts or details
examples
cause and effect (reasons or results)
process
contrast

1. paragraph 3   _____

2. paragraph 4   _____

3. paragraph 14   _____

4. paragraph 15   _____

5. paragraph 27   _____

F. UNDERSTANDING VOCABULARY

Look through the paragraphs listed by number in brackets and find a word that matches each definition. Refer to a dictionary if necessary. An example has been done for you.

Ex. traditional word for a poet [paragraphs 1–2]   *bard*

1. slang word meaning personal names [3–4] _____

2. words made from the initial letters of a
   name [7–8] _____

3. short, often endearing forms of names [7–8] _____

4. given the name of, often facetiously [7–8] _____

5. well-informed, perceptive, shrewd [9–10] _____

6. describing a person who likes to overthrow
   established traditions [14–15] _____

7. breaking with convention or tradition [16–20] _____

8. innumerable, a large indefinite number [24–25] _____

9. describing a stupid, clumsy person [27–29] _____

10. call forth, draw out [32–33] _____

G. USING VOCABULARY IN CONTEXT

From the following list of vocabulary words, choose a word that fits in each blank according to both the grammatical structure of the sentence and the context. Use each word in the list only once. Do not change the form of the word. (Note that there are more words than blanks.)

cosmically	oafish	obscure	devastated
homogeneous	ironic	correlation	sophisticated
singular	crucial	taunts	stereotype

1. Flora writes that parents are choosing _____ names as a
   way of rebelling against what she calls our _____ strip-mall
   culture.

2. In the past children with unusual names might suffer _____
   from other children on the playground, but she says that today's children are
   cruel in more _____ ways.

3. Kent Evans, a professor of psychology, says that the urge to give children
   unusual or _____ names actually started in the 1960s when it
   became less _____ to give children traditional family names.

4. Although Olaf is a common Scandinavian name, to non-Scandinavians
   it sounds _____, nor does the name Bertha fit the
   _____ of a classical ballerina.

H. ANNOTATING EXERCISE

For this exercise, assume that you are preparing to write an essay on the question of whether one's name affects—whether positively or negatively—one's self-image or self-esteem. Go through the article and locate any piece of information that supports this idea. To identify it, put a star in the margin next to the sentence or bracket the words.

I. TOPICS FOR DISCUSSION

1. Why is it so hard for parents to name their children? What does the writer say about this problem? What are some other reasons that it exists?
2. In *Romeo and Juliet,* Shakespeare asked, "What's in a name? That which we call a rose by any other name would smell as sweet." The writer alludes to this quotation in paragraph 2. If the flower we know as a rose were called, say, a skunk cabbage flower, would it alter our perception of its essence? This is the central question Flora poses in her article: To what extent do our names affect our concept of ourselves and others' perception of us?
3. What are some truly awful names of people you know or have heard of?

J. TOPICS FOR WRITING

1. Do some research on your first name. You can consult your parents or other family members or use one of the online sites listed in the Explore the Web section. Then write an essay in which you explain the origin of your name, its meaning, why the name was given to you, and finally, your feelings about it.
2. If friends told you that they were going to name their child something you consider outlandish, how would you respond? Write a paragraph or two in which you address this question. Your focus should be on warning them against choosing such a name.

EXPLORE THE WEB

- Information about baby's names—their origin, meanings, rankings, and popularity—can be found at these two sites. Both are easy to navigate.

  www.babynamesworld.com

  www.thinkbabynames.com

- The Social Security Administration maintains an extensive website (mentioned in paragraph 6) that tracks the popularity of names going back 100 years to 1911. In 2010, Emily and Madison lost out to these top five names for girls: Isabella, Sophia, Emma, Olivia, and Ava. The top five boys' names were Jacob, Ethan, Michael, Jayden, and William. The site allows you to see how a name's ranking has changed over the years, among other interesting name-related facts.

  www.ssa.gov/OACT/babynames

- For another perspective on this matter of giving odd names to children, read the article in the following New York Times link below about how Germany regulates the naming of children. In Germany, children's names must be approved by a local authority, according to the article, guided by a reference book, *The International Handbook of Forenames.* The article cites two interesting examples. The second one is particularly amusing: "In 2003, an appellate court ruled that a boy could not be named 'Anderson,' because it was a last name in Germany. And the Constitutional Court ruled in 2004 to limit the number of forenames a child could have, capping at five the number a mother could give her son, to whom she had tried to bequeath the 12-part

'Chenekwahow Tecumseh Migiskau Kioma Ernesto Inti Prithibi Pathar Cha-jara Majim Henriko Alessandro,' to protect the child." What do you think about this prohibition against so-called chain names? Should the state intervene in cases like this, or should parents have the right to name their children whatever they want as a matter of personal expression?

www.nytimes.com/2009/05/06/world/europe/06germany.html

25 The Bystander's Dilemma: Why Do We Walk on By?

MARC IAN BARASCH

Marc Ian Barasch, a former editor for Psychology Today, studied literature, philosophy, and film at Yale University. A practicing Buddhist, Barasch has written a book titled Field Notes on the Compassionate Life: A Search for the Soul of Kindness. The book is about empathy, altruism, and compassion—an exploration into human conduct based on acting from unselfish motives and with sensitivity to others' problems. This selection was adapted from the book and was later reprinted in a magazine titled Greater Good, published by the Center for the Development of Peace and Well-Being at the University of California, Berkeley. In the essay, which I have slightly condensed, Barasch examines the "bystander's dilemma"—why we often fail to come to the aid of someone in trouble. In this excerpt, Barasch describes his experiment—what it is like to panhandle on the streets of Denver.

Vocabulary Preview

WORD PARTS

equi- [17] When we *equivocate*, we use language that avoids making a clear statement or that misleads, from Latin *equi-* ("equal") + *voc-* ("lito call"). In other words, equivocation involves saying two things at the same time rather than being decisive.

Some other words that begin with this prefix, signifying either equal or equality, are these:

equivalent	having equal value
equity	the state of being fair and impartial
equilibrium	state of balance due to the equal action of opposing forces

If your house is *equidistant* from your college and your place of work, what does that mean? _____

potent [paragraph 2] The homeless often smell bad, or as Barasch says, their smell is *potent* because it intrudes so strongly on passersby. *Potent* means "powerful," derived from the Latin root *patens*, or "power." Here are two other words in this family:

impotent	the opposite of potent, often referring to a man who is incapable of sexual activity
potential	having the power or capacity for future development

What is a potentate? _____

MARC IAN BARASCH

The Bystander's Dilemma: Why Do We Walk on By?

1   It was one of those small encounters that lodges in the mind like a pebble in the shoe: A few years ago, walking back from the market at dusk, I heard a muffled keening coming from a pile of discarded coats on the sidewalk 20 yards ahead. The sound became more intense as I approached, a kind of Doppler effect, until I made out a man about my age, wrapped in layers of outerwear, loudly demanding a handout. I gave him a dollar and, for good measure, dug into my bag for an apple. But my conscience was hardly appeased.

2   Street people. The homeless. Truth be told, most of us find them an annoyance. They barge into public space (sometimes their smell, supernally potent, intrudes first), interrupting our train of thought or flow of conversation. Haven't they brought this on themselves in some way (in some way *we* clearly haven't)? Why don't they get a job, bootstrap themselves out of purgatory? We avert our eyes, feign sudden deafness, sidestep them as they sprawl at our feet. We're as eager to cross paths with them as we would be with Marley's Ghost.[1]

3   That I had barely helped the man had a sting of irony, as I'd just begun researching a new book on empathy, altruism, and compassion. Browsing for quotes, I'd stumbled on *Works of Love*, a tome by the alternately cranky and transcendent 19th century philosopher Søren Kierkegaard,[2] whose moral scolding had instantly gotten under my skin. When he mocked that person who is "never among the more lowly"; who "will go about with closed eyes . . . when he moves around in the human throng"; and jeered the existential snob who "thinks he exists only for the distinguished, that he is to live only in the alliance of their circles," well . . . I couldn't pretend I didn't know whom he was talking about.

---

[1] Jacob Marley, or Marley's Ghost, a character in Charles Dickens's *A Christmas Carol*, appears before Ebenezer Scrooge at the beginning of the novel to warn him. Scrooge thinks that the ghost is merely a figment of his imagination. (Ed.)

[2] Søren Kierkegaard (1813–1855) was a Danish philosopher and thinker, often called the father of existentialism. He advocated a passionate commitment to others and taking responsibility for one's own actions while rejecting traditional rationalism. (Ed.)

4   In fact, I was anticipating a rather gala break in my writing schedule: a trip to Cannes and then on to a farmhouse in glorious Provence, an offer from a jetsetting filmmaker buddy I could hardly refuse.

5   But then another invitation had suddenly cropped up in the same calendar slot, this one from a group called the Zen Peacemaker Order, to go on what they called a "street retreat." With the back of my neck still prickling under Kierkegaard's gaze (to say nothing of my editor's), I decided to stay on the ground. Literally. The retreat rules were simple: Hit the pavement unbathed and unshaven, Without money or change of clothes, joining for the better part of a week the ranks of those whom life had kicked to the curb. A sojourn in the land of *ain't got nothin', got nothin' to lose* might, I thought, pierce my bystander's armor. . . .

BEARING WITNESS

6   The street retreats are the brainchild of Bernie Glassman. A bearded, portly former aerospace engineer ordained as a Buddhist *roshi*,[3] Bernie had been looking for ways to integrate spiritual practice with compassionate social action. Sometime in the 1980s, he decided to spend a few months walking aimlessly around the inner-city Bronx neighborhood that abutted his meditation center, hanging out, talking with people in his cannily receptive way, listening to their problems. Out of this had grown, as naturally and prolifically as a zucchini patch, a sprawling multimillion-dollar social organization serving the rebuked and the scorned.

7   First there was the Greyston Bakery, which employed people just getting out of prison or off the street. The business grew, eventually snagging a contract to make brownies for Ben and Jerry's Ice Cream. But it soon came smack up against the endemic problems of the neighborhood. People missed work because of drug problems. Batches of dough were ruined because employees lacked basic math skills to measure ingredients or the reading skills to decipher labels on cans. But each problem had suggested, after trial and error, its own solution. The Greyston Mandala that emerged from Bernie's first street-scuffing walkabout now trains, employs, houses, and provides health services to hundreds of the formerly marginal, as well as offering care and housing to people with AIDS on the site of a former Catholic nunnery.

8   When Bernie's 55th birthday rolled around, rather than resting on his laurels, he decided to spend a few days sitting homeless on the steps of the Capitol, figuring out what next to do with his life. During what turned out to be Washington, D.C.'s coldest, snowiest week in half a century, he dreamed up the multifaith Peacemaker Order, a spiritual path based on just bearing witness and seeing what happened.

9   "When we bear witness," he wrote, "when we become the situation—homelessness, poverty, illness, violence, death—then right action arises by itself. We don't have to worry about what to do. We don't have to figure out solutions ahead of time. . . . It's as simple as giving a hand to someone who stumbles, or picking up a child who has fallen on the floor."

---

[3] In Zen Buddhism a *roshi* is a spiritual leader. (Ed.)

10   You could say, "Witness, *schmitness*."[4] Fine for Bernie, with his track record of weaving straw into gold. But if he hadn't recommended it, I'd be hard put to justify my week of taking to the streets in a bum costume, as if I and my fellow retreatants didn't have somewhere better to go. What I had to tell myself was, at least for this interlude, there would be no "better," and no worse.

THE HAUNTED STREET

11   And so I find myself living on the streets of Denver, dressed in ratty, stinking clothes, a toothbrush in my pocket and a week's worth of stubble on my cold-reddened cheeks. I'm hoping to discover some way to be a little less full of myself; to see if more kindness might arise if I persuade Mr. Ego to move out for a week.

12   But what I find arising is my innate irritability. I can be impatient, and homelessness involves lots of waiting: waiting for a soup kitchen to open, then waiting for your number to be called for a meal; waiting for the rain or snow to let up, or for a cop to stop looking your way. It's a different map of the world: Which Starbucks has a security guard who'll let you use the bathroom? How long can you linger in this place or that before you're rousted? It's pretty much a stray dog's life, sniffing for a bone to gnaw, a tree to piss on, knowing nobody wants you, wary of the company you keep.

13   And what to make of my new company? My friend Søren K.,[5] in his tough-old-bird fashion, argued against harboring any delusions that "by loving some people, relatives and friends, you would be loving the neighbor." No, he squawked, the real point is "to frighten you out of the beloved haunts of preferential love." Most of my new neighbors *are* haunted. Life has failed them, or they've failed it. A tall, stringy young man with lank, black-dyed hair, tattooed like a Maori, tells me, "If you see Sherry, tell her Big John's back from Oklahoma." His eyes have the jittery glint of crank, each pupil a spinning disco ball, fitfully sparkling. An alcoholic Indian vet yanks open his shirt to show me his scars—the roundish puckers from shrapnel, the short, telegraphic dashes from ritual piercing at a Sun Dance—weeping over a life he no longer wants.

14   An angry-looking man approaches me to ask—to demand—that I give him a plastic fork, purpose unknown. When I demur, he stalks over to the dumpster and scrabbles through it unproductively.

15   "I'm sorry," I say.

16   "I'll just *bet* you are," he snarls, then raises both middle fingers, staring into my eyes with cold fury.

17   I can't say I'm pleased to meet him, but WWKD: What Would Kierkegaard Do?[6] "Root out all equivocation and fastidiousness in loving them!" *Sir, yes-sir.* The Buddhist sage Atisha recommended a prayer upon encountering those folks who mess with our minds: *When I see beings of a negative disposition, or*

---

[4]"Witness, schmitness" is an example of a Yiddish expression in which one says a word and then repeats it, but this time changing the first consonant to "schm." The phrase thus dismisses the idea. (Ed.)
[5]Søren Kierkegaard. (Ed.)
[6]A play on a common question asked by Christians: WWJD? or What Would Jesus Do? (Ed.)

those oppressed by negativity or pain, may I, as if finding a treasure, consider them precious.

18   Every cerebral word of this homily is *not* running through my head as I step toward my new neighbor with a little faux-nod of appreciation, hoping he hasn't stashed a ball-peen hammer in his coat. But he backs away, lips curled, then turns and runs, pursued by some host of invisibles. At least, I tell myself, I've managed to become more curious about him than repulsed, mindful that the more I amp up my judgment of others, the more I empower that ogre of criticism that grinds my own bones to make its bread. Really, I don't know how these guys drove their lives into the ditch, or how to winch them out. I try to stay present, feeling my heart's systole and diastole, its sympathies opening, closing, opening, closing.

THE DEBT OF LOVE

19   I'm willing to practice extending those sympathies to my street neighbors. But I'm not nearly as enthusiastic about doing what the Zen Peacemaker Order refers to as "begging practice." The thought horrifies me. Sure, I've done that high-class begging known as fundraising, palm outstretched for checks written out to high-minded projects. But I've always felt it was worth the other person's while; there were good deeds to show for it. Here on the street I, the beggar, have nothing to offer the beggee. There is no mutual exchange, just an imbalance of boons. I'm a walking bundle of needs, and it galls me.

20   Besides, it isn't easy to get those needs met. Faces turn to stone at my plea for food money. Eyes flicker sideways, ahead to the middle distance, to the ground, anywhere but the empty space where I'm standing. The Confucians of the Sung Dynasty compared not feeling compassion for a stranger to not feeling that your own foot's caught fire, and too many of us seem to have gone numb. (I think of an acquaintance of mine, a much-awarded designer of leafy town squares in the New Urbanist style. "Of course," he once said to me ruefully, "the more open space, the bigger the quotient of 'bummage.'")

21   Bummage I am. I supplicate downtown pedestrians, dauntingly busy on their way from here to there, clutching purses and shopping bags and cell phones and lovers' waists. I recognize the filmy bubble of self-concept that surrounds them, that protective aura of specialness. How often do most of us secretly say to ourselves that we're smarter, stronger, taller, more charming than average; have a cooler job, a more lovely spouse, more accomplished children; that we are (somehow) more spiritual, even more selfless? Anything is grist for the mill of selfhood versus otherness, of the gourmet-flavored me versus plain-vanilla everyone else. I too, have achieved my differentiation at some cost and considerable effort; even here, hugging the ground, I resist inhabiting the same universe as the full-time failures.

22   But I'm already there in one respect: My panhandling talents are nil. Each rejection thuds like a body blow. I can see the little comic-strip thought balloon spring from people's brows—*Get a job; I work!* It occurs to me to just forget it. Though we've agreed that during the week we'd each scrape up $3.50 for the bus fare home, throwing any extra into the kitty for the homeless shelter, I think, *Why put myself through it? I'll send a check when I get home.*

23   But I'm hungry *now*. I'm also starting to realize that there's more to "begging practice" than meets the eye. Roshi Bernie Glassman has explained it with disarming simplicity: "When we don't ask, we don't let others give. When we fear rejection, we don't let generosity arise." I realize that the street, much like a meditation cushion, has put my issues on parade, and this begging routine's got them goose-stepping smartly past the reviewing stand. There's the Humiliation Battalion. The Fear of Rejection Brigade. The Undeserving Auxiliary. And of course, the Judgment Detachment—for I find I'm even judging my potential donors (are *they* good enough to give *me* a dollar?).

24   My profound reluctance to ask passersby for help feels not unlike my aversion to calling friends when I'm needful in other ways, those times when I'm feeling sad, lost lonely, bereft. I prize autonomy; I'm overly proud of it. I don't *want* to owe people for my well-being. Or just maybe I don't want to owe them my love. I wonder suddenly if I'm not rejecting gratitude itself, that spiritual 3-in-1 oil said to open the creakiest gate around the heart? Aren't we all in debt to our parents, teachers, friends, and loved ones—for our very existence?

25   But dear Søren Kierkegaard thought even *this* was a crock. Sure, he said, we think the person who is loved owes a debt of gratitude to the one who loves them. There is an expectation that it should be repaid in kind, on installment, "reminiscent," he says sarcastically, "of an actual bookkeeping arrangement." Instead, he turns the whole thing on its head: "No, the one who loves runs into debt; in feeling himself gripped by love, he feels this as being in an infinite debt. Amazing!"

26   *Amazing.* It is his most radical proposition: We owe those who elicit love from us for allowing us to be overfilled with the stuff. We owe a debt to those who suffer because they draw forth our tenderness. (Do I think that by avoiding others' suffering, I can hoard my stash of good feelings and not get bummed out? The "helper's high" phenomenon suggests the opposite: It's giving that turns on the juice, taps us into the infinite current.) Giving and taking start to seem less like zero-sum transactions than some universal love-circuitry, where what goes around not only comes around but comes back redoubled.

27   Still, "How'd you like to enter into Kierkegaard's infinite debt of love?" is not going to win Year's Best Panhandling Line. I ask a stylish young guy—*No War: Not in Our Name* button on his fawn-colored coat, canvas messenger bag in muted gray—if he can spare a little change for food. He calls out chidingly over his shoulder, "I don't give *on the street*." Fair enough. But the bank building's LED thermometer reads 25 degrees, and the sun still hasn't gone down. I haven't had dinner. Sleeping on the street is a frigid proposition, and body heat requires calories. Then I realize I'm judging him and everyone else, defeating the whole purpose of the exercise. I make a point to mentally bless all comers and goers.

28   I approach a bearded guy in a fringed suede jacket. He declines, but hangs around as if waiting for someone. A few minutes later, hearing me unsuccessfully petition a half dozen more people, he comes over and hands me two dollars, cautioning *sotto voce*, "Don't tell anyone I gave it to you," as if worried I'd alert a Fagin's gang of accomplices.[7]

---

[7]Another reference to a Dickens novel, in this case *Oliver Twist*. Fagin is a criminal who recruits little boys and teaches them to be thieves and pickpockets. (Ed.)

29   I've now streamlined my pitch: "I'm sleeping on the street tonight, I'm hungry. I wonder if you could help me out at all?" Most people's eyes still slam down like steel shutters over a storefront at closing time, but then, ". . . Could you help me out?" and a man who's just passed me with a curt *No* pivots abruptly, yanked like a puppet by his heartstrings, and walks back with a green bill. "On second thought, I can." And I see in that moment how much more effort it takes to resist the raw tug of each other's existence.

30   I strike out another 20 or 30 times before a crisp-looking gent crosses my palm with silver. "Thanks so much, it's chilly out tonight," I mumble, surprised after so many averted gazes. "It *is* cold," he says sympathetically, and those three words restore my faith.

SMALL CHANGE

31   A week later, back home again, I'm delighted to be sleeping in my own bed. Bathed, shaved, fed, dressed, I take a walk on the mall with a friend. He looks at me askance as I press a dollar into a panhandler's palm and then, seeing how browbeaten the man looks, peel off another two and chat with him for a while.

32   I'm trying to become insufferably virtuous, I tell my friend. How am I doing?

33   Great, he replies, you're getting on my nerves.

34   These days, I give money to the people with cardboard signs who stake out corners on trafficked streets, remembering when I was stranded once on the highway, having to scare up a ride with my own magic-markered plea. One guy comes up to the window to recite his story as my car idles at a light. He's a former truck driver with a neck injury, he says, saving up for surgery. He seems utterly sincere, though I'm not sure that matters: I know he must have his reasons. I hand him a bill and drive off. Then, feeling suddenly touched, I circle the block and cut recklessly through two lanes of traffic to give him another. "For your medical fund," I yell, practically hurling a tenner at him to beat the light. "God bless you, you and your family," he yells after me; and yes, I think, he's for real, and yes, I also think, how Dickensian: *Oh, kind sir.* But I also mentally thank him for helping me sink deeper into that debt that swallows all others and makes them small—small, and of no consequence.

35   I won't claim I've evolved that much. Not in a week or two; not in a few months. Sure, I help out, sometimes, at the local soup kitchen; kick in for the anti-homelessness coalition. But I do feel as if my inner pockets have been turned inside out, shaking loose some small change in my life. I've developed an ineluctable soft spot. I can't help but notice the people at the margins, the ones who used to be the extras in my movie. Knowing a little of how they feel makes me an easy touch. The money I give out sometimes mounts up, 20, 30 bucks a month, unburdening the wallet, filling the heart's purse. Until I figure out what I can do to really change things—or until the world becomes a different place—this feels better than okay.

Marc Ian Barasch, "The Bystander's Dilemma: Why Do We Walk on By?" from *Greater Good* (Fall/Winter 2006-2007). Reprinted with the permission of the author.

Exercises

Do not refer to the selection for Exercises A and B unless your instructor directs you to do so.

A. DETERMINING THE MAIN IDEA AND PURPOSE

Choose the best answer.

_____ **1.** The main idea of the selection is that
   a. homelessness is an endemic, persistent problem in American cities.
   b. there is a great deal of disagreement among social thinkers and philosophers about how we should respond to the homeless.
   c. for the writer, panhandling for a week gave him a new perspective and newfound compassion for the homeless.
   d. street retreats are a novel way to integrate spiritual practice with compassionate social action.

_____ **2.** With respect to the presence of the homeless in his community, the writer's purpose is to
   a. discuss various methods that communities have used to deal with the issue.
   b. describe his search for both a philosophic and a practical response to them.
   c. explain the philosopher Søren Kierkegaard's thinking about compassion.
   d. urge cities and municipal governments to establish more programs to help them.

B. COMPREHENDING MAIN IDEAS

Choose the correct answer.

_____ **1.** Barasch's encounter with a homeless man who asked for money was ironic because
   a. he was researching a book on compassion at the time.
   b. he had recently been homeless himself.
   c. he had never thought much about the homeless problem before.
   d. he had never given money to panhandlers before.

_____ **2.** The purpose of the street retreat sponsored by the Zen Peacemaker Order was to
   a. teach people a workable and compassionate response to the homeless by following the thinking of Søren Kierkegaard.
   b. sponsor job training programs and improved accommodations for the homeless.
   c. ask participants to panhandle and live on the streets for a week.
   d. offer religious services for the homeless.

_____3.   Bernie Glassman's project, the Greyston Bakery, was unusual because it
  a. was immediately successful, far beyond what anyone expected.
  b. was the first project to be sponsored by Buddhists.
  c. made ice cream for Ben & Jerry's.
  d. gave former prisoners and homeless people an opportunity for employment.

4.   Underlying Bernie Glassman's project, sponsored by the Peacemaker Order, was the philosophic idea to "bear witness," which means that participants _____.

5.   According to Barasch, the daily life of a homeless person consists of a great deal of _____.

_____ 6.   Because of Barasch's experience on the streets of Denver, he now
  a. talks to panhandlers and learns their stories before deciding whether to give money.
  b. notices people who live on the margins and often gives them money.
  c. refuses to hand out money to those who can't get their lives together.
  d. hands out pamphlets telling panhandlers where they can get help.

COMPREHENSION SCORE

Score your answers for Exercises A and B as follows:

A. No. right _____ × 2 = _____

B. No. right _____ × 1 = _____

Total points from A and B _____ × 10 = _____ percent

C. LOCATING SUPPORTING DETAILS

For the main ideas from the selections paraphrased here, find two relevant details that support each one.

1.   The Greyston Bakery employed people newly released from prison or trying to find a new life off the streets. However, it soon came smack up against the endemic problems of the neighborhood. [paragraph 7]

a.   _____

b.   _____

2.   The writer recognized the "filmy bubble of self-concept" that surrounds the people on the street, that "protective aura of specialness." [paragraph 21]

a.   _____

_____

b. _____

_____

D. INTERPRETING MEANING

1. Look again at the quotations Barasch cites from the philosopher Søren Kierkegaard in paragraph 3. Explain in your own words what they mean.

_____

_____

2. In paragraph 20, Barasch cites the opinion of an acquaintance, an urban designer, who observes the following: "the more open space, the bigger the quotient of 'bummage.'" What does he mean, and why would this be the case? _____

_____

3. Paragraphs 25 and 26 present what Barasch calls a "radical proposition" that "we owe a debt to those who suffer because they draw forth our tenderness." What exactly does he mean? _____

_____

E. UNDERSTANDING VOCABULARY

Look through the paragraphs listed by number in brackets and find a word that matches each definition. Refer to a dictionary if necessary. An example has been done for you.

Ex. soothed relieved [paragraphs 1–2]   _____*appeased*_____

1. identification with another's situation or feelings [3]   _____

2. cleverly, shrewdly [6]   _____

3. describing those who live on the edges of society or at the lower limits of social acceptability [7]   _____

4. prevalent or established in a particular area [7]   _____

5. careful, watchful [12]   _____

6. inborn, natural, inherent [12]   _____

7. French for fake, false [18—here used as part of a compound word]   _____

8. impressively, in a commanding way [21]   _____

9. deprived, abandoned, lacking what is needed [24]   _____

10. bring or draw out [26]   _____

F. SMALL GROUP ACTIVITY—UNDERSTANDING SLANG AND IDIOMATIC EXPRESSIONS

Barasch uses several informal and slang expressions. Consider these expressions in their context and then, working in small groups, try to determine their meaning. The paragraph number where each occurs is included. You might try the dictionary if you are unsure, or ask your instructor for help.

1. *bootstrap* themselves out of purgatory [2—more commonly, to *pull themselves up by their bootstraps*] _____

2. I'd *stumbled on* [3] _____

3. whose moral scolding had *gotten under my skin* [3] _____

4. another invitation *cropped up* [5] _____

5. the street retreats are the *brainchild* of Bernie Glassman [6] _____

6. the business grew, eventually *snagging* a contract [7] _____

7. rather than *resting on his laurels* [8] _____

8. the more I *amp up* my judgment [18] _____

9. how these guys *drove their lives into the ditch* [18] _____

10. throwing any extra into *the kitty* [22] _____

11. Kierkegaard thought even this was *a crock* [25] _____

12. not *get bummed out* [26] _____

13. I've now *streamlined my pitch* [29] _____

14. hurling *a tenner* at him [34] _____

15. makes me *an easy touch* [35] _____

G. ANNOTATING EXERCISE

The title of the essay, "The Bystander's Dilemma," refers to a situation that involves two or more unfavorable alternatives. What exactly was the dilemma that Barasch experienced when homeless people panhandled him for money? What dilemma did he experience when he himself panhandled? Look through the essay again and annotate it, but this time making notes only on those portions of the essay pertaining to this concept.

H. PARAPHRASING EXERCISE

Here are some sentences from the selection. Write a paraphrase of each passage in the space provided.

1. Out of this had grown, as naturally and prolifically as a zucchini patch, a sprawling multimillion-dollar social organization serving the rebuked and the scorned.

_____

_____

2. I've done that high-class begging known as fundraising, palm outstretched for checks written out to high-minded projects. But I've always felt it was worth the other person's while; there were good deeds to show for it. Here on the street I, the beggar, have nothing to offer the beggee. There is no mutual exchange, just an imbalance of boons. I'm a walking bundle of needs, and it galls me. _____

_____

_____

_____

_____

3. It is his [Kierkegaard's] most radical proposition: We owe those who elicit love from us for allowing us to be overfilled with the stuff. We owe a debt to those who suffer because they draw forth our tenderness.

_____

_____

I. TOPICS FOR DISCUSSION

1. Consider again the subtitle of this selection. Why *do* we just walk on by?
2. To what extent do you think Barasch's opinion changed to compassion because of his own experience on the street? If you don't routinely give spare change to panhandlers, how much do you think your attitude would change if you had to panhandle for a week?
3. Does one have the "right" to be homeless, to refuse shelter? This question involves civil liberties, and it has been a thorny one that many communities have been dealing with, with varying degrees of success. If streets are considered "public," that is, if they belong to the people, does that fact include the right to live on them?
4. Barasch cites the thinking of Danish philosopher Søren Kierkegaard in his revised response to the homeless and in his newfound empathy toward their plight. How do you respond to the homeless, specifically to their panhandling (assuming that this is a common occurrence in your community)? Do you give them money or not? Do you listen to their stories? Whatever your usual reaction, what is the philosophical basis for it?

J. TOPICS FOR WRITING

1. What was your attitude toward the homeless before reading this article? Examine your thinking in some depth. Has this article in any way changed your thinking? If a homeless person were to come up to you on the street today and ask you for a dollar or some spare change (for whatever reason), what would you do? Write an essay setting forth your attitudes and your explanations for them.
2. To what extent is homelessness a problem in your community? Do some investigation, either by making firsthand observations or by reading about the issue in your local newspaper. If it is a problem, what factors contribute

to it? If it is not a problem, what factors contribute to its absence? Write a short paper presenting your findings.

EXPLORE THE WEB

- This article was published in the Fall/Winter 2006–2007 issue of *Greater Good* magazine, along with six other essays on subjects relating to the greater good. One of them, "Playground Heroes" by Ken Rigby and Bruce Johnson, deals with the increasing problem of bullying in schools. You can access the entire issue at this address:

  http://greatergood.berkeley.edu/greatergood/archive/2006fallwinter/

26 My Teacher Is an App

Stephanie Banchero is a reporter for the Wall Street Journal, *but previously she had extensive journalism experience as education reporter for the* Chicago Tribune. *She has degrees in journalism from the University of Utah and the Columbia Graduate School of Journalism, and she is also the current president of the Education Writers Association. Her cowriter, Stephanie Simon, also a reporter for the* Wall Street Journal, *began her career at the* Los Angeles Times, *where she covered the O. J. Simpson murder trial and the Columbine High School massacre. This article was published in the* Journal's Life and Style *section in November 2011. The online version received seven pages of comments. (See Explore the Web.)*

Vocabulary Analysis

WORD PARTS

The prefix *cyber-* The prefix *cyber-* is a relatively recent addition to English. Like its counterparts, *virtual*, *e-*, and *digital*, when added to a root word, *cyber-* refers to activities carried out on a computer network or using an electronic medium. The writers use three words with this prefix: *cybercourses* (paragraph 6), *cyberschools* (11), and *cyberlearning* (34). Two other words with this prefix are *cyberbullying* and *cyberspace*. *Cyberspace* is distinguished from its opposite, *bricks-and-mortar* (see paragraph 5), which refers to an actual physical place, like Macy's, a Barnes & Noble bookstore, or a school campus. (It's also interesting to note that we say *cybercash* and *cyberworld*, but not *cyberbook* or *cybercommerce*. *E-book* and *e-commerce* seem to be the terms most English speakers have adopted).

WORD FAMILIES

utilitarian One of the biggest criticisms cited in this article is that cyberlearning "turns education into a largely *utilitarian* pursuit. Learn content, click ahead." The adjective *utilitarian* derives from the Latin root *utilis*, meaning "useful." In English, the word conveys the idea of both practicality and usefulness. Other words in this linguistic family are *utility*, *useful*, *utilitarianism*, and *utilize*.

STEPHANIE BANCHERO AND STEPHANIE SIMON

My Teacher Is an App

1   It was nearing lunchtime on a recent Thursday, and ninth-grader Noah Schnacky of Windermere, Fla., really did not want to go to algebra. So he didn't.

2   Tipping back his chair, he studied a computer screen listing the lessons he was supposed to complete that week for his public high school—a high school conducted entirely online. Noah clicked on his global-studies course. A lengthy article on resource shortages popped up. He gave it a quick scan and clicked ahead to the quiz, flipping between the article and multiple-choice questions until he got restless and wandered into the kitchen for a snack.

3   Noah would finish the quiz later, within the three-hour time frame that he sets aside each day for school. He also listened to most of an online lecture given by his English teacher; he could hear but not see her as she explained the concept of a protagonist to 126 ninth graders logged in from across the state. He never got to the algebra.

4   His sister Allison, meanwhile, has spent the past two hours working on an essay in the kitchen. She has found a new appreciation of history. At her old school, she says, the teacher stood at the blackboard and droned, and history was "the boringest class ever." Now, thanks to the videos she's been watching on ancient Egypt, she loves it.

5   In a radical rethinking of what it means to go to school, states and districts nationwide are launching online public schools that let students from kindergarten to 12th grade take some—or all—of their classes from their bedrooms, living rooms and kitchens. Other states and districts are bringing students into brick-and-mortar schools for instruction that is largely computer-based and self-directed.

6   In just the past few months, Virginia has authorized 13 new online schools. Florida began requiring all public-high-school students to take at least one class online, partly to prepare them for college cybercourses. Idaho soon will require two. In Georgia, a new app lets high-school students take full course loads on their iPhones and BlackBerrys. Thirty states now let students take all of their courses online.

7   Nationwide, an estimated 250,000 students are enrolled in full-time virtual schools, up 40% in the last three years, according to Evergreen Education Group, a consulting firm that works with online schools. More than two million pupils take at least one class online, according to the International Association for K-12 Online Learning, a trade group.

8   Although some states and local districts run their own online schools, many hire for-profit corporations such as K12 Inc. of Herndon, Va., and Connections Academy in Baltimore, a unit of education services and technology company Pearson PLC. The companies hire teachers, provide curriculum, monitor student performance—and lobby to expand online public education.

9   It's all part of a burst of experimentation in public education, fueled in part by mounting budgetary pressures, by parental dissatisfaction with their kids'

schools and by the failure of even top-performing students to keep up with their peers in other industrialized countries. In the nation's largest cities, half of all high-school students will never graduate.

10   Advocates say that online schooling can save states money, offer curricula customized to each student and give parents more choice in education.

11   A few states, however, have found that students enrolled full-time in virtual schools score significantly lower on standardized tests, and make less academic progress from year to year, than their peers. Critics worry that kids in online classes don't learn how to get along with others or participate in group discussions. Some advocates of full-time cyberschools say that the disappointing results are partly because some of the students had a rough time in traditional schools, and arrive testing below grade level in one or more subjects.

12   The experimental schools draw a diverse lot. Some students were previously home-schooled, some are high achievers and others have erratic schedules because of sports training or health problems. Many are ordinary kids who didn't prosper in traditional schools or whose parents want to shelter them from bullying and peer pressure. They are, however, less likely to be poor or to have special needs than the general public-school population, according to data from state education officials and from online schools.

13   One promising approach, many experts say, is hybrid schools, which blend online study with face-to-face interaction with teachers.

14   In California, Rocketship Education, a chain of charter hybrid schools that serves mostly poor and minority kids, has produced state test scores on par with some of the state's wealthiest schools. Rocketship students spend up to half of each school day in computer labs playing math and literacy games that adjust to their ability level.

15   At Southwest Learning Centers, a small chain of charter schools in Albuquerque, N.M., standardized test scores routinely outpace state and local averages, according to data provided by the schools. Students complete most lessons online but come into class for teacher support and hands-on challenges, such as collaborating to design and build a weight-bearing bridge. The high school recently received a statewide award for its students' strong scores on the ACT college admissions test.

16   Allison Brown, a Georgia mother of three, says that she intended to enroll her son in the local public school for kindergarten last year until she met with an administrator there to discuss how the school might accommodate his advanced reading skills. She says the teacher told her that her son would be challenged— by helping other kids to learn their letters. So she enrolled her son in an online school where he could advance rapidly into higher grade levels.

17   Her son, Aarington, is now in first grade at Georgia Cyber Academy, and she has also enrolled her twins there for kindergarten. Ms. Brown has set up her basement as a mini-school, complete with counting blocks, reading nook and blackboard, and she tutors the kids through their online curriculum for most of each day. She says they're all thriving, and she plans to keep them in a full-time online school at least for the next several years.

18   "I don't think learning has to happen at school, in a classroom with 30 other kids and a teacher. . . corralling all children into learning the same thing at

the same pace," she says. "We should rethink the environment we set up for education."

19   Colleges and universities have offered online courses for decades. The practice first cropped up in secondary schools in the early 1990s, when a few states began offering virtual Advanced Placement and foreign-language classes to high-school students. Cybercourses were also promoted as a convenient way for students who had failed a class to make up the credit.

20   The amount of teacher interaction varies. At online-only schools, instructors answer questions by email, phone or the occasional video conference; students will often meet classmates and teachers on optional field trips and during state exams. Southwest Learning Centers requires just 14 hours a week of classroom time and lets students set their own schedules, deciding when—or whether—to come in on any given day. And in Miami, students at iPrep Academy work in free-flowing "classrooms" with no doors or dividing walls but plenty of beanbag chairs and couches. Teachers give short lectures and offer one-on-one help, but most learning is self-directed and online.

21   "If it seems strange, that's because it is strange," says Alberto Carvalho, superintendent of the Miami schools. But he sees no point in forcing the iPod generation to adapt to a classroom model that has changed little in 300 years.

22   Noah Schnacky, 14, says he likes expressing his thoughts at the keyboard instead of in a crowded classroom.

23   The drive to reinvent school has also set off an explosive clash with teachers unions and backers of more traditional education. Partly, it's a philosophical divide. Critics say that cyberschools turn education into a largely utilitarian pursuit: Learn content, click ahead. They mourn the lack of discussion, fear kids won't be challenged to take risks, and fret about devaluing the softer skills learned in classrooms.

24   "Schools teach people the skills of citizenship—how to get along with others, how to reason and deliberate, how to tolerate differences," says Jonathan Zimmerman, a professor of educational history at New York University.

25   The growth of cybereducation is likely to affect school staffing, which accounts for about 80% of school budgets. A teacher in a traditional high school might handle 150 students. An online teacher can supervise more than 250, since he or she doesn't have to write lesson plans and most grading is done by computer.

26   In Idaho, Alan Dunn, superintendent of the Sugar-Salem School District, says that he may cut entire departments and outsource their courses to online providers. "It's not ideal," he says. "But Idaho is in a budget crisis, and this is a creative solution."

27   Other states see potential savings as well. In Georgia, state and local taxpayers spend $7,650 a year to educate the average student in a traditional public school. They spend nearly 60% less—$3,200 a year—to educate a student in the statewide online Georgia Cyber Academy, saving state and local tax dollars. Florida saves $1,500 a year on every student enrolled online full time.

28   For individual school districts, though, competition from online schools can cause financial strain. The tiny Spring Cove School District in rural Pennsylvania lost 43 of its 1,850 students this year to online charter schools. By law, the district

must send those students' share of local and state tax dollars—in this case $340,000—to the cyberschool. Superintendent Rodney Green, already struggling to balance the budget, cut nine teaching jobs, eliminated middle-school Spanish and French and canceled the high-school musical, "Aida."

29   Dennis Van Roekel, president of the National Education Association, the nation's largest teachers union, says that his organization opposes full-time online schools but supports integrating virtual lessons into classrooms. "Obviously, we all want to save money," he says. "But to replace teachers with online learning is a mistake."

30   Online advocates note that teachers are still involved, delivering optional online lectures and answering questions by phone, text and email. Former Florida Gov. Jeb Bush, who co-founded the Foundation for Excellence in Education, which promotes online schools nationwide, says learning will be "digitized" with or without cooperation from the unions. "I'm happy to go to war over this," he says.

31   Rupert Murdoch, chief executive officer of News Corp., which owns The Wall Street Journal, has been an advocate of digital education. Last year News Corp. bought a 90% stake in Wireless Generation, an education-technology company that sells hand-held computers to teachers to help monitor student performance.

32   Two companies, K12 and Connections Academy, dominate the market for running public cyberschools. Full-time enrollment in online schools using the K12 curriculum has doubled in the past four years, to 81,000, the company says. K12's revenue grew 35% to $522 million in its fiscal year ended June 30, when it reported net income of $13 million.

33   At some K12 schools, academic struggles have followed rapid growth. Colorado Virtual Academy, launched in 2001, notched strong test scores initially. But enrollment has soared to nearly 5,000—and scores have plummeted. The school falls below Colorado averages on nearly every standardized test at every grade level, with particularly big deficits in math and writing. Outside Colorado, too, many K12 schools have poor results on state standardized tests.

34   K12 officials say state scores can be misleading because students often enroll midyear and take the tests after just a few months online. They say that the longer kids stick with cyberlearning, the better they do: Only 39% of students pass state math exams when they've been enrolled in K12 schools for less than a year, compared to 48% for kids enrolled at least one full school year. The same trend holds true for reading.

35   Tim Booker, an insurance agent who presides over the school board at Colorado Virtual Academy, says he fears that the program simply attracts too many kids who aren't suited to online learning. He now has deep concerns about whether full-time cyberschools are a viable model. "The jury's still out," he says.

36   Ron Packard, chief operating officer of K12, acknowledges that achievement has declined at some schools, which he attributes to explosive growth in the number of struggling students who register. K12 has become a "school of last resort" for many, he says. Traditional schools are best for most students, he says, but for some, "online education is a powerful choice."

37   Poor scores aren't unique to K12. In Minnesota, full-time online students in grades 4 through 8 made half as much progress in math during the 2009-

10 school year, measured by annual state exams, as their peers in traditional schools, though they were about equal in reading. A September report by the Office of the Legislative Auditor also found that 25% of high-school seniors in virtual schools dropped out, compared to 3% of seniors statewide.

38   Nonetheless, many parents and pupils who have tried online education tout its benefits. The curriculum is flexible, so a second-grader can enroll in fourth-grade math. And while many lessons look like digitized workbooks, some online classes are more creative.

39   At Florida Virtual School, which has 4,300 full-time students, up from about 1,500 last year, high-school students can earn a U.S. history credit by playing a semester-long video game that whisks them through the historical milestones. Biology students don 3-D glasses to dissect a virtual frog.

40   Noah and Allison Schnacky, aspiring actors who travel frequently, initially chose Florida Virtual for its flexibility. Noah says that he likes expressing his thoughts at the keyboard, alone in his room, instead of in a crowded class. But there are downsides. After falling behind in algebra, he tried to set up a 15-minute call with his teacher. She was booked solid—for a month. Florida Virtual says that was an anomaly and most students can set up calls within three days. Teachers also answer emails daily.

41   Miami's iPrep Academy, which blends online learning with in-person instruction, is so new that students have taken just one standardized test in science, where they handily topped state averages. The unstructured days let teachers work one-on-one with struggling students; the free-form classrooms hum with conversations and impromptu lessons.

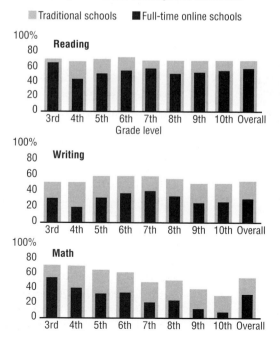

Virtual Classroom

Number of students enrolled in full-time cyberschools

175,000   200,000   250,000

2008-09   2009-10   2010-11*

*Some states have not reported final totals
Source: Evergreen Education Group

Percentage of Students Meeting State Standards:

Traditional schools   ■ Full-time online schools

Reading

100% 80 60 40 20 0

3rd 4th 5th 6th 7th 8th 9th 10th Overall
Grade level

Writing

100% 80 60 40 20 0

3rd 4th 5th 6th 7th 8th 9th 10th Overall

Math

100% 80 60 40 20 0

3rd 4th 5th 6th 7th 8th 9th 10th Overall

42   In the end, virtual schooling "comes down to what you make of it," says Rosie Lowndes, a social-studies teacher at Georgia Cyber Academy. Kids who work closely with parents or teachers do well, she says. "But basically letting a child educate himself, that's not going to be a good educational experience." The computer, she says, can't do it alone.

Exercises

You may refer to the selection to complete these exercises except for Exercise B.

A. COMPREHENDING MAIN IDEAS

Write the answers for these questions in the space provided using your own words.

1. Florida recently began requiring all high school students to take at least one class online. Why?

2. Enrollment in virtual schools has increased 40 percent in the last three years. List two reasons that taking classes online has become more popular during this period.

3. The writers mention several benefits of online education. Identify two.

4. Test scores apparently are lower for students enrolled in online courses than for students who attend traditional brick-and-mortar schools. Advocates of online education dismiss these concerns by citing two reasons to explain lower test scores. And officials for K12, one of the largest online education companies, cite other reasons to explain the same problem. Identify any two of these reasons mentioned.

5. What is a "charter hybrid school" such as that offered by Rocketship Education?

6. What is the primary reason that many states, for example, Georgia and Florida, have embraced cybereducation?

7. The writers quote Tim Booker, a school board member at Colorado Virtual Academy, who says that some kids just aren't suited to online learning, and he expresses concerns about the long-term benefits: "The jury's still out," he says. What does he mean by this phrase?

_____

8. What happened when Noah Schnacky, who was falling behind in algebra, tried to set up a 15-minute call with his teacher?

_____

B. SEQUENCING

These sentences from one paragraph in the selection may have been scrambled. Read the sentences and choose the sequence that puts them back into logical order. Do not refer to the original selection.

1 The drive to reinvent school has also set off an explosive clash with teachers unions and backers of more traditional education. **2** Partly, it's a philosophical divide. **3** Critics say that cyberschools turn education into a largely utilitarian pursuit: Learn content, click ahead. **4** They mourn the lack of discussion, fear kids won't be challenged to take risks, and fret about devaluing the softer skills learned in classrooms.

_____ Which of the following represents the correct sequence for these sentences?
  a. 1, 3, 2, 4
  b. 3, 1, 2, 4
  c. 2, 1, 4, 3
  d. 2, 3, 1, 4
  e. Correct as written.

C. DISTINGUISHING BETWEEN FACT AND OPINION

For each of the following statements from the selection, write F if the statement represents a factual statement that can be verified or O if the statement represents the writer's or someone else's subjective interpretation.

_____ 1. In a radical rethinking of what it means to go to school, states and districts nationwide are launching online public schools that let students from kindergarten to 12th grade take some—or all—of their classes from their bedrooms, living rooms and kitchens.

_____ 2. Other states and districts are bringing students into brick-and-mortar schools for instruction that is largely computer-based and self-directed.

_____ 3. In Georgia, a new app lets high-school students take full course loads on their iPhones and BlackBerrys.

_____ 4. In the nation's largest cities, half of all high school students will never graduate.

_____ 5. "I don't think learning has to happen at school, in a classroom with 30 other kids and a teacher . . . corralling all children into learning the same thing at the same pace," says Allison Brown. "We should rethink the environment we set up for education."

_____ 6. "If it seems strange, that's because it is strange," says Alberto Carvallo, superintendent of the Miami schools. But he sees no point in forcing the iPod generation to adapt to a classroom model that has changed little in 300 years.

_____ 7. Noah Schnacky, 14, says he likes expressing his thoughts at the keyboard instead of in a crowded classroom.

_____ 8. "Schools teach people the skills of citizenship—how to get along with others, how to reason and deliberate, how to tolerate differences," says Jonathan Zimmerman, a professor of educational history at New York University.

_____ 9. "It's not ideal," says Alan Dunn [superintendent of Idaho's Sugar-Salem School District.] "But Idaho is in a budget crisis, and this is a creative solution."

_____ 10. Rosie Lowndes, a social-studies teacher at Georgia Cyber Academy, says that kids who work closely with parents or teachers do well. "But basically letting a child educate himself, that's not going to be a good educational experience." The computer, she says, can't do it alone.

D. ANNOTATING AND LOCATING INFORMATION

This exercise asks you to evaluate the article in terms of balance—that is, if it presents both sides of the issue fairly—so that one side is not favored over the other. To complete this task, go through the article again, first annotating it carefully, noting each argument for online learning for K-12 students (not college students) and noting each argument against. You will use the information that you write in this exercise for class discussion. See Topics for Discussion.

Benefits—Arguments For   **Drawbacks—Arguments Against**

_____   _____

_____   _____

_____   _____

_____   _____

_____   _____

_____   _____

_____   _____

E. UNDERSTANDING GRAPHIC MATERIAL

Study the two graphs that appear at the end of the article to answer these questions.

1. Look at the first graph, labeled "Virtual Classroom." What does the graph depict?

    _____

2. Which two-year period had the biggest growth in full-time online enrollment?

    _____

3. Why might the figures for 2010–2011 not be completely reliable?

    _____

4. Now examine the second graph, labeled "Testing Trouble." State what the graph depicts.

    _____

5. Based on the figures for reading scores, in which grade were reading test scores highest?

    _____

6. In which grade did online students do most poorly in reading?

    _____

7. Now look at the bar graphs representing students' writing scores. What does this line of bars depict? What conclusion do these figures lead to?

    _____

8. Finally, look at the last row of figures that represent math scores. Describe the trend, both for traditional students and for full-time online students that the graphs depict.

    _____

F. UNDERSTANDING VOCABULARY IN CONTEXT

Here are a few vocabulary words from the selection along with their definitions. Study these definitions carefully. Then write the appropriate word in each space provided according to the context, the way it is used. Note: You will use only four of the five words in each set.

lobby (verb)	attempt to influence the thinking of public officials for a particular cause
radical	revolutionary, departing from the ordinary
on par with	equal in value or status
launch	introduce to the market or to the public
thrive	grow well, succeed, flourish

1. Online education for grades K through 12 offers students a _____ way to get an education. Online schools have become big business, with

companies like K12 and Connections Academy, working to _____ states to adopt their program. Not all schools, however, produce results that are _____ those of public school students, and it's also clear not all students will _____ in the virtual classroom.

divide (noun)	a dividing point in a conflict, split
erratic	not fixed, lacking consistency, order, or uniformity
fret	feel uneasy or troubled, worry
anomaly	departure from the normal, something irregular or abnormal
advocate (noun)	one who supports or argues for a cause

2. Rupert Murdoch, CEO of News Corporation (which owns *The Wall Street Journal*) has been a leading _____ of digital education. He and other supporters argue that online education can help those with _____ schedules or health problems. But teachers and teachers unions are on the other side of this philosophical _____. They _____ about lack of socialization that online students experience and even the lack of sufficiently rigorous intellectual challenge.

hybrid	something of mixed origin, here, something that combines two features
plummeted	declined suddenly and steeply
viable	capable of developing or of succeeding
touted	promoted, praised, publicized
droned	spoken in a monotone

3. Some online schools, for example, Colorado Virtual Academy, have dramatically increased the number of students enrolled in their curriculum, but at the same time math and writing scores have _____. Online school officials who have _____ their benefits offer the explanation that these test scores are misleading since some students have enrolled in school for only half a year. Perhaps a good alternative to full-time online enrollment is the so-called _____ school, which combines online instruction with interaction with real teachers in a classroom. It remains to be seen how _____ a model cyberschools are.

G. TOPICS FOR DISCUSSION

1. Return to the list you made for Exercise D. Have the writers achieved balance in their article or not? Can you tell which side, if any, they favor?
2. Which argument(s) for online education seem most compelling? Which seem weakest? On balance, do you think online or virtual learning for K-12 students is a good idea or not? Examine your thinking.
3. Do you know anyone who has enrolled in a virtual K-12 school? If so, what was his or her experience? Comment on the examples of Noah Schnacky and his sister Allison that the writers provide at the beginning and end of the article. What purpose do these examples serve?
4. It may be financially sound to adopt online learning, as various states—Colorado, Georgia, Florida, Idaho and others—have done, but is it a better way to educate students than the traditional classroom? Test scores for online

students are apparently lower, but is this the only measure of academic success?

5. The graphic material showing test scores reveals particularly low writing scores for online students. What might be the reason for this?

6. Assume that you are in favor of online learning for elementary and high school students. What restrictions would you put on a system should it be adopted in your community?

H. TOPICS FOR WRITING

1. Write a summary of this article, being sure to include the most important arguments for and against online learning for K-12 students. The article is 2400 words in length, so your summary should be 300–400 words long.

2. Write an essay in which you argue for or against online education for elementary and high school students. You may use the arguments embedded in the article, but you may also use your own arguments as well as material from your own observations and experience.

3. If you have ever taken an online college class, write about that experience. What was the subject? How was the class conducted? What did the online material consist of? Did you learn as much or more than you would have in a traditional classroom? What is your final estimation of the process?

4. Read the comments, following the directions in Explore the Web below. Then write a short essay summarizing the remarks both for and against online education. Which side engendered more comments? Which side was more persuasive?

EXPLORE THE WEB

- This article engendered numerous comments. You can read the comments online. In the search box, type in this information: "Stephanie Banchero, Stephanie Simon, My Teacher Is an App." The first link provides the article: "Online Education: My Teacher Is an App – WSJ.com." Click on that link and then, under the title, click on "Comments."

JARED DIAMOND

Easter's End

Jared Diamond is currently a professor of geography at UCLA. He began his academic career in physiology, but later expanded his area of interest into evolutionary biology and biogeography, in the course of which he made several trips to New Guinea and the Solomon Islands. His book, Guns, Germs, and Steel: The Fates of Human Societies *(1997), which investigates the role of geography on human societies and their evolution, was awarded the Pulitzer Prize in 1998 in the category of general nonfiction.*

"Easter's End," first published in Discover, *is a thought-provoking essay describing the civilization that flourished on Easter Island (an island that belongs to Chile) in Polynesia. When the culture on Easter Island reached its peak from A.D. 1200 to 1500, it was particularly noteworthy for the hundreds of mysterious and huge stone statues along the coast, called* moai. *But the civilization—including both human and plant life—eventually declined. Diamond offers some hypotheses to explain the reasons for its decline. In telling Easter Island's story, he finds a grim parallel for modern human civilization. An expanded version of this material is included in Diamond's most recent book,* Collapse: How Societies Choose to Fail or Succeed *(2005).*

Vocabulary Analysis

WORD PARTS

The prefix *extra-* In English, many compound words are formed with the prefix *extra-*, meaning "outside" or "beyond." The word *extraterrestrial* describes an inhabitant of another world, a combination of the prefix and *terra*, the Latin root for "earth." Other words beginning with this prefix are *extraordinary*, *extramarital*, *extracurricular*, and *extrasensory*.

WORD FAMILIES

revive In selections 1 and 15 you were introduced to the prefix *re-*, meaning "again," and the root *vivere*, meaning "to live." *Revive* (paragraph 4) combines these two word parts to form a verb meaning "to bring back to life." This verb and the noun *vita* ("life") have given rise to other words in this linguistic family, among them: *vital* (essential for life), *vitamin* (an essential food element), *revitalize* (to give new life to), and *vivacious* (full of life and spirit).

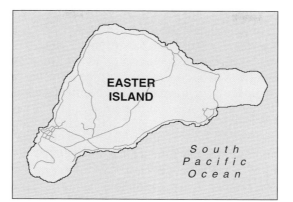

Mysterious statues, called *moai*, on Easter Island.

JARED DIAMOND

Easter's End

1 Among the most riveting mysteries of human history are those posed by vanished civilizations. Everyone who has seen the abandoned buildings of the Khmer, the Maya, or the Anasazi is immediately moved to ask the same question: Why did the societies that erected those structures disappear?

2 Their vanishing touches us as the disappearance of other animals, even the dinosaurs, never can. No matter how exotic those lost civilizations seem, their framers were humans like us. Who is to say we won't succumb to the same fate? Perhaps someday New York's skyscrapers will stand derelict and overgrown with vegetation, like the temples at Angkor Wat and Tikal.

3   Among all such vanished civilizations, that of the former Polynesian society on Easter Island remains unsurpassed in mystery and isolation. The mystery stems especially from the island's gigantic stone statues and its impoverished landscape, but it is enhanced by our associations with the specific people involved: Polynesians represent for us the ultimate in exotic romance, the background for many a child's and an adult's vision of paradise. My own interest in Easter was kindled over 30 years ago when I read Thor Heyerdahl's fabulous accounts of his *Kon-Tiki* voyage.

4   But my interest has been revived recently by a much more exciting account, one not of heroic voyages but of painstaking research and analysis. My friend David Steadman, a paleontologist, has been working with a number of other researchers who are carrying out the first systematic excavations on Easter intended to identify the animals and plants that once lived there. Their work is contributing to a new interpretation of the island's history that makes it a tale not only of wonder but of warning as well.

5   Easter Island, with an area of only 64 square miles, is the world's most isolated scrap of habitable land. It lies in the Pacific Ocean more than 2,000 miles west of the nearest continent (South America), 1,400 miles from even the nearest habitable island (Pitcairn). Its subtropical location and latitude—at 27 degrees south, it is approximately as far below the equator as Houston is north of it—help give it a rather mild climate, while its volcanic origins make its soil fertile. In theory, this combination of blessings should have made Easter a miniature paradise, remote from problems that beset the rest of the world.

6   The island derives its name from its "discovery" by the Dutch explorer Jacob Roggeveen, on Easter (April 5) in 1722. Roggeveen's first impression was not of a paradise but of a wasteland: "We originally, from a further distance, have considered the said Easter Island as sandy; the reason for that is this, that we counted as sand the withered grass, hay, or other scorched and burnt vegetation, because its wasted appearance could give no other impression than of a singular poverty and barrenness."

7   The island Roggeveen saw was a grassland without a single tree or bush over ten feet high. Modern botanists have identified only 47 species of higher plants native to Easter, most of them grasses, sedges, and ferns. The list includes just two species of small trees and two of woody shrubs. With such flora,[1] the islanders Roggeveen encountered had no source of real firewood to warm themselves during Easter's cool, wet, windy winters. Their native animals included nothing larger than insects, not even a single species of native bat, land bird, land snail, or lizard. For domestic animals, they had only chickens.

8   European visitors throughout the eighteenth and early nineteenth centuries estimated Easter's human population at about 2,000, a modest number considering the island's fertility. As Captain James Cook recognized during his brief visit in 1774, the islanders were Polynesians (a Tahitian man accompanying Cook was able to converse with them). Yet despite the Polynesians' well-deserved fame as a great seafaring people, the Easter Islanders who came out to Roggeveen's and Cook's ships did so by swimming or paddling canoes that Roggeveen described

---

[1] Plants as a group; often used with *fauna*, or animals as a group. (Ed.)

as "bad and frail." Their craft, he wrote, were "put together with manifold small planks and light inner timbers, which they cleverly stitched together with very fine twisted threads. . . . But as they lack the knowledge and particularly the materials for caulking and making tight the great number of seams of the canoes, these are accordingly very leaky, for which reason they are compelled to spend half the time in bailing." The canoes, only ten feet long, held at most two people, and only three or four canoes were observed on the entire island.

9   With such flimsy craft, Polynesians could never have colonized Easter from even the nearest island, nor could they have traveled far offshore to fish. The islanders Roggeveen met were totally isolated, unaware that other people existed. Investigators in all the years since his visit have discovered no trace of the islanders' having any outside contacts: not a single Easter Island rock or product has turned up elsewhere, nor has anything been found on the island that could have been brought by anyone other than the original settlers or the Europeans. Yet the people living on Easter claimed memories of visiting the uninhabited Sala y Gomez reef 260 miles away, far beyond the range of the leaky canoes seen by Roggeveen. How did the islanders' ancestors reach that reef from Easter, or reach Easter from anywhere else?

10   Easter Island's most famous feature is its huge stone statues, more than 200 of which once stood on massive stone platforms lining the coast. At least 700 more, in all stages of completion, were abandoned in quarries or on ancient roads between the quarries and the coast, as if the carvers and moving crews had thrown down their tools and walked off the job. Most of the erected statues were carved in a single quarry and then somehow transported as far as six miles— despite heights as great as 33 feet and weights up to 82 tons. The abandoned statues, meanwhile, were as much as 65 feet tall and weighed up to 270 tons. The stone platforms were equally gigantic: up to 500 feet long and 10 feet high, with facing slabs weighing up to 10 tons.

11   Roggeveen himself quickly recognized the problem the statues posed: "The stone images at first caused us to be struck with astonishment," he wrote, "because we could not comprehend how it was possible that these people, who are devoid of heavy thick timber for making any machines, as well as strong ropes, nevertheless had been able to erect such images." Roggeveen might have added that the islanders had no wheels, no draft animals, and no source of power except their own muscles. How did they transport the giant statues for miles, even before erecting them? To deepen the mystery, the statues were still standing in 1770, but by 1864 all of them had been pulled down, by the islanders themselves. Why then did they carve them in the first place? And why did they stop?

12   The statues imply a society very different from the one Roggeveen saw in 1722. Their sheer number and size suggest a population much larger than 2,000 people. What became of everyone? Furthermore, that society must have been highly organized. Easter's resources were scattered across the island: the best stone for the statues was quarried at Rano Raraku near Easter's northeast end; red stone, used for large crowns adorning some of the statues, was quarried at Puna Pau, inland in the southwest; stone carving tools came mostly from Aroi in the northwest. Meanwhile, the best farmland lay in the south and east, and the

best fishing grounds on the north and west coasts. Extracting and redistributing all those goods required complex political organization. What happened to that organization, and how could it ever have arisen in such a barren landscape?

13   Easter Island's mysteries have spawned volumes of speculation for more than two and a half centuries. Many Europeans were incredulous that Polynesians—commonly characterized as "mere savages"—could have created the statues or the beautifully constructed stone platforms. In the 1950s, Heyerdahl argued that Polynesia must have been settled by advanced societies of American Indians, who in turn must have received civilization across the Atlantic from more advanced societies of the Old World. Heyerdahl's raft voyages aimed to prove the feasibility of such prehistoric transoceanic contacts. In the 1960s the Swiss writer Erich von Däniken, an ardent believer in Earth visits by extraterrestrial astronauts, went further, claiming that Easter's statues were the work of intelligent beings who owned ultramodern tools, became stranded on Easter, and were finally rescued.

14   Heyerdahl and Von Däniken both brushed aside overwhelming evidence that the Easter Islanders were typical Polynesians derived from Asia rather than from the Americas and that their culture (including their statues) grew out of Polynesian culture. Their language was Polynesian, as Cook had already concluded. Specifically, they spoke an eastern Polynesian dialect related to Hawaiian and Marquesan, a dialect isolated since about A.D. 400, as estimated from slight differences in vocabulary. Their fishhooks and stone adzes resembled early Marquesan models. Last year DNA extracted from 12 Easter Island skeletons was also shown to be Polynesian. The islanders grew bananas, taro, sweet potatoes, sugarcane, and paper mulberry—typical Polynesian crops, mostly of Southeast Asian origin. Their sole domestic animal, the chicken, was also typically Polynesian and ultimately Asian, as were the rats that arrived as stowaways in the canoes of the first settlers.

15   What happened to those settlers? The fanciful theories of the past must give way to evidence gathered by hardworking practitioners in three fields: archeology, pollen analysis, and paleontology.

16   Modern archeological excavations on Easter have continued since Heyerdahl's 1955 expedition. The earliest radiocarbon dates associated with human activities are around A.D. 400 to 700, in reasonable agreement with the approximate settlement date of 400 estimated by linguists. The period of statue construction peaked around 1200 to 1500, with few if any statues erected thereafter. Densities of archeological sites suggest a large population; an estimate of 7,000 people is widely quoted by archeologists, but other estimates range up to 20,000, which does not seem implausible for an island of Easter's area and fertility.

17   Archeologists have also enlisted surviving islanders in experiments aimed at figuring out how the statues might have been carved and erected. Twenty people, using only stone chisels, could have carved even the largest completed statue within a year. Given enough timber and fiber for making ropes, teams of at most a few hundred people could have loaded the statues onto wooden sleds, dragged them over lubricated wooden tracks or rollers, and used logs as levers to maneuver them into a standing position. Rope could have been made from

the fiber of a small native tree, related to the linden, called the hauhau. However, that tree is now extremely scarce on Easter, and hauling one statue would have required hundreds of yards of rope. Did Easter's now barren landscape once support the necessary trees?

18   That question can be answered by the technique of pollen analysis, which involves boring out a column of sediment from a swamp or pond, with the most recent deposits at the top and relatively more ancient deposits at the bottom. The absolute age of each layer can be dated by radiocarbon methods. Then begins the hard work: examining tens of thousands of pollen grains under a microscope, counting them, and identifying the plant species that produced each one by comparing the grains with modern pollen from known plant species. For Easter Island, the bleary-eyed scientists who performed that task were John Flenley, now at Massey University in New Zealand, and Sarah King of the University of Hull in England.

19   Flenley and King's heroic efforts were rewarded by the striking new picture that emerged of Easter's prehistoric landscape. For at least 30,000 years before human arrival and during the early years of Polynesian settlement, Easter was not a wasteland at all. Instead, a subtropical forest of trees and woody bushes towered over a ground layer of shrubs, herbs, ferns, and grasses. In the forest grew tree daisies, the rope-yielding hauhau tree, and the toromiro tree, which furnishes a dense, mesquite-like firewood. The most common tree in the forest was a species of palm now absent on Easter but formerly so abundant that the bottom strata of the sediment column were packed with its pollen. The Easter Island palm was closely related to the still-surviving Chilean wine palm, which grows up to 82 feet tall and 6 feet in diameter. The tall, unbranched trunks of the Easter Island palm would have been ideal for transporting and erecting statues and constructing large canoes. The palm would also have been a valuable food source, since its Chilean relative yields edible nuts as well as sap from which Chileans make sugar, syrup, honey, and wine.

20   What did the first settlers of Easter Island eat when they were not glutting themselves on the local equivalent of maple syrup? Recent excavations by David Steadman, of the New York State Museum at Albany, have yielded a picture of Easter's original animal world as surprising as Flenley and King's picture of its plant world. Steadman's expectations for Easter were conditioned by his experiences elsewhere in Polynesia, where fish are overwhelmingly the main food at archeological sites, typically accounting for more than 90 percent of the bones in ancient Polynesian garbage heaps. Easter, though, is too cool for the coral reefs beloved by fish, and its cliff-girded coastline permits shallow-water fishing in only a few places. Less than a quarter of the bones in its early garbage heaps (from the period 900 to 1300) belonged to fish; instead, nearly one-third of all bones came from porpoises.

21   Nowhere else in Polynesia do porpoises account for even 1 percent of discarded food bones. But most other Polynesian islands offered animal food in the form of birds and mammals, such as New Zealand's now extinct giant moas and Hawaii's now extinct flightless geese. Most other islanders also had domestic pigs and dogs. On Easter, porpoises would have been the largest animal available—other than humans. The porpoise species identified at Easter, the common

dolphin, weighs up to 165 pounds. It generally lives out at sea, so it could not have been hunted by line fishing or spearfishing from shore. Instead, it must have been harpooned far offshore, in big seaworthy canoes built from the extinct palm tree.

22 In addition to porpoise meat, Steadman found, the early Polynesian settlers were feasting on seabirds. For those birds, Easter's remoteness and lack of predators made it an ideal haven as a breeding site, at least until humans arrived. Among the prodigious numbers of seabirds that bred on Easter were albatross, boobies, frigate birds, fulmars, petrels, prions, shearwaters, storm petrels, terns, and tropic birds. With at least 25 nesting species, Easter was the richest seabird breeding site in Polynesia and probably in the whole Pacific.

23 Land birds as well went into early Easter Island cooking pots. Steadman identified bones of at least six species, including barn owls, herons, parrots, and rail. Bird stew would have been seasoned with meat from large numbers of rats, which the Polynesian colonists inadvertently brought with them; Easter Island is the sole known Polynesian island where rat bones outnumber fish bones at archeological sites. (In case you're squeamish and consider rats inedible, I still recall recipes for creamed laboratory rat that my British biologist friends used to supplement their diet during their years of wartime food rationing.)

24 Porpoises, seabirds, land birds, and rats did not complete the list of meat sources formerly available on Easter. A few bones hint at the possibility of breeding seal colonies as well. All these delicacies were cooked in ovens fired by wood from the island's forests.

25 Such evidence lets us imagine the island onto which Easter's first Polynesian colonists stepped ashore some 1,600 years ago, after a long canoe voyage from eastern Polynesia. They found themselves in a pristine paradise. What then happened to it? The pollen grains and the bones yield a grim answer.

26 Pollen records show that destruction of Easter's forests was well under way by the year 800, just a few centuries after the start of human settlement. Then charcoal from wood fires came to fill the sediment cores, while pollen of palms and other trees and woody shrubs decreased or disappeared, and pollen of the grasses that replaced the forest became more abundant. Not long after 1400 the palm finally became extinct, not only as a result of being chopped down but also because the now ubiquitous rats prevented its regeneration: of the dozens of preserved palm nuts discovered in caves on Easter, all had been chewed by rats and could no longer germinate. While the hauhau tree did not become extinct in Polynesian times, its numbers declined drastically until there weren't enough left to make ropes from. By the time Heyerdahl visited Easter, only a single, nearly dead toromiro tree remained on the island, and even that lone survivor has now disappeared. (Fortunately, the toromiro still grows in botanical gardens elsewhere.)

27 The fifteenth century marked the end not only for Easter's palm but for the forest itself. Its doom had been approaching as people cleared land to plant gardens; as they felled trees to build canoes, to transport and erect statues, and to burn; as rats devoured seeds; and probably as the native birds died out that had pollinated the trees' flowers and dispersed their fruit. The overall picture is

among the most extreme examples of forest destruction anywhere in the world: the whole forest gone, and most of its tree species extinct.

28   The destruction of the island's animals was as extreme as that of the forest: without exception, every species of native land bird became extinct. Even shellfish were overexploited, until people had to settle for small sea snails instead of larger cowries. Porpoise bones disappeared abruptly from garbage heaps around 1500; no one could harpoon porpoises anymore, since the trees used for constructing the big seagoing canoes no longer existed. The colonies of more than half of the seabird species breeding on Easter or on its offshore islets were wiped out.

29   In place of these meat supplies, the Easter Islanders intensified their production of chickens, which had been only an occasional food item. They also turned to the largest remaining meat source available: humans, whose bones became common in late Easter Island garbage heaps. Oral traditions of the islanders are rife with cannibalism; the most inflammatory taunt that could be snarled at an enemy was "The flesh of your mother sticks between my teeth." With no wood available to cook these new goodies, the islanders resorted to sugarcane scraps, grass, and sedges to fuel their fires.

30   All these strands of evidence can be wound into a coherent narrative of a society's decline and fall. The first Polynesian colonists found themselves on an island with fertile soil, abundant food, bountiful building materials, ample lebensraum,[2] and all the prerequisites for comfortable living. They prospered and multiplied.

31   After a few centuries, they began erecting stone statues on platforms, like the ones their Polynesian forebears had carved. With passing years, the statues and platforms became larger and larger, and the statues began sporting ten-ton red crowns—probably in an escalating spiral of one-upmanship, as rival clans tried to surpass each other with shows of wealth and power. (In the same way, successive Egyptian pharaohs built ever-larger pyramids. Today Hollywood movie moguls near my home in Los Angeles are displaying their wealth and power by building ever more ostentatious mansions. Tycoon Marvin Davis topped previous moguls with plans for a 50,000-square-foot house, so now Aaron Spelling has topped Davis with a 56,000-square-foot house. All that those buildings lack to make the message explicit are ten-ton red crowns.) On Easter, as in modern America, society was held together by a complex political system to redistribute locally available resources and to integrate the economies of different areas.

32   Eventually Easter's growing population was cutting the forest more rapidly than the forest was regenerating. The people used the land for gardens and the wood for fuel, canoes, and houses—and, of course, for lugging statues. As forest disappeared, the islanders ran out of timber and rope to transport and erect their statues. Life became more uncomfortable—springs and streams dried up, and wood was no longer available for fires.

33   People also found it harder to fill their stomachs, as land birds, large sea snails, and many seabirds disappeared. Because timber for building seagoing canoes vanished, fish catches declined and porpoises disappeared from the table. Crop yields also declined, since deforestation allowed the soil to be eroded by rain and wind, dried by the sun, and its nutrients to be leeched from

---

[2] German word meaning "living space." (Ed.)

it. Intensified chicken production and cannibalism replaced only part of all those lost foods. Preserved statuettes with sunken cheeks and visible ribs suggest that people were starving.

34   With the disappearance of food surpluses, Easter Island could no longer feed the chiefs, bureaucrats, and priests who had kept a complex society running. Surviving islanders described to early European visitors how local chaos replaced centralized government and a warrior class took over from the hereditary chiefs. The stone points of spears and daggers, made by the warriors during their heyday in the 1600s and 1700s, still litter the ground of Easter today. By around 1700, the population began to crash toward between one-quarter and one-tenth of its former number. People took to living in caves for protection against their enemies. Around 1770 rival clans started to topple each other's statues, breaking the heads off. By 1864 the last statue had been thrown down and desecrated.

35   As we try to imagine the decline of Easter's civilization, we ask ourselves, "Why didn't they look around, realize what they were doing, and stop before it was too late? What were they thinking when they cut down the last palm tree?"

36   I suspect, though, that the disaster happened not with a bang but with a whimper. After all, there are those hundreds of abandoned statues to consider. The forest the islanders depended on for rollers and rope didn't simply disappear one day—it vanished slowly, over decades. Perhaps war interrupted the moving teams; perhaps by the time the carvers had finished their work, the last rope snapped. In the meantime, any islander who tried to warn about the dangers of progressive deforestation would have been overridden by vested interests of carvers, bureaucrats, and chiefs, whose jobs depended on continued deforestation. Our Pacific Northwest loggers are only the latest in a long line of loggers to cry, "Jobs over trees!" The changes in forest cover from year to year would have been hard to detect: yes, this year we cleared those woods over there, but trees are starting to grow back again on this abandoned garden site here. Only older people, recollecting their childhoods decades earlier, could have recognized a difference. Their children could no more have comprehended their parents' tales than my eight-year-old sons today can comprehend my wife's and my tales of what Los Angeles was like 30 years ago.

37   Gradually trees became fewer, smaller, and less important. By the time the last fruit-bearing adult palm tree was cut, palms had long since ceased to be of economic significance. That left only smaller and smaller palm saplings to clear each year, along with other bushes and treelets. No one would have noticed the felling of the last small palm.

38   By now the meaning of Easter Island for us should be chillingly obvious. Easter Island is Earth writ small. Today, again, a rising population confronts shrinking resources. We too have no emigration valve, because all human societies are linked by international transport, and we can no more escape into space than the Easter Islanders could flee into the ocean. If we continue to follow our present course, we shall have exhausted the world's major fisheries, tropical rain forests, fossil fuels, and much of our soil by the time my sons reach my current age.

39   Every day newspapers report details of famished countries—Afghanistan, Liberia, Rwanda, Sierra Leone, Somalia, the former Yugoslavia, Zaire—where

soldiers have appropriated the wealth or where central government is yielding to local gangs of thugs. With the risk of nuclear war receding, the threat of our ending with a bang no longer has a chance of galvanizing us to halt our course. Our risk now is of winding down, slowly, in a whimper. Corrective action is blocked by vested interests, by well-intentioned political and business leaders, and by their electorates, all of whom are perfectly correct in not noticing big changes from year to year. Instead, each year there are just somewhat more people, and somewhat fewer resources, on Earth.

40 It would be easy to close our eyes or to give up in despair. If mere thousands of Easter Islanders with only stone tools and their own muscle power sufficed to destroy their society, how can billions of people with metal tools and machine power fail to do worse? But there is one crucial difference. The Easter Islanders had no books and no histories of other doomed societies. Unlike the Easter Islanders, we have histories of the past—information that can save us. My main hope for my sons' generation is that we may now choose to learn from the fates of societies like Easter's.

Jared Diamond, "Easter's End," *Discover*, August 1995. Copyright © 1995 by Jared Diamond. Reprinted with permission of the author.

Exercises

Do not refer to the selection for Exercises A and B unless your instructor directs you to do so.

A. DETERMINING THE MAIN IDEA AND WRITER'S PURPOSE

Choose the best answer.

_____ **1.** The main idea of the selection is that, among all vanished civilizations, the former Polynesian society on Easter Island remains unsurpassed in mystery and isolation, and it
   a. sparks our imagination and interest in other remote and vanished civilizations.
   b. offers paleontologists a place to conduct research to identify the plants and animals that once flourished there.
   c. is the world's most isolated scrap of habitable land.
   d. recently offered us a new interpretation of the island's history that parallels the dangers confronting modern civilization.

_____ **2.** The author's purpose is to
   a. warn us that the disaster and chaos that befell Easter Island could happen to us.
   b. trace the history of human civilization on Easter Island.
   c. describe the statues on Easter Island and explain how they were built and erected.
   d. show the painstaking work and important scientific contribution that paleontologists add to the world's store of knowledge.

B. COMPREHENDING MAIN IDEAS

Choose the correct answer.

_____ 1.   Which geographical characteristics of Easter Island's should have made it a "miniature paradise, remote from problems that beset the rest of the world"?
   a. Its fertile soil and ample water supply.
   b. Its remoteness, fertile soil, and mild climate.
   c. Its industrious population and position as a regional trading center.
   d. Its bountiful food supply and convenient location for nearby islands.

_____ 2.   When the Dutch explorer Jacob Roggeveen arrived on Easter Island in 1722, he found
   a. a paradise.
   b. densely forested land.
   c. well-tended, productive farm plots.
   d. a wasteland.

3.   What was the biggest mystery surrounding the huge stone statutes lining Easter Island's coastline?

   _____

_____ 4.   Researchers in archeology, pollen analysis, and paleontology excavating Easter Island have found that it had, in fact,
   a. been barren for years, thus deepening the mystery.
   b. at one time been extensively forested with various kinds of trees.
   c. been colonized by advanced societies of American Indians.
   d. contained plants and animals never identified or associated with any other Polynesian island.

5.   The Easter Islanders whom explorers encountered in the 1700s paddled frail, rickety canoes rather than large, sturdy seagoing canoes that other Polynesian islanders constructed. Why were the Easter Islanders' canoes of such poor quality?

   _____

_____ 6.   Diamond speculates that Easter's civilization declined
   a. so slowly that the residents didn't realize from generation to generation what was really happening.
   b. very quickly, wiped out by a combination of unfortunate and cataclysmic events.
   c. despite the residents' best efforts to regenerate it.
   d. in the same fashion and for the same reasons that all the other civilizations in Polynesia declined.

COMPREHENSION SCORE

Score your answers for Exercises A and B as follows:

A. No. right _____ × 2 = _____

B. No. right _____ × 1 = _____

Total points from A and B _____ × 10 = _____ percent

You may refer to the selection as you work through the remaining exercises.

C. DISTINGUISHING BETWEEN MAIN IDEAS AND SUPPORTING DETAILS

The following sentences come from paragraphs 27 and 28. Label them as follows: MI if the sentence represents a *main idea* and SD if the sentence represents a *supporting detail*.

1. _____ The fifteenth century marked the end not only for Easter's palm but for the forest itself.

2. _____ Its doom had been approaching as people cleared land to plant gardens; as they felled trees to build canoes, to transport and erect statues, and to burn; as rats devoured seeds; and probably as the native birds died out that had pollinated the trees' flowers and dispersed their fruit.

3. _____ The overall picture is among the most extreme examples of forest destruction anywhere in the world: the whole forest gone, and most of its tree species extinct.

4. _____ The destruction of the island's animals was as extreme as that of the forest: without exception, every species of native land bird became extinct.

5. _____ Even shellfish were overexploited, until people had to settle for small sea snails instead of larger cowries.

6. _____ Porpoise bones disappeared abruptly from garbage heaps around 1500; no one could harpoon porpoises anymore, since the trees used for constructing the big seagoing canoes no longer existed.

D. DRAWING CONCLUSIONS

Place an X beside each statement that represents a reasonable conclusion you can draw from this selection.

1. _____ The most serious threat to our survival lies in overpopulation.

2. _____ Reconstructing the civilization on Easter Island and the reasons for its decline would not have been possible without the research done by paleontologists and biologists.

3. _____   Those Easter Islanders who tried to warn the younger generation about their harmful practices were dismissed as eccentrics or doomsayers.

4. _____   The people who inhabit Easter Island today are making every attempt to recapture its past glory.

5. _____   It is not within our power to change the course of civilization; cultures are born, flourish, and die, just as all life on earth does, and human intervention in a society's evolution is futile.

6. _____   Written records—the mark of literate societies—are a better way of preserving descriptions of an area's landscape than are oral tales handed down from generation to generation.

7. _____   Despite the technological advancements that our civilization has produced, it is likely that Earth in the future—with its billions of people and dwindling resources—could succumb to the same fate that befell the Easter Islanders.

E. INTERPRETING MEANING

Where appropriate, write your answers for these questions in your own words.

1. _____   Which of the following would be a good title for paragraph 3?
   a. "Mysterious Stone Statues"
   b. "Easter Island: A Place of Exotic Romance"
   c. "Easter Island: A Vanished Civilization of Mystery and Isolation"
   d. "Polynesian Paradise"

2. Describe the kinds of evidence that Diamond uses to reinforce his theory that Easter Island, at one time, was a fertile, productive island, capable of sustaining life. _____

3. In paragraph 36, what words and phrases show us that Diamond's ideas are hypothetical and not factual?_____

_____

4. Find the quotation and identify the number of the paragraph that represents the *single* most important reason Diamond cites to explain Easter Island's demise. _____

5. Look again at almost any of the paragraphs throughout the body of the article and determine what they have in common structurally. _____

_____

6. _____   Which of the following best describes Diamond's tone, or emotional attitude, toward his subject in this piece?
   a. neutral, informative, objective
   b. somber, concerned, and admonishing

    c. philosophical, reflective, and pensive

    d. provocative, shrill, inflammatory

F. UNDERSTANDING VOCABULARY

Look through the paragraphs listed by number in brackets and find a word that matches each definition. Refer to a dictionary if necessary. An example has been done for you.

Ex. suitable for living [paragraphs 4–5]   *habitable*

1. many and varied [8–9]   _____

2. completely lacking, without [10–11—phrase]   _____

3. skeptical, disbelieving [12–13]   _____

4. practicability, likelihood [12–13]   _____

5. passionate, enthusiastic [12–13]   _____

6. horizontal layers, bands, or beds [18–19]   _____

7. easily sickened or disgusted [22–23]   _____

8. immense, huge [22–23]   _____

9. untouched, unspoiled [25–26]   _____

10. grandiose, pretentiously showy [30–31]   _____

G. PARAPHRASING AND SUMMARIZING EXERCISE

1. Paraphrase these sentences from paragraph 38.

By now the meaning of Easter Island for us should be chillingly obvious. Easter Island is Earth writ small. Today, again, a rising population confronts shrinking resources. _____

_____

2. Paragraph 36 is one of the most moving passages in the article. Summarize it in 25 to 30 words. _____

_____

_____

EXPLORE THE WEB

- Information about Easter Island is available online. Easter Island's home page includes several links. In the search box type in "Easter Island Home Page." Here is another site that lists four topics for further exploration of the subject—The Story, Island Tour, Controversies, and Easter Island Books and Travel Info.

    www.mysteriousplaces.com/Easter_Island.html

PART FIVE

Reading about Issues

Persuasive Writing and Opinion Pieces

In this introductory section, you will learn about these topics:

- The principles of persuasive writing
- The aims of persuasive writing
- How to read persuasive writing
- Types of claims
- Kinds of evidence
- The refutation
- The structure of an argument
- Bias

The Principles of Persuasive Writing

As you will recall from the introduction to Part One, to *persuade* is one of the primary purposes of nonfiction prose. The art of persuasion is a worthwhile skill to develop. Consider its usefulness in practical terms. Let's say that you have been working at your current part-time job for a year, you think you have done a good job, you take on new responsibilities willingly and without complaint, you arrive on time, and you don't fool around on the job. But your boss has never given you a raise. How would you approach your boss to ask for a higher salary? And what reasons would you give to support your request?

You would certainly wait to make sure that he or she was in a good mood and not stressed out about meeting deadlines or dealing with grumpy customers. You might point to your fine qualities listed above. You would mention your loyalty, your dedication to the job, and other stellar traits. And if you were lucky, you might succeed in getting that raise. This real-life example shows that understanding the tactics of persuasion can yield tangible rewards.

Learning to read persuasive prose with understanding and a critical eye also yields rewards. It is the basis on which our democratic society is built. A significant part of being a good citizen is learning about the issues of the day, weighing the arguments for and against proposed policies, and coming to a decision on your own, not one imposed by someone else. The right to make an informed decision on one's own is one of many rewards of living in a democratic country with a free press and the freedom to express oneself without fear of punishment, retaliation, or censorship, as occurs in repressive societies or in dictatorships. In sum, learning to see issues from a variety of perspectives, not merely from one person's (or our own) point of view, is an important part of becoming an educated citizen.

The Aims of Persuasive Writing

Persuasive writing essentially aims to convince you in various ways of something. A person may try to convince you to accept his or her point of view. Politicians do this all the time, when they try to persuade us that they are the best candidate for public office. Someone may try to persuade us to change our behavior—for example, to get us to exercise more, to stop smoking, to get better grades, to protest against the war in Iraq, to volunteer to work in a soup kitchen—or simply to consider that another point of view has merit. All of these are common aims of persuasion and of persuasive writing as well.

AIMS OF PERSUASIVE WRITING

- To convince you to accept a particular point of view
- To convince you to change your thinking
- To convince you to take action
- To convince you to at least consider that another point of view has merit

---

What follows is a brief discussion of the component parts of opinion pieces, typically found on the op-ed pages of newspapers, in magazines, on websites, or in blogs. This discussion is followed by a practice editorial that I have annotated to show you how an experienced reader might read and analyze an opinion piece. Part Five concludes with 5 pieces of persuasive writing from print and online sources. The pieces take up some issues that I hope you will find interesting and provocative and worth considering. All relate to the future of our society and our way of life: the value of a college education, the decline in morality among the young, a subtle yet damaging and troubling form of racial discrimination, unruly sports fans and hooliganism, and the dwindling possibility of achieving the American dream.

How to Read Persuasive Writing

When you read the opinion pieces in this text and in other sources like your daily newspaper, first you decide on the aim of the article or opinion piece. By definition, persuasive writing presents a controversial issue that is open to discussion. Also by definition, a persuasive piece presents the writer's subjective opinions. But there is wide latitude in what persuasive writers do: Some writers present two or even three points of view and leave you to make up your own mind about where you stand. Other writers present only one side, an obvious attempt to change your mind or to get you to adopt their position. Still other writers may resort to bias, slanted language, emotional appeals, and other manipulative devices.

Whichever technique the opinion writer uses, the most important step—and your starting point—is to determine his or her central *argument*, also called the *claim*—the proposition or idea to be backed up and defended—that lies at the heart of the piece. Like the thesis statement in an informative or expository essay (discussed in Part One), the claim or argument in a persuasive piece may be *stated* directly or implied. Those who study argumentation classify claims into three types: *claims of fact*, *claims of value*, and *claims of policy*. Study the explanations and examples that follow.

Types of Claims

Claims of fact can be verified, measured, tested, and proved by citing factual evidence, the results of scientific research, or in the case of predictions, by the passage of time. *Claims of value* involve matters of taste, morality, opinion, and ideas about right and wrong, and because of this, they are harder to prove than are claims of fact. The support for a claim of value is usually in the form of reasons, examples, reference to a book of rules or other work (such as the Bible, the Koran, or the Constitution), and personal experience. *Claims of policy* argue for a recommended course of action, propose a change or a new policy, or identify a problem that needs a solution. Note that claims of policy may include a word like "should," "must," or "ought to." They are typically supported by good reasons, facts and statistics, examples, or the testimony of authorities or experts. Study the examples in these three charts so that you can practice distinguishing among them.

CLAIMS OF FACT
• Smoking causes numerous health problems for long-term smokers.
• Genetically modified crops will help feed Third World nations.
• The Boston Patriots will win the Super Bowl again.

CLAIMS OF VALUE
• Community colleges offer students a good education at relatively little cost.
• Broccoli tastes better than spinach.
• *Juno* is an intriguing, engaging movie about a serious subject—a teenage girl's unwanted pregnancy and the decision she makes.

CLAIMS OF POLICY
• Because of overcrowded classes, Centerville Community College should raise its tuition so that more teachers can be hired.
• Elementary schools must do their part to discourage obesity in the nation's children by removing candy and soft drink machines from campuses.
• High schools ought to require students to complete a course in consumer economics before they graduate.

One area of environmental concern is the problem of plastic water bottles in the nation's landfills. The exercise that follows presents several claims relating to this issue of proliferating water bottles. Study them and then in the space provided write whether it represents a claim of fact, a claim of value, or a claim of policy.

1. _____ Bisphenol A (BPA), a compound in hard, clear plastics, should be banned from containers such as baby bottles and water bottles.

2. _____ The drinking water in metropolitan areas like New York City and the San Francisco Bay Area tastes just as good as, if not better than, the water you buy in plastic bottles like Evian, Calistoga, Dasani, or Crystal Geyser.

3. _____ BPA is a potentially harmful chemical found in hard, clear plastic water bottles that has been associated with some types of cancer and with early onset of puberty.[1]

4. _____ Discarded plastic water bottles pose a serious problem because they clog our nation's landfills.

5. _____ Municipalities should encourage people to give up drinking water from plastic bottles by installing public drinking fountains on city sidewalks.

6. _____ Portland, Oregon, is one city that has installed drinking fountains on city sidewalks, and because many of them were designed by artists, they are not only useful but also aesthetically pleasing.

Kinds of Evidence

After you have located the writer's argument or claim in an opinion piece, then you can identify and evaluate the *evidence* used to support it. Writers of opinion pieces may use a single kind of evidence, or they may combine various kinds. Here are the most common: facts and statistics, which may derive from scientific studies, research reports, government-sponsored investigations or surveys, census reports, clinical tests, and so forth; examples and observations from the writer's experience or from reading; rational, plausible explanations (good reasons) that answer the question "why?"; and finally, quotation or testimony from authorities and experts in a particular field. This chart summarizes each kind:

KINDS OF EVIDENCE USED IN PERSUASIVE WRITING
• **Facts and statistics:** From scientific studies and research reports
• **Examples and observations:** From the writer's experience and/or reading
• **Good reasons:** Rational explanations that answer the question "why?"
• **Quotation or testimony:** The opinion of experts

The first step in reading opinion pieces is to locate the *claim* and then identify the *supporting evidence*. Try to separate the two, because some writers mix the claim and the evidence in the same sentence, for example:

Because obesity has become such a serious health risk for our nation's children (the government estimates that 11 percent of American children are obese), our public schools should encourage children to walk or ride their bikes to school and should eliminate candy and snack food machines from school grounds.

---

[1]There is a great deal of information available online about the health effects of bisphenol A. Type in the term in the search box, and you will find many links to reputable scientific studies about this chemical and its dangers.

Which part of the sentence represents the claim and which part represents the evidence? Write the claim in the first space.

Claims: _____

_____

Evidence: _____

_____

The Refutation

The final step in reading persuasive pieces is to look for a *refutation*, wherein the writer deals with the opposing side. Note that many editorial writers do not include a refutation, but if there is one, it might look like this: First the writer *concedes* that there is some merit to the opposing side. (After all, every question has two sides, and often more.) The writer then takes one or two of the opposition's major arguments and *refutes* them, offering counterarguments against them.

An example from real life will help you understand this process better. Let's say that there is a dangerous intersection near campus where some students have been injured while they were trying to cross the street. You get some concerned students and citizens to request a meeting of the municipal transportation and safety board. At the meeting your group explains the problem, gives evidence that the problem is serious, and offers a solution—that is, you present your claim of policy: The intersection needs a stoplight, so someone doesn't get killed.

The safety director counters your proposal by saying that the city's budget is tight, that a new light will cost $100,000, and that the community has more pressing needs to meet. For example, the city has just committed the same amount of money to an after-school program for disadvantaged boys and girls. Hard to argue against that!

Still, you and your fellow students are convinced that your position is right. You prepare your refutation and come up with the following counterarguments:

1. An after-school program for disadvantaged youth is surely a worthy cause (your concession), but the board needs to reexamine its priorities. Saving the lives of students who attend the local college is more important. Also, a stoplight is the city's responsibility; an after-school club is not. It would be more appropriate to seek funding for a club from private grants and charitable foundations. (This is your first counterargument.)

2. Your second counterargument appeals to the board's conscience: If a stoplight isn't installed, more injuries will occur, and someone might die. Although $100,000 might seem like a lot of money for a simple stoplight, it will be money well spent. A human life is more precious than the $100,000 saved by not installing one. How many people must die or be seriously injured before the board decides that a light is necessary?

3. Your third counterargument appeals to the emotions: It's unconscionable that the board is willfully ignoring traffic hazards.

4. Finally, you offer some hard evidence refuting the board's contention that the town doesn't have enough money in its budget for the project: Recently, the local newspaper ran a series of articles criticizing frivolous expenditures at city hall. For example, the mayor redecorated her office at taxpayer expense, buying leather couches, matching chairs, an expensive Persian rug, and installing a bar; she also requisitioned a new limousine. Surely pedestrians' lives are more important than an elegant mayor's office and a fancy car.

Your refutation might work, or it might not, but at least you have dealt with your opponent's primary objections to spending this money.

The refutation or counterargument can take many forms. The writer may agree that there is some merit to the opposition but that the issue is more serious or complicated than the opponent realizes. The writer may argue that the opposing argument is somehow flawed. Finally, and probably most effective, the writer may admonish the opponent by warning of the consequences of not acting. Or the reverse might be appropriate. For example, when George W. Bush and many Republican supporters argued for going to war to remove the Iraqi leader, Saddam Hussein, many writers, scholars, and government officials argued for *not* acting because attacking Iraq would have severe political and economic consequences. This is a good example of a claim of fact that proved to be true by virtue of the passage of time.

When you read persuasive pieces, look for a refutation. The best opinion writers anticipate their opponents' objections and offer a rebuttal.

The Structure of an Argument

An argumentative piece must be clearly organized if the writer is to get the point across effectively and to convince the audience to adopt the particular claim. Most good opinion pieces contain the elements you have examined above—a claim, evidence, and a refutation. How these elements are arranged depends on convention and to some extent on the writer's personal preference. Practicing locating the component parts in opinion pieces is an excellent way to sharpen your thinking skills, and at the same time, to make you more aware of the problems that abound in today's world.

A conventional opinion piece might follow this organizational scheme: The introduction provides background, introduces the subject, and perhaps engages the reader's attention with a meaningful anecdote. The introduction *may* also contain the claim. The body of the opinion piece contains evidence to support or to prove the claim along with a *refutation*, a section (usually quite short) in which the writer considers *opposing views* and offers a counterargument against them. (Note, however, that many writers do not include refutations.) Finally, the conclusion, which also may contain the claim, recommends future action, gives a warning about what will happen if the claim is not accepted, or states the seriousness of the problem. Here, again in chart form, is a summary of the arrangement of elements in opinion pieces.

- **Introduction:** Provides background for the subject and may contain the argument or claim
- **Body:** Contains the evidence—various kinds of material to support or prove the claim
- **Refutation:** Contains opposing views or a counterargument against the claim
- **Conclusion:** May contain the claim; also may recommend future action or give a warning

Not every argument you read will be arranged like this, since some writers prefer to begin with the evidence and end with the claim. Still, these are the elements to look for when you read opinion pieces.

Bias

Last, when you read opinion pieces, look for evidence of *bias*—prejudice or unfair preconceived ideas. Obviously, complete objectivity is humanly impossible, since we are all the products of our environment, ethnic and religious heritage, social class, and the like. Yet a writer should not come across as having an axe to grind— a particular point of view that he or she bludgeons the reader with. Nor should the writer stand to gain (or lose) economically if the reader accepts the argument. For example, if Elizabeth Royte were an artist who designed public water fountains, bias might be evident in her editorial. Since she is not, and since she has written two books on environmental matters pertaining to garbage, you can safely assume that her opinion piece is motivated by environmental concerns, not by her desire to profit personally.

Therefore, you can ask yourself if the writer treats the issue fairly, whether there is sufficient evidence to support the argument, and whether the writer appeals to your sense of reason or to your emotions (or perhaps to both). There is nothing wrong with a writer's appealing to the emotions, as long as you are aware that it is going on.

A Practice Editorial

ELIZABETH ROYTE

A Fountain on Every Corner

Let us consider the issue of plastic water bottles. We see people carrying them everywhere, and though the single water bottle you carry with you to class or to the gym might not seem to constitute a serious problem like war, hunger, the price of gasoline, AIDS, or the melting of the Arctic ice cap and its effects on the polar bear population, the issue is in fact serious. It is aptly illustrated in this photograph:

© Digital Vision/Punchstock

The photo accompanying this article underscores the problem of plastic bottles that end up in landfills. Estimates about the percentage of water bottles recycled range from 28 to 32 percent, a significant increase from the previous edition of this book, but still troubling. You can find a great deal of information online about the cumulative effects of plastic bottles and plastic shopping bags online.

This practice editorial gives you the opportunity to study the structure of a typical opinion piece. Written by Elizabeth Royte and published on the New York Times *editorial page, the editorial examines what New York City is doing to encourage people to abandon their plastic water bottles. Royte is the author of* Garbage Land: On the Secret Trail of Trash *and* Bottlemania: How Water Went on Sale and Why We Bought It *(2005). This information suggests that she is a reliable authority on the subject. I have annotated the piece for you, paragraph by paragraph, pointing out the significant elements.*

1 Establishes background & states claim of policy.

2 A concession—water bottles are convenient. Evidence—the 50 billion bottles have a big economic and environmental impact. Most important reason—tap water tastes good and is free.

1   Water fountain season is here. New York City workers have turned on bubblers in the parks, and the Icelandic artist Olafur Eliasson has begun to erect four enormous waterfalls in the harbor, each 90 to 120 feet high, that are scheduled to flow from July to October. The shimmering cascades will cost the city nothing (the $15 million cost is being paid by private donations to the Public Art Fund), but here's a better idea for a civic-minded organization or person interested in celebrating water: sidewalk fountains in places outside the parks.

2   Convenience is said to be one of bottled water's greatest allures: we're a grab-and-go society, consuming roughly 50 billion bottles of water a year. But as awareness of the product's economic and environmental impact has escalated, mayors across the nation (although not Michael Bloomberg of New York) have canceled city contracts with bottled water purveyors, citing the expense of hauling away empties (less than 20 percent make it into recycling systems); the vast amounts of oil used in producing, transporting and refrigerating the bottles; and the hypocrisy of spending taxpayer dollars on private water while touting the virtues of public supplies. Last summer,

New York City spent $700,000 on a campaign reminding New Yorkers that their tap water is tasty and affordable.

3 Delivered by gravity, tap water generates virtually no waste. All that, and it contains no calories, caffeine or colorants either. (Yes, New York's water—like that of other cities—contains trace amounts of drugs, but we lack proof, so far, that exposure at these low levels is a human health risk.)

4 Bottled water's main virtue, it seems, is convenience, especially for people at large in the city. As the editor of Beverage Digest told The Times, "It's not so easy, walking down Third Avenue on a hot day, to get a glass of tap water."

5 But it needn't be so. Paris has its ornate cast-iron Wallace fountains (donated in the late 19th century by a wealthy philanthropist hoping to steer the homeless from alcohol toward a healthier beverage); Rome its ever-running street spigots; Portland, Ore., its delightful four-bowl Benson Bubblers.

6 In the 1880s, several American cities had "temperance fountains," paid for by the philanthropist (and dentist) Henry D. Cogswell of San Francisco. New York City had six of these, placed at busy corners: "In the brief space of 10 minutes one morning 40 persons were recently observed to stop for a refreshing drink," observed an officer of the New York Association for Improving the Condition of the Poor, which helped place the fountains.

7 Such fountains have largely disappeared (although the temperance fountain in Tompkins Square Park still stands). Today, we've got plenty of bubblers in parks, but Midtown is a Sahara for parched pedestrians, who don't even think of looking for public sources of tap water.

8 An entire generation of Americans has grown up thinking public faucets equal filth, and the only water fit to drink comes in plastic, factory sealed. It's time to change that perception with public fountains in the city's busiest quadrants, pristine bubblers that celebrate the virtues of our public water supply, remind us of our connection to upstate watersheds and reinforce our commitment to clean water for all.

9 On a more practical note: let's make them easy to maintain, with water pressure adequate to fill our reusable bottles. And germophobes, relax: city water is chlorinated, and experts report that pathogens impolitely left on spigots by the lips of preceding drinkers don't creep down into pipes. In other words, the bubbling water is clean, so get over it.

10 Minneapolis recently committed to spending $500,000 on 10 artist-designed fountains that will be placed in areas of high foot and bike traffic. Mayor Gavin Newsom of San Francisco, archenemy of bottled water, is pursuing a similar plan. New York and other cities should swiftly follow suit, if not with fancy fountains then with several dozen off-the-shelf models. Wheelchair-accessible, and vandal- and frost-resistant, they can be had for less than $2,000 apiece (plumbing not included). It's a small price to pay to quench thirst, reduce bottle litter, slash our collective carbon footprint and reaffirm our connection with the city's most valuable resource: its public water supply.

First, read the annotations in the margin alongside the editorial. Be sure that you know the meanings of any unfamiliar words in them. Then in your own words, state the primary *claim* in this editorial. Then identify the type of claim—fact, value, or policy. (Note that there may be a primary claim and a secondary one, as well.) Be sure not to include any supporting evidence in this section.

Claims _____

_____

Now list four pieces of supporting evidence. Use the annotations to help you. After you write each one, identify the type of evidence according to this list: facts and statistics; examples and observations; good reasons; or quotation or testimony.

Evidence _____

_____

_____

_____

_____

_____

_____

Finally, look through the editorial again, this time locating three ideas Royte uses as a concession or a refutation—that is, objections those opposed to her proposal might raise and her counterarguments against them.

Refutation _____

_____

_____

_____

The exercises in Part Five differ markedly from those in the earlier sections of the book. Each editorial asks you to perform several analytical tasks: identify the claim; locate the evidence and, if there is one, the refutation; and identify any solutions the writer includes. One short vocabulary exercise rounds out the exercises. Finally, there is a section called "What More Do I Need to Know?" The purpose of this section is to show you that, generally with controversial issues, there are more questions than answers. Part of being a good college student is learning to ask the right questions both to help you become the best critical thinker you can be and to learn how to solve problems. Solving problems begins with asking questions.

28 JOHN STOSSEL
The College Scam

John Stossel is an author, journalist, and columnist espousing libertarian issues. After working for several years at ABC News, he left to join the Fox Business Channel and Fox News Channel. He has also appeared on The O'Reilly Factor, *and he writes a blog for Fox News called "John Stossel's Take." His brand of journalism is called advocacy journalism, in which he takes on unpopular points of view and challenges widely held assumptions. This opinion piece was published online at www.RealClearPolitics.com, a site that publishes material across the political spectrum, though it tends toward conservatism.*

Vocabulary Analysis

WORD ORIGINS

scam This word, prominent in the editorial, is a relatively recent yet obscure addition to the English language. Some dictionaries say that the origin is unknown, but the website dictionary.com traces its origin to the 1960s from carnival argot, meaning a specialized language that members of a particular group use. As a noun, *scam* refers to a confidence game or fraudulent scheme, done in order to make a profit, in other words, to swindle. As a verb, *scam* means to cheat or to defraud.

WORD FAMILIES

education, the root *duc-* The Latin verb root *ducere* ("to lead") forms the basis of a large number of words in English. Let's start with the word *education*. It derives from the prefix *e-* ("out of") + *ducere*. The word literally means "leading out," from ignorance or the dark, in other words, gaining knowledge. *Conduct* means "leading into," *abduct* means "to lead away," and an *aqueduct* refers to a passage carrying water.

JOHN STOSSEL

The College Scam

1 What do Michael Dell, Mark Zuckerberg, Bill Gates and Mark Cuban have in common?

2 They're all college dropouts.

3 Richard Branson, Simon Cowell and Peter Jennings have in common? [sic]

4 They never went to college at all.

5 But today all kids are told: To succeed, you must go to college.

6 Hillary Clinton tells students: "Graduates from four-year colleges earn nearly twice as much as high school graduates, an estimated $1 million more."

7 We hear that from people who run colleges. And it's true. But it leaves out some important facts.

8 That's why I say: For many people, college is a scam.

9 I spoke with Richard Vedder, author of "Going Broke by Degree: Why College Costs Too Much," and Naomi Schafer Riley, who just published "Faculty Lounges and Other Reasons Why You Won't Get the College Education You Paid For."

10 Vedder explained why that million-dollar comparison is ridiculous:

11 "People that go to college are different kind of people. . . (more) disciplined . . . smarter. They did better in high school."

12 They would have made more money even if they never went to college.

13 Riley says some college students don't get what they pay for because their professors have little incentive to teach.

14 "You think you're paying for them to be in the classroom with you, but every hour a professor spends in the classroom, he gets paid less. The incentives are all for more research."

15 The research is often on obscure topics for journals nobody reads.

16 Also, lots of people not suited for higher education get pushed into it. This doesn't do them good. They feel like failures when they don't graduate. Vedder said two out of five students entering four-year programs don't have a bachelor's degree after year six.

17 "Why do colleges accept (these students) in the first place?"

18 Because money comes with the student—usually government-guaranteed loans.

19 "There are 80,000 bartenders in the United States with bachelor's degrees," Vedder said. He says that 17 percent of baggage porters and bellhops have a college degree, 15 percent of taxi and limo drivers. It's hard to pay off student loans with job like those. These days, many students graduate with big debts.

20 Entrepreneur Peter Thiel, who got rich helping to build good things like PayPal and Facebook, is so eager to wake people up to alternatives to college that he's paying students $100,000 each if they drop out of college and do something else, like start a business.

21   "We're asking nothing in return other than meetings so we make sure (they) work hard, and not be in school for two years," said Jim O'Neill, who runs the foundation.

22   For some reason, this upsets the left. A Slate.com writer called Thiel's grant a "nasty idea" that leads students into "halting their intellectual development . . . maintaining a narrow-minded focus on getting rich."

23   But Darren Zhu, a grant winner who quit Yale for the $100,000, told me, "Building a start-up and learning the sort of hardships that are associated with building a company is a much better education path."

24   I agree. Much better. Zhu plans to start to biotech company.

25   What puzzles is me is why the market doesn't punish colleges that don't serve their customers well. The opposite has happened: Tuitions have risen four times faster than inflation.

26   "There's a lot of bad information out there," Vedder replied. "We don't know . . . if (students) learned anything" during their college years.

27   "Do kids learn anything at Harvard? People at Harvard tell us they do. . . . They were bright when they entered Harvard, but do . . . seniors know more than freshmen? The literacy rate among college graduates is lower today than it was 15 or 20 years ago. It is kind of hard for people to respond in market fashion when you don't have full information."

28   Despite the scam, the Obama administration plans to increase the number of students getting Pell grants by 50 percent. And even a darling of conservatives, New Jersey Gov. Chris Christie, says college is must: "Graduating from high school is just the first step."

29   We need to wake people up.

Exercises

A. IDENTIFYING THE CLAIM

1.   Using your own words as much as possible, write the writer's central claim or proposition. Also indicate the number of the paragraph where it is located.

2.   Then decide if the claim is a claim of fact, a claim of value, or a claim of policy. Remember that an argument may have a secondary claim as well.

B. LOCATING EVIDENCE AND THE REFUTATION

1.   One piece of evidence is listed for you. List two or three other major pieces of evidence that the writer uses to support the claim. Also characterize each

piece of evidence according to whether it represents facts and statistics; examples and observations; good reasons; or quotation or testimony.

a. Michael Dell, Mark Zuckerberg, Bill Gates, Mark Cuban, Richard Branson, Simon Cowell, and Peter Jennings—all leading entrepreneurs or celebrities of some sort—either never attended college or dropped out. (facts)

b. _____

c. _____

d. _____

e. _____

2.   Finally, if there is a refutation, list that as well.

_____

C. IDENTIFYING SOLUTIONS

1.   Does the writer provide a solution to the problem he discusses? If so, write it in the space provided. Be sure to use your own words.

_____

_____

2.   What is your proposal to help solve this problem?

_____

_____

D. UNDERSTANDING VOCABULARY

Choose the best definition according to an analysis of word parts or the context.

_____ **1.**   the _incentives_ are all for more research [paragraph 14]
   a. motivations
   b. salaries
   c. responsibilities
   d. impulses

_____ **2.**   _obscure_ topics for journals nobody reads [15]
   a. challenging
   b. little known
   c. significant
   d. worthy of study

_____ **3.**   _entrepreneur_ Peter Thiel [20]
   a. media tycoon
   b. philanthropist, a person who donates money to a cause
   c. a person who starts a business venture
   d. social critic

_____ **4.**   a *darling* of conservatives [28]
   a. beloved person in a romantic relationship
   b. enemy, one who is distrusted
   c. spokesperson, one who represents
   d. favorite, someone highly regarded

E. WHAT MORE DO I NEED TO KNOW?

For this exercise, think about the editorial and the questions it raises. Then write two or three questions that you would like to find answers to or information you would like to have before you accept or reject the writer's claim.

_____

_____

_____

_____

F. TOPICS FOR DISCUSSION

1. John Stossel is described as a libertarian. What do libertarians believe in? How is this philosophy reflected in his opinion piece?
2. What is Stossel's underlying assumption—the premise from which he begins his editorial—about the purpose and value of a college education? Why does he believe that students are being swindled? Do you find the reasons he presents convincing? Why or why not?
3. Stossel criticizes college faculty for spending too much time on research and not enough time in the classroom and for writing articles on obscure topics in journals that nobody reads. Is this an accurate portrayal of your college teachers? Why or why not?
4. What counterarguments can you supply to Stossel's opinion?

G. TOPICS FOR WRITING

1. Why are you attending college? What is your goal? What do you think the purpose of a college education is? Write an essay in which you address these questions, using specific examples from your own observations and experience.
2. Write a rebuttal to Stossel's opinion piece.
3. Stossel calls college a "scam." Write a paragraph in which you defend his use of this word to describe college today, or take the opposite approach, and write a critique of his use of the word.

EXPLORE THE WEB

- A recent *Wall Street Journal* article reported these figures: College tuition has increased 136 percent over the past 20 years when adjusted for inflation. A student who graduated in 2010 on average carries a $25,250 debt load from student loans. Tuition, especially at state colleges and universities, has risen dramatically because 40 states have cut their funding for higher education.

If you type in the following term in the search box of your favorite search engine, you will find a lot of statistics and further information to explain this situation: "rising college tuition—reasons."

Study this cartoon by David Horsey, cartoonist for Hearst Newspapers. How does it connect to the claim Stossel makes in his editorial?

David Horsey/Seattlepi.com © 2011 Hearst Newspapers, LLC.

29 JOHN EDGAR WIDEMAN
The Seat Not Taken

John Edgar Wideman has taught English at the University of Massachusetts at Amherst. Currently, he is professor of Africana at Brown University in Providence, Rhode Island. Wideman is an eminent social critic, novelist, and essayist, and also the second African-American to win a Rhodes scholarship for graduate study at Oxford University. This editorial was published in the New York Times.

Vocabulary Analysis

WORD PARTS

the suffixes *-able* + *-ly* You are probably well aware that the suffix *–able* means "able to" or "capable of" and that the suffix *–ly* indicates an adverb. It's easy to determine the meaning of easy words with these suffixes, for example, *reliably* or *predictably*. But for English-language learners, in particular, deciphering words with these prefixes may pose a challenge. In paragraph 3 Wideman uses the word *invariably*. Here is how to break down the word: *in- + vary + -able + -ly.*

First, strip away the prefix *in-*, which means "not." Next, consider the root, *vary*, which means to change. Add to that the two suffices, and the adverb describes a situation that is not able to be changed, in other words, something that happens almost all the time.

What do the following words mean? Refer to a dictionary if you are unsure.

infallible _____

invincible _____

inimitable _____

indubitable _____

JOHN EDGAR WIDEMAN

The Seat Not Taken

1   AT least twice a week I ride Amtrak's high-speed Acela train from my home in New York City to my teaching job in Providence, R.I. The route passes through a region of the country populated by, statistics tell us, a significant segment of its most educated, affluent, sophisticated and enlightened citizens.

2   Over the last four years, excluding summers, I have conducted a casual socio-logical experiment in which I am both participant and observer. It's a survey I began not because I had some specific point to prove by gathering data to sup-port it, but because I couldn't avoid becoming aware of an obvious, disquieting truth.

3   Almost invariably, after I have hustled aboard early and occupied one half of a vacant double seat in the usually crowded quiet car, the empty place next to me will remain empty for the entire trip.

4   I'm a man of color, one of the few on the train and often the only one in the quiet car, and I've concluded that color explains a lot about my experience. Unless the car is nearly full, color will determine, even if it doesn't exactly clar-ify, why 9 times out of 10 people will shun a free seat if it means sitting beside me.

5   Giving them and myself the benefit of the doubt, I can rule out excessive body odor or bad breath; a hateful, intimidating scowl; hip-hop clothing; or a hideous deformity as possible objections to my person. Considering also the cost of an Acela ticket, the fact that I display no visible indications of religious pref-erence and, finally, the numerous external signs of middle-class membership I share with the majority of the passengers, color appears to be a sufficient reason for the behavior I have recorded.

6   Of course, I'm not registering a complaint about the privilege, conferred upon me by color, to enjoy the luxury of an extra seat to myself. I relish the opportu-nity to spread out, savor the privacy and quiet and work or gaze at the scenic New England woods and coast. It's a particularly appealing perk if I compare the train to air travel or any other mode of transportation, besides walking or bicycling, for negotiating the mercilessly congested Northeast Corridor. Still, in the year 2010, with an African-descended, brown president in the White House and a nation confidently asserting its passage into a postracial era, it strikes me as odd to ride beside a vacant seat, just about every time I embark on a three-hour journey each way, from home to work and back.

7   I admit I look forward to the moment when other passengers, searching for a good seat, or any seat at all on the busiest days, stop anxiously prowling the quiet-car aisle, the moment when they have all settled elsewhere, including the ones who willfully blinded themselves to the open seat beside me or were unconvinced of its availability when they passed by. I savor that precise moment when the train sighs and begins to glide away from Penn or Providence Sta-tion, and I'm able to say to myself, with relative assurance, that the vacant place

beside me is free, free at last, or at least free until the next station. I can relax, prop open my briefcase or rest papers, snacks or my arm in the unoccupied seat.

8   But the very pleasing moment of anticipation casts a shadow, because I can't accept the bounty of an extra seat without remembering why it's empty, without wondering if its emptiness isn't something quite sad. And quite dangerous, also, if left unexamined. Posters in the train, the station, the subway warn: if you see something, say something.

"The Seat Not Taken" by John Edgar Wideman. Copyright © 2010 by John Edgar Wideman, used by permission of The Wylie Agency LLC. From *The New York Times*, October 6, 2010.

Exercises

A. IDENTIFYING THE CLAIM

1. Using your own words as much as possible, write the writer's central claim or proposition. Also indicate the number of the paragraph where it is located.

   _____

   _____

2. Then decide if the claim is a claim of fact, a claim of value, or a claim of policy. Remember that an argument may have a secondary claim as well.

   _____

   _____

B. LOCATING EVIDENCE AND THE REFUTATION

1. One piece of evidence is listed for you. List two or three other major pieces of evidence that the writer uses to support the claim. Also characterize each piece of evidence according to whether it represents facts and statistics; examples and observations; good reasons; or quotation or testimony.

   a. Wideman has concluded that his skin color is the only factor that distinguishes him from other Amtrak passengers in the quiet car.

   b. _____

   c. _____

   d. _____

2. Finally, if there is a refutation, list that as well.

   _____

C. IDENTIFYING SOLUTIONS

1. Does the writer provide a solution to the problem he discusses? If so, write it in the space provided. Be sure to use your own words.

   _____

2. What is your proposal to help solve this problem?

   _____

D. UNDERSTANDING VOCABULARY

Look through the paragraphs listed by number in brackets and find a word that matches each definition. Refer to a dictionary if necessary. An example has been done for you.

Ex. almost always [paragraphs 2–3]   _____ *invariably* _____

1. troubling, worrisome [2–3]   _____

2. reject, deliberately avoid [3–4]   _____

3. look of anger or disapproval [5]   _____

4. bestowed, given [6]   _____

5. cruel, terrible, unending [6]   _____

6. benefit, something expected as due to us [informal—6]   _____

7. board a vehicle, start on a trip [6]   _____

8. appreciate fully, enjoy [6—two possible answers]   _____

9. purposely, deliberately [7]   _____

10. something given liberally or freely, a reward [8]   _____

E. WHAT MORE DO I NEED TO KNOW?

For this exercise, think about the editorial and the questions it raises. Then write two or three questions that you would like to find answers to or information you would like to have before you accept or reject the writer's claim.

_____

_____

_____

_____

F. TOPICS FOR DISCUSSION

1. How would you characterize Wideman's tone, or emotional attitude, in this editorial? Does he sound rational, angry, judgmental, bitter, or hostile? Show examples of his writing style that point to your answer.
2. Why does Wideman include paragraph 5? What it its purpose?
3. What does the term *postracial* mean? See paragraph 6.
4. Comment on Wideman's observation and his method of examining it. He says that he finds the experience of having an empty seat next to him "odd." Why does he use this word to describe his feeling?
5. Read the last paragraph again. What do posters on subways and trains that he mentions in the last sentence actually refer to? What does Wideman mean about our heeding the warning: "if you see something, say something."

Does this observation explain why he wrote this editorial? What is he advocating?

G. TOPICS FOR WRITING

1. Write a short essay in which you relate an experience that you had recently that exemplified a subtle form of racial discrimination.
2. The election of Barack Obama, the first African-American president in American history, signaled a *postracial era*, as Wideman observes in paragraph 6. What gains do you think African-Americans have achieved from Obama's being elected president? Do you think blacks' economic and social situation has changed for the better, for the worse, or stayed the same? Examine your thinking by citing examples and observations from around you.

EXPLORE THE WEB

- An extensive biography of Wideman is available at www.aalbc.com, also a good site to explore in depth the subject of African-American literature.

30 ANDY BROOKS AND STEVE WEBER
Disarming the Hooligans Among Us

Sports fans Andy Brooks and Steve Weber wrote this opinion piece for Open Forum, On Sports and Culture, for the San Francisco Chronicle *where it was published on 2012's Super Bowl weekend. Brooks is a doctoral student at U.C. Berkeley's School of Information, and Weber is a faculty member at the same school. Brooks is a fan of the San Francisco 49ers and the Oakland A's, while Weber is a New York Giants and New York Yankees fan. This editorial addresses the causes of hooliganism at sporting events. Hooliganism refers to violent behavior by sports fans; those who engage in such tough, aggressive behavior are called* hooligans.

Vocabulary Analysis

The Latin phrase *de facto* In paragraph 8 the writers mention the bad economy as one reason that today's sports fans are so volatile. Citing the *de facto* recession of 2011 as one reason, they mean a recession that exists as a fact or in reality, even though it was never officially named a recession. During the civil rights struggle of the 1960s, there existed segregation that was *de facto*. This means that it existed in practice even though it was illegal. Legal segregation would be called *de jure* because it was based on law.

ANDY BROOKS AND STEVE WEBER

Disarming the Hooligans Among Us

1   On any given Sunday, you never know who will win an NFL game.
2   But if you've been to the 'Stick'[1] or many other stadiums this year, you know one thing: Fans' actions toward the opposing team's fans will go beyond just emotional or angry to sometimes threatening and even violent.

---

[1]The "'Stick" refers to Candlestick Park, the 49ers stadium in San Francisco. The team, however, is scheduled to move to Santa Clara after that city builds a new stadium

3   And it's not just in the United States: A riot after a soccer game in Egypt this week left 74 dead when local fans chased the supporters of the visiting team with knives, clubs and stones up against a locked gate at an exit.

4   Is the behavior at U.S. football stadiums hooliganism in the making? That's what the British called the unruly behavior that came to dominate their soccer stadiums in the early 1980s. Police in riot gear had to escort each team's fans to and from games. At the stadium, a wall of riot police stood between opposing fans. A game meant tear gas obstructing the field, home made explosives lobbed at opposing fans and players, and racist chants.

5   Things have improved in the United Kingdom since then. But is this the NFL's future?

6   There's an element of human nature at play here because people naturally take to us-versus-them dynamics. You can create hostile tribes among college students in psychology laboratories by assigning them stunningly simple differences—even just calling one group A and another group B. But these tribes don't physically attack each other. They might though if enough anger were thrown into the mix.

7   Britain in the early 1980s was certainly an angry place. The economy was in a recession, unemployment was stuck around 12 percent, and the two major political parties—Labor and Conservative—were battling it out brutally in the House of Commons, with verbal insults escalating to interruptions of Prime Minister Margaret Thatcher's speeches.

8   The United States today is also an angry place. We have some of the same ingredients as 1980s Britain—a de facto recession, high unemployment and vicious politics. Democrats and Republicans regularly call each other "idiots," "wing nuts" and other less complimentary names. A congressman interrupts a president's State of the Union address with a shout of "You Lie!" It's not a long leap from that kind of invective to what feels like violence-inducing hatred between 49ers fans and fans of the Giants, Saints or other teams.

9   But this isn't Britain in the 1980s, and the NFL doesn't have to let football games lead to police states. To be a football fan today is a very different experience, and that means we can stop the descent into hooliganism.

10   Today's fans are engaged at a higher level. We pay a lot more for tickets. The vast majority watch on high-def television, soon to become 3-D and social television, where we'll be able to yell and cheer with our friends as if we're together. We manage fantasy teams for bragging rights. We comment on our team's Facebook updates—and on any news articles about them—and follow our favorite players on Twitter. The game starts weeks before the coin toss, and it's not over when the clock expires. For fans, there's really no offseason—we're constantly engaged.

11   This new virtual stadium certainly can be a nasty place. It's no holds barred on some teams' Facebook pages, and you don't have to look hard to find videos of fan-on-fan violence on YouTube. Kyle Williams, the 49ers' kick returner, received death threats on Twitter. It's almost routine to dehumanize the other team, its fans, and officials who make "bad calls." It's not a huge leap from accepting that kind of rhetoric as commonplace to real violence when the opportunity presents itself.

12   Let's not fool ourselves—this is a form of free speech. No one can control how fans use social media. But the NFL, teams and players can step up and use these same channels to set the tone and shape the behavior of fans. They're certainly good at using them to get us revved up for the game. How about reminding us what it means to be a good fan, a civil fan, a true sportsperson? If Eli Manning and Alex Smith jointly recognized and rewarded fans who act as role models, we think that would make a real difference.

13   Ultimately it's on all of us. We, the fans, can stop the hooligans because they're some of us. Think twice before posting that nasty message, "liking" a fellow fan's expletive-ridden diatribe or sharing a video of fan-on-fan violence. On social media, we don't have to risk getting our nose broken when we break up a fight. So tell your Facebook friends who do those angry unacceptable things that you'll not be a part of it. You—we—are better than that.

Andy Brooks and Steve Weber, "Disarming the Hooligans Among Us," *San Francisco Chronicle*, February 3, 2012. © 2012 by Andy Brooks and Steve Weber. Reprinted by permission of the authors.

Exercises

A. IDENTIFYING THE CLAIM

1. Using your own words as much as possible, state the writers' central claim or proposition. Also indicate the number of the paragraph where it is located.

_____

_____

2. Then decide if the claim is a claim of fact, a claim of value, or a claim of policy. Remember that an argument may have a secondary claim as well.

_____

_____

B. LOCATING EVIDENCE AND THE REFUTATION

1. One piece of evidence is listed for you. List two or three other major pieces of evidence that the writers use to support the claim. Also characterize each piece of evidence according to whether it represents facts and statistics; examples and observations; good reasons; or quotation or testimony.

   a. American fans' behavior is beginning to look like that of the hooligans whose unruly behavior at English soccer games became dominant in the early 1980s.

   b. _____

   c. _____

   d. _____

2. Finally, if there is a refutation, list that as well.

_____

C. IDENTIFYING SOLUTIONS

1. Do the writers provide a solution to the problem they discuss? If so, write it in the space provided. Be sure to use your own words.

   _____

2. What is your proposal to help solve this problem?

   _____

D. UNDERSTANDING VOCABULARY

Look through the paragraphs listed by number in brackets and find a word that matches each definition. Refer to a dictionary if necessary. An example has been done for you.

Ex. violent, thuggish behavior [paragraphs 4 and 9]   *hooliganism*

1. impossible to control or discipline [4]   _____

2. blocking with obstacles [4]   _____

3. increasing, intensifying [7]   _____

4. abusive language [8]   _____

5. leading to, producing [8]   _____

6. lower in status, make less than human [11]   _____

7. made livelier, increased [12—two-word phrase]   _____

8. following accepted social rules, polite, not rude [12] _____

9. bitter, abusive denunciation; hostile speech [13]   _____

10. obscene word, profanity [13]   _____

E. WHAT MORE DO I NEED TO KNOW?

For this exercise, think about the editorial and the questions it raises. Then write two or three questions that you would like to find answers to or information you would like to have before you accept or reject the writer's claim.

   _____

   _____

   _____

   _____

F. TOPICS FOR DISCUSSION

1. If you live near the headquarters of an NFL team, how prevalent is hooliganism at its games?
2. Comment on the structure of this opinion piece. Why do the writers use British soccer fans in the 1980s as an example? What does the British experience with hooliganism have to do with American fans and their behavior?
3. Comment on the quality of the evidence—the reasons—that the writers supply to explain hooliganism in this country. What are some other factors that have contributed to the increasingly brutish behavior among football fans?
4. What is it about football fans that makes them so unruly, as opposed to, say, baseball or basketball or even ice hockey fans?
5. Evaluate the writers' solution to the problem of fan violence. Can you devise other, less abstract solutions for this problem?

G. TOPICS FOR WRITING

1. Describe an experience where you witnessed or experienced fan violence. What triggered it? What was the specific behavior? How did the incident end?
2. If fan violence has been a problem with a team that you follow, write a short proposal in which you offer some suggestions for stopping the unruly behavior.
3. Is the problem of fan violence exaggerated, so that just a few bad apples are responsible for the behavior? Write a short essay in which you defend such behavior as being part of the spectacle, part of the sport.

EXPLORE THE WEB

- After the Canucks lost in Game 7 to the Boston Bruins in the 2011 Stanley Cup finals, residents of Vancouver, Canada, went on a rampage. An account of the riot by Canucks' fans and an analysis of how a crowd can become a mob in an instant was published in the *Los Angeles Times* (June 17, 2011). In the search box of your favorite search engine, type in "Sam Farmer, Sports Can Be an Excuse to Riot, Los Angeles Times."

- If you are interested in the subject of hooliganism, the classic book on the subject was written by Bill Buford. Called *Among the Thugs* (2001), Buford, who was living in England at the time, writes a first-hand account of his experience at British soccer (which they call football) matches. You can read reviews of his book to see if the subject is worth pursuing. In the search box, type in "Bill Buford, Among the Thugs, Reviews."

DAVID BROOKS

If It Feels Right . . .

David Brooks has written columns for the op-ed page of the New York Times *since 2003. He was formerly an editor at the* Evening Standard *and at the* Atlantic *as well as serving as a commentator on* The Newshour *with Jim Lehrer on PBS. Brooks is sometimes described as the "liberals' favorite conservative" because of his rational and calm approach to the issues of the day. Brooks's most recent book is* The Social Animal: The Hidden Sources of Love, Character and Achievement *(2011).*

Vocabulary Analysis

The suffix *–ism*—Part 1 Since Brooks uses four words that end with this common suffix, it's a good place to study its meaning and use. Frequently attached to nouns, *-ism* indicates a doctrine, practice, theory, or principle. *Relativism, individualism,* and *nonjudgmentalism* (paragraph 9) and *consumerism* (paragraph 10) all refer to a practice or belief. For example, *relativism* is the belief that morality is relative; *individualism* is the belief that the individual is of primary importance. This suffix appears in many English words, among them *terrorism, realism, romanticism, barbarism, Catholicism, sexism,* and *totalitarianism,* just to cite a few.

DAVID BROOKS

Clear Sense of Morality Lacking in Young Adults

1   During the summer of 2008, the eminent Notre Dame sociologist Christian Smith led a research team that conducted in-depth interviews with 230 young adults from across America. The interviews were part of a larger study that Smith, Kari Christoffersen, Hilary Davidson, Patricia Snell Herzog and others have been conducting on the state of America's youth.

2   Smith and company asked about the young people's moral lives, and the results are depressing.

3   It's not so much that these young Americans are living lives of sin and debauchery, at least no more than you'd expect from 18- to 23-year-olds. What's disheartening is how bad they are at thinking and talking about moral issues.

4   The interviewers asked open-ended questions about right and wrong, moral dilemmas and the meaning of life. In the rambling answers, which Smith and company recount in a new book, "Lost in Transition," you see the young people groping to say anything sensible on these matters. But they just don't have the categories or vocabulary to do so.

5   When asked to describe a moral dilemma they had faced, two-thirds of the young people either couldn't answer the question or described problems that are not moral at all, like whether they could afford to rent a certain apartment or whether they had enough quarters to feed the meter at a parking spot.

6   "Not many of them have previously given much or any thought to many of the kinds of questions about morality that we asked," Smith and his co-authors write. When asked about wrong or evil, they could generally agree that rape and murder are wrong. But, aside from these extreme cases, moral thinking didn't enter the picture, even when considering things like drunken driving, cheating in school or cheating on a partner. "I don't really deal with right and wrong that often," is how one interviewee put it.

7   The default position, which most of them came back to again and again, is that moral choices are just a matter of individual taste. "It's personal," the respondents typically said. "It's up to the individual. Who am I to say?"

8   Rejecting blind deference to authority, many of the young people have gone off to the other extreme: "I would do what I thought made me happy or how I felt. I have no other way of knowing what to do but how I internally feel."

9   Smith and company found an atmosphere of extreme moral individualism—of relativism and nonjudgmentalism. Again, this doesn't mean that America's young people are immoral. Far from it. But, Smith and company emphasize, they have not been given the resources—by schools, institutions and families—to cultivate their moral intuitions, to think more broadly about moral obligations, to check behaviors that may be degrading. In this way, the study says more about adult America than youthful America.

10   Smith and company are stunned, for example, that the interviewees were so completely untroubled by rabid consumerism. (This was the summer of 2008, just before the crash.)

11   Many of these shortcomings will sort themselves out, as these youngsters get married, have kids, enter a profession or fit into more clearly defined social roles. Institutions will inculcate certain habits. Broader moral horizons will be forced upon them. But their attitudes at the start of their adult lives do reveal something about American culture. For decades, writers from different perspectives have been warning about the erosion of shared moral frameworks and the rise of an easygoing moral individualism.

12   In most times and in most places, the group was seen to be the essential moral unit. A shared religion defined rules and practices. Cultures structured people's imaginations and imposed moral disciplines. But now more people

are led to assume that the free-floating individual is the essential moral unit. Morality was once revealed, inherited and shared, but now it's thought of as something that emerges in the privacy of your own heart.

Exercises

A. IDENTIFYING THE CLAIM

1. Using your own words as much as possible, write the writer's central claim or proposition. Also indicate the number of the paragraph where it is located.

_____

2. Then decide if the claim is a claim of fact, a claim of value, or a claim of policy. Remember that an argument may have a secondary claim as well.

_____

B. LOCATING EVIDENCE AND THE REFUTATION

1. One piece of evidence is listed for you. List two or three other major pieces of evidence that the writer uses to support the claim. Also characterize each piece of evidence according to whether it represents facts and statistics; examples and observations; good reasons; or quotation or testimony.

   a. Although students aren't living lives of sin and debauchery, they are bad at thinking about and articulating moral issues.

   b. _____

   c. _____

   d. _____

2. Finally, if there is a refutation, list that as well.

_____

C. IDENTIFYING SOLUTIONS

1. Does the writer provide a solution to the problem he discusses? If so, write it in the space provided. Be sure to use your own words.

_____

_____

2. What is your proposal to help solve this problem?

_____

D. UNDERSTANDING VOCABULARY IN CONTEXT

Here are a few vocabulary words from the selection along with their definitions. Study these definitions carefully. Then write the appropriate word in each space provided according to the context, the way it is used. **Note:** You will use only three of the four words in each set.

dilemmas	situations that require a choice between two equally undesirable courses
inculcate	teach by instruction and repetition
deference	yielding to another's judgment or opinion
interviewees	those who were interviewed

1. It appears that parents and teachers have failed to _____ moral values and a vocabulary to discuss moral _____ intelligently. Young people have rejected blind _____ to authority, instead substituting an extreme form of individualism to judge their and others' actions.

disheartening	discouraging
eminent	prominent, outstanding in one's field
debauchery	indulgence in sexual pleasure, dissipation
degrading	tending to lower one's status or moral character

2. A study by the _____ sociologist, Christian Smith, from the University of Notre Dame, found that, although young people aren't leading lives of _____, their inability to discuss moral issues intelligently is quite _____.

E. WHAT MORE DO I NEED TO KNOW?

For this exercise, think about the editorial and the questions it raises. Then write two or three questions that you would like to find answers to or information you would like to have before you accept or reject the writer's claim.

_____

_____

_____

_____

F. TOPICS FOR DISCUSSION

1. Whom does Brooks hold responsible for the decline in morality among young adults?

2. Provide an example of a moral dilemma. Be sure you understand the true meaning of a dilemma. (See Exercise D above.) What makes this situation a dilemma? How would you go about choosing a course of action to resolve the dilemma?

3. Brooks says that young people lack the vocabulary to talk intelligently about matters of right and wrong and about moral dilemmas. What is the reason for this, if his observation is true? Is it our rampant consumerism, lack of education (lack of a vocabulary with which to discuss moral matters), our reliance on the individual to form moral standards, or something else?

4. Is Brooks overstating young adults' supposed lack of morality, or do you find truth in what he says?

5. *Should* we be troubled by "rabid consumerism"? Has our interest in consuming, in buying material things, diminished since the recent Great Recession? If so, how?

6. The title of this editorial, "If It Feels Right. . . ," is from the original New York Times piece. However, it was reprinted in two Bay Area newspapers with different titles: "Clear Sense of Morality Lacking in Young Adults" and "Adults Fail to Give Children a Clear Sense of Morality." Which of these titles is more accurate in describing Brooks's claim?

G. TOPICS FOR WRITING

1. Write a short essay about a moral dilemma you faced and how you resolved it.

2. Write a rebuttal to Brooks's essay. Show that young people do, in fact, have moral standards and that they are well aware of the difference between right and wrong. Use your own experience and observations of young adults as support.

3. If you have lived in or traveled in another country, write a short essay in which you compare consumer behavior among people there with Americans. What are the consequences of what Brooks calls "rabid consumerism"?

EXPLORE THE WEB

• David Brooks's editorials are readily available online. Type in the search box "David Brooks, New York Times," and you will find a complete index of his columns.

32 Is the American Dream a Delusion?

COURTNEY E. MARTIN

Social critic Courtney E. Martin is an adjunct professor of Women's Studies at Hunter College. She is also the author of five books, among them Perfect Girls, Starving Daughters: The Frightening New Normalcy of Hating Your Body *(2007) and of* Project Rebirth: Survival and the Strength of the Human Spirit from 9/11 Survivors *(2011). This opinion piece was published on AlterNet (www.AlterNet.org), an e-zine and online community devoted to publishing original journalism from a variety of independent media sources. Its mission is to challenge readers to take action on a variety of social issues, among them the environment, civil liberties, social justice, and the like, and to help people "navigate a culture of information overload and providing an alternative to the commercial media onslaught."*

When this was published in 2006, Martin could not have predicted the Occupy movement of 2011 and 2012, which organized protests around the country against the growing gap in income and wealth in this country. The slogan of the Occupy movement, first started in New York City, is "We are the 99 percent," as distinguished from the 1 percent who are the wealthiest members of the population.

Vocabulary Analysis

WORD FAMILIES

mobility [paragraph 3] From the Latin verb *movere* meaning "to move," this word has a number of related words in the English language. *Mobility* refers to the ability to move. *Mobile*, the adjective form, can apply to a person who is capable of moving on his or her own, to a type of house, or, as a noun, to an art form—a type of sculpture with movable elements, often used in a baby's crib. The opposite of *mobile* is *immobile*. The verb *mobilize* means to assemble or to prepare, usually for war.

What is the derivation of the word *automobile*? _____

COURTNEY E. MARTIN

Is the American Dream a Delusion?

1   "My uncle came to this country with nothing. Nothing. And now he has a lucrative carpet business and season tickets to the Mets," says one of my students, a wide-eyed, 18-year-old Pakistani immigrant, on a Monday evening in room 605, the light just disappearing behind the Manhattan skyscrapers through the windows.

2   As a gender studies professor at Hunter College—one of the most ethnically diverse schools in the nation—I am used to provoking passionate and often personal reactions in my students. We drift onto some fairly dangerous ground—abortion, rape, love, war—but after two and half years of teaching this material I have realized that I am never so uncomfortable as when class discussion turns to the American Dream.

3   You know the story: Once upon a time there was a hardworking, courageous young man, born in a poor family, who came to America, put in blood, sweat and tears, and eventually found riches and respect. But knowing the statistics on social mobility and the ever-widening gap between rich and poor, I just can't stomach this "happily ever after" scenario. It is too clean. Real life is full of messy things like racism and the wage gap and child care and nepotism.

4   The working-class students in my class are often struggling, and sometimes failing, with full-time jobs and full-time academic loads. You might predict that they would welcome the idea that if you're born poor, no matter how hard you work, sometimes success is still outside your grasp.

5   But semester after semester, student after student, when I suggest that the American Dream might be more fairy tale and less true story, I encounter the opposite reaction. As if by gut survival instinct, students hold up their favorite uncle or a distant cousin, or my personal favorite, Arnold Schwarzenegger, as evidence that the American Dream is alive and well.

6   Part of me wants to cringe, lecture them about how one success story is dangled in front of a struggling public so they won't get angry enough to revolt against an unfair system. How oppression can so easily be mistaken for personal failure. How many employers won't even look at their resumes if they don't see an Ivy League college at the top. But another part of me wants to keep my white, upper-middle-class mouth shut.

7   Many of these students' parents—some of whom have left behind mothers, friends, respect and status in their countries of origin—have sacrificed their lives on the altar of the American Dream. Some of my students are recent immigrants themselves, so relieved to have made it out of violent and poverty-stricken places like Haiti and Colombia that they aren't ready to criticize the country that is their haven. Others, American as apple pie, are the first to go to college in their families and believe ardently that this guarantees a better life. At what cost do I ask them to question their beliefs? What right do I have to deconstruct one of the foundations they stand on?

8   Discomfort produces learning; Piaget taught me that. When I ask my students to read about intersexuality, I know that they will be surprised and "weirded out," as they often put it, that sex may be more accurately thought of as a spectrum rather than a binary. This, of course, shatters their previous understanding of male and female, blue and pink, penis and vagina, but I find that they can usually process this exploration with a bit of distanced wonder. It doesn't appear to threaten their sense of self, as much as expand it.

9   But when it comes to exploring the validity of the American Dream, I find myself—perhaps too sensitively—afraid of breaking them. I can see that their feverish daily schedules from home to daycare to work to school to daycare to home, repeat, are running not on caffeine or a love of learning, but on potent "someday" dreams. They have landed in my class not by accident, but as one more small step in their destiny to make it big, they believe.

10   And maybe this is the crux of it after all. "Making it big," for my wide-eyed, 18-year-old Pakistani student, is not Bill Gates or Bill Clinton or even Bill Cosby. It is getting to see the Mets whenever he wants. For him, the American Dream is not so damaging because he has revisioned its scope.

11   But at the risk of falling into the same trap that my students sometimes do, I have to attest that he is not the rule. Many have dreams of Hummers and fame and multiple vacation homes. I don't want to be the pinprick that lets the air out of the swollen balloon of hope, but at the same time I desperately want them to see that their wholehearted belief in the American Dream is actually doing more to benefit people far richer and whiter than they are.

12   As long as they are distracted by their own dedication, they won't stop to question why the richest people in this country pay far less in taxes, proportionally, than the middle class. They won't have the time to organize against elitist candidates because they will be too busy working dead-end jobs. As a friend once explained to me, "The proletariat didn't rise up like Marx predicted because he was too tired after work. All he wanted to do was watch TV and have a beer."

13   I want to give my students an intellectual tool that can serve as an emotional cushion, convincing them that it isn't "all their fault" if things don't work out exactly as planned. I want them to imagine living in a genuinely more equal society, not just one that pays lip service to it. What could they accomplish if it didn't take a million-dollar budget to run for political office, and if people didn't hire their friends' kids, and if college was free?

14   So I push. I push beyond my own comfort zone. I certainly push beyond theirs. In fact, I put faith in my own version of the American Dream—that dialogue makes people smarter, kinder, happier—and hope that my students don't prove it a myth.

Exercises

You may refer to the selection as you complete these exercises. Write your answers to these questions in the spaces provided.

A. IDENTIFYING THE CLAIM

1. Using your own words as much as possible, write Martin's central claim or proposition. Also indicate the number of the paragraph where it is located.

   _____

   _____

   _____

2. Then decide if the claim is a claim of fact, a claim of value, or a claim of policy. Remember that an argument may have a secondary claim as well.

   _____

B. LOCATING EVIDENCE AND THE REFUTATION

1. One piece of evidence is listed for you. List two other major pieces of evidence that the writer uses to support the claim. Also characterize each piece of evidence according to whether it represents facts and statistics; examples and observations; good reasons; or quotation or testimony.

   a. Martin is always uncomfortable when the subject of the American dream comes up in class because she understands that, despite the fact that it motivates her students, at the same time she also knows that it's more a myth than a reality. (observation)

   b. _____

   _____

   c. _____

   _____

2. Finally, if there is a refutation, list that as well. _____

   _____

   _____

   _____

   _____

C. IDENTIFYING SOLUTIONS

1. Does Martin provide a solution to the problem she discusses? If so, write it in the space provided. Be sure to use your own words. _____

   _____

_____

_____

_____

2. What is your proposal to help solve this problem? _____

D. USING VOCABULARY

From the following list of vocabulary words, choose a word that fits in each blank according to both the grammatical structure of the sentence and the context. Use each word in the list only once. Do not change the form of the word. (Note that there are more words than sentences.)

lucrative	mobility	scenario	elitist
nepotism	ardently	potent	crux
spectrum	validity	proletariat	myth

Martin writes about her students' hopes of achieving the American Dream—upward social _____ and a fulfilling and _____ career, yet she wonders if this dream isn't more of a _____ than reality. Working-class people, also known as the _____, are too busy working and therefore don't have the time or energy to campaign against _____ candidates, rich men for the most part who have no idea about what working-class people face every day. Still, her students _____ believe in the American Dream, and it remains a _____ motivation for them. Martin concludes that the _____ of the matter is that they have reimagined the dream and narrowed its scope.

E. WHAT MORE DO I NEED TO KNOW?

For this exercise, think about the editorial and the questions it raises. Then write two or three questions that you would like to find answers to or information you would like to have before you accept or reject the writer's claim.

_____

_____

_____

F. TOPICS FOR DISCUSSION

1. Is Martin overstating the situation? Do you accept her characterization—that working-class people don't recognize oppression, which allows the ruling elite to keep people in their place and to blame their problems on personal failure?

2. Martin is obviously biased. Characterize her bias. Is it fair or unfair? That is, is her bias rooted in a desire to do good or to achieve personal gain? What measures does she take to mitigate, or to soften, this bias?

G. TOPICS FOR WRITING

1. Write a rebuttal to Martin's editorial, in particular focusing on her claims that for working-class people the American dream is a delusion.

2. Choose a relative, friend, co-worker, or acquaintance who immigrated to this country and who achieved the American dream. Write a short essay in which you examine the person's experience in this country—including his or her motivations for coming here and to what extent the person bears out Martin's observations about the lure of the myth of the American dream. Be sure to define the dream as you interpret it.

EXPLORE THE WEB

- The website where this editorial was published offers a compendium of articles and editorials from a liberal perspective on a variety of topics—hunger, immigration, the wage gap, politics, health, and the environment, just to name a few.

    www.AlterNet.org

33 | PETER TURNLEY
The Line—Photographs from the U.S.–Mexican Border

© Peter Turnley/Corbis

Ubencia Sanchez, from the Chiapas region of Mexico, peers over a border fence in Tijuana, looking into the United States for the first time.

In October 2006, Harper's Magazine *contributing editor Peter Turnley published a photo essay of images taken along the U.S.–Mexican border. Turnley is a photographer based in New York City and Paris. Reprinted here are three photographs from the essay. Your college library should be able to provide you with a physical copy of the magazine if you want to see the entire collection.*

Unable to cross the border, a couple meet at the fence in San Diego.

A memorial in Tijuana for a Mexican who was killed in an incident with the Border Patrol in 2005.

Exercises

A. TOPICS FOR DISCUSSION

Study each photograph carefully, noting the composition of the photograph—that is, the dominant image the photographer captures, the background scene, the point of view reflected, and the situation or scene that the photo depicts. Then consider these questions:

1. Concerning photograph 1, what do you think the woman in the foreground is thinking as she looks at the United States for the first time? How old does

she appear to be? How would you characterize the landscape around her? How would you describe the fence that borders the two countries as it is depicted here?

2. Now consider the second photograph. What does it depict? Why do you suppose this couple must meet at the border fence in this way?

3. The third photograph shows some rocks and a white cross commemorating a Mexican killed by Border Patrol agents. What is the emotional impact of this photo? One sees these roadside memorials often, where a victim's relatives and friends commemorate a loved one's death as the result of an automobile accident. How is this memorial different? Finally, comment on the appearance of the fence. Does it look intimidating and secure? Would a person of average height be able to scale it?

B. TOPICS FOR WRITING

1. After you have examined the three photographs carefully, write an essay in which you set forth your ideas about the validity and effectiveness of the fence as a way to stop illegal immigrants from sneaking across the border into the United States.

2. Write a paragraph or two about these photographs as they demonstrate the human impact of the border fence.

3. Using the cartoon by Nick Anderson in the following section, write a short essay examining America's ambivalence about illegal immigrants.

This cartoon by Nick Anderson was published in the *Houston Chronicle*. Questions for analysis follow.

Nick Anderson Editorial Cartoon used with the permission of Nick Anderson, the Washington Post Writers Group and the Cartoonist Group. All rights reserved.

QUESTIONS FOR ANALYSIS

1. What is this cartoon about? Explain what is going on in the cartoon's two panels.
2. Political cartoons are meant to call attention to folly, to poke fun at current events and current attitudes. What is Anderson poking fun at in this cartoon?
3. What does this cartoon reveal about American attitudes toward immigrants and toward immigration?

PART SIX

Reading Short Fiction

In this section of the book are four short stories to read for pleasure. They represent a variety of themes, giving you an opportunity to see how fictional characters respond to conflict. The conflict may lie within the character's soul or spirit, or it may lie outside—with other people, with the environment, or with a philosophical principle. Seeing how literary writers use conflict to explore human behavior is an excellent and enjoyable way to learn what it is to be human, to see how characters have dealt with and solved age-old problems.

In addition, the stories represent a variety of styles, giving you an opportunity to become familiar with fictional techniques—plot, theme, narration, setting, as well as conflict and its resolution. Questions for thought and discussion follow each selection. These stories cover a wide spectrum—from very short fiction—"Town Life" by J. Robert Lennon, what is sometimes called "flash fiction"—to Guy de Maupassant's "The Necklace," and Jack London's classic, "To Build a Fire." Also included is "Souvenir," a story set in modern China by a contemporary Chinese-American writer, Yiyun Li.

If you enjoy the stories in this section of the book, one easy way to become more familiar with classic short stories is, of course, to ask your instructor for recommendations and to visit your local library. But you can also find stories online. One source is the Literature Network, whose address is www.online-literature.com/author_index.php.

34

J. ROBERT LENNON

Town Life

Flash fiction is a subgenre of fiction—meaning a subdivision of a literary type. Flash fiction is very short fiction, sometimes called microfiction, short short stories, and even sudden fiction. There is no general agreement on what constitutes flash fiction in terms of length. But its popularity has surely increased with Internet exposure. If you are interested in reading other examples, there are many sources available online. The classic example of flash fiction is this one attributed to Ernest Hemingway, who supposedly wrote this six-word short short story: "For sale: baby shoes, never worn."

J. Robert Lennon is an American writer best known for his collection of 100 literary anecdotes, Pieces for the Left Hand: 100 Anecdotes *(2005). Set in an unnamed American town, the style is casual, almost conversational. Each story reveals something unexpected and telling about human nature. Lennon currently teaches creative writing at Cornell University.*

J. ROBERT LENNON

Town Life

A small town not far from here gained some small notoriety when a famous movie actress, fed up with the misanthropy and greed of Hollywood, moved there with her husband, children, and many dogs and horses. In an interview published in a popular national magazine, the actress said that she was sick of being recognized by tourists on the street, approached by scheming strangers at restaurants, and generally restricted in her activities by her own popularity. The nearby town, she said, offered ample privacy and a beautiful natural setting; most importantly, she added, she would not be bothered there by slimy, self-interested people more concerned with what she represented than who she was.

Hearing this, the denizens of the small town resolved to make her residence pleasant, and agreed they would welcome her in the same way they would welcome anyone who moved there; that is, the chamber of commerce sent her a package of advertising circulars, her neighbors engaged her in lively debates about the borders of her property, the police solicited her for tickets to the annual charity ball, and she was encouraged in town to apply for shopping club memberships, coffee punch cards and home improvement loans.

Respectful of her fame and her unwillingness to acknowledge it, the towns-people averted their eyes when she passed them on the street and made no mention of her films, which everyone of course had seen. When her new movie debuted, the town filled up with reporters and photographers, but all requests for comment on the actress were rebuffed, and a few dedicated townspeople even claimed to be unaware that she lived there. The local paper printed no arti-cles about the national press presence, and ran only a short wire-service review of the new film.

Not long after, a terrible scene erupted in the diner when the actress threw down her utensils in the middle of an otherwise unremarkable meal and shouted something to the effect that the townspeople were the unfriendliest bunch of stuck-up bastards she'd ever encountered. Within weeks she had sold her enor-mous house in the hills and returned to California.

The nearby town is still baffled by her strange behavior. As for the actress, she has said nothing about her experience in our area, except that she was unac-customed to town life and was glad to be back where she belonged.

Questions for Thought and Discussion

1. In leaving Hollywood for the small town, what was the actress, the protago-nist or main character, trying to escape?
2. How did the townspeople treat the actress after her arrival? And why did they behave this way toward her? What were they trying to accomplish?
3. Comment on this phrase about the townspeople's attitude toward the actress: "respectful of her fame and her unwillingness to acknowledge it." Do you think this accurately represents how the actress felt about herself? Did the townspeople misinterpret her wish to be left alone, or did the actress expect an entirely different sort of reception?
4. Read again the passage where the actress erupted and caused a terrible scene in the diner. She calls the townspeople "the unfriendliest bunch of stuck-up bastards she'd ever encountered." Is this characterization fair?
5. Why were the townspeople "baffled" by the actress's decision to return to Hollywood? And for the actress, what is ironic about her reaction to her experience among the townspeople?
6. What does the story reveal about the nature of celebrity status?

35

Souvenir

A native of Beijing, China, and a graduate of the highly regarded Iowa Writers' Workshop, Yiyun Li was named one of the best American novelists under 35 in 2007. She is the author of two novels, A Thousand Years of Good Prayers *and* The Vagrants, *as well as* Gold Boy, Emerald Girl, *the collection of short stories from which this selection is reprinted. Li teaches writing at the University of California at Davis.*

YIYUN LI

Souvenir

THE MAN NOTICED the girl first, moving cautiously from one storefront to the next, not glancing even once at the shop windows. She wore a white dress, more like a smock, with a pink and purple floral print, and her bare arms and ankles were innocent as a small girl's, bony and smooth. The man watched her walk past him on the roadside bench and stood up. You remind me of my wife when she was your age, he practiced in his mind. His cane bumped into the backpacks on the ground, which belonged to the two college students sitting next to him on the bench, and they looked at him with disapproval before resuming their intimate conversation, the boy's lips touching the girl's earlobe. They had hinted, when he had first taken the seat next to them on the bench, at their unhappiness at his intrusion, but he had refused to leave, having every right to the bench as much as the young couple did.

You remind me of my wife when she was your age, he said now to the girl. It was not the first time he had started a conversation with a young woman with the line, but he meant it more than any time before. The way she maneuvered through the late-afternoon street—vigilant, as if she was aware that anyone, anything, could run her over without the slightest idea of her existence—was how he remembered his wife—not only as a young woman when they had first met but also as an older woman in the next forty years of their marriage. She had been taken advantage of by many unfriendly strangers cutting into the lines in front of her, colleagues getting promotions that belonged to her, three miscarriages, and a tumor in her liver.

She passed away six months ago, the man added now. We don't have children.

The girl looked at the old man, unconvinced by his widower's sorrow. This was not the first time she had been approached this way, older men claiming that she reminded them of their dead wives and first loves. She was never harsh with them. Even with her physics professor, who took every opportunity to touch the arms and backs of his female students, she did not flinch as the other girls did; the graze of his hands was no more harmful than another man's recognition of his own dead wife in her. They were in as much pain as she was, and they did not add to her suffering.

Have you tried the chrysanthemum tea? the man said, pointing to the window display of the pharmacy where the girl had stopped. My wife used to say it helped to get any poison out of someone's system.

The girl sighed noticeably. She would learn every bit of information about his wife if she did not stop him; not that she minded being told about and compared to a dead woman, but she had her own love to take care of on this evening. She nodded to the man and went for the door of the pharmacy, wishing that he would take his leave and find another girl in the street.

The man followed her into the store. Fluorescent lamps lit the place from the ceiling and from underneath the glass counters. Two middle-aged women, one sitting behind the cash register and one behind the counter at the opposite side of the store, exchanged information about their husbands' annoying habits, agreeing and encouraging each other as if they were deeply engaged in a verbal Ping-Pong game. Another customer listened while studying pairs of reading glasses but then left without buying. It was one of those long evenings, the man thought.

The girl walked from counter to counter and feigned interest in various products. She did not know how to stop the man from following her, since he had every right to be standing in the same store that she was, but soon it would be nightfall and the women would close the shop without asking her what she needed. The girl looked at the clock on the wall and panicked. It was all as she had planned it, that the pharmacy would be free of prying eyes in the last ten minutes before closing and she would be spared embarrassment; she did not foresee the tenacity of a lonely man.

There's a good wonton stand across the street and I'll buy you a bowl of wonton soup, the man said to the girl.

His wife must have liked wonton soup, or else she must have cooked good wonton soup for him. The girl thought about being old and having few comforts to hold on to. She was twenty-two and found it hard to be comforted by the little things in life. For the past two years she had seen bigger events than she had been prepared for, protests that led to bloodshed that led to arrests and interrogations; the tragedies would not be personal if not for her having fallen for a boy hero—she had not been the only one to admire his flamboyant gestures in front of Western reporters' cameras, but two years later, she was the only one to go to his parents' flat and sit with him every night. Don't keep your hope high, his mother had warned the girl earlier on, but she had not believed that the spirit he had shown in the square would be so easily crushed by the interrogations. She had gone to his parents and begged to see him until they had to accept her presence; still, they told her that the boy, officially a madman now, would not pass the test for a permit to get married.

Marriage is for those who still believe in the mundane, she replied and later told her parents so. She went to sit with the boy and listen to his long monologues on history and philosophy and the fatality of humankind; she noticed repetitions but did not point them out to him, nor did she ask what he thought of her presence in his bedroom. Perhaps she blended in with the furniture well, but even a piece of good furniture might save someone's life by miracle. He touched her face and arms sometimes, absentmindedly, as someone deep in thought would stroke a cat. The tenderness of his hands kept her hopeful of his recovery; after all, he had not been handled with any consideration in the two-month detention.

It's just a bowl of wonton soup, the old man said, more vehemently than he had intended. The girl's quiet rejection shamed him; his wife would have smiled and thanked him because she knew the invitation bore no ill intention. Even if she were indeed unable to join him, she would have given him a good excuse instead of letting him stand in the middle of the shop like an idiot. The world is not as bad as you think it is, he said to the girl. Enough young women these days were treating him as if he were as old and non-feeling as a half-dead tree, but he could not stand that she, who reminded him of his wife in another life, was being one of them.

The girl looked at the man. His sudden rudeness was a relief. She did not have to be responsible for his feelings, after all, even if he had not lied about his wife. The girl moved closer to the cash register, where in a locked glass case packs of condoms were on display. The girl glanced at the half-naked men and women, all foreign with blond hair, printed on the packages. A pack of those, comrade, she said, and wished that only she herself noticed the trembling in her voice.

What are those? We don't sell "those" here, the woman behind the cash register said.

The condoms, the girl said.

Which one?

That pink pack.

What size? They come in three different sizes, the woman said, and the other woman laughed audibly across the store.

The medium size, the girl said.

Are you sure?

The man watched the girl's face and neck burn with shame. Such a young woman, he thought, not experienced enough to know that all married people with respectable jobs had condoms distributed monthly to them by the birth control officers in their working units. He wished the women would be adamant in not selling the condoms to the girl; he wanted to suggest they require her marriage certificate, but before he opened his mouth the woman asked for the marked price and then threw the pack to the girl. It slid on the glass counter and then fell onto the floor.

Young girl, the man said. Do you know what you're doing?

The girl watched the man step on the naked couple with one foot. Please, sir, I paid for them, she said. They belong to me.

She's not like my wife, the man thought. He remembered one time running out of the monthly ration of condoms from his work; he had begged his wife to ask the birth control officer in her working unit, but she had cried and said she would rather die instead of going to ask a man for them. He would rather die now, the man thought, to make her alive again, but what was the point of wishing for that? It was a better arrangement that he was left behind; without him she would be bullied every day by people like those women behind the counters.

Please, it's getting late, the girl said. Had she been a different person she would have found a sharp voice and ordered the man to return to her what by law belonged to her; she would have turned to the two women, who were enjoying the scene for their end-of-the-day shift, and told them that they had better stop feeling good about themselves, because after all, they were old and loose and not as desirable as she was. The women would curse her as if she were a madwoman, and they would try to get rid of her and pretend that they were not stung by her words, but for the rest of the evening they would stay furious and their meals would remain undigested, a big lump of stone in their stomachs where her poisonous words sat, and she would walk away with a triumphant pleasure, but the truth was, she was not that person. She was the girl who went to buy condoms and planned to give herself to the boy she loved; the boy had been beaten so badly that he would never become a husband, his parents had told her, but she was the kind of girl who did not believe their words. She believed that her love would save and change him.

The old man moved away his foot. He could go on chiding the girl but he was tired. Perhaps it was good that they had not had children; his wife would be heartbroken if their daughter had turned out to be like the girl in front of him.

The girl bent down to pick up the condoms and clutched the pack in her fist. Someday, when she became an old woman, she would show the pink pack to her children, a souvenir of her hopeful youth. She was aware of the old man's shaking hands, just an arm's length away from her, and she was aware of the two women watching with ridicule, behind the counters. She wondered how much they understood love, and love despite the fatality of humankind.

Questions for Thought and Discussion

1. In what period of Chinese history does this story take place? How can you tell? What do the "bigger events," the "protests" that the young woman thinks about as she stands in the pharmacy refer to?
2. Why does the man initiate a conversation with the young woman? What is he looking for?
3. How would you characterize the girl's response to the man's overtures? How do her responses change during the course of the story?
4. Who is her "boy hero"? What has happened to him? What turned him "officially" into a "madman"?
5. Why has she come to the pharmacy? How is the man interfering with her business there?
6. The girl goes often to sit with the boy, to listen to his monologues on history and philosophy and the "fatality of humankind." Yet he doesn't seem to notice that she is anything more than a piece of furniture. So why does she persist in making these visits?
7. What features of Chinese society in this period are revealed in this story? Are there any references that, if you are a Western reader, are surprising to you?
8. Why does the old man step on the package of condoms and initially refuse to give them to the girl? Is he watching out for her morality, or is something else at play?
9. How would you describe the theme of this story? What does it say about the relationships between two generations? What is the old man searching for? the young woman?
10. In what ways is the girl set apart from the two store clerks and from the old man? What does she understand and believe about love herself? Is this a story more about love than loss, or is it more about loss than love? At the end of the story, has the meaning of the key phrase, "the fatality of humankind," changed in any significant way?

36 GUY DE MAUPASSANT
The Necklace

Considered one of the world's great masters of the short story, French writer *Guy de Maupassant (1850–1893) published "The Necklace" in a Paris newspaper,* Le Gaulois, *in 1884. The piece is now included in his short story collection,* Tales of Day and Night. *It remains as relevant today as it did when it was published over a century and a quarter ago. Maupassant is associated with the Naturalist school of writing, which uses ordinary episodes from daily life, described in an objective and highly detailed manner. This story ends with a twist, a reversal of fortune, similar to that employed by the American writer O. Henry and by H. H. Munro, the Scottish writer who published stories under the pseudonym Saki. A complete collection of Maupassant stories can be found online courtesy of the Gutenberg Project (www.gutenberg.org).*

GUY DE MAUPASSANT

The Necklace

She was one of those pretty and charming girls who, as if through some blunder of fate, are born into a family of pen pushers. She had no dowry, no prospects, no possibility of becoming known, appreciated, loved, of finding a wealthy and distinguished husband. And so she settled for a petty clerk in the Ministry of Education.

Unable to adorn herself, she remained simple, but as miserable as if she'd come down in the world. For women have no caste or breed; their beauty, their grace, and their charm serve them in lieu of birth and family background. Their native finesse, their instinct for elegance, their versatile minds are their sole hierarchy, making shopgirls the equals of the grandest ladies.

She suffered endlessly, feeling that she was meant for all delicacies and all luxuries. She suffered from the poverty of her apartment, the dinginess of the walls, the shabbiness of the chairs, the ugliness of the fabrics. All these things, which wouldn't have even been noticed by any other woman of her station, tortured her and infuriated her. The sight of the Breton girl who did her humble housework aroused woeful regrets in her and desperate dreams. She fantasized about hushed antechambers with Oriental hangings, illuminated by high, bronze torchères, and with a pair of tall footmen wearing knee breeches and napping in spacious easy chairs because of the air made heavy by the heater. She fantasized about large drawing rooms lined with ancient silk, about fine furniture carrying priceless knickknacks, about small, fragrant, dainty parlors meant for five o'clock chats with the most intimate friends, well-known and sought-after men whose attention was envied and desired by all women.

Whenever she sat down for supper at the circular table covered with the same tablecloth for three days, she faced her husband, who, removing the lid from the tureen, ecstatically declared: "Ah! A good stew! I don't know of anything better!"

But she fantasized about elegant dinners, about shiny silverware, about tapestries filling the walls with ancient figures and exotic birds in the midst of a magic forest; she fantasized about exquisite courses served in wondrous vessels, about gallantries whispered and listened to with sphinxlike smiles, while the diners consumed the rosy flesh of a trout or the wings of a grouse.

She had no wardrobe, no jewels, nothing. And those things were all that she loved; she felt that they were what she'd been born for. She so dearly wanted to be liked, to be envied, to be seductive and in demand.

She had a rich friend, from convent-school days, whom she stopped visiting because she suffered so deeply upon coming home. And she'd weep for entire days, weep with chagrin, with regret, with despair, and with distress.

—

Now, one evening, her husband came home exuberantly, clutching a large envelope. "Look," he said, "here's something for you."

She ripped it open and pulled out a printed card bearing these words:

THE MINISTER OF EDUCATION AND MADAME GEORGES RAMPONNEAU
ASK MONSIEUR AND MADAME LOISEL FOR THE PLEASURE OF THEIR COMPANY
AT A SOIRÉE AT THE MINISTRY ON MONDAY, 18TH OF JANUARY.

Instead of being thrilled, as her spouse had hoped, she resentfully hurled the invitation on the table, muttering: "What do you want me to do with this?"

"But darling, I thought you'd be pleased. You never go out, and this is an occasion, a wonderful occasion! I went to endless trouble to get our names on the list. Everyone wants an invitation. They're greatly desired, and not too many clerks are invited. You'll see the entire official world there."

She glared at him, irritated, and snapped impatiently: "What do you expect me to wear?"

Her spouse hadn't considered that; he stammered: "Why, the gown you wear to the theater. It strikes me as very nice. . . ."

He held his tongue, stupefied, bewildered, upon seeing his wife crying. Two big tears rolled slowly from the corners of her eyes toward the corners of her mouth. He stuttered: "What's wrong? What's wrong?"

But with a violent effort, she repressed her pain, and, wiping her moist cheeks, she answered in a calm voice: "Nothing's wrong. Except that I've got nothing to wear and consequently I can't go to that ball. Give your card to some colleague whose wife's got a better wardrobe than I."

He was desolated. He went on: "Look, Mathilde. How much would it cost—a suitable gown that you could use on other occasions, something very simple?"

She mulled for several instants, making estimates in her head, trying to hit on a figure that she could ask for without drawing an immediate refusal and terrified exclamation from the frugal clerk.

At last, she hesitantly responded: "I'm not sure about an exact sum, but I think I could manage with four hundred francs."

He blanched slightly, for he had saved up that very amount to buy himself a rifle and go hunting that summer on the plain of Nanterre, with friends who'd be shooting larks on Sundays.

Nevertheless he said: "Fine. I'll give you four hundred francs. But try to have a beautiful gown."

———

The night of the ball was approaching, and Madame Loisel appeared sad, worried, anxious. Still, her gown was ready.

One evening, her husband said to her: "Listen, what's wrong? You've been acting funny for three days now."

And she replied: "I'm annoyed that I don't have any jewelry—not a single gem, nothing to put on. I'll look downright poverty-stricken. I'd almost rather not go to the ball."

He rejoined: "You'll wear real flowers. They're very chic this season. For ten francs you'll have two or three magnificent roses."

She wasn't convinced. "No. . . . There's nothing more humiliating than looking like a pauper in the middle of rich women."

But her husband exclaimed: "How silly you are. Go to your friend Madame Forestier and ask her to lend you some jewelry. The two of you are close enough for you to do that."

She uttered a cry of joy. "You're right! It didn't occur to me!"

The next day, she went to her friend and explained her distress. Madame Forestier went to a mirrored armoire, removed a large case, brought it over, opened it, and said to Madame Loisel: "Take your pick, my dear."

Madame Loisel looked first at some bracelets, then at a pearl necklace, then at a marvelously crafted Venetian cross made up of gold and precious stones. She tried the pieces on before the mirror, wavering, unsure whether to keep them or leave them. She kept asking: "Don't you have anything else?"

"Of course. Keep searching. I can't tell what you'll like."

All at once, in a black satin box, Madame Loisel unearthed a superb diamond necklace, and her heart began pounding with unrestrained desire. Her hands trembled when she picked up the necklace. She placed it on her throat, against her high-necked dress, and remained ecstatic in front of her reflection. Then, hesitant and fearful, she asked: "Can you lend me this, nothing but this?"

"Of course, by all means."

Madame Loisel flung her arms around her friend, hugged her passionately, then fled with her treasure.

———

The night of the ball arrived. Madame Loisel was a grand success. She was love-lier than any other woman, elegant, gracious, smiling, and wild with joy. All the men gazed at her, asked for her name, and tried to get introduced. All the cabinet attachés wanted to waltz with her. The minister noticed her.

She danced, intoxicated, swept away, heady with pleasure, thinking of nothing, in the triumph of her beauty, in the glory of her conquest, in something like a cloud of happiness made of all that homage, all that admiration, all that awoken yearning, all that complete victory that is so dear to a woman's heart.

She left around four in the morning. Since midnight her husband had been dozing in a small, deserted salon with three other men whose wives were having a wonderful time.

Monsieur Loisel, bringing the wraps for their exit, tossed them over her shoulders: they were the modest garments of ordinary life, their poverty clashing with the elegance of the ball gown. She sensed the discord and wanted to flee, to avoid being noticed by the other women, who were bundling up in expensive furs.

Loisel held her back: "Just wait. You'll catch cold out there. I'll hail a cab."

But she didn't listen, she hurried down the stairs. Out in the street, they couldn't find a cab; so they began searching, shouting at the drivers whom they saw riding by in the distance.

They walked down to the Seine, desperate, shivering. Finally, on a quay, they found one of those old, nocturnal broughams that you see in Paris only at night as if they were ashamed of their squalor by day. It brought them to their front door on Rue des Martyrs, and they sadly trudged up to their apartment. It was all over for her. And as for him, he knew he had to be at the Ministry by ten A.M.

Stripping off the wraps that had enveloped her shoulders, she stood in front of the mirror to view herself in her glory again. But suddenly she uttered a cry. The necklace was gone from her neck!

Her husband, already half undressed, asked her: "What's the matter?"

She turned toward him, panic-stricken: "I . . . I . . . I don't have Madame Forestier's necklace."

He rose in horror: "Huh? What do you mean?! That's impossible!. . ."

And they searched the folds of her gown, the folds of her coat, the pockets—everywhere. They did not find the necklace.

He asked her: "Are you sure you had it when we left the ball?"

"Yes, I touched it in the vestibule of the Ministry."

"Well, if you'd lost it in the street, we'd have heard it fall. It must be in the cab."

"Yes. Probably. Did you jot down the number?"

"No. What about you? Did you get it?"

"No."

Their eyes locked in terror. Finally Loisel put his clothes back on.

"I'm going to scour the entire distance that we walked—I'll see if I can find it."

And he left. Too feeble to go to bed, she remained in her gown, sprawling on a chair, her heart inert, her mind blank.

Her husband returned at around seven. He had found nothing.

He went to the police station, to the cab companies, to the newspapers, promising a reward—he went wherever a glimmer of hope beckoned.

She waited all day, still bewildered by that dreadful disaster.

Loisel came back in the evening, his face gaunt and pale; he had discovered nothing.

"You have to write your friend," he said, "that you broke the clasp of her necklace and that you're having it fixed. That'll buy us some time."

She wrote as he dictated.

———

By the end of a week, they had lost all hope.

And Loisel, who had aged five years, declared: "We have to see about replacing the necklace."

The next day they took the jewel case to the jeweler whose name was inside. He consulted his books.

"Madame, I'm not the one who sold this necklace, I only furnished the case."

So, both of them sick with chagrin and anguish, they traipsed from jeweler to jeweler, seeking a necklace that looked like the other one, consulting their memories.

In a boutique at the Palais-Royal, they found a diamond chaplet that struck them as entirely similar to the one they were searching for. The price was forty thousand francs. They could have it for thirty-six thousand.

They begged the jeweler to put it on reserve for three days. And he agreed to take it back for thirty-four thousand if the first necklace were found by the end of February.

Loisel had eighteen thousand francs that his father had left him. He would borrow the rest.

He borrowed, asking for a thousand francs from one person, five hundred from another, five louis here, three louis there. He signed promissory notes, accepted ruinous conditions, dealt with usurers, with all the races of moneylenders. He compromised his entire life, risked his signature without even knowing if he could honor it; and, terrified at the thought of future anguish, the black misery that would overwhelm him, the prospect of all the physical deprivations and all the mental tortures, he went to pick up the new necklace, placing thirty-six thousand francs on the merchant's counter.

When Madame Loisel returned the necklace to Madame Forestier, the latter said, with a slight show of annoyance: "You should have brought it back sooner, I might have needed it."

Madame Forestier did not open the case, which her friend had feared she would do. Had she detected the substitution, what would she have thought? What would she have said? Wouldn't she have taken Madame Loisel for a thief?

———

Madame Loisel now knew the horrible life of necessity. However, she did her part, thoroughly, heroically. The ghastly debt had to be repaid. She would repay it. They dismissed the maid; they moved to a garret.

She performed the gross household tasks, the odious kitchen chores. She washed the dishes, wearing down her rosy nails on greasy pots and on the bottoms of pans. She washed the dirty linen, the shirts and the dishcloths, and let them dry on a line. She lugged the garbage down to the street every morning and hauled up the water, stopping at every landing to catch her breath. And, dressed like a pauper, she went to the produce store, the grocer, the butcher, her basket on her arm, haggling, insulted, defending her miserable cash sou by sou.

Every month, they had to pay off some IOUs, renew others, gain time.

The husband worked evenings, putting a businessman's accounts in order, and spent many nights doing copies at five sous a page.

And this life dragged on for ten years.

At the end of ten years, they had repaid everything, everything, at the rates of loan sharks and with the accumulation of compound interest.

Madame Loisel looked old now. She had become the strong, and hard, and crude woman of poor households. Her hair ill kempt, her skirts awry, and her hands red, she spoke loudly and she washed the floors with big buckets of water. But sometimes, when her husband was at the office, she would sit down at the window and daydream about that long-ago ball, where she had been so beautiful and so celebrated.

What would have happened if she hadn't lost the necklace? Who knows? Who knows? How strange life is, how full of changes! How little it takes to doom you or save you!

—

Now one Sunday, as she was walking along the Champs-Élysées, trying to recover from her weekday chores, she suddenly noticed a woman strolling with a child. It was Madame Forestier, still young, still beautiful, still seductive.

Madame Loisel felt a surge of emotion. Should she speak to her? Yes, of course. And now that she had paid off her debt, she would tell Madame Forestier everything. Why not?

She walked over.

"Good day, Jeanne."

The other woman didn't recognize her, she was astonished at being addressed so familiarly by this housewife. She stammered: "But . . . Madame! . . . I don't know . . . You must be mistaken."

"No. I'm Mathilde Loisel."

Her friend uttered a cry: "Oh! . . . My poor Mathilde, how you've changed!. . ."

"Yes, I've had a hard life since I last saw you. And lots of misery. . . . And all because of you!. . ."

"Because of me? . . . What are you saying?"

"Do you recall that diamond necklace you lent me to attend the ball at the Ministry?"

"Yes. What about it?"

"Well, I lost it."

"What? But you returned it to me."

"I brought you a different one, identical with yours. And we've been paying it off for the past ten years. You realize it wasn't easy for us, we had nothing. . . . At last it's over, and I'm thoroughly glad of it."

Madame Forestier paused.

"You say you bought a diamond necklace to replace mine?"

"Yes. You didn't catch on, did you? They were fairly alike."

And she smiled with a proud and naïve joy.

Madame Forestier, deeply moved, took hold of Madame Loisel's hands.

"Oh, my poor Mathilde! My necklace was paste. It was worth at most five hundred francs!. . ."

From *The Works of Guy de Maupassant* (New York and London: Classic Publishing Company, 1911).

Questions for Thought and Discussion

1. From the telling details in the first two paragraphs of the story, how would you characterize Mathilde? Describe her background. What does it mean to be "born into a family of pen-pushers"? What motivates her behavior, and what does she aspire to?

2. In what way does Mathilde see herself as set apart from others of her station and class? What is the nature of her fantasies?

3. What do expensive possessions mean to her? Why does she stop visiting her rich friend from her convent days?

4. How does Mathilde react when her husband shows her the invitation to the soirée (a fancy ball) at the ministry where he works? How does she "play" him to get what she wants?

5. In borrowing her friend's diamond necklace, what fundamental moral error or error in judgment does Mathilde make? What does this decision reveal about her value system?

6. How does the loss of the diamond necklace change Mathilde? What is the irony of the situation that Mathilde now finds herself in, as she performs "the gross household tasks," scrimps, saves, and borrows money to repay their debts incurred by having to replace the necklace? How well does she accept the necessity of living as they must for ten years?

7. Comment on the pathos—or emotional sadness—that Mathilde experiences as she occasionally daydreams about the night of the ball and how her life might have been different had she not lost the necklace.

8. When Mathilde meets Mme. Forestier along the Champs-Élysées, what does the woman notice immediately about Mathilde's appearance? What is the deeper significance—in the fact that, despite her wretched appearance, Mathilde allows herself to explain what really happened to the necklace?

9. How would you characterize the ending—the revelation that the necklace was only "paste," worth no more than 500 francs? Clearly, irony is involved, but of what sort? How would you explain exactly what this irony involves, beyond the obvious surprise revelation?

10. What is the narrator implying about material goods and their value? Is Mathilde a better human being at the end of the story than she is at the beginning? What moral lesson or value do you think Maupassant intends us to take away from this story?

37 JACK LONDON
To Build a Fire

American writer Jack London (1876–1916) is best known for his depictions of the North American wilderness. Among his most famous novels are Call of the Wild *(1903) and* White Fang *(1908). Long admired for his prodigious literary output, Jack London was an adventurer and hard-living fixture on the San Francisco waterfront at the turn of the century. (In fact, Jack London Square, a complex along the Oakland Estuary on San Francisco Bay, is named after him.) "To Build a Fire" is perhaps London's best known story. First published in* The Youth's Companion *in 1902, London rewrote the story and changed the ending for this version, published in 1908 in* The Century Magazine. *This story is one of the best for depicting the conflict between man and nature, but this nature is not butterflies, glistening raindrops, and snowy mountaintops. The nature depicted here is menacing and unforgiving.*

Library of Congress

Jack London

JACK LONDON

To Build a Fire

Day had broken cold and gray, exceedingly cold and gray, when the man turned aside from the main Yukon trail and climbed the high earth bank, where a dim and little-traveled trail led eastward through the fat spruce timberland. It was a steep bank, and he paused for breath at the top, excusing the act to himself by looking at his watch. It was nine o'clock. There was no sun nor hint of sun, though there was not a cloud in the sky. It was a clear day, and yet there seemed an intangible pall over the face of things, a subtle gloom that made the day dark, and that was due to the absence of sun. This fact did not worry the man. He was used to the lack of sun. It had been days since he had seen the sun, and he knew that a few more days must pass before that cheerful orb, due south, would just peep above the skyline and dip immediately from view.

The man flung a look back along the way he had come. The Yukon lay a mile wide and hidden under three feet of ice. On top of this ice were as many feet of snow. It was all pure white, rolling in gentle undulations where the ice-jams of the freeze-up had formed. North and south, as far as his eye could see, it was unbroken white, save for a dark hair-line that curved and twisted from around the spruce-covered island to the south, and that curved and twisted away into the north, where it disappeared behind another spruce-covered island. This dark hair-line was the trail—the main trail—that led south five hundred miles to the Chilcoot Pass, Dyea, and salt water; and that led north seventy miles to Dawson, and still on to the north a thousand miles to Nulato, and finally to St. Michael on Bering Sea, a thousand miles and half a thousand more.

But all this—the mysterious, far-reaching hair-line trail, the absence of sun from the sky, the tremendous cold, and the strangeness and weirdness of it all—made no impression on the man. It was not because he was long used to it. He was a newcomer in the land, a *chechaquo,* and this was his first winter. The trouble with him was that he was without imagination. He was quick and alert in the things of life, but only in the things, and not in the significances. Fifty degrees below zero meant eighty-odd degrees of frost. Such fact impressed him as being cold and uncomfortable, and that was all. It did not lead him to meditate upon his frailty as a creature of temperature, and upon man's frailty in general, able only to live within certain narrow limits of heat and cold; and from there on it did not lead him to the conjectural field of immortality and man's place in the universe. Fifty degrees below zero stood for a bite of frost that hurt and that must be guarded against by the use of mittens, earflaps, warm moccasins, and thick socks. Fifty degrees below zero was to him just precisely fifty degrees below zero. That there should be anything more to it than that was a thought that never entered his head.

As he turned to go on, he spat speculatively. There was a sharp, explosive crackle that startled him. He spat again. And again, in the air, before it could fall to the snow, the spittle crackled. He knew that at fifty below spittle crackled on the snow, but this spittle had crackled in the air. Undoubtedly it was colder than fifty below—how much colder he did not know. But the temperature did not matter. He was bound for the old claim on the left fork of Henderson Creek, where the boys were already. They had come over across the divide from the Indian Creek country, while he had come the roundabout way to take a look at the possibilities of getting out logs in the spring from the islands in the Yukon. He would be in to camp by six o'clock; a bit after dark, it was true, but the boys would be there, a fire would be going, and a hot supper would be ready. As for lunch, he pressed his hand against the protruding bundle under his jacket. It was also under his shirt, wrapped up in a handkerchief and lying against the naked skin. It was the only way to keep the biscuits from freezing. He smiled agreeably to himself as he thought of those biscuits, each cut open and sopped in bacon grease, and each enclosing a generous slice of fried bacon.

He plunged in among the big spruce trees. The trail was faint. A foot of snow had fallen since the last sled had passed over, and he was glad he was without a sled, traveling light. In fact, he carried nothing but the lunch wrapped in the handkerchief. He was surprised, however, at the cold. It certainly was cold, he concluded, as he rubbed his numb nose and cheek bones with his mittened hand. He was a warm-whiskered man, but the hair on his face did not protect the high cheek bones and the eager nose that thrust itself aggressively into the frosty air.

At the man's heels trotted a dog, a big native husky, the proper wolf-dog, gray-coated and without any visible or temperamental difference from its brother, the wild wolf. The animal was depressed by the tremendous cold. It knew that it was no time for traveling. Its instinct told it a truer tale than was told to the man by the man's judgment. In reality, it was not merely colder than fifty below zero; it was colder than sixty below, than seventy below. It was seventy-five below zero. Since the freezing point is thirty-two above zero, it meant that one hundred and seven degrees of frost obtained. The dog did not know anything about thermometers. Possibly in its brain there was no sharp consciousness of a condition of very cold such as was in the man's brain. But the brute had its instinct. It experienced a vague but menacing apprehension that subdued it and made it slink along at the man's heels, and that made it question eagerly every unwonted movement of the man, as if expecting him to go into camp or to seek shelter somewhere and build a fire. The dog had learned fire, and it wanted fire, or else to burrow under the snow and cuddle its warmth away from the air.

The frozen moisture of its breathing had settled on its fur in a fine powder of frost, and especially were its jowls, muzzle, and eyelashes whitened by its crystalled breath. The man's red beard and mustache were likewise frosted, but more solidly, the deposit taking the form of ice and increasing with every warm, moist breath he exhaled. Also, the man was chewing tobacco, and the muzzle of ice held his lips so rigidly that he was unable to clear his chin when he expelled the juice. The result was that a crystal beard of the color and solidity of amber was increasing its length on his chin. If he fell down it would shatter itself, like glass, into brittle fragments. But he did not mind the appendage. It was the

penalty all tobacco-chewers paid in that country, and he had been out before
in two cold snaps. They had not been so cold as this, he knew, but by the spirit
thermometer at Sixty Mile he knew they had been registered at fifty below and
at fifty-five.

He held on through the level stretch of woods for several miles, crossed a
wide flat of nigger-heads, and dropped down a bank to the frozen bed of a small
stream. This was Henderson Creek, and he knew he was ten miles from the
forks. He looked at his watch. It was ten o'clock. He was making four miles an
hour, and he calculated that he would arrive at the forks at half-past twelve. He
decided to celebrate that event by eating his lunch there.

The dog dropped in again at his heels, with a tail drooping discouragement,
as the man swung along the creek bed. The furrow of the old sled trail was
plainly visible, but a dozen inches of snow covered the marks of the last run-
ners. In a month no man had come up or down that silent creek. The man held
steadily on. He was not much given to thinking, and just then particularly he
had nothing to think about save that he would eat lunch at the forks and that at
six o'clock he would be in camp with the boys. There was nobody to talk to; and,
had there been, speech would have been impossible because of the ice muzzle on
his mouth. So he continued monotonously to chew tobacco and to increase the
length of his amber beard.

Once in a while the thought reiterated itself that it was very cold and that he
had never experienced such cold. As he walked along he rubbed his cheek bones
and nose with the back of his mittened hand. He did this automatically, now
and again changing hands. But rub as he would, the instant he stopped his cheek
bones went numb, and the following instant the end of his nose went numb. He
was sure to frost his cheeks; he knew that, and experienced a pang of regret that
he had not devised a nose strap of the sort Bud wore in cold snaps. Such a strap
passed across the cheeks, as well, and saved them. But it didn't matter much,
after all. What were frosted cheeks? A bit painful, that was all; they were never
serious.

Empty as the man's mind was of thoughts, he was keenly observant, and he
noticed the changes in the creek, the curves and bends and timber-jams, and
always he sharply noted where he placed his feet. Once, coming around a bend,
he shied abruptly, like a startled horse, curved away from the place where he
had been walking, and retreated several paces back along the trail. The creek,
he knew, was frozen clear to the bottom,—no creek could contain water in that
arctic winter,—but he knew also that there were springs that bubbled out from
the hillsides and ran along under the snow and on top of the ice of the creek.
He knew that the coldest snaps never froze these springs, and he knew likewise
their danger. They were traps. They hid pools of water under the snow that
might be three inches deep, or three feet. Sometimes a skin of ice half an inch
thick covered them, and in turn was covered by the snow. Sometimes there were
alternate layers of water and ice skin, so that when one broke through he kept
on breaking through for a while, sometimes wetting himself to the waist.

That was why he had shied in such panic. He had felt the give under his feet
and heard the crackle of a snow-hidden ice skin. And to get his feet wet in such
a temperature meant trouble and danger. At the very least it meant delay, for he

would be forced to stop and build a fire, and under its protection to bare his feet while he dried his socks and moccasins. He stood and studied the creek bed and its banks, and decided that the flow of water came from the right. He reflected a while, rubbing his nose and cheeks, then skirted to the left, stepping gingerly and testing the footing for each step. Once clear of the danger, he took a fresh chew of tobacco and swung along at his four-mile gait.

In the course of the next two hours he came upon several similar traps. Usually the snow above the hidden pools had a sunken, candied appearance that advertised the danger. Once again, however, he had a close call; and once, suspecting danger, he compelled the dog to go on in front. The dog did not want to go. It hung back until the man shoved it forward, and then it went quickly across the white, unbroken surface. Suddenly it broke through, floundered to one side, and got away to firmer footing. It had wet its forefeet and legs, and almost immediately the water that clung to it turned to ice. It made quick efforts to lick the ice off its legs, then dropped down in the snow and began to bite out the ice that had formed between the toes. This was a matter of instinct. To permit the ice to remain would mean sore feet. It did not know this. It merely obeyed the mysterious prompting that arose from the deep crypts of its being. But the man knew, having achieved a judgment on the subject, and he removed the mitten from his right hand and helped tear out the ice particles. He did not expose his fingers more than a minute, and was astonished at the swift numbness that smote them. It certainly was cold. He pulled on the mitten hastily, and beat the hand savagely across his chest.

At twelve o'clock the day was at its brightest. Yet the sun was too far south on its winter journey to clear the horizon. The bulge of the earth intervened between it and Henderson Creek, where the man walked under a clear sky at noon and cast no shadow. At half-past twelve, to the minute, he arrived at the forks of the creek. He was pleased at the speed he had made. If he kept it up, he would certainly be with the boys by six. He unbuttoned his jacket and shirt and drew forth his lunch. The action consumed no more than a quarter of a minute, yet in that brief moment the numbness laid hold of the exposed fingers. He did not put the mitten on, but, instead, struck the fingers a dozen sharp smashes against his leg. Then he sat down on a snow-covered log to eat. The sting that followed upon the striking of his fingers against his leg ceased so quickly that he was startled. He had had no chance to take a bite of biscuit. He struck the fingers repeatedly returned them to the mitten, baring the other hand for the purpose of eating. He tried to take a mouthful, but the ice muzzle prevented. He had forgotten to build a fire and thaw out. He chuckled at his foolishness and as he chuckled he noted the numbness creeping into the exposed fingers. Also he noted that the stinging which had first come to his toes when he sat down was already passing away. He wondered whether the toes were warm or numb. He moved them inside the moccasins and decided that they were numb.

He pulled the mitten on hurriedly and stood up. He was a bit frightened. He stamped up and down until the stinging returned into the feet. It certainly was cold, was his thought. That man from Sulphur Creek had spoken the truth when telling how cold it sometimes got in the country. And he had laughed at him at the time! That showed one must not be too sure of things. There was no mistake about it, it *was* cold. He strode up and down, stamping his feet and threshing his arms, until reassured by the returning warmth. Then he got out matches and proceeded to make a fire. From the undergrowth, where high water of the previous spring had lodged a supply of seasoned twigs, he got his firewood. Working carefully from a small beginning, he soon had a roaring fire, over which he thawed the ice from his face and in the protection of which he ate his biscuits. For the moment the cold of space was outwitted. The dog took satisfaction in the fire, stretching out close enough for warmth and far enough away to escape being singed.

When the man had finished, he filled his pipe and took his comfortable time over a smoke. Then he pulled on his mittens, settled the ear-flaps of his cap firmly about his ears, and took the creek trail up the left fork. The dog was disappointed and yearned back toward the fire. This man did not know cold. Possibly all the generations of his ancestry had been ignorant of cold, of real cold, of cold one hundred and seven degrees below freezing point. But the dog knew; all its ancestry knew, and it had inherited the knowledge. And it knew that it was not good to walk abroad in such fearful cold. It was the time to lie snug in a hole in the snow and wait for a curtain of cloud to be drawn across the face of outer space whence this cold came. On the other hand, there was no keen intimacy between the dog and the man. The one was the toil-slave of the other, and the only caresses it had ever received were the caresses of the whip-lash and of harsh and menacing throat sounds that threatened the whip-lash. So the dog made no effort to communicate its apprehension to the man. It was not concerned in the welfare of the man; it was for its own sake that it yearned back toward the fire. But the man whistled, and spoke to it with the sound of whip-lashes, and the dog swung in at the man's heels and followed after.

The man took a chew of tobacco and proceeded to start a new amber beard. Also, his moist breath quickly powdered with white his mustache, eyebrows, and lashes. There did not seem to be so many springs on the left fork of the Henderson, and for half an hour the man saw no signs of any. And then it happened. At a place where there were no signs, where the soft, unbroken snow seemed to advertise solidity beneath, the man broke through. It was not deep. He wet himself halfway to the knees before he floundered out to the firm crust.

He was angry, and cursed his luck aloud. He had hoped to get into camp with the boys at six o'clock, and this would delay him an hour, for he would have to build a fire and dry out his foot-gear. This was imperative at that low temperature—he knew that much; and he turned aside to the bank, which he climbed. On top, tangled in the underbrush about the trunks of several small spruce trees, was a high-water deposit of dry fire-wood—sticks and twigs, principally, but also larger portions of seasoned branches and fine, dry, last year's grasses. He threw down several large pieces on top of the snow. This served for a foundation and prevented the young flame from drowning itself in the snow it otherwise would melt. The flame he got by touching a match to a small shred of birch-bark that he took from his pocket. This burned even more readily than paper. Placing it on the foundation, he fed the young flame with wisps of dry grass and with the tiniest dry twigs.

He worked slowly and carefully, keenly aware of his danger. Gradually, as the flame grew stronger, he increased the size of the twigs with which he fed it. He squatted in the snow, pulling the twigs out from their entanglement in the brush and feeding directly to the flame. He knew there must be no failure. When it is seventy-five below zero a man must not fail in his first attempt to build a fire—that is, if his feet are wet. If his feet are dry, and he fails, he can run along the trail for half a mile and restore his circulation. But the circulation of wet and freezing feet cannot be restored by running when it is seventy-five below. No matter how fast he runs, the wet feet will freeze the harder.

All this the man knew. The old-timer on Sulphur Creek had told him about it the previous fall, and now he was appreciating the advice. Already all sensation had gone out of his feet. To build the fire he had been forced to remove his mittens, and the fingers had quickly gone numb. His pace of four miles an hour had kept his heart pumping blood to the surface of his body and to all the extremities. But the instant he stopped, the action of the pump eased down. The cold of space smote the unprotected tip of the planet, and he, being on that unprotected tip, received the full force of the blow. The blood of his body recoiled before it. The blood was alive, like the dog, and like the dog it wanted to hide away and cover itself up from the fearful cold. So long as he walked four miles an hour, he pumped that blood, willy-nilly, to the surface; but now it ebbed away and sank down into the recesses of his body. The extremities were the first to feel its absence. His wet feet froze the faster, and his exposed fingers numbed the faster, though they had not yet begun to freeze. Nose and cheeks were already freezing, while the skin of all his body chilled as it lost its blood.

But he was safe. Toes and nose and cheeks would be only touched by the frost, for the fire was beginning to burn with strength. He was feeding it with twigs the size of his finger. In another minute he would be able to feed it with branches the size of his wrist, and then he could remove his wet foot-gear, and, while it dried, he could keep his naked feet warm by the fire, rubbing them at first, of course, with snow. The fire was a success. He was safe. He remembered the advice of the old-timer on Sulphur Creek, and smiled. The old-timer had been very serious in laying down the law that no man must travel alone in the Klondike after fifty below. Well, here he was; he had had the accident; he was alone; and he had saved himself. Those old-timers were rather womanish, some of them, he thought. All a man had to do was to keep his head, and he was all right. Any man who was a man could travel alone. But it was surprising the rapidity with which his cheeks and nose were freezing. And he had not thought his fingers could go lifeless in so short a time. Lifeless they were, for he could scarcely make them move together to grip a twig, and they seemed remote from his body and from him. When he touched a twig he had to look and see whether or not he had hold of it. The wires were pretty well down between him and his finger-ends.

All of which counted for little. There was the fire, snapping and crackling and promising life with every dancing flame. He started to untie his moccasins. They were coated with ice; the thick German socks were like sheaths of iron halfway to the knees; and the moccasin strings were like rods of steel all twisted and knotted as by some conflagration. For a moment he tugged with his numb fingers, then, realizing the folly of it, he drew his sheath-knife.

But before he could cut the strings, it happened. It was his own fault, or, rather, his mistake. He should not have built the fire under the spruce tree. He should have built it in the open. But it had been easier to pull the twigs from the brush and drop them directly on the fire. Now the tree under which he had done this carried a weight of snow on its boughs. No wind had blown for weeks, and each bough was fully freighted. Each time he had pulled a twig he had communicated a slight agitation to the tree—an imperceptible agitation, so far as he was concerned, but an agitation sufficient to bring about the disaster. High up in the tree one bough capsized its load of snow. This fell on the boughs beneath, capsizing them. This process continued, spreading out and involving the whole tree. It grew like an avalanche, and it descended without warning upon the man and the fire, and the fire was blotted out! Where it had burned was a mantle of fresh and disordered snow.

The man was shocked. It was as though he had just heard his own sentence of death. For a moment he sat and stared at the spot where the fire had been. Then he grew very calm. Perhaps the old-timer on Sulphur Creek was right. If he had only had a trail-mate he would have been in no danger now. The trail-mate could have built the fire. Well, it was up to him to build the fire over again, and this second time there must be no failure. Even if he succeeded, he would most likely lose some toes. His feet must be badly frozen by now, and there would be some time before the second fire was ready.

Such were his thoughts, but he did not sit and think them. He was busy all the time they were passing through his mind. He made a new foundation for a fire, this time in the open, where no treacherous tree could blot it out. Next he gathered dry grasses and tiny twigs from the high-water flotsam. He could not bring his fingers together to pull them out, but he was able to gather them by the handful. In this way he got many rotten twigs and bits of green moss that were undesirable, but it was the best he could do. He worked methodically, even collecting an armful of the larger branches to be used later when the fire gathered strength. And all the while the dog sat and watched him, a certain yearning wistfulness in its eyes, for it looked upon him as the fire-provider, and the fire was slow in coming.

When all was ready, the man reached in his pocket for a second piece of birch-bark. He knew the bark was there, and, though he could not feel it with his fingers, he could hear its crisp rustling as he fumbled for it. Try as he would, he could not clutch hold of it. And all the time, in his consciousness, was the knowledge that each instant his feet were freezing. This thought tended to put him in a panic, but he fought against it and kept calm. He pulled on his mittens with his teeth, and threshed his arms back and forth, beating his hands with all his might against his sides. He did this sitting down, and he stood up to do it; and all the while the dog sat in the snow, its wolf-brush of a tail curled around warmly over its forefeet, its sharp wolf ears pricked forward intently as it watched the man. And the man, as he beat and threshed with his arms and hands, felt a great surge of envy as he regarded the creature that was warm and secure in its natural covering.

After a time he was aware of the first far-away signals of sensation in his beaten fingers. The faint tingling grew stronger till it evolved into a stinging ache that was excruciating, but which the man hailed with satisfaction. He stripped the mitten from his right hand and fetched forth the birchbark. The exposed fingers were quickly going numb again. Next he brought out his bunch of sulphur matches. But the tremendous cold had already driven the life out of his fingers. In his effort to separate one match from the others, the whole bunch fell in the snow. He tried to pick it out of the snow, but failed. The dead fingers could neither touch nor clutch. He was very careful. He drove the thought of his freezing feet, and nose, and cheeks, out of his mind, devoting his whole soul to the matches. He watched, using the sense of vision in place of that of touch, and when he saw his fingers on each side the bunch, he closed them—that is, he willed to close them, for the wires were down, and the fingers did not obey. He pulled the mitten on the right hand, and beat it fiercely against his knee. Then, with both mittened hands, he scooped the bunch of matches, along with much snow, into his lap. Yet he was no better off.

After some manipulation he managed to get the bunch between the heels of his mittened hands. In this fashion he carried it to his mouth. The ice crackled and snapped when by a violent effort he opened his mouth. He drew the lower jaw in, curled the upper lip out of the way, and scraped the bunch with his upper teeth in order to separate a match. He succeeded in getting one, which he dropped on his lap. He was no better off. He could not pick it up. Then he devised a way. He picked it up in his teeth and scratched it on his leg. Twenty times he scratched before he succeeded in lighting it. As it flamed he held it with his teeth to the birch-bark. But the burning brimstone went up his nostrils and into his lungs, causing him to cough spasmodically. The match fell into the snow and went out.

The old-timer on Sulphur Creek was right, he thought in the moment of controlled despair that ensued: after fifty below, a man should travel with a partner. He beat his hands, but failed in exciting any sensation. Suddenly he bared both hands, removing the mittens with his teeth. He caught the whole bunch between the heels of his hands. His arm muscles, not being frozen, enabled him to press the hand heels tightly against the matches. Then he scratched the bunch along his leg. It flared into flame, seventy sulphur matches at once! There was no wind to blow them out. He kept his head to one side to escape the strangling fumes, and held the blazing bunch to the birch-bark. As he so held it, he became aware of sensation in his hand. His flesh was burning. He could smell it. Deep down below the surface he could feel it. The sensation developed into pain that grew acute. And still he endured it, holding the flame of the matches clumsily to the bark that would not light readily because his own burning hands were in the way, absorbing most of the flame.

At last, when he could endure no more, he jerked his hands apart. The blazing matches fell sizzling into the snow, but the birch-bark was alight. He began laying dry grasses and the tiniest twigs on the flame. He could not pick and choose, for he had to lift the fuel between the heels of his hands. Small pieces of rotten wood and green moss clung to the twigs, and he bit them off as well as he could with his teeth. He cherished the flame carefully and awkwardly. It meant life, and it must not perish. The withdrawal of blood from the surface of his body now made him begin to shiver, and he grew more awkward. A large piece of green moss fell squarely on the little fire. He tried to poke it out with his fingers, but his shivering frame made him poke too far, and he disrupted the nucleus of the little fire, the burning grasses and tiny twigs separating and scattering. He tried to poke them together again, but, in spite of the tenseness of the effort, his shivering got away with him, and the twigs were hopelessly scattered. Each twig gushed a puff of smoke and went out. The fire-provider had failed. As he looked apathetically about him, his eyes chanced on the dog, sitting across the ruins of the fire from him, in the snow, making restless, hunching movements, slightly lifting one forefoot and then the other, shifting its weight back and forth on them with wistful eagerness.

The sight of the dog put a wild idea into his head. He remembered the tale of the man, caught in a blizzard, who killed a steer and crawled inside the carcass, and so was saved. He would kill the dog and bury his hands in the warm body until the numbness went out of them. Then he could build another fire. He spoke to the dog, calling it to him; but in his voice was a strange note of fear that frightened the animal, who had never known the man to speak in such way before. Something was the matter, and its suspicious nature sensed danger—it knew not what danger, but somewhere, somehow, in its brain arose an apprehension of the man. It flattened its ears down at the sound of the man's voice, and its restless, hunching movements and the liftings and shiftings of its forefeet became more pronounced; but it would not come to the man. He got on his hands and knees and crawled toward the dog. This unusual posture again excited suspicion, and the animal sidled mincingly away.

The man sat up in the snow for a moment and struggled for calmness. Then he pulled on his mittens, by means of his teeth, and got upon his feet. He glanced down at first in order to assure himself that he was really standing up, for the absence of sensation in his feet left him unrelated to the earth. His erect position in itself started to drive the webs of suspicion from the dog's mind; and when he spoke peremptorily, with the sound of whip-lashes in his voice, the dog rendered its customary allegiance and came to him. As it came within reaching distance, the man lost his control. His arms flashed out to the dog, and he experienced genuine surprise when he discovered that his hands could not clutch, that there was neither bend nor feeling in the fingers. He had forgotten for the moment that they were frozen and that they were freezing more and more. All this happened quickly, and before the animal could get away, he encircled its body with his arms. He sat down in the snow, and in this fashion held the dog, while it snarled and whined and struggled.

But it was all he could do, hold its body encircled in his arms and sit there. He realized that he could not kill the dog. There was no way to do it. With his helpless hands he could neither draw nor hold his sheath-knife nor throttle the animal. He released it, and it plunged wildly away, with tail between its legs, and still snarling. It halted forty feet away and surveyed him curiously, with ears sharply pricked forward. The man looked down at his hands in order to locate them, and found them hanging on the ends of his arms. It struck him as curious that one should have to use his eyes in order to find out where his hands were. He began threshing his arms back and forth, beating the mittened hands against his sides. He did this for five minutes, violently, and his heart pumped enough blood up to the surface to put a stop to his shivering. But no sensation was aroused in the hands. He had an impression that they hung like weights on the ends of his arms, but when he tried to run the impression down, he could not find it.

A certain fear of death, dull and oppressive, came to him. This fear quickly became poignant as he realized that it was no longer a mere matter of freezing his fingers and toes, or of losing his hands and feet, but that it was a matter of life and death, with the chances against him. This threw him into a panic, and he turned and ran up the creek-bed along the old dim trail. The dog joined in behind and kept up with him. He ran blindly, without intention, in fear such as he had never known in his life. Slowly, as he plowed and floundered through the snow, he began to see things again,—the banks of the creek, the old timber-jams, the leafless aspens, and the sky. The running made him feel better. He did not shiver. Maybe, if he ran on, his feet would thaw out; and, anyway, if he ran far enough, he would reach the camp and the boys. Without doubt he would lose some fingers and toes and some of his face; but the boys would take care of him, and save the rest of him when he got there. And at the same time there was another thought in his mind that said he would never get to the camp and the boys; that it was too many miles away, that the freezing had too great a start on him, and that he would soon be stiff and dead. This thought he kept in the background and refused to consider. Sometimes it pushed itself forward and demanded to be heard, but he thrust it back and strove to think of other things.

It struck him as curious that he could run at all on feet so frozen that he could not feel them when they struck the earth and took the weight of his body. He seemed to himself to skim along above the surface, and to have no connection with the earth. Somewhere he had once seen a winged Mercury, and he wondered if Mercury felt as he felt when skimming over the earth.

His theory of running until he reached camp and the boys had one flaw in it: he lacked the endurance. Several times he stumbled, and finally he tottered, crumpled up, and fell. When he tried to rise, he failed. He must sit and rest, he decided, and next time he would merely walk and keep on going. As he sat and regained his breath, he noted that he was feeling quite warm and comfortable. He was not shivering, and it even seemed that a warm glow had come to his chest and trunk. And yet, when he touched his nose or cheeks, there was no sensation. Running would not thaw them out. Nor would it thaw out his hands and feet. Then the thought came to him that the frozen portions of his body must be extending. He tried to keep this thought down, to forget it, to think of something else; he was aware of the panicky feeling that it caused, and he was afraid of the panic. But the thought asserted itself, and persisted, until it produced a vision of his body totally frozen. This was too much, and he made another wild run along the trail. Once he slowed down to a walk, but the thought of the freezing extending itself made him run again.

And all the time the dog ran with him, at his heels. When he fell down a second time, it curled its tail over its forefeet and sat in front of him, facing him, curiously eager and intent. The warmth and security of the animal angered him, and he cursed it till it flattened down its ears appeasingly. This time the shivering came more quickly upon the man. He was losing in his battle with the frost. It was creeping into his body from all sides. The thought of it drove him on, but he ran no more than a hundred feet, when he staggered and pitched headlong. It was his last panic. When he had recovered his breath and control, he sat up and entertained in his mind the conception of meeting death with dignity. However, the conception did not come to him in such terms. His idea of it was that he had been making a fool of himself, running around like a chicken with its head cut off—such was the simile that occurred to him. Well, he was bound to freeze anyway, and he might as well take it decently. With this new-found peace of mind came the first glimmerings of drowsiness. A good idea, he thought, to sleep off to death. It was like taking an anæsthetic. Freezing was not so bad as people thought. There were lots worse ways to die.

He pictured the boys finding his body next day. Suddenly he found himself with them, coming along the trail and looking for himself. And, still with them, he came around a turn in the trail and found himself lying in the snow. He did not belong with himself any more, for even then he was out of himself, standing with the boys and looking at himself in the snow. It certainly was cold, was his thought. When he got back to the States, he could tell the folks what real cold was. He drifted on from this to a vision of the old-timer on Sulphur Creek. He could see him quite clearly, warm and comfortable, and smoking a pipe.

"You were right, old hoss; you were right," the man mumbled to the old-timer of Sulphur Creek.

Then the man drowsed off into what seemed to him the most comfortable and satisfying sleep he had ever known. The dog sat facing him and waiting. The brief day drew to a close in a long, slow twilight. There were no signs of a fire to be made, and, besides, never in the dog's experience had it known a man to sit like that in the snow and make no fire. As the twilight drew on, its eager yearning for the fire mastered it, and with a great lifting and shifting of forefeet, it whined softly, then flattened its ears down in anticipation of being chidden by the man. But the man remained silent. Later, the dog whined loudly. And still later it crept close to the man and caught the scent of death. This made the animal bristle and back away. A little longer it delayed, howling under the stars that leaped and danced and shone brightly in the cold sky. Then it turned and trotted up the trail in the direction of the camp it knew, where were the other food-providers and fire-providers.

Questions for Thought and Discussion

1. Where does the story take place? What time of year is it?
2. What is the man's flaw? What is he lacking in? How does the narrator reveal it?
3. How is nature portrayed in this story? In what ways is nature an antagonist?
4. In what way is his canine companion more attuned to the environment than the man is? What is the "vague but menacing apprehension" that the

dog senses? Describe the relationship between the man and the dog as it is revealed throughout the story.

5. What particular danger do springs under the snow pose for the winter traveler in this environment?

6. While the man is eating his lunch, he realizes that he has forgotten to build a fire. How does he respond to this realization? What does this response reveal about his character?

7. How aware is the man of the danger he is in? Point to instances in the story that suggest an answer.

8. In the middle of the story, the man recounts the advice the old-timer from Sulphur Creek had given him about not traveling alone in the Klondike when the temperature is below 50 degrees below zero. What does his reaction in recounting this advice suggest about the man's character? What mistake best demonstrates that, in fact, the man isn't so smart after all in thinking that the "womanish" advice of the old-timer wasn't worth listening to? What would a trail-mate with more experience have told him, warned him about?

9. At what point in the story is there an epiphany, a sudden realization of what is to come? Does he accept this eventuality completely or not?

10. Physically, what is the effect of extreme cold on the human body? What physical changes is the man's body subject to throughout the story? How do these physical changes defeat his determination to build a fire?

11. The man does at least one or two things right as he tries to solve his predicament. What are they?

12. The ancient Greeks used the term *hubris*, meaning overbearing pride or arrogance, to describe a character flaw that led to a tragic end. To what extent does this term explain the misfortune that besets the man in this story?

13. How, if at all, does the man change at the end of the story? Why do you suppose London didn't give the character a name?

14. This story was published over a century ago. The writing style was quite different then. Comment on the difference in style between, say, J. Robert Lennon and Jack London. London is often accused of overwriting, of being too florid in his prose style. Do you think this problem is evident in this story? Is the criticism justified in this case?

PART SEVEN

Everyday Reading

New to this edition, Part Seven gives you an opportunity both to learn the importance of flexibility in tackling various reading assignments and to practice comprehension skills with various kinds of reading that we all encounter in our everyday lives. News articles (whether in print or online), credit card provisions, package labels, even recipes, require reading, but reading of a different sort than what you have practiced thus far.

Throughout this book, you have been in training, so to speak—learning to identify main ideas, inferences, patterns of development, distinguishing between fact and opinion, and so forth. There hasn't been much room for flexibility, because the goal throughout has been the same: to help you become the best college reader possible so that you can succeed in your college classes.

But the material we encounter in our daily lives outside the classroom is different, and we need to read it for different purposes and in different ways. The key concept is *flexibility*, the realization that we shouldn't be reading everything the same way. We surely don't read the sports pages or a review of a TV program or movie we might want to watch in the same depth or with the same focus as we do a reading selection for an English class—or at least we shouldn't. In the case of the former, we most likely skim through, looking for information about how our favorite football or basketball team did or what their prospects are for the next game. We get a general sense of the movie or program, but we don't *analyze* the material as you have learned to do in earlier sections of the text. We read for information or for answers to specific questions.

What follows, then, are several short reading assignments, in most cases followed by some basic comprehension questions or questions for discussion and analysis.

Reading Newspaper and Magazine Articles (Print or Online)

Whether you read the daily paper or magazines in a print edition or online, the task remains the same—to get an understanding of the writer's main point. Typically, however, we don't subject a newspaper article to the analytical scrutiny that you have practiced in this book. Your task is to find out what happened and why before you move on to the next item.

DAVID BROWN

Test Rat a Good Samaritan,
The Washington Post

At the very least, the new experiment reported in *Science* is going to make people think differently about what it means to be a "rat." Eventually, though, it may tell us interesting things about what it means to be a human being

In a simple experiment, researchers at the University of Chicago sought to find out whether a rat would release a fellow rat from an unpleasantly restrictive cage if it could. The answer was yes.

The free rat, often hearing distress calls from its compatriot, learned to open the cage and did so with greater efficiency over time. It would release the other animal even if there wasn't the payoff of a reunion with it. Astonishingly, if given access to a small hoard of chocolate chips, the free rat would usually save at least one treat for the captive—which is a lot to expect of a rat.

The researchers came to the unavoidable conclusion that what they were seeing was empathy, and apparently selfless behavior driven by that mental state.

"There is nothing in it for them except for whatever feeling they get from helping another individual," said Peggy Mason, the neurobiologist who conducted the experiment along with graduate student Inbal Ben-Ami Bartal and fellow researcher Jean Decety.

The idea that animals have emotional lives and are capable of detecting emotions in others has been gaining ground for decades.

Empathic behavior has been observed in apes and monkeys, and testified to by numberless pet owners (especially dog owners). Recently, scientists demonstrated "emotional contagion" in mice, a situation in which one animal's stress worsens another's. But empathy that leads to helping activity—what psychologists term "pro-social behavior"—hasn't been formally shown in non-primates until now.

If this experiment reported Thursday holds up under scrutiny, it will give neuroscientists a method to study empathy and altruism in a rigorous way.

Do age and sex affect empathic behavior? Will a rat free a rat it doesn't know? Is more help offered to individuals an animal is related to, either directly or as a member of the same genetic tribe? What are the genes, and their variants, that determine whether one animal helps another and how much? Answering those questions becomes possible now that there is an animal "model" for this behavior.

COMPREHENSION QUESTIONS

1. What does the term "Good Samaritan" in the title refer to? Consult a dictionary if necessary.

    _____

2. What was the purpose of the study? How was it conducted?

    _____

    _____

3. What conclusion did the researchers draw from the rat's behavior?

    _____

4. Why was this experiment a breakthrough?

    _____

5. Are its findings conclusive or definitive? How do you know?

    _____

    _____

LISA M. KRIEGER

Uncovering Glimpse of Young Universe, *San Jose Mercury News*

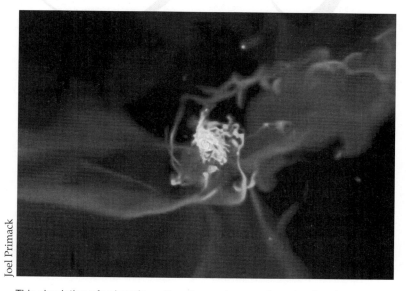

Joel Primack

This simulation of galaxy formation shows streams of gas feeding the growing galaxy. The newly discovered gas clouds may be part of a "cold flow" of gas similar to these streams.

For the first time, astronomers have detected ancient and pristine clouds of primordial gas, conceived when the universe was a very young, dark and lonely place.

This long-sought discovery of 12-billion-year-old pockets of gas by UC Santa Cruz scientists offers a stunning snapshot of early cosmic history—and adds more support to the widely accepted big bang theory about the origin of elements in our universe.

"It's thrilling. It describes all that we've been looking for," said J. Xavier Prochaska, professor of astronomy and astrophysics, whose study is published in Thursday's issue of the journal *Science*.

Staring into deep time within two patches of dark sky—one in the constellation Leo and the other Ursa Major—the team found clouds of hydrogen and a hydrogen isotope, called deuterium. Those two original elements, relics of the big bang—a mega-explosion that led to the expansion of the universe—are uncontaminated by more recent elements like carbon, nitrogen and oxygen.

The ancestral clouds are very, very faint, not visible to the naked eye. But powerful computers in a UC Santa Cruz basement can analyze their spectral images, captured by Hawaii's Keck Telescope.

The discovery is significant because it props up the big bang theory of the origin of the elements. In the beginning, according to the hypothesis, hydrogen and helium were created during "the dark ages" of the universe—through nuclear reactions in the first few moments of creation.

But that could not be proven until now, because astronomers were able to detect only much newer elements, such as our beloved oxygen.

The primordial gas provided fuel for the very first stars—lighting up the darkness. These early stars were monsters that burned hot, lived fast and died young. Their deaths sent newer elements exploding into space, seeding galaxies with everything necessary for life.

More profoundly, the UCSC discovery is a reminder of the illuminating power of human reason, and how scientists can overcome seemingly insoluble problems using technology.

"We've been trying to find such pockets, because there was good reason to think they exist," said Prochaska. "We've been aggressively looking for material that would match the theory.

"This is very pristine gas—exactly what the theory predicts," he said. "It's material not polluted by stars or galaxies."

Turning the scientific process on its head, the discovery was made by the actual absence of data—what couldn't be seen.

Light is absorbed by gas. So when light can't be found, it reveals the composition of that gas.

All gases, and other elements, have unique "spectral" fingerprints. So the UCSC team did a spectrographic analysis of the fingerprints of the light. The light came from a super-bright quasar; fortunately, the clouds happened to be right in front of it.

The scientists' computers spread out this light into a broad spectrum of different wavelengths—making it possible to identify which wavelengths were absorbed by the gas.

Looking for wavelengths of hydrogen, "we don't see it. That light is removed," meaning it is contained within the clouds, Prochaska said.

Ditto for deuterium. Scientists believe that the universe once had more deuterium than it does today—and the deuterium-to-hydrogen ratio in the gas clouds matches big bang predictions.

"It's doing astronomy backwards," explained Prochaska. "Most people look at stars, galaxies—things like color, shape, whatever. . . . But we don't care about the light we receive. We care about light that we don't receive. The dark spots."

He added, "We're doing science in silhouette—studying that light that doesn't get here, due to the gas.

"We get excited about nothing," he joked. "When it was immediately clear that nothing was there, that really floored us."

Poignantly, these clouds likely no longer exist.

Powerful telescopes see distant objects as they were far back in time, not now. It takes a long time for light to travel across the universe.

"It's very different today," said Prochaska. "They're probably not there at all."

COMPREHENSION QUESTIONS

1. What did UC Santa Cruz scientists recently discover?

   _____

2. What does the word *primordial* mean? Why have these clouds of primordial gases remained pristine? How old are they?

   _____

   _____

3. Why is this discovery significant?

   _____

4. What is the "big bang" explanation of how the universe was created?

   _____

5. The writer states that the scientists were studying clouds of gas they couldn't see without the aid of powerful telescopes and that no longer exist. What surprise does the conclusion suggest?

   _____

"Comfort Food on the Brain," *Utne Reader*

On a stressful or depressing day, the gut goes straight for comfort food: potatoes and gravy, meatloaf, or, for the veggies, a grilled cheese sandwich piled high with cheddar, provolone, or mozzarella. The more the cheese oozes, the better the day gets. In an emerging field dubbed neurogastroenterology, scientists are finding that the stomach knows more than we give it credit for. "The gut can work independently of any control by the brain in your head—it's functioning as a second brain," Michael Gershon, professor of pathology and cell biology at Columbia University, tells Dan Hurley in *Psychology Today* (Nov.–Dec. 2011). The brain in the gut, called the enteric nervous system (ENS), is made up of 100 million neurons and can work on its own, without any direction from your upper half. And like the mind, it can control mood. The ENS manufactures serotonin identical to that in the head, Hurley reports, and "tinkering with the second brain in our gut has lately been shown to be a potent tool for achieving relief from major depression." Autism has also been found to be wrapped up in the neurobiology of the stomach, with many parents finding that a gluten- and dairy-free diet calms obsessive behavior and reduces social withdrawal. So what comfort food works best to bolster moods: Mashed potatoes? Macaroni and cheese? Mainlined ice cream sundaes? Any of these can work, according to researchers in Belgium, as long as they contain plenty of fat. After participants in the Belgian study were fed either a saline solution or an infusion of fatty acids and then listened to neutral or melancholy music, they were interviewed and given MRI scans. Researchers found that the fatty acids activated the brain regions that regulate emotions and reduced feelings of sadness by about half. "It's an important demonstration that in a nonconscious way, without knowing whether you are getting the fat or the salt water, something you put in your stomach can change your mood," Giovanni Cizza of the National Institute of Diabetes and Digestive and Kidney Diseases tells Hurley. So go on and take solace in comfort food. As it turns out, cravings aren't all in the head.

"Comfort Food on the Brain." Originally published in *Utne Reader*, March/April 2012, p. 19. Reprinted with permission. www.utne.com

COMPREHENSION QUESTIONS

1. What do you think a neurogastroenterologist studies?

    _____

2. When Michael Gershon says that the stomach functions like a "second brain," what does he mean? What specifically enables the enteric nervous system (ENS) to work on its own?

    _____

3. What is the relationship between so-called comfort foods and mood?

    _____

4. One ingredient is essential in comfort food. What is it?

    _____

5. What's the main point of the article, and where does it appear?

    _____

Reading a Credit Card Insert

What do you normally do with the inserts that come with your credit card bill? If you're like millions of American consumers, you probably never give them a second glance and place them in the recycling container. Recently, I applied for a new credit card, Chase's Sapphire card, and while searching for a suitable item for this section of the book, I came across the bank's protection in case my identity is stolen.

Chase Sapphire Visa Credit Card— Identity Theft Protection

What is the Personal Identity Theft benefit?

The Personal Identity Theft benefit offers reimbursement for covered expenses you incur to restore your identity, up to a maximum of $5,000, as a result of a Covered Stolen Identity Event.

Who is eligible for this benefit?

To be eligible for this benefit, you must be a valid cardholder whose name is embossed on an eligible U.S.-issued card and reside in the United States or Canada.

What is a Covered Stolen Identity Even?

"Covered Stolen Identity Event" means the theft or unauthorized or illegal use of your name, transaction card account or account number, Social Security number, or any other method of identifying you.

What is covered?

Covered Losses under the Personal Identity Theft benefit are:

- Costs you incur for re-filing applications for loans, grants, or other credit or debt instruments that are rejected solely because the lender received incorrect information as a result of a Covered Stolen Identity Event.
- Costs for notarizing affidavits or other similar documents, long distance telephone calls, and postage reasonably incurred as a result of your efforts to report a Covered Stolen Identity Event or to amend or rectify records as to your true name or identity as a result of a Covered Stolen Identity Event.
- Costs incurred by you for a maximum of four (4) credit reports, requested as a result of a Covered Stolen Identity Event, from any entity approved by the Benefit Administrator.
- Actual lost wages for time taken away from your work premises solely as a result of your efforts to amend or rectify records as to your true name or identity as a result of a Covered Stolen Identity Event.
- Costs for reasonable fees for an attorney appointed by the Benefit Administrator and related court fees you incur with the consent of the Benefit Administrator for suits brought against you by a creditor or collection agency or similar entity acting on behalf of a creditor for nonpayment of goods or services or default on a loan as a result of a Covered Stolen Identity Event.

What is *not* covered?
- Any dishonest, criminal, malicious, or fraudulent acts by you.
- Any damages, loss, or indemnification unless otherwise stated in this disclosure.
- Costs associated with any legal action or suit other than those set forth under Covered Losses.
- Sick days and any time taken from self-employment.
- Any losses as a result of theft or unauthorized use of an account by a person to whom the account has been entrusted.

Is there a charge for these services?
No. Your financial institution provides this benefit to you at no additional cost.

When and where am I covered?
Payment for Covered Losses will be limited to losses incurred in the United States, its territories and possessions, Puerto Rico, or Canada for a loss occurring during the benefit period.

How do I file a claim?
Call our Benefit Administrator immediately when you reasonably believe a Covered Stolen Identity Event has occurred and provide information including, but not limited to, how, when, and where the Covered Stolen Identity Event occurred. The Benefit Administrator may also require other reasonable information or documents regarding the loss.

What documents do I need to submit with my claim?
A signed, sworn proof of loss or affidavit containing the information requested by the Benefit Administrator must be submitted within sixty (60) days.

How will I be reimbursed?
Once your claim has been verified, under normal circumstances, reimbursement will be initiated within five (5) business days of receipt and approval of all required documents.

Do I have to do anything else?
- If you reasonably believe that a law may have been broken, you must promptly file a report with the police.
- You must take all reasonable steps to mitigate possible losses, including cancellation of any affected debit, credit, or similar card in the case of a Covered Stolen Identity Event.

Additional Provisions for Personal Identity Theft: This benefit applies only to you, the primary eligible cardholder. You must use due diligence and do all things reasonable to avoid or diminish any loss of or damage to property protected by the benefit.

If you make any claim knowing it to be false or fraudulent, no coverage shall exist for such claim and your benefits may be canceled. Each cardholder agrees that representations regarding claims will be accurate and complete. Any and all relevant provisions shall be void in any case of fraud, intentional concealment, or misrepresentation of material fact by the cardholder.

Once you report a Covered Stolen Identity Event, a claim file will be opened and shall remain open for six (6) months from the date of the Covered Stolen Identity Event. No payment will be made on a claim that is not completely substantiated in the manner required by the Benefit Administrator with six (6) months of the Covered Stolen Identity Event.

After the Benefit Administrator has paid your claim of loss or damage, all your rights and remedies against any party in respect of this loss or damage will be transferred to the Benefit Administrator to the extent of the payment made to you. You must give the Benefit Administrator all assistance as may reasonably be required to secure all rights and remedies.

No legal action for a claim may be brought until sixty (60) days after we receive a Proof of Loss. No legal action against us may be brought more than two (2) years after the time for giving Proof of Loss. Further, no legal action may be brought against us unless all the terms of this Guide to Benefit have been complied with fully.

This benefit is provided to eligible cardholders at no additional cost and is in effect for acts occurring while the benefit is in effect. The terms and conditions contained in this Guide to Benefit may be modified by subsequent endorsements. Modifications to the terms and conditions may be provided via additional Guide to Benefit mailings, statement inserts, or statement messages. The benefit described in this Guide to Benefit will not apply to cardholders whose accounts have been suspended or canceled.

Termination dates may vary by financial institutions. Your financial institution can cancel or non-renew this benefit, and if we do, we will notify you at least thirty (30) days in advance. This information is a description of the benefit provided to you as a cardholder. It is insured by Indemnity Insurance Company of North America.

FORM #VPID (07/08)

COMPREHENSION QUESTIONS

1. How does Chase define a "Covered Stolen Identity Event"?

_____

_____ **2.** Which of these expenses are *not* covered if your identity is stolen?
   a. You have to hire an attorney if a collection agency or other creditor files a suit against you if you don't pay charges that were actually incurred by the person who stole your identity?
   b. Moving expenses associated with your wanting to start a new life after the identity theft.
   c. Securing an unlimited number of credit reports so that you can re-establish your good name.

      d. Fuel costs associated with remedying the Identity Theft Event.

      e. Taking days off from work or sick days to deal with the problem.

      f. Reimbursing you for charges made by your brother to whom you gave the card.

3. How much does identity theft protection cost?

_____

4. If you are traveling in Asia or in Europe and your identity is stolen, are you covered?

_____

5. How do you go about reporting an Identity Theft Event? Once you report such an occurrence, how long will the case stay open?

_____

6. Should you file a police report?

_____

Reading and Comparing Package Labels

Consumers who want to eat a healthy diet or who have food restrictions consult the nutrition facts on food packages to determine their contents. Others are concerned about artificial additives, color agents, and sweeteners in food, and so they read the side panels of food packages to determine if any are included. The FDA (Food and Drug Administration) is the federal agency that regulates food processors in the United States. By law, the FDA requires food producers to list ingredients on their packages in an identical format. But what many consumers don't know is that the ingredients must be listed in order of quantity. Therefore, the first ingredient listed is the main ingredient, the second ingredient listed is the next ingredient by quantity, and so on.

For the past 20 years or so, food producers have also been required to list nutrition facts like calories and grams and percentages of sodium, fat, and sugar as part of the so-called "daily value," along with a brief summary of two representative dietary requirements. The third newspaper article you read in this section about comfort food prominently mentions macaroni and cheese, an American staple and certainly a staple in the college student's cupboard. Packaged macaroni and cheese is cheap (Kraft dinner costs $1.29, while the organic or "natural" brand, Annie's, costs $2.29 at the local Safeway). Reprinted here side by side are the side panels showing nutrition facts and ingredients for each. Study the information carefully, and then answer the questions that follow.

Kraft Macaroni and Cheese

Nutrition Facts

Serving size 2.5 oz
(70g / about 1/3 Box)
(Makes about 1 cup)
Servings Per Container about 3

Amount per serving	As Packaged	As Prepared
Calories	260	400
Calories from Fat	30	170

	% Daily Value**	
Total Fat 3.5g*	5%	29%
Saturated Fat 1.5g	8%	23%
Trans Fat 0g		
Cholesterol 15mg	5%	5%
Sodium 580mg	24%	30%
Total Carbohydrate 47g	16%	16%
Dietary Fiber 1g	4%	4%
Sugars 6g		
Protein 10g		
Vitamin A	0%	15%
Vitamin C	0%	0%
Clacium	10%	15%
Iron	10%	15%

*Amount in Box. Margarine and 2% Reduced Fat Milk preparation adds 15.5g total fat (3g sat fat, 4g trans fat), 130mg sodium, 2g total carbohydrate (1g sugars), and <1g protein.

**Percent Daily Values are based on a 2,000 calorie diet. Your daily values may be higher or lower depending on your calorie needs:

		Calories: 2,000	2,500
Total Fat	Less than	65g	80g
Sat Fat	Less than	20g	25g
Cholest	Less than	300mg	300mg
Sodium	Less than	2,400mg	2,400mg
Total Carb		300g	375g
Dietary Fiber		25g	30g

INGREDIENTS: ENRICHED MACARONI PRODUCT (WHEAT FLOUR, NIACIN, FERROUS SULFATE [IRON], THIAMIN MONONITRATE [VITAMIN B1], RIBOFLAVIN [VITAMIN B2], FOLIC ACID); CHEESE SAUCE MIX (WHEY, MILKFAT, MILK PROTEIN CONCENTRATE, SALT, SODIUM TRIPOLYPHOSPHATE, CONTAINS LESS THAN 2% OF CITRIC ACID, LATRIC ACID, SODIUM PHOSPHATE, CALCIUM PHOSPHATE, YELLOW 5, YELLOW 6, ENZYMES, CHEESE CULTURE).

CONTAINS: WHEAT, MILK.

KRAFT FOODS GLOBAL, INC.
NORTHFIELD, IL 60093-2753 USA

kraft foods

Annie's Macaroni and Cheese

Nutrition Facts

Serving Size 2.5 oz (71g)
About 1 cup prepared
Servings About 2.5

Amount Per Serving	Mix	As Prepared
Calories	270	280
Fat Cal.	40	40

	% Daily Value**	
Total Fat 4g*	6%	7%
Sat. Fat 2.5g	13%	13%
Trans Fat 0g		
Cholest. 10mg	3%	3%
Sodium 510mg	21%	22%
Total Carb. 46g	15%	16%
Dietary Fiber 2g	8%	8%
Sugars 5g		
Protein 10g	11%	13%
Vitamin A	2%	2%
Vitamin C	0%	0%
Calcium	10%	15%
Iron	4%	4%
Thiamin (Vit. B1)	10%	10%
Folic Acid	10%	10%

*Amount in Mix. Prepared with 3 Tbsp lowfat milk adds 10 Calories, 0.5g Total Fat, 10mg Sodium, 1g Total Carbohydrate (1g Sugars), 1g Protein

**Percent Daily Values (DV) are based on a 2,000 calorie diet. Your daily values may be higher or lower depending on your calorie needs:

		Calories: 2,000	2,500
Total Fat	Less than	65g	80g
Sat. Fat	Less than	20g	25g
Cholest.	Less than	300mg	300mg
Sodium	Less than	2,400mg	2,400mg
Total Carb.		300g	375g
Fiber		25g	30g
Protein		50g	65g

BEST INGREDIENTS: ORGANIC WHEAT MACARONI, CHEDDAR CHEESE (CULTURED PASTEURIZED MILK, SALT, NON-ANIMAL ENZYMES), WHEY, NONFAT MILK, BUTTER, SALT, CULTURED WHOLE MILK, SODIUM PHOSPHATE, ANNATTO EXTRACT FOR COLOR.

CONTAINS MILK AND WHEAT INGREDIENTS.

MADE ON SHARED EQUIPMENT THAT ALSO PROCESSES EGG AND SOY.

MANUFACTURED FOR: ANNIE'S HOMEGROWN © 2012 ANNIE'S, INC. 1610 5th STREET BERKELEY, CA 94710 MADE IN USA

Certified Organic by Oregon Tilth

We source only ingredients stated to be free of genetically modified organisms.

Keep in a Cool, Dry Place

QUESTIONS FOR INTERPRETATION AND ANALYSIS

1. At the top of each package label, compare the amounts of calories, including calories from fat. Which contains more in both categories? _____

2. Now do the same for the number of milligrams of sodium and the percentages recommended for the "daily value." Which brand contains more sodium? _____

3. Let's assume that your optimal dietary intake per day is 2,000 calories. What is the recommended number of milligrams of carbohydrates for such a diet?

   _____

   Next, let's assume that over a period of two days, you eat one serving of each brand of macaroni and cheese. How many grams of carbohydrates are contained in each serving? _____ Last, what percentage of the daily value does this amount of carbs represent? _____

4. Now look at the list of ingredients for each product, specifically at the description of the macaroni and cheese, the obvious ingredients in both products. Which one offers a more complete description? _____ Which product seems to have more additives and artificial colorings? How can you tell? _____

   _____

5. Comment on the information these side panels present. Is the information easy to understand for the general reader or not? What difficulties do you note? Are these nutrition labels helpful for someone who is trying to avoid eating, for example, a lot of fat or sugar or sodium? _____

   _____

6. Annie's is labeled "organic." What agency or organization certifies this? What do you think this organization does? It might be worth checking it out online.

   _____

   Finally, compare the promotional material on the back side of each package, again reprinted side by side for easy comparison.

Kraft Macaroni and Cheese

imported from your childhood.

congratulations. you just picked up a box of **deliciously gooey** macaroni & cheese dinner. chances are you'll be serving it to your kids but at the same time **helping yourself to a spoonful or two.**

don't worry, we understand. it's the same **classic cheesy taste** you know and love from your own childhood. so go ahead, **dig in.** your kids may be the perfect age to enjoy the **gooey, cheesy goodness**—but remember: **you were there first.**

kraftmacandcheese.com/facebook

KRAFT Macaroni & Cheese is a registered trademark of Kraft Foods Inc. and is used with permission.

Annie's Macaroni and Cheese

Dear Friend,

I've been in the food business for over twenty years and a mom and organic farmer for nearly ten. My three roles as mom, organic grower, and "Annie" are very much intertwined. I've discovered that some of the same skills apply to both raising children and raising vegetables. With love, patience, and respect, both children and vegetables flourish. The more experience I gain from being a mom and organic grower, the more these two roles influence my role as "Annie."

As you know, I've always relied on your thoughts and suggestions to shape our decisions. And that leads me to this box. . . Annie's blue box. We've received hundreds of requests for a product with elbow macaroni and a milder, mellower cheese. Here it is. Annie's "true blue" version of the macaroni & cheese you may have grown up with.

Like all of Annie's products, our new Macaroni & Cheese contains ingredients all found in nature. No weird chemicals. No artificial anything—just smooth, mild, all-natural cheese. . .mmmm. And the pasta is certified organic. It's produced by family farmers who farm without harsh pesticides or fertilizers, who respect the environment and have an understanding of our interconnectedness with all life on this planet. I invite you to read about Annie's organic growers and learn more about the organic movement at www.Annies.com.

This is the real deal. Our "true blue." Please tell us what you think.
Bye for now.

Annie

© 2012 Annie's, Inc. Reprinted with permission.

QUESTIONS FOR DISCUSSION AND ANALYSIS

1. The back panels of these two products are very different. Comment on their content, tone, purpose, as well as what is emphasized in the advertising copy (the promotional material) on each package. Which one is more effective? Do either of these descriptions persuade you to buy one brand over the other? Is Annie's worth the extra $1.00, based on all the information you have studied? Does the more flowery description on the Annie's package appeal to you or not? Is it effective in convincing you that it is the superior product? What other factors might influence your decision to buy one brand over the other?

2. The back panel of Annie's mentions that the product contains "no weird chemicals" or "artificial anything." Is this true? What other information might you need to answer this question?

3. Comment on the names of the two products' websites. What would you expect to find on the two websites listed? After you answer this question, type in both websites in the search box of your favorite search engine. What did you find? Comment on these findings.

Reading Recipes

Now that you have studied the nutritional content and promotional material for two common food products, why not make your own? People often say that anyone can cook as long as he or she can follow a recipe. But is this really true? What is the difference between ordinary everyday reading and reading a recipe?

This is a reading text, not a cookbook, but if you are a beginning cook, you need to know three crucial things about how to read a recipe: Since a recipe provides a step-by-step explanation of a process, first you need to read it through completely to be sure that you understand the steps involved. Second, you need to read the list of ingredients carefully to be sure that you have everything on hand. There is nothing worse, in the middle of making a new dish, than discovering that you are out of eggs or garlic or cinnamon.

Last, knowing the meaning of cooking terms is also critical. The first recipe printed here says that the onion should be "minced," while the second one says that the onion should be "finely chopped." What's the difference? And to complicate matters, some recipes also ask that onions be "roughly chopped" or "diced." Each one is different. Most standard cookbooks define and illustrate these terms, and of course, websites on cooking abound.

Two Macaroni and Cheese Recipes

First is Macaroni and Cheese from the *Better Homes and Gardens New Cook Book*.

Macaroni and Cheese

$1^1/_2$ cups elbow macaroni
3 tablespoons butter or margarine
3 tablespoons all-purpose flour
2 cups milk
$^1/_2$ teaspoon salt
Dash pepper
$^1/_4$ cup minced onion (optional)
2 cups shredded sharp process cheese

OVEN 350°

Cook macaroni in boiling, salted water till tender; drain.

Melt butter; blend in flour. Add milk. Cook and stir till thick. Add salt, pepper, onion, and cheese; stir till cheese is melted.

Mix sauce with macaroni. Turn into $1^1/_2$-quart casserole. If you like, sprinkle tomato slices with salt; arrange on top, pushing edge each slice into macaroni. Bake in moderate oven (350°) about 45 minutes, or till bubbly and browned. Makes 6 to 8 servings.

The second is from *The Essential New York Times Cookbook*.

Macaroni with Ham and Cheese

Salt
$^1/_2$ pound macaroni (about 2 cups)
$^3/_4$ pound sliced cooked ham ($^1/_2$-inch-thick)
$^1/_3$ pound mushrooms
$^1/_2$ pound sharp cheddar cheese
3 tablespoons unsalted butter
1 tablespoon all-purpose flour
2 cups whole milk
$^3/_8$ teaspoon freshly grated nutmeg
Freshly ground black pepper
$^1/_2$ cup finely chopped onion
$^1/_8$ teaspoon cayenne pepper, or more to taste
1 cup heavy cream
3 tablespoons freshly grated Parmesan cheese

1. Heat the oven to 425 degrees. Bring 3 quarts of water to a boil in a large pot. Add salt to taste. Add the macaroni and cook for 10 to 12 minutes, or until tender. Drain and return to the pot.
2. Meanwhile, cut the ham into $^1/_2$-inch cubes. There should be about 2 cups. Set aside.
3. Slice the mushrooms. There should be about 2 cups. Set aside.
4. Cut the cheddar into slices about $^1/_4$ inch thick. Stack the slices and cut them into $^1/_4$-inch-wide strips. Cut the strips into $^1/_4$-inch cubes. There should be about 2 cups.
5. Melt 2 tablespoons butter in a medium saucepan over medium heat. Add the flour, stirring with a wire whisk, and cook for about a minute, then add the milk, whisking rapidly. Let simmer for about 1 minute, and add the nutmeg, cheddar cheese, and salt and black pepper to taste, whisking until smooth. Remove from the heat.
6. Melt the remaining tablespoon of butter in a skillet. Add the onion and mushrooms and cook, stirring, until the mushrooms are wilted, 5 to 7 minutes. Add the ham and cook, stirring, for about 1 minute. Add the cheese sauce, cayenne, and cream and cook, stirring, for about 1 minute. Taste, adding more cayenne if needed.
7. Add the macaroni to the sauce and mix well. Transfer to a buttered 3-quart baking dish. Sprinkle the top with the Parmesan cheese, and bake for 10 minutes.
8. Turn the broiler to high. Brown the macaroni and cheese under the broiler until the top is nicely browned, 2 to 3 minutes.

Serves 6 as a main course

Serving Suggestions

Mezzaluna Salad (p. 185), Tangerine Sherbet (p. 734),
Brownies (p. 684)
JANUARY 6, 1988: "60-MINUTE GOURMET," BY PIERRE
FRANEY.
—1988

QUESTIONS FOR INTERPRETATION

1. Which of the two recipes seems more appropriate for the beginning cook?
2. Which recipe is easier to follow, in terms of clear steps and directions?
3. Finally, compare the cost of preparing the first recipe (with its fewer ingredients) to the cost of Kraft and Annie's Macaroni and Cheese dinner packages. Would the packaged dinner be more or less expensive to make than the first recipe? How important is cost to you? What other factors do you need to consider?

Reading Blogs

Blogs are relatively new in cyberspace. There are blogs, which refer to "weblogs," on virtually any subject you can think of, and on subjects that you probably have never thought of. It is impossible to generalize about blogs and about how to read them, however, because people who write blogs are as diverse as the human population is diverse. Also, anything that I write in the summer of 2012 may have changed by the time you read this text.

However, two important things to remember about reading blogs are (1) that they are generally more informal in construction and in expression than material published in print or in online news sources, and (2) that they represent personal opinion, experience, observation, and judgments that have not been subjected to editorial scrutiny, oversight, or editing the way that newspaper and magazine articles are. This means that you have to be extra careful about accepting (or reject-ing) the opinions expressed. If it's a truism that you can't believe everything in print, it's even truer with blogs!

An amazing number of the living writers represented in this book write blogs. Among them are Luis J. Rodriguez; David Sedaris; Sherman Alexie; Colby Buz-zell; Caroline Hwang (on the Ms.blog); Elizabeth Bernstein (at *WSJ* blogs); Olivia Wu; "The Waiter" (the original blog called "Waiter Rant" and a newer one under his real name, Steve Dublanica); Debra Dickerson; Tamara Lush; Carlin Flora; and Courtney Martin, to name just a few.

Naturally, some of these writers will let their blogs lapse, making them obso-lete, or they may contribute to them only sporadically. But if you are unfamiliar with the blogosphere, any of these writers—particularly the ones whom you enjoyed reading—would be a good place to start.

In addition, you can find blogs on subjects you are interested in pursuing at the following addresses:

- www.blogspotsearch.com
- www.blogsearchengine.com
- www.google.com/blogsearch

Note: Return to the cartoon in Part One on page 80 by Roz Chast called "Blog Breakdown." What makes this cartoon particularly amusing?

Reading Graphic Material—Pie Charts, Bar Graphs, and Line Graphs

Graphic material often accompanies magazine and newspaper articles. Graphs present statistical information, especially the results of surveys, in an easy-to-understand format. There are three kinds of graphs—line graphs, pie charts, and bar graphs. You can "read" a graph just as you can read other material, but the reading process is somewhat different. We'll start with the pie chart, because it is the easiest to understand. This kind of chart presents data graphically in triangu-lar sections or wedges, just like the pieces of a pie.

The following chart accompanied an article called "Young, Underemployed and Optimistic: Coming of Age, Slowly, in a Tough Economy," a PewResearch-Center Publication (February 9, 2012). You can locate this article online easily by typing in this link:

- www.pewresearch.org
  Then in the site search box, type in 2191 pubs.
  Here is the chart:

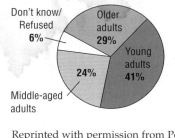

Reprinted with permission from Pew Research Center, Pew Social & Demographic Trends Project. *Young, Underemployed and Optimistic* (February 9, 2012), p. 19. http://pewresearch.org/pubs/2191/young-adults-workers-labor-market-pay-careers-advancement-recession

To read any kind of chart, first start with the title, "Young Adults Hardest Hit." Then read the question below the title. Finally, study the relative size of the pieces of the pie and their numbers. In this case, the numbers bear out the article's title—41 percent of young adults are having a tough time. The other two groups cited are faring somewhat better—only 29 percent of older adults and 24 percent of middle-aged adults report economic distress. (The accompanying article defines "young adults" as those between 18 and 34.)

Next is the bar chart, which is used to present more complicated material, usually statistics that span several years. In this case, bars are used to represent shifts in attitude, opinion, practices, and the like. Consider this bar chart from *The Wall Street Journal*, which accompanied an article titled "Survey Says: Cellphones Annoy Pollsters." The article discusses the problem public-opinion pollsters are increasingly encountering, as more Americans are abandoning their telephone landlines. (It helps to know that federal regulations prevent pollsters from using automated dialing services to cell phone numbers; they have to dial numbers by hand.) But demographics also play a role, as pollsters know that relying only on people with landlines can skew the results of their polls, as this chart clearly indicates. Study the chart, and then read the commentary that follows.

Cutting the Wire

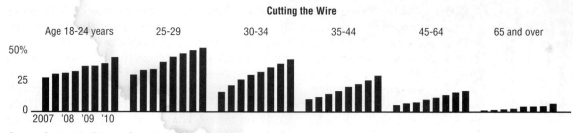

Source: Centers for Disease Control and Prevention

From Carl Bialik, "Survey Says: Cellphones Annoy Pollsters," *The Wall Street Journal*, December 3-4, 2011. Reprinted by permission of The Wall Street Journal, Copyright © 2011 by Dow Jones & Company, Inc. All Rights Reserved Worldwide. License numbers 2923361119102 and 2923361408360.

As before, look at the title first, "Cutting the Wire," and then read the sentence directly above the chart. This chart presents statistics on the percentage of adults who live in cell phone–only households, meaning that they no longer have a landline. Then look at the bottom left-hand side. Each bar represents one-half of a year, ranging from 2007 to 2010. Next, look at the age groups represented, which are divided into six groups. Finally, look at the vertical numbers on the left side of the graph, which indicate numbers from 0 percent to 50 percent. The chart shows clearly that three groups are leading this trend, in this order: (1) 25–29; (2) 18–24); and (3) 30–34. Very few people aged 45 to 64 or over 65 live in cell phone–only households. You can see why pollsters would find this information of use and the difficulties it presents.

Last is the line chart. This particular graph appeared alongside an article, also published by the Pew Research Center on February 7, 2012 (pubs/2190), during the Republican presidential primary season. The title of the article is "Cable Leads the Pack as Campaign News Source." Look at the chart in relation to the commentary that follows.

Campaign News Sources: Internet Cable Flat, Others Decline

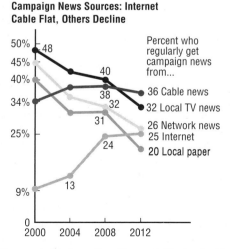

Reprinted with permission from Pew Research Center for The People & The Press. *Cable Leads the Pack as Campaign News Source: Twitter, Facebook Play Very Modest Roles* (February 7, 2012), p. 1. http://www.people-press .org/2012/02/07/cable-leads-the-pack-as-campaign-news-source

Begin with the title as you did before. This graph depicts the shift in news sources, where people get campaign news. Next, look at the dates covered—four-year periods from 2000 to 2012, representing four presidential election years. Then look at the percentage numbers listed vertically on the left side. Finally, look at what the various lines represent—news sources representing cable news, local TV news, network news, Internet, and the local newspaper. The line graph clearly shows the decline in public reliance on local and network TV and the daily newspaper and the increasing reliance on the Internet, from 13 percent in 2000 to 25 percent today. Cable news has held relatively steady.

While only 25 percent of the people surveyed get their information from the Internet, more surprising is the number of people who have abandoned the newspaper as a primary political news source—from 40 percent to half that, 20 percent, over the 12-year period. But consider this: None of these sources reaches 50 percent, which means that more than half the population isn't getting any campaign news at all, if I am reading the graph correctly. There is clearly room for discussion here.

E-Readers—An Overview

As I prepare this revision of *Improving Reading Skills*, the book is not yet available in electronic form, but by the time you are assigned this book, it may be. If you are thinking of buying an e-reader, I urge you to try the major models out before making a decision rather than relying on a friend's recommendation or on advertising pitches. Your choice will depend on the features you most want as well as on price. And prices are coming down all the time. As of this writing, in summer 2012, there are several good e-readers available, and whatever I write today will probably be outdated by the time you read this.

First, we must distinguish between tablet computers and e-readers. The former are mini-computers, capable of doing much more than a dedicated e-reader, but of course, they cost more. E-readers include the Amazon Kindle and the Kindle Fire, Barnes and Noble's Nook (also available in color as the Nook Color), and the Sony Reader. Tablets include the Apple iPad and the Samsung Galaxy. Prices range from $79 for e-readers to $500 or more for tablets, depending on the model and features.

In addition to trying them out, do some research. One good source for complete and up-to-date reviews of these devices is www.reviews.cnet.com. At the top, click on Reviews and then click on E-Readers. Factors to consider are price, manufacturer, weight, and other features, in addition to what you will use it for as well as where and for what. If your budget allows for a tablet, Cnet also has reviews of tablet computers, with useful categories like "Best Tablet Computers," "Best Android Tablets," "Best 7-inch Tablets," and so forth. But no amount of research can substitute for trying out the device before you buy.

Some features to look for are screen size, weight, ease of use, clarity of print, backlighting, battery life, the cost of downloading books, and miscellaneous features such as whether or not the device allows you to bookmark a page and whether or not you can look up words in the dictionary. The iPad, which I own, is more expensive than a regular e-reader because it is more versatile, allowing me to access the Internet, check e-mail, store photos, listen to music, play the highly addictive Scrabble-like game Words with Friends, and watch instantly streamed movies via Netflix, in addition to reading books, newspapers, and magazines. On the iPad, when I read a book I have downloaded from the Kindle app or the iTunes Store, I can touch an unfamiliar word, click on "Dictionary," and receive a full definition with pronunciation. See if this feature is available on the device you are considering purchasing. I can also adjust the font and font size, the amount of backlighting, particularly useful if you are reading in dim light, for example, in a camping tent. However, unlike the Kindle, the iPad can't be used outdoors in the bright sunlight.

There is no question that e-readers will change the nature of reading. The question is how much and to what degree. My friends and colleagues have all shared my experience: These devices are made for distraction. If I'm reading a book on the iPad, it's very easy to say, "Oh, I should check my e-mail," or "I need to look up a recipe for dinner tonight." The experience of luxurious, sustained, deep reading is somehow diminished. It's important to guard against this very real possibility by setting aside a specific time for checking e-mail or for playing games so that your reading concentration isn't compromised.

Whether or not you will enjoy reading printed material on an e-reader is a matter of personal taste and preference. My experience is that, initially, I didn't concentrate as well while reading on a tablet device, but eventually my concentration returned to normal. But these are only one person's experiences. I still prefer printed matter, but it is also wonderful to have another way to access reading material.

Is this what the future of reading will look like?

© Ward Sutton/The New Yorker Collection/www.cartoonbank.com

Index

Index of Vocabulary Preview Words

Reading Comprehension Progress Chart

To calculate your progress, find the number of the selection at the top and the number representing your percentage of correct answers at the left. At the square where the two numbers meet, shade it in with a pencil. This will allow you to keep track of the progress you make during the term. Remember that a score of 70 percent or above is considered acceptable and that since the selections become progressively more difficult, a constant score of 70 percent throughout the text indicates improvement.